❖ A SPLENDID SAVAGE ❖

A
SPLENDID
SAVAGE

The Restless Life of
Frederick Russell Burnham

STEVE KEMPER

260626

W. W. NORTON & COMPANY ✣ *Independent Publishers Since 1923*
NEW YORK ✣ LONDON

For information about permission to reproduce selections from this book,
write to Permissions, W. W. Norton & Company, Inc., 500 Fifth Avenue,
New York, NY 10110

For information about special discounts for bulk purchases, please contact
W. W. Norton Special Sales at specialsales@wwnorton.com or 800-233-4830

Manufacturing by RR Donnelley, Harrisonburg, VA
Book design by Dana Sloan
Production manager: Anna Oler

ISBN 978-0-393-23927-0

W. W. Norton & Company, Inc.
500 Fifth Avenue, New York, N.Y. 10110
www.wwnorton.com

W. W. Norton & Company Ltd.
Castle House, 75/76 Wells Street, London W1T 3QT

1 2 3 4 5 6 7 8 9 0

For my parents,
who let their children roam

CONTENTS

❖ A SPLENDID SAVAGE ❖

PROLOGUE

SHE STOOD IN the doorway of the log cabin, nervously brushing her hair as dusk fell over forest and clearing. She would feel safer tomorrow when her husband returned with bullets and powder. Her mother's old pewter, lovingly carried to this new country from England, had long since been melted down for slugs.

A flicker of movement at the wood's edge caught her eye, then sent her heart racing: Sioux braves, painted for war.

She snatched up her infant son and fled toward the corn field. Not far into it, an awful truth struck her: she could not escape carrying her fifteen-month-old baby. The braves would run her down and kill them both. She stooped and pushed the infant into a shock of freshly-cut stalks. Don't move or make any noise, she instructed him, until I come back for you. Then she ran.

At the brush line along the creek, she looked back. Some Sioux were entering the cabin. Others had noticed her trail. With chilling howls, they began trotting in her direction, heads tilted to study the ground.

She bolted into the cottonwoods. Youth and fear gave her feet wings. When darkness finally obscured her trail, she paused to catch her breath. Above the trees, in the direction of her cabin, the night sky glowed orange. She prayed that the green corn shocks would refuse to burn. Perhaps her child would survive, if he didn't cry out. Later that night she reached a barricaded cabin six miles from her own.

At dawn she rushed back with armed men. They passed the smoking remains of a neighboring cabin. Near it were the scalped and tortured bodies of a man and woman. Their child lay nearby, head cracked open from being swung by the legs against a tree.

At her homestead the timbers were smoldering. She ran to the corn shock and shoved apart its scorched stalks. There lay the boy, calmly gazing up at her with bright blue eyes.

It was 1862 on the Minnesota frontier and the child's name was Frederick Russell Burnham. This was the first in a lifetime of narrow escapes on violent frontiers in the United States, Africa, Mexico, and the Klondike. Burnham's life was so crammed with adventure that his friend H. Rider Haggard, author of popular exotic tales such as *She* and *King Solomon's Mines*, remarked, "In real life he is more interesting than any of my heroes of romance."

Burnham was once world-famous as "the American scout." His expertise in woodcraft, learned from Indians and frontiersmen in the American West, helped inspire another of his friends, Robert Baden-Powell, to found the Boy Scouts. A best-selling book called *Real Soldiers of Fortune* (1911) by Richard Harding Davis, a prominent journalist, included Burnham among six larger-than-life figures profiled, along with Winston Churchill and the rogue provocateur William Walker. According to John Hays Hammond, a wealthy investor and advisor to several presidents, Burnham was one of the only people who could turn their garrulous mutual friend Theodore Roosevelt into a listener.

Burnham's story seems almost too far-fetched for credibility, as if an old newsreel got mashed up with a Saturday matinee thriller. In fact, his critics, despite thin evidence, have called him a fabricator. His life included Indian wars and range feuds in the American West; booms and busts in mining camps across African veldts, the U.S. Southwest, Mexican sierras, and Yukon tundra; explorations of remote regions in east, west, and central Africa; death-defying feats in African wars that brought him high military honors, including the Distinguished Service Order from King Edward

VII; and finally, in his sixties, wealth. Other men of his era had a few such adventures, but Burnham had them all.

In outline he resembled a comic-book swashbuckler, yet he often mocked such images as melodramatic clichés. As a scout, he preferred to sidestep danger, not rush into it. He survived so many extraordinary adventures because of intensive training and experience, not bravado.

He was quintessentially American. His optimism, like the man himself, was unkillable. Again and again he shook off disappointment, failure, tragedy. He was endlessly willing to set off into the unknown and start over. His natural habitat was the frontier, a place of escape and hope and violence. "Sometimes I wish I had never learned to read or form any conception of duty, civilization, religion," he once wrote to his mother, "for I would have been and am at heart a splendid savage, nothing more."

Two intermixed urges—one monetary, one idealistic—drove his restlessness. He constantly dreamed of a big strike, but also chased history's leading edge, where the future felt up for grabs and values worth dying for were at stake. Burnham purposefully skated these edges as a scout, prospector, pioneer, explorer, and imperialist soldier. On many of his adventures he was accompanied by his intrepid wife Blanche, who could charm high society or handle a shotgun, depending on what was needed.

Burnham believed deeply in certain values that he found among frontiersmen, soldiers, and certain native tribes: courage, sacrifice, self-discipline, self-reliance, physical and mental toughness. For him these weren't platitudes or abstractions but daily practices that could determine the fate of individuals and nations. He lamented what he saw as their decay in the twentieth century.

Alongside his admirable traits ran others that justified the subjugation of native peoples and the confiscation of their lands. Like most whites shaped by the late nineteenth century, including Churchill and Roosevelt, Burnham was sure that Indians and blacks belonged to inferior races. He assumed that race plus ancestry equaled something close to historic destiny. For him, this assumption explained not only the arc of his life but the larger arcs of history

in which he participated. He knew that before Mexican and American pioneers swarmed into the Southwest, the Apaches had pushed out the region's
weaker tribes. If the Apaches could have annihilated the whites, they would
have; they certainly tried. Likewise, in southern Africa, he knew that the
belligerent Ndebeles had overrun the softer Shonas. The weak gave way to
the strong; the strong gave way to the stronger. Progressive white civilization
naturally triumphed over primitive native cultures, and the British naturally
triumphed over cruder white cultures such as that of the Boers.

As an agent of this triumph, Burnham believed he was furthering high
ideals through practical actions that demanded a steep toll of sacrifice and
bloodshed. After conquest came responsibility to the conquered, what
Kipling called the white man's burden. To preserve civilized values against
ever-prowling chaos and savagery required vigilance and sometimes violence. All of these values and attitudes helped shape the continent and the
world we inherited.

The past is often depicted through a single lens in which the actors are
portrayed as heroes or racist imperialists, victors or victims, as if historical
truth is a crisp choice between fixed positions. But the past, like everything
made by humans, is far more muddled and thorny than that, by turns
admirable, misguided, appalling, inspiring. Much like Frederick Russell
Burnham.

———

A word about sources: aside from Burnham's two memoirs, *Scouting on Two
Continents* and *Taking Chances*, the first twenty-five years of his life are
sparsely documented. For that reason the early chapters here are more heavily contextual than later ones. Recorded historical events provide some clear
markers, like navigational buoys in a fog. By comparing these to Burnham's
memoirs, it's possible to chart a rough map of his locations and activities, not
accurate in every detail, during his early years of drift and conflict.

CHAPTER ONE

CHILD OF THE FRONTIER

Burnham considered himself a link in a long line of wanderers and pioneers. In the first sentence of his memoir *Scouting on Two Continents*, published in 1926 when he was sixty-five, he wrote, "My adventurous ancestors, migrating from England during the turbulent religious wars, carried a fierce love of freedom and great physical energy into the New World." His forebears pioneered from Connecticut into Kentucky, then crossed the Mississippi to the frontier hamlet of Le Claire, Iowa, where Burnham's mother learned to read in a log schoolhouse with a boy named Cody, known to fame as Buffalo Bill. By paragraph three of *Scouting on Two Continents* the Sioux are scalping settlers on the Minnesota frontier, and Burnham's mother has stashed him in a corn shock before outrunning a war party.

Restlessness, dislocation, independence, violence: Burnham saw these as his heritage and implicit destiny. He was proud that his ancestry combined the learned and the martial, the book and the gun. His original American ancestor, a lawyer named Thomas Burnham, left England in 1635 in search of religious freedom. He landed in the new settlement of Hartford, Connecticut, where his independent views soon nettled the authorities. In 1645 he defended a woman accused of witchcraft and saved her from hanging, which so irritated the Puritan inquisitors that they banned him from the court.

Burnham's great-grandfather, Abner Burnham, was born in Hartford and fought for the colonists in the Revolutionary War before settling in Madison, New York. Abner's son Frederick was seriously wounded in the War of 1812. Afterward he moved his wife Harriet and his medical practice to Ghent, Kentucky, a frontier settlement on the Ohio River. Frederick's son Edwin Otway Burnham (Burnham's father) was born there in 1824. Six years later Edwin and his younger sisters Harriet and Caroline were orphans. They were sent back east to their grandfather Abner Burnham, who died soon thereafter.

Nevertheless, Edwin, a young man of ample physical and intellectual energy, graduated from both Oberlin College and Hamilton College, and then enrolled in Union Theological Seminary in New York City. In 1855, after three years there, he was licensed as a preacher of the Gospel. The following year he took all this higher education to the Minnesota frontier, becoming a missionary to the Winnebago Indians on their reservation at Tivoli (now the town of Le Ray). He set about saving heathen souls.

In nearby Sterling Center, a restless British immigrant named William Russell ran a general store. William and his second wife Rebecca had left England in 1845 with their young daughter and William's four sons from a previous marriage. They started a farm in New York state, but in 1849 moved to the frontier, first in Iowa and then in Minnesota. Like the Burnhams, the Russells were deeply religious Congregationalists. William was also a passionate abolitionist who later wrote strong-minded essays for newspapers.

Edwin Burnham must have approved of the Russells' rigorous Christian values. He definitely approved of their teenaged daughter Rebecca. He and Rebecca married in 1860 when she was eighteen, half his age. They set up house on the reservation. Ten months later, on May 11, 1861, a month after Confederate forces fired on Fort Sumter, the couple's first child was born among Indians. They named him to honor the merged streams of his ancestry: Frederick Russell Burnham. Not long after his birth, they left the reservation for a homestead with a one-room cabin about twenty miles from Mankato. It would soon be torched by rampaging Sioux.

———

Like many bloody encounters between settlers and Native Americans, the Dakota War of 1862 began with a spontaneous stupidity bred of resentment. On August 17 of that year, when Burnham was fifteen months old, four Dakota Sioux braves were returning to their reservation in southern Minnesota from a hunting trip. About eighty miles west of St. Paul, they came across a clutch of chicken eggs near the fence of a homesteader they knew. One of the braves scooped up an egg. His companion warned him against stealing a white man's property. The egg thief mocked his cautious friend as a coward. To regain face, the insulted man proposed killing the egg's owner right then, and challenged the others to join him. They accepted the dare. Soon the homesteader, his wife, son, stepdaughter, and a visitor lay dead.

Of course that wasn't the real start of hostilities; their roots were old and deep. In the early 1850s, after decades of friction between Indians and white settlers encroaching into the Territory of Minnesota, several bands of eastern Dakota Sioux signed treaties giving them large reservations and annual federal stipends of food and cash. The following decade brought the federal government's usual litany of broken promises, including reductions of the Indians' reservations and stipends, which were further reduced by corrupt Indian agents and extortionate reservation storekeepers.

In 1862 the federal annuity due in late June or early July was tardy again, stalled in a Congress distracted by the Civil War. The Sioux depended on the money to buy food and supplies, so by August they were hungry and angry. Meanwhile the traders' warehouses on the reservations were full of provisions guarded by soldiers. At a tense gathering at the Lower Sioux Agency on August 15, the Indians asked the traders to advance them food on credit until the annuity arrived. Andrew J. Myrick's response on behalf of himself and the other three storekeepers was translated to the crowd: "If they are hungry, let them eat grass."

The next day, August 16, the federal payment to the Sioux of $71,000 in gold coins reached St. Paul. It was too late. On August 17 an egg and an insult sparked the massacre that would lead to war, atrocity, and vengeance, events that would become foundational memories for young Fred Burnham.

The four Sioux who killed the homesteaders fled to their village and described what they had done. At a council that night, some braves wanted to turn over the killers. Others urged war against the intruders who had lied to them, stolen their land, and now were starving them by reneging on the promise of money to buy food. The pro-war faction pressed the others to reclaim Sioux honor and territory while so many white men were away at their Civil War.

The main chief, Little Crow, wavered. As the homesteaders were being murdered that Sunday, Little Crow had been attending the Episcopalian service on the reservation. He had turned himself into a farmer. He was building a brick house and he liked his white man's bed. He had been photographed wearing a cravat, button coat, and high starched collar, and he had visited Washington, D.C. several times as the Sioux's representative. But he believed that Sunday's massacre would end the federal stipend and bring down the white man's wrath. He agreed to lead his people into war.

Early the next morning Sioux in war paint attacked the Lower Agency, shocking the whites there. One of the first targets was the storekeeper Myrick. The Indians riddled him with arrows and stuffed his mouth with grass, perhaps not in that order. About two dozen other whites, all well-known to the Indians, were murdered as well. Some Christian Indians saved several settlers from death.

From there the warriors spread to the townships and isolated homesteads such as the Burnhams'. They killed the men and captured the women, raping some. They slaughtered some children and left others clinging to their mothers. Barns and crops were burned. In Milford the braves murdered fifty German settlers. Other townships were wiped out and razed. Outside of Fort Ridgely, a large party of warriors overtook thirteen white families in flight. The Sioux's leader spoke English and had often hunted with the leader of the refugees. The Indian warned his white friend to beware of the Chippewas, who were on the warpath. When the settlers relaxed, the Sioux killed twenty-five of them, male and female, and took some women captive.

As news of the uprising spread on August 18, panicky settlers fled to the barricaded settlement of New Ulm, which soon contained more than a thousand people. Few had guns or bullets, which suggests how completely stunned they were by the uprising. The refugees exchanged horrifying stories about pregnant women cut open, babies nailed to trees, young girls brutally raped. On August 19 about 500 Indians with firearms attacked the settlement, whose defenders mustered half that many guns. In two days of fighting, twenty-six whites were killed and at least twice that many were wounded. The Sioux's casualties were unknown. Much of the town was burned.

Over the next few days Sioux war parties terrified the Minnesota River Valley. Settlers in twenty-three counties fled their townships and homesteads. But the Indians' main weapon—surprise—was gone. When the whites finally responded with militia and soldiers, the Indians were quickly outnumbered and outgunned. In late September, less than six weeks after the uprising began, it effectively ended with the capture and surrender of 303 Sioux warriors and the recovery of 269 captives. Another 1,500 Indian women, children, and elderly braves were placed in custody. Many had nothing to do with the violence. Some had opposed it. The whites didn't care about such distinctions. All Sioux were the same. Little Crow fled and escaped.

Hysteria inflated the number of dead settlers into the thousands. (The true number was somewhere between 450 and 800.) Rumor also exaggerated the number of rapes and mutilations, though enough of these had been survived or witnessed to create horror beyond mere figures.

The settlers also felt betrayed. They had assumed the Sioux were peaceable neighbors living contentedly on gifts from the federal government: land, housing, medical care, a yearly stipend. "Our nation's pampered protégés," complained one contemporary commentator. Neighborliness and generosity had been paid back with vicious treachery, proving the Indians' irredeemable savagery. The Sioux were labeled fiends, demons, beasts deserving extermination.

This volatile mix of grief and outrage led to calls for vengeance. A mob carrying axes and clubs tried to break through the troops protecting the Indian prisoners, and killed one of them. Most people in Minnesota wanted all the imprisoned braves hanged.

The warriors were tried by a military court in November 1862. They weren't provided lawyers. All 303 were quickly found guilty of rape and murder, and were sentenced to death. Eastern Quakers and philanthropes, as well as the Episcopal bishop of Minnesota, implored President Lincoln to pardon the Indians on grounds of humanitarianism and years of white provocations. Lincoln agreed to look into the matter, enraging people in Minnesota. The state's governor, Alexander Ramsey, warned the president that if the federal government didn't kill the Indians legally, the incensed people of his state might do so illegally. When word reached Minnesota that Lincoln was leaning toward pardons, a drunken mob marched on the Indian prison in Mankato but was dispersed by the U.S. Cavalry.

Lincoln decided that the evidence proved only two Indians guilty of rape and forty of "wanton murder." Of these forty, he commuted the sentence of one man to ten years and ordered the other thirty-nine to be hung. He nullified the death sentences of the other imprisoned braves.

Minnesota again felt betrayed, this time by its federal government, in cahoots with Eastern do-gooders, neither of which had any understanding of Indians or life on the frontier—Western resentments that would persist long after the frontier disappeared. "While [the Indian] still lies in wait for our heart's blood, sympathy for the 'poor, wronged red man,' is being roused, in some parts of our nation," wrote Harriet E. Bishop in the first history of the uprising, *Dakota War Whoop, or, Indian Massacres and War in Minnesota, of 1862–3* (1864). "Had the tragic scenes, of which we have given but a faint outline, been concentrated for one stereoscopic view, in any Eastern city, had their streets been drenched with blood, as were our prairies, had fire and ravishment come to their homes, as to ours, we think we know the New England heart well enough to say, that quite as little leniency would have been desired for the perpetrators, as by us."

On December 26, 1862, a crowd that included Burnham's parents gathered in Mankato to watch the Indians hang. One of the thirty-nine condemned had been reprieved. Most of the other thirty-eight had agreed to be baptized. They painted their faces and ascended the gallows chanting their eerie death song, which silenced the crowd. Bags were placed over their heads, nooses tightened around their necks. A drum was beaten slowly three times. Each Indian reached out and clasped hands with his companions to either side. A settler whose wife and children had been burned alive was given the honor of cutting the rope to open the scaffold. The hangings in Mankato remain the largest mass execution in U.S. history.

"I remember hearing my parents relate vividly how the braves met their fate," wrote Burnham six decades later, "singing the Sioux war song; undaunted, exultant, and defiant to the end.... Those were rough days and fierce resentments. Today, recalling all the crimes of the Indians, which were black enough, one cannot but cast up in their behalf the long column of wrongs and grievances they suffered at the hands of the whites. Then hatred dies, and I can entertain the honest hope that they have all reached the Happy Hunting Ground of their dreams."

At the time, a darker mood prevailed. President Lincoln had stopped the execution of the other imprisoned warriors, but the people of Minnesota demanded that these braves and all other Dakota Sioux be expelled from the state, a pattern that would be repeated throughout the West. The warriors were shipped to a prison in Illinois. Their families went to a temporary internment camp. In April 1863 the U.S. Congress annulled all treaties with the tribe and sold its reservation. The interned families were sent to a bleak reservation in the Dakota Territory, then moved three years later to another reservation in Nebraska.

Meanwhile in July 1863 the state hired hunters and trappers to track down any Dakota Sioux left in Minnesota. The government offered a bounty of $25 for every dead male, payable upon proof such as a scalp. Most of the surviving Sioux had fled the state, so few bounties were collected.

The most notable bounty went to a settler who shot and killed a brave as he was collecting raspberries with his teenaged son in a forest west of St. Paul. The dead man turned out to be Chief Little Crow, who had slipped back into Minnesota. State officials triumphantly displayed his skull and scalp in the capital city.

—·—

The Dakota War was the last spasm of the frontier era in Minnesota, which helped give it the aura of myth. Burnham was too young to have his own memories of it, but it colored his childhood. He grew up hearing firsthand stories about Indian treachery and massacred settlers, retribution and Eastern arrogance, the deadly consequences of lax vigilance.

Though the real frontier had moved west by the 1860s, Minnesota was far from settled. The Sioux had been killed or expelled, but other Indians remained a common presence, and Burnham grew up playing with Indian children. For settlers such as Edwin and Rebecca Burnham, self-reliance was still essential for survival. Pioneers carved small homesteads from forest and prairie by felling trees and sawing boards for houses, barns, and fences. They cleared and plowed the land, grew crops and raised livestock for food and trade. Currency was rare. Instead, people bartered—muskrat skins for eggs, beaver pelts for grain.

Most of the Burnhams' clothing came from wool spun from a small flock owned by Rebecca's brother. Young Burnham's aunt taught him to spell three-letter words as she turned wool into yarn for mittens and clothing. The family made their own soap, sugar, candles, and dyes, and tanned their own leather from cattle and deer. Boys ran traplines for otter, mink, beaver, wolf, sable, and muskrat.

With a wife and son to feed, Edwin had given up missionary work for farming. He threshed wheat with a simple flail and hauled his surplus by ox wagon to market at Red Wing, about 100 miles away. Though a farmer in the hinterland, Edwin maintained a steady correspondence with educated men back east such as Horace Greeley, whose letters often contained packets of seeds or cuttings of new plants. After moving to a new farm near Wilton, Minnesota, Edwin tired of the flail and brought in the area's first McCormick reaper. Curious neighbors came to watch the newfangled contraption work.

The Minnesota winters were brutal. Snowed-in settlers regularly froze in their cabins. Cattle left outside became ice sculptures; their horns would sometimes freeze and burst. Burnham recalled one snowstorm that lasted several weeks and reduced the family to a diet of boiled turnips. Starving timber wolves howled at their front door and tried to get at the livestock protected by makeshift shelters made of rails and straw.

After the long confining winters, spring and summer were joyous for the children. They transformed their parents' frightening stories into play. "Our games generally patterned on some form of Indian warfare," wrote Burnham, "and whoever was 'It' had to submit to being 'scalped,' and prisoners must allow themselves to be tied to the stake, along with other penalties suggestive of frontier incidents."

Social gatherings typically had a practical justification—a barn raising, a quilting bee, or, in autumn, a corn husking that turned drudgery into a competition. Sometimes the gatherings included wrestling, stone throws, and other physical contests.

The adult activity that most interested young Burnham was trick shooting, another skill with a utilitarian purpose. Edwin Burnham was a scholarly man of God, but he also excelled at marksmanship. He passed his passion for it along to his son, who got his first rifle at age eight. Edwin could split a soft lead bullet on an axe blade. To verify the deed, he positioned a big kettle behind the axe to catch the bullet's two ringing halves. He could also make a bullet snuff a candle or drive a nail, feats that Burnham would later perform in Africa to amaze British soldiers. The most rigorous test of a marksman's ability was the autumn turkey shoot. A live turkey was tied behind a log or some other barrier so that only the bird's bobbing head sporadically showed. The men used muzzle-loaders charged with black powder and homemade round bullets. The best marksmen, according to Burnham, could hit a turkey's head at 200 yards.

Occasionally there was a dance. Young Burnham knew about dancing through his father's abomination of it. Edwin Burnham, recalled his son, divided the community into two groups, the godly and the ungodly. "The crimes of the ungodly," wrote Burnham, "in the order of importance were—first and worst, they danced. For awhile I did not know what that terrible sin was, but I suspected it was worse than murder."

One summer, soon after his father left on a short trip, someone organized a dance in a grove about two miles from the Burnham homestead. "This was my mother's chance to dare to be young and gay," wrote Burnham. She not only risked perdition, she brought along her son. Young Fred never forgot it. "There was an amazing number of those lost souls whirling around," he wrote, "and they seemed to be astonishingly happy. It was the first time I ever heard a fiddle." It all enthralled him.

Edwin Burnham's list of ungodly vices, in addition to dancing and music, was long: smoking, drinking, gambling, swearing, and card-playing. The ungodly fished and hunted on the Sabbath. They invited hellfire by kissing and sparking before marriage. They also indulged in the frivolous temptations of novels and poetry. These sinners could be redeemed, preached Edwin, by going to revival, renouncing Satan, and embracing Jesus.

"As for the Godly people," wrote Burnham, "they were 'Don'ts' personified. It seemed that anything one really wanted to do was ungodly and most of the things one hated to do were Godly. Happily, there were a few liberal spirits in my clan, and my mother was one of them." Though

Rebecca Burnham was a Bible-reading Christian and a regular at temperance meetings, her faith didn't prohibit joy and amusement. She secretly read her son thrilling melodramas such as Longfellow's "Evangeline" ("This is the forest primeval") and "The Song of Hiawatha."

Once the boy could read on his own, Edwin believed the Good Book was sufficient and required him to memorize verses. But "some blessed soul put into my hands a child's edition of Greek mythology that gave me a hint of another world of ideas, strange and exciting." Six decades later he still fondly recalled the people who gave him glimpses of a life beyond the terrors and constraints of his father's severe Christianity. In a letter written late in life he remembered a kind teacher in Minnesota who sat him on her knee "and told me the wonders of the stars and a hundred illuminating things of life. It was my first conception of God as different from a dangerous angry monster wanting to send me to hell." He was so grateful for her liberating gift that he earnestly offered her a potato wrapped in brown paper.

Books helped release Burnham from his father's constrictions and also fueled his dreams. "As a boy I was always hungry for books full of action and shy on preachment." He doesn't mention particular titles, but in the 1860s, when he was learning to read, the action category was dominated by highly embroidered biographies of famous frontiersmen such as Kit Carson, Daniel Boone, and Davy Crockett, and by dime novels, which began appearing in the 1860s, about sensational Wild West adventurers with names such as Deadwood Dick, Mustang Sam, and Duke Darrall, hero of W. J. Hamilton's *Old Avoirdupois; or, Steel Coat, the Apache Terror*.

For a boy who read avidly and dreamed of adventure, just the titles must have fired the imagination. Burnham probably knew the popular "frontier thrillers" of Charles Wilkins Webber, such as *Old Hicks the Guide, or Adventures in the Comanche Country in Search of a Gold-Mine*, and *The Prairie Scout, or Agatone the Renegade: a Romance of Border Life*. He was probably familiar with the equally popular adventure books of "Captain" Mayne Reid, such as *The Scalp Hunters: or, Romantic Adventures in Northern*

Mexico, and *The Boy Hunters, or, Adventures in Search of a White Buffalo* (a particular favorite of Theodore Roosevelt).

The formulaic heroes of these potboilers were always brave and unflappable. Most were absurdly virtuous, never cussing or drinking. They were intimate with Mother Nature but never with wholesome women, whose decency transformed even the roughest of them into gentlemen. Regrettably—though to great commercial success—these paragons also were obliged to kill hundreds or even thousands of outlaws and Indians. This mixture of morals and mayhem contributed to Burnham's conceptions of manhood and the West. The romantic myths about the frontier that suffused these books colored his boyhood dreams and later tinted his perceptions about his own experiences.

In *Scouting on Two Continents* he ascribed his most influential literary moment to a brief stay with a family in Mankato, where a sixteen-year-old girl read aloud every evening from a book about the adventures of two boys in the wilds of the Orange Free State in South Africa. "Then and there," he wrote, "I made a solemn resolve to become a scout, to trek to South Africa, and to see the whole world and its wonderful life."

Other influences closer to home fed his dreams about scouting and the West. A harvest hand who claimed to have wandered the Rocky Mountains told the marveling prairie boy about great peaks sprinkled with gold and silver, prowled by fierce Indians and bears as big as cows. The neighboring Indians also inspired him. "The small boys of my day got much of their education through their interest in Indian ways," he wrote, "and we played with Indians at every opportunity." Burnham decided that the best way to turn his dreams about scouting and Africa into reality was to assimilate the Indians' woodcraft and physical toughness. This meant disciplining himself to go without food, water, or sleep, and to endure pain without flinching, for instance by pushing pins into his flesh. He eventually perfected these skills to an astonishing degree.

Other forces were shaping Burnham's future as well. Edwin Burnham, carrying a timber for a new cabin, slipped on ice. The timber crushed his chest and fractured a rib, puncturing his lung. He seemed unable to recover his strength. Domestic sorrows piled up. The Burnhams' second child, Edward, born in November 1863, died in September 1866. A third child, Mary, died in July 1868 at eight months old. Another child, Mather Howard Burnham, arrived in May 1870.

By the end of that year Edwin had decided that a warmer climate might improve his health and fortunes. In December the Burnhams traveled on the new transcontinental railroad across endless plains still dotted with buffalo. On New Year's Day the train crossed into the state where the family hoped to find a new life: California.

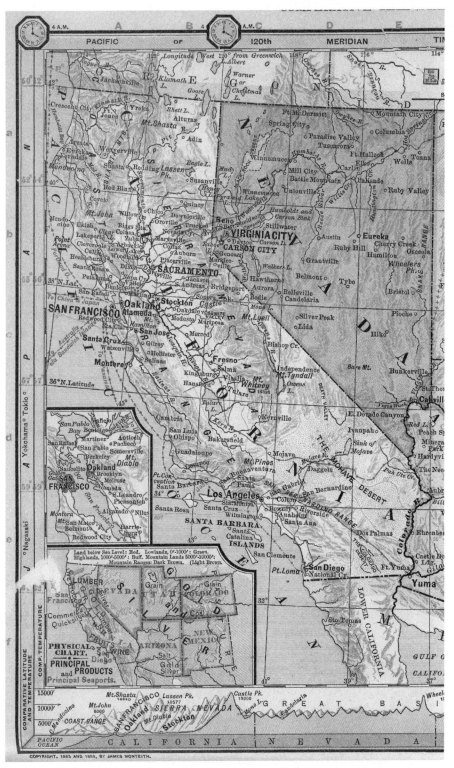

California. (From *Barnes's Complete Geography* by James Monteith, 1885.)

CHAPTER TWO

A PUEBLO AND
SOME PURITANS

THE RAILROAD JOURNEY took two weeks and ended at San Francisco. This humming place, still expanding from the big bang of the gold rush, bustled with 150,000 go-getters. It was by far the biggest city young Burnham had ever seen. The family boarded a small paddle-wheeler bound down the coast to San Pedro. From there, a twenty-five-mile stagecoach ride through tawny hills and ranches speckled with livestock brought them to a sleepy collection of flat-roofed adobes. Residents called it El Pueblo. To newcomers it was Los Angeles. The majority of its citizens were Mexican and Spanish. The 1870 census listed 5,728 inhabitants.

To young Burnham it seemed close to paradise. Los Angeles improved in every way on the climate and austerities of Minnesota. "For the greater part of the year," he wrote, "California was one long summer afternoon." Life there seemed soft and golden. Fruits were plentiful; the sea teemed with fish, the hills with game. Even the new language that he heard everywhere, Spanish, sounded gently sibilant, a pleasing contrast to the gutturals and clotted consonants of Minnesota's Germans and Scandinavians. The salubrious air and easy abundance kindled hopes of restoring his father's health and reviving the family's fortunes. At the least, his father wouldn't have to exhaust his waning energy wresting a living from soil that froze six months a year.

California had been part of the United States since the end of the Mexican–American War more than twenty years earlier. The Mexican presence remained strong. Burnham marveled at the big clanking spurs and silver-tooled saddles, tall sombreros and wooden-wheeled *carretas* pulled by donkeys. El Pueblo was also a frontier town with rough customs. Young Fred never forgot one popular spectacle. The vaqueros would rope a grizzly, truss it with rawhide, and load the roaring beast into a *carreta* bound for an adobe bear pit near what became Elysian Park. The grizzly's opponent was a long-horned wild bull. The bull always charged. The grizzly stood waiting like a patient boxer, usually dodging the horns as neatly as a matador, then swatting viciously at the bull's jaw. If the grizzly miscalculated, the bull drove a horn up through the bear's armpit.

Inspirations for a boy's imagination were easy to find among Angelenos. An old sea captain named Will Tell, who had a house at what is now Playa del Rey, fascinated Burnham with tales about whale hunting. Burnham resolved to go to sea, catch whales, and train them to carry him to Japan, where he would become a samurai who flashed two swords and cut men in half with one stroke.

Burnham also enjoyed listening to the ramblings of a drayman named Wood, who hauled small loads with his one-horse, two-wheeled cart. Wood's shack on the edge of town was fronted by a crude ramada made of sticks and willow branches. He lived there with an Indian woman whose considerable dimensions were equal in all directions. "But she had a most wonderful smile, beautiful teeth, and kindly eyes," remembered Burnham, "and she had that subtle way of treating a kid as if he were a titled Don." The old drayman, lying on his bull-hide couch while recovering from his frequent five-day toots, dissected the flaws of the town's great men and described the coming days when people would fly like eagles and probe the depths of the sea. He also dispensed practical advice, such as how to sit a horse and "If you must steal eggs, be sure and hide the shells."

It was a boy's paradise. Yet frictions that would blister it were already chafing—for instance, disputes over water. Farmers and ranchers north of town built diversion dams out of brush, boards, and rocks to tap water from the Los Angeles River. Every summer, people downstream got fed up with the leftover trickle and went upriver to tear out some dams. They were occasionally stopped, sometimes fatally, by buckshot from the riverside willows. Burnham remembered a heated town meeting that he evidently attended with his father, in which the leading citizens discussed the chronic water shortage and the possibility of storing water in nearby canyons. They concluded that the pueblo's lack of water would keep its population under 40,000.

As more Anglos migrated into Spanish Southern California, land disputes flared. The 1848 treaty that ended the Mexican–American War stipulated that the old Spanish land grants would be honored, but newcomers began challenging or ignoring them. Edwin Burnham attempted to arbitrate a quarrel between some Mexicans and Americans about a land-grant boundary. One day, with young Fred beside him, he drove a buckboard to the Mexicans' ranch. An American man, a party to the dispute, was so anxious to hear the Mexicans' response that, without Edwin's knowledge, he tailed the wagon and waited on a hillside to get the news. The palaver must not have gone well, because the Mexicans, armed with rifles, escorted Edwin to the edge of the ranch. When they spotted the American, they smelled collusion and opened fire. Bullets pattered the dust all around the buckboard. The horse bolted. No one was hit.

Most people who come under fire hope it never happens again. Not young Fred. The incident "stirred my pulses in a most lively manner," he recalled, "and indeed influenced my entire career."

It's unknown how Edwin Burnham spent his time in Los Angeles, but the Golden State failed to revive him and his fortunes. On August 1, 1873, after two and a half years there, he died of tuberculosis at age forty-nine. He left a thirty-one-year-old widow and two young boys—Fred was twelve, Howard three—but no money. Rebecca Burnham's brothers were now living in Iowa, and they offered her family a home there. To accept, Rebecca had to borrow $125 from a friend in Los Angeles for the train fare.

Fred told her he wasn't leaving California. He intended to find work and repay his mother's debt. Boys shouldered responsibilities early in those days. For Fred this had been accelerated by Edwin's long enfeeblement in Minnesota and California. Still, the boy had just turned twelve, rather early to declare complete self-reliance. Rebecca probably objected, yet she also disliked owing a large debt that she couldn't hope to repay. Perhaps she extracted a promise from Fred to join them in Iowa once the sum was paid. At any rate, she and Howard left for Iowa without him.

He was alone, nearly 2,000 miles from his family, essentially an orphan at age twelve. Such circumstances would have frightened most boys. To Burnham they meant liberation. "Certain incidents return to mind of this first year of being my own master," he wrote in a passage deleted from his memoir. "My father had held me in subjection by stern measures but now I was restrained only by my mother's love and gentle persuasion."

Liberty, however, required hard work. After three years in California Burnham was an excellent rider, so he got a job as a messenger for Western Union Telegraph. The company's wire ended in the old pueblo of Los Angeles. From there riders delivered messages to towns and haciendas for thirty miles in all directions—Anaheim, Santa Monica, San Pedro. The pay was $20 a month. Burnham had a string of four horses. He often exhausted all of them to collect extra pay for riding up to sixteen hours per day, from dawn into the night. "While doing this work," he wrote, "I first discovered that I had more endurance than other boys."

He paid off his mother's debt in less than a year. Next he wanted work with less regimentation and more adventure. During his rides across Los Angeles he often saw massive freight wagons with wheels six feet high, water barrels strapped to the tall sides, pulled by huge teams of straining mules—fourteen to twenty in a span, all of them obeying a single jerk-line held by the teamster. Entering Los Angeles the wagons were heavy with 15,000 pounds of silver and lead bullion from the mines at Cerro Gordo (Fat Hill) in the Inyo Mountains, 250 miles to the northeast. On the return trip the wagons carried equipment and local products such as fruit, nuts, vegetables, wine, brandy—things craved by miners in an isolated place.

The Cerro Gordo mines had developed quickly, following the usual pattern. In earlier years Indians and Mexicans had scratched the area for silver, without much effect aside from a few prospectors killed by irritated Indians. Then in 1865 a Mexican prospector discovered a promising seam of silver and iron ore (the two often occur together). The news spread, and by 1867 miners had rushed in to stake claims and dig. By 1870 three smelters were processing tons of ore into ingots of bullion weighing about eighty-five pounds, with "ears" on each side for lifting.

The smelters allowed higher production, necessitating more miners. Keeping the smelters' fires burning required an army of woodcutters and charcoal makers. Hauling the bullion required another army of freighters. Wherever such men congregated, merchants followed to sell the boomtown essentials: food, gear, liquor, gambling, and women. Slightly bigger boomtowns offered the next tier of amenities: stagecoach stop, mail, hotel, newspaper, jail, graveyard.

Getting the ore from Cerro Gordo to Los Angeles took enormous labor. The raw ore had to be dug from shafts sunk into the mountains, then transported down a steep twisty road carved from the rock. To slow the descent, the teamsters locked their back wheels, but mules and wagons sometimes took accidental shortcuts off the cliff. Smelters on the eastern shore of Owens Lake burned thousands of dollars of charcoal each month to turn the ore into heavy bars of bullion. Teamsters loaded these bars, cracked a blacksnake whip above their mules, and began the long haul to Los Angeles. About 100 mule teams worked the route. At first the mule skinners had to go around the upper end of Owens Lake. Today the lake is a dust bowl—it was drained long ago by the thirst of Los Angeles—but in the 1870s it was filled with blue water twenty-five miles long and ten miles wide. In 1872 a go-getter built wharves on opposite sides of the lake and launched a steam barge. It was soon carrying tons of bullion per day across the water to Cartago on the western shore. This cut three days from the trip.

From Cartago the freighters went down the baking Owens Valley, then across the sand and alkali wastes of the western Mojave, and finally over the San Gabriel Mountains to Los Angeles. Bullion freighters were catnip to bandits, so before long most wagons carried guards armed with shotguns loaded with buckshot. At one point, miners at the Comstock Lode got so frustrated by bullion bandits that they began smelting their silver into balls weighing 450 pounds, far too heavy for highwaymen on horses.

The 250-mile trip from Cerro Gordo to Los Angeles took three weeks. Every month, about 200 tons of silver and lead bullion rumbled into Los Angeles and then on to the port at San Pedro. There the ingots were loaded onto a steamer and shipped to San Francisco for further refining before being transformed into the machines, buildings, and ornaments of the Gilded Age.

In just a few years, Cerro Gordo's bullion began changing Los Angeles. Brick started replacing adobe. New merchants who catered to some part of the mining operation, or to the consumers making money from it, opened storefronts. "What Los Angeles is, is mainly due to [the bullion trade]," said the *Los Angeles Daily News* in the early 1870s. "It is the silver cord that binds our present existence. Should it be uncomfortably severed, we would inevitably collapse."

Collapse did threaten several times when other ambitious burgs, such as Ventura and Bakersfield, tried to snatch away the bullion traffic. The trade was also threatened by merchants along the routes, who began gouging the freighters for hay and barley to feed their mules. Some freighters left in disgust to work in Nevada, hauling borax or bullion from the Comstock Lode. Soon there weren't enough mule teams to haul the wealth coming out of Cerro Gordo's smelters. The ingots piled up on the shore of Owens Lake. Workers began building shelters made of silver bars and canvas roofs. By May 1873 more than 20,000 ingots were stranded at Owens Lake waiting to be pulled to Los Angeles. The owners of the mines and smelters were desperate.

A freighter named Remi Nadeau, who had earlier abandoned the route, reentered the picture. He made a deal with the owners of two smelters to become partners in a freight company and to build a dozen stations along the bullion trail to Los Angeles. By September 1873 Nadeau had eighty mule teams working the route. About fifty teams carried bullion, each one pulling three huge wagons loaded with 170 bars weighing more than seven tons. The other teams hauled food to the stations for the teamsters and their mules.

Each segment between stations was a one-day trip, worked by four teams. Every day two teams per segment headed north and two headed south, passing each other in opposite directions. Nadeau's system was remarkably efficient. The stacks of ingots on the wharves at Owens Lake rapidly shrank, and the smelters doubled their production. All of it rolled through Los Angeles, enriching people along the way.

Sometime in 1874, when he was thirteen, Burnham began working for Nadeau's operation as a freelance hunter. He supplied fresh game to the teamsters who lived at the company's remote stations in the wild mountains and deserts north of Los Angeles. The stations' names hint at the allure of the job for a boy seeking adventure: Nine Mile Canyon, Barrel Springs, Red Rock Canyon, Cow Holes, Willow Springs, Forks-of-the-Road, Coyote Holes, Tujunga Pass. "Along this route," wrote Burnham, "I explored and hunted, often alone for weeks at a time."

During this period he met several old scouts and Indian fighters, and had a short conversation with General George Crook, famous for his recent campaigns against the Apaches in Arizona. The conversation with Crook "set me afire to reach the still little-known frontiers of Arizona and old Mexico," wrote Burnham. One scout he came across had served with General Zachary Taylor during the Mexican–American War. Burnham attached himself to this taciturn man and gleaned what he could during the intervals when liquor had loosened the scout's tongue but not yet left him incoherent.

At a campfire during a trip into the San Gabriel Mountains, the scout used corncobs to explain some of Vauban's principles of fortification. An educated man, he loaned Burnham books on similar subjects, as well as William H. Prescott's histories of the conquests of Mexico and Peru, the lives of Hannibal and Cyrus the Great, and the works of the African explorer and missionary David Livingstone. Burnham became a lifelong student of military tactics, battles, and soldiers; his writings are filled with references to them.

During this time he also had a brush with one of the state's most notorious bandits, Tiburcio Vásquez. Vásquez's long career as an outlaw began as a teenager in 1854, when he got mixed up in a fatal quarrel between Californios and Americanos over some señoritas at a fandango. For nearly twenty years, interrupted by stints in San Quentin prison, Vásquez was a busy but common thief, stealing horses and cattle, breaking into houses, holding up stores, wagons, and stagecoaches.

But in 1873, around the time Burnham began riding for Western Union, Vásquez became infamous. While raiding a town in Fresno County, his gang killed three bystanders. This was the first in a spree of brazen sackings that alarmed the entire state and made news across the country. By the end of 1873 the California legislature had authorized the immense sum of $15,000 for Vásquez's capture, and the governor had put a bounty on him, $8,000 if alive, $6,000 if dead. Despite some chases and gunfire, Vásquez eluded all pursuers, hiding in the San Joaquin Valley and in the forests and canyons of the rugged San Gabriel and Verdugo Mountains.

Burnham, thirteen at the time, was in the Verdugos hunting game for Nadeau's stations. One evening he tethered his black horse in a side canyon and made camp. At four the next morning he rose to stake out a water hole for deer. A few hours later, when he went to get his horse, it was gone. Mingled with its hoofprints were impressions left very recently by the small heels of Mexican boots. Burnham tried to intercept the thief by running two miles up a peak and down to the trail. There he found fresh tracks made by his horse, leaving the canyon. Walking out, he came across some Mexican woodcutters who told him that he had just missed seeing the famous bandit Vásquez ride by on a handsome black horse.

Burnham soon came across Vásquez again. Dozens of men were hunting the outlaw. In the spring of 1874 he went to ground at the adobe home of Giorgios Caralambo in the northwest corner of Rancho La Brea (named after the tar pits there), in what is now West Hollywood. Caralambo, better known as "Greek George," had come to America as a camel driver for the U.S. Army's short-lived Camel Corps.

The idea for the corps arose after the Mexican–American War, when the United States found itself in possession of vast stretches of Southwestern desert. Someone convinced U.S. Secretary of War Jefferson Davis that the best way to move military supplies and communications across such wastes was the camel. In the mid-1850s Congress funded the idea and the army sent someone to the Middle East to buy camels and recruit drivers. Thirty-three dromedaries survived a trip to Texas, soon followed by forty-four more. The imported camel drivers, aside from Greek George, included another man who became famous in the West, Hajj Ali, whose name the Americans transformed into Hi Jolly. The drivers trained soldiers how to handle and pack the camels.

In June 1857 the Camel Corps left Texas for California. The camels quickly demonstrated their value. They could walk thirty miles a day carrying three or four times the load of a mule, could go for days without water, and could survive on the thorniest desert scrub. There was talk of importing another 1,000 camels and building camel stations across the Great American Desert for military operations and delivery of mail. But Congress got distracted by the divisions leading up to the Civil War and failed to approve more funding. In the early 1860s the army auctioned off the camels. Hajj Ali bought a few to run freight between the Colorado River and mining camps in Arizona, but the business failed and he released his camels into the Sonoran Desert in southwestern Arizona. Burnham once chased one for five days there, and travelers reported sightings into the twentieth century.

During the years of the Camel Corps, a wealthy lawyer and landowner in Los Angeles named Henry Hancock had noticed Greek George Caralambo's skill with the animals. When the corps disbanded, Hancock hired Caralambo to look after livestock on his property at Rancho La Brea. Hence Greek George's adobe house there, where the outlaw Vásquez was holed up in May 1874.

The sheriff of Los Angeles got a tip about Vásquez's whereabouts. Some accounts say a disgruntled member of his gang betrayed him; others credit the family of one of the many young women Vásquez had seduced and abandoned. On May 14 a posse raided Greek George's rancho and surprised the bandit, who dove out a window and got peppered with six shots before surrendering. His capture was reported as far away as New York City.

Vásquez spent nine days in jail in Los Angeles. His visitors included Burnham, who reminded the bandit about the black horse stolen in the Verdugos. Vásquez laughed and offered Burnham his own pinto, demonstrating some of his famous charm. According to Burnham, the sheriff allowed him to ride the horse proudly around Los Angeles.

Vásquez was transferred to San Jose, where he was nursed back to health so he could be tried and hung. Meanwhile, he proved adept at operating in that peculiar American zone where criminality becomes indistinguishable from celebrity. Handsome and courtly, fluent in Spanish and English, he often attracted hundreds of visitors a day, many of them women, who brought flowers and other gifts. He posed for photographs and sold autographed copies from his prison window. He hand-picked reporters to do interviews and used his soapbox to claim that he had spent his life fighting against gringo discrimination and in support of the return of California to Mexico, but unfortunately he had been the victim of greedy Anglos who had left him no choice but a life of crime. Some Mexican Americans, eager for a hero, swallowed Vásquez's malarkey and esteemed him as a champion who had stood up to the land-hungry Americanos. In his understanding of media and the manipulation of public opinion, he was visionary.

Vásquez admitted some of his crimes but, despite considerable evidence, denied killing anyone. The jury needed only two hours to disagree, convicting him of murder. He was hanged on March 19, 1875.

Soon after Vásquez swung, Burnham got a letter from Iowa. His mother must have been worried about him. Her brothers, highly Christian men, certainly considered it improper that a boy barely into his teens was roving unsupervised among Satan's blandishments in California. One of these uncles, Josiah Russell, sent for Burnham and offered to pay for schooling. This patriarchal summons, accompanied by the insinuation that, unlike his ancestors, young Fred was neglecting his education, altered the boy's course. In the spring of 1875, at age fourteen, he left the mountains and deserts of golden California and took a train back to his family on the plains of the Midwest.

———

Clinton, Iowa, population around 7,500, sat on the Mississippi River at the state's eastern edge. Whatever pleasure Burnham got from reuniting with his mother and brother was soon dampened by life in his new home. Aside from an exciting visit by his mother's old school friend Buffalo Bill Cody, Burnham found Clinton a dreary burg. In *Scouting on Two Continents* he disguised the place with the pseudonym Montville to ease the sting of his comments.

"The town was just old enough to have lost its rugged pioneers and Indian fighters," he wrote, "and had become a strange combination of materialism and intolerant religiosity. When the inhabitants were not trying to reform one another, they were wholly bent on making a lot of money."

To a boy fresh from the bustling diversity of Los Angeles, and from sharing campfires with old scouts in wild mountains, Clinton felt like a monochrome jail. Fun and free spirits were shushed and punished. A grim schoolmarm pounded the three Rs into Clinton's students. "Sunday was an awful day," wrote Burnham. "No one dared swim in the river, fish, or go boating. Baseball or football on that day would have led to immediate arrest." Burnham often found himself standing in front of the local bank's big chromolithographs of mountains in Colorado, like a prisoner staring through bars at lost freedom.

Clinton's teenaged boys were bursting with energy, but the town's stifling religious decorum gave them few chances to release it. Burnham lit the fuse. He organized secret societies, such as Indian tribes and a Trappers' League. The members made moccasins and dugout canoes, and practiced marksmanship with .22 pistols. To toughen themselves, they lashed one another with hickory switches until they could withstand the pain without crying or flinching.

Naturally, this band of brothers carried out missions worthy of their training. Some of their shenanigans were simple pranks, but others required know-how and planning. They used a block-and-tackle to drop wagons on top of barns, and moved other heavy objects to comical new locations around town. The adults were not amused. Despite severe parental interrogations, during which the training with hickory switches came in handy, the tribe preserved a code of silence.

Teenaged boys have a metaphorical kinship with explosives, and when the tribe learned how to make nitroglycerin, the next step was clear. Their target: a peevish deacon who often chased them out of his woodlot, not because they were damaging his property but "because he hated to see us having such a good time." One Sunday afternoon, while people in their church clothes strolled through the nearby graveyard, the tribe saturated cotton with nitro, snuck into the deacon's woods, and wrapped the bomb around one of his trees. The saboteurs withdrew about eighty yards. From there Burnham fired a rifle shot to detonate the nitro. The tree became toothpicks. Shocked but thrilled, the tribe quickly reverted to innocent bystanders and joined the crowd rushing to see what had happened. They survived strong suspicions and a furious investigation.

Then Sister Maggie Newton Van Cott—"the first lady licensed to preach in the Methodist Episcopal Church in the United States," according to her biographer—brought her revival tent to town. After several nights of brimstone, one of Burnham's young braves felt scorched by hellfire. He dragged his sins to the mourners' bench and spilled every classified secret. The tribe was soon in disarray.

"Through all this nonsense," wrote Burnham, "matters were coming to a real crisis with me. Games began to pall. I felt an urge to do bigger things." His uncles agreed it was high time for this young savage to give up monkeyshines and buckle down. They laid out their plan for his life, which excluded any foolishness about scouting or Africa. "The consensus of opinion," wrote Burnham, "was that I should have a strong-handed guardian who would see that every hour of my day should bring its appointed task and who would give constant attention to my spiritual instruction."

For a time he submitted, out of deference to the debt he owed his uncles for the ticket from California and a year of education. He was also held in Clinton by a pretty, spirited girl named Blanche Blick, who seemed excited by his wide-horizon dreams about scouting and Africa. But when his uncles apprenticed him to one of Clinton's dreary money-grubbers, something snapped.

"I cut the knot of all my difficulties," wrote Burnham, "by taking to the great river in a canoe, one dark night. Then, abandoning the river, I headed for the plains—the Southwest and Freedom." He was fifteen.

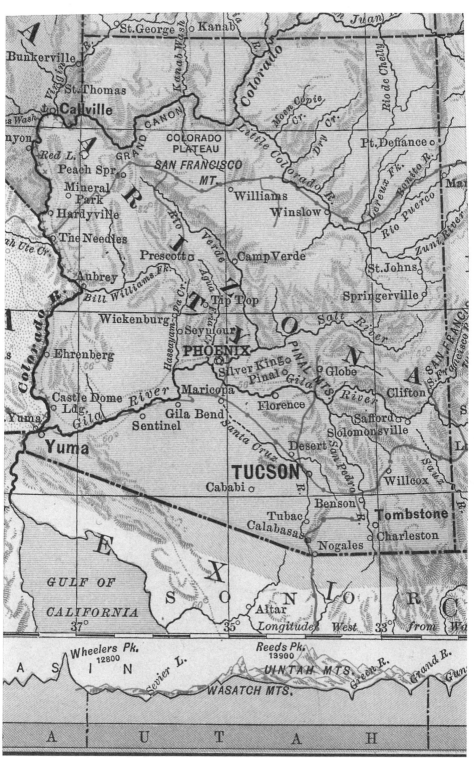

Arizona Territory. (From *Barnes's Complete Geography* by James Monteith, 1885.)

CHAPTER THREE

WANDERINGS AND APPRENTICESHIPS

AFTER ESCAPING IOWA, Burnham began what he called "a period of glorious wandering." He drifted southwest across Missouri, Kansas, and Oklahoma, sometimes trailing remnant herds of the once-countless buffalo. Once, when he and several companions were surprised by a blizzard in the Texas panhandle, they swaddled themselves and their horses in green buffalo hides, hair side in. The hides froze solid but saved their lives.

Burnham paused in Texas, working as a cowpuncher, driving herds to slaughterhouses in Kansas. To make a stake, he ran a string of mustangs from Texas to Missouri. He blew his take on fancy spurs and other cowboy trappings, and was soon adrift again. At some point during these years, he and a boyhood friend named Homer Blick briefly returned to Iowa—not to Clinton, to see Burnham's family, but to Prescott, 275 miles west of there, where Blick's parents had moved with his sister, Blanche, the Clinton girl who had listened eagerly to Burnham's dreams about scouting and Africa. "The schoolgirl sister still remembered me," wrote Burnham, "and when again I rode into the wilderness, there was much in my heart to disturb my plans for the future—but I rode alone and far."

His direction was southwest. Tales remembered from his California days pulled him toward the unruly frontier there. "No charm could hold me long against the lure of New and Old Mexico and Arizona."

He made his way to Sante Fe, where lures were in short supply. So were lawful opportunities. He heard that mining camps were sprouting farther west, so he headed for Prescott, a gold-rush town barely fifteen years old, yet the capital of the sparsely populated Territory of Arizona. Soon after he set off, someone stole his only horse, leaving him worse than broke. Prescott was 500 miles away, across snow-covered mountains and country made hazardous by the latest Apache outbreak. He started walking. To avoid Indians, he traveled mostly at night, which also kept him from freezing in the winter dark. During the day he rested on a "Tucson bed," made by using his back for a mattress and his belly for a blanket.

It's hard to nail down a timeline for Burnham's whereabouts during these years. His memoirs are little help, jumping around chronologically. But taken together with other references, his mention of Apaches raiding and haunting the mountains on the Arizona–New Mexico border probably refers to the rampage led by Victorio from September 1879 to October 1880. Since the mountains were covered with snow during Burnham's trek, he likely made it in late 1879 or early 1880 when he was eighteen.

Cold, hunger, Indians, and frigid rivers almost did him in, but he also marveled at sights along the way: petrified forests, the Painted Desert, abandoned cliff dwellings. After a month or so he walked into Prescott. Gold had been discovered nearby in 1863, which led in 1864 to the nearly simultaneous founding of Prescott and its protective outpost, Fort Whipple. Both were in territory claimed by Apaches. The gold miners promptly ruined relations with the Indians by killing two Apache boys who wandered into a camp on the boomtown's edge. The Apaches retaliated by massacring some miners. This violent cycle, constantly renewed by fresh blood, would send waves of terror through the region for the next twenty years.

By 1870, to serve its population of 668 plus itinerant prospectors,

Prescott offered ten saloons, twice that many gambling halls, and one "eating house" in a log cabin, run by a woman called Virgin Mary. Her posted menu:

Breakfast: *Fried venison and chili, bread, coffee, goat milk*
Dinner: *Roast venison and chili, bread, coffee, goat milk*
Supper: *Chili*

When Burnham arrived a decade later, the town had grown to about 1,800. He may have crossed paths with Virgil Earp, who lived there in 1879 before leaving to meet Wyatt and his other brothers in a southerly boomtown named Tombstone, where Burnham certainly knew them.

Meanwhile, in Prescott, he met two men who furthered his education in scouting. The first was an old-timer named Holmes who had served with John C. Fremont and Kit Carson during some of Fremont's explorations and blunders in the 1840s. Holmes's family had been wiped out by Indians, and he was half broken in body and mind. Before he died he wanted to pass on some of his woodcraft, but he was often so vehemently demeaning to the boys drawn to him that they soon avoided him.

Except Burnham. When Holmes cursed that young Fred didn't know how to saddle a horse properly, or to hobble it properly, or to braid a proper rope to use as a hobble, or to tie the right knot with his poorly braided rope, Burnham didn't slouch off but listened and learned, and then showed up the next day for more. Holmes began to take him seriously. He and his eighteen-year-old apprentice traveled into the mountains of Arizona, New Mexico, and northern Mexico for six months of advanced training in hunting, tracking, and woodcraft.

Holmes flooded Burnham with information and scorched him with criticism. There was a right way, a precise way, to do everything. One small error, one careless moment, could have devastating consequences, especially in hostile territory. Saddling a horse improperly, for instance, overtaxed its muscles, which affected its gait and durability and might even cause lameness. A horse improperly hobbled, or hobbled with a poorly braided rope, could break free when spooked, leaving its owner on foot.

Holmes also taught Burnham survival skills that often saved him in future years: how to protect himself from snakes, floods, and forest fires; the best way to ascend and descend cliffs; how to find water in the desert and to forage for food; how to travel by the stars and maintain direction during daylight without a compass; how to double back, avoid ambush, and hide his trail.

The tracks of other horses brimmed with information. How many horses had passed? When? Were they walking, trotting, or galloping? Was it a war party or a hunting party? If a single horse, was it running free or carrying a rider? Was it tired or fresh? Holmes could study a horse's tracks and follow them even when mixed with hundreds of others. This may seem unbelievable but was not uncommon among good trackers, who could trail a horse for hundreds of miles. "The [horse] thieves had three days start and the trail had grown somewhat cold and in places obliterated by the passage of other stock over it," began a story with the headline "Good Work Done by Good Men: Horse Thieves Caught and Stock Recovered!" in the *Arizona Silver Belt* in February 1883, "but the pursuers were no novices, and so they never lost the tracks. One of the animals stolen . . . had a mule shoe on the off fore foot, which, on account of its greater squareness at the toe made it easier tracking."

The same was true for human footprints. Even when someone tried to eliminate tracks by covering his shoes or moccasins with burlap, he compressed the desert's surface and left a smooth "shine" that, in slanting sunlight, contrasted with untrod ground.

Tracks also disclosed a timeline. Were the tracks' edges collapsing or still sharp? If it had rained recently, were the tracks mottled and eroded or untouched by raindrops? Had night animals or insects left sign atop or beneath the tracks? Horse droppings, too, were time capsules—how far toward their center were they dry, relative to the temperature and other conditions? Likewise broken twigs—was the end fresh or dried out? A skilled tracker only needed a few clues: fibers caught on bushes, pebbles overturned or pressed into the ground.

Animals spoke to the attentive scout. The alarm cry of a bird, the clatter of a panicked deer, a sudden pause in the chorus of droning insects— these were alerts. Burnham also learned to pay close attention to his horse, a sentinel with superior hearing. If your horse dilated its nostrils, or lifted its head and pointed its ears in a particular direction, heed the signal. If your horse stopped grazing, note the direction of its cocked ear. If it resumed feeding, relax; if it didn't, investigate.

To the observant, said Holmes, the tiniest details carried messages. A broken cobweb indicated that someone or something recently passed by during daylight, since most webs were spun overnight. Other signs of passage: scuff marks, bent grass, small stones dislodged from their cradles, a disturbed ants' nest. Airflow, Holmes told Burnham, resembles a river whose currents carry sensory information—a tip that would save Burnham's life in South Africa when he avoided blundering into a group of Boers because their camp smoke drifted down a ravine. A scout was someone on whom nothing was lost. Every sign was a word, and the words accumulated into a story.

Burnham's second mentor in Prescott was "Dead Eye" Lee, who had scouted for George Crook in his first campaign against the Apaches from 1872 to 1873. Like most men in Arizona Territory, Lee had gold fever and was now trying his luck at prospecting. Burnham was eager to learn that skill as well as everything Lee could teach him about scoutcraft. Lee took Burnham into the Santa Maria Mountains northwest of Prescott, "a rough desert land of wide mesas covered with boulders or lava and cleft by tortuous canyons hundreds of feet deep."

Lee taught him that these desert slot canyons, barely touched by the sun and impenetrable by a horse, often held water at their lowest point. He advised carrying a piece of canvas or rubber cloth to lug this hidden water to your horse. Absent those, he showed Burnham how to use a saddle blanket or even his clothing to absorb a gallon or two that could be transported to a horse, without too much loss, by turning the sopping bundle over and over in a ball as he walked, then wringing it out into a hat or rock hollow. Agaves could save a thirsty man; their basal leaves sometimes held pockets of old rainwater that could be sipped through a reed straw. An Apache on the move would sometimes fill a dead horse's intestines with water and wrap them around his body. If desperate, you could chew the inside of certain cactuses, especially barrel cactus, for moisture.

The other necessity was food, for man and mount. To travel into dangerous country where a gunshot or a fire was inadvisable, a frontiersman carried nutritious prepared food. In Arizona, the preferred ration called for grinding dried venison into powder, adding an equal amount of flour, and baking the mixture into hard loaves that fit into saddlebags. "Ten pounds of this concentrated food," wrote Burnham, "would, at a pinch, last a man ten days and keep him in strength, albeit lean and hungry." Apaches often made do with a bag of pinole, maize flour mixed with dried crushed seeds and mesquite beans. Later, in Africa, Burnham would become familiar with the "iron rations" of other cultures—for the Maasai, the milk and blood of cows; for the Bedouin, dates and camel's milk.

In a harsh land where inexperienced people who ran out of food would starve, Indians and frontiersmen could sustain themselves by foraging. The plentiful yucca offered edible fruit and flowers, and the seeds could be ground into flour. Wild potatoes, berries, and squash grew for those who knew how to find them, and ground bees would lead you to honey. Even the soft inner bark of the pine could be chewed for sustenance. To survive, a scout trained his stomach to digest almost anything.

Lee had hunted Apaches for Crook in Arizona's rough canyon country, where the Indians seemed to vanish. One way Lee tracked them was through their staple food, hearts of mescal, which they roasted in great mounds and occasionally fermented into a liquor. The Apaches were expert at concealing the smoke from these bakes, but they couldn't hide the aroma, which wafted down narrow canyons on air currents and could be traced to its source.

Lee, like Holmes, used this example to underscore two things for young Burnham. First, a scout must develop and train all five senses to the highest degree, not just sight and hearing but smell, touch, and taste. Each of these senses would one day save Burnham's life. He trained his peripheral vision to almost 180 degrees, a skill he later demonstrated to incredulous journalists. "He can stroll casually through a street of fifty shops," wrote a London reporter after Burnham returned from the Boer War, "and tell you at the other end the name, business, and principal articles exhibited in connection with each establishment."

To keep his senses sharp, Burnham early on gave up tobacco. Likewise alcohol, which saturated mining camps and boomtowns. Men who didn't drink were often mocked, but Burnham avoided liquor as detrimental to a scout's perceptions. (Temperance had nothing to do with this; he later opposed Prohibition. He also served alcohol to guests, and on rare occasions had a glass of wine or beer, but he seems to have gotten tipsy just once, when he accidentally took a big gulp of a friend's cocktail. "And it has made me woozy," he wrote to his wife. "If you were here now you would see [me] nearer drunk than you ever did in your life, a delightfully swaying sensation in the head, but a great desire left to see you right away and *now*. We must have one drunk together just to know what it is before we cross to the great unknown." It was 1911 and he was fifty.)

Whatever dulled the senses was hazardous to the scout. For that reason it was necessary to train yourself to endure deprivation for long periods— hunger, thirst, sleeplessness, absolute stillness—while remaining alert. The hardest of these to defeat was lack of sleep. Burnham eventually disciplined himself to operate without it for two nights and part of another day. The worst hours to get through were three o'clock to five o'clock in the morning, when pinches and pinpricks and bitten lips no longer worked. Then he switched to harsher reminders: sharp raps with a knuckle on the back of the head, or a borrowed bit of tobacco rubbed near the eyes. "By thus torturing myself," he wrote, "I kept going."

Second, Lee emphasized that in addition to physical and observational skills, a scout needed psychological insight. It was vital to learn everything possible about a foe's culture, tactics, social customs, and superstitions. Such intelligence was as valuable as woodcraft or knowledge of landscape because it offered clues about how that foe would act and react in various circumstances.

To all these things the scout must add the skills of deduction and improvisation—the ability, wrote Burnham, "to interpret and to act," sometimes instantaneously, in response to the unexpected.

Even mastering all this, instructed Lee, was not enough. The scout also needed to develop the psychological strength to spend long periods by himself. "Ten days in the mountains alone," said Lee, "especially if it is hostile country, will teach you more than I can tell you in six months." In his writings, Burnham often refers to this lesson. A scout spent most of his time alone, completely self-reliant, amid enemies who wanted to kill him. Essentially, the scout had to accustom himself to being prey.

"There is nothing that sharpens a man's senses so acutely," wrote Burnham, "as to know that bitter and determined enemies are in pursuit of him night and day. In many lines of endeavour, errors may be repeated without fatal results, but in an Indian or savage war, or in a bitter feud, one little slip entails the 'Absent' mark for ever against a man's name."

Learning to endure isolation was essential but painful. "The lash of solitude," wrote Burnham, was "one of the greatest ordeals in the world." It intensified everything, from perceptions to mental stress. Only in solitude could a scout learn to concentrate his mind for hours on one focus, yet too much isolation could destroy a scout's mental balance. Inability to bear solitude led to mistakes. A lapse in alertness or patience, a surrender to boredom, meant missed clues, which could be fatal. For most men, the combination of physical hardship, imminent menace, and solitude was intolerable.

"What the white scout has to learn from the Indian," wrote Burnham, "is the power to endure loneliness, as well as the stoical indifference to physical pain. The Boers of the high veldt, the Tauregs and Beduoins of the desert, and the Apaches, have this power in superlative degree." These tribes, especially the Apaches, exemplified Burnham's scouting ideals: iron bodies, iron wills, and encyclopedic mastery of their environments.

———

After his apprenticeships with the old scouts, Burnham set out on his own. As usual, he was broke. Penniless young men in Arizona who preferred lawful work often did odd jobs until they could scrape together a few dollars for some salt, flour, coffee, fatty bacon, and beans ("Arizona strawberries"). To these they added a pick, a shovel, a miner's pan, and a horn spoon. This latter was essential for detecting gold, evinced by the common oath, "I swear by the great horn spoon." It was a cow's horn cut in half lengthwise to produce a curved shallow vessel. Prospectors put promising ore into their horn spoons, added water, then gently swirled, hoping for glitter. They loaded their tools and supplies onto a horse or mule, along with their dreams, and disappeared into the mountains to prospect for gold and silver. A friend of Burnham's wrote of those days, "Travel—it was the impulse and the act and the life. There were fairly no moorings: neither home nor bonnet nor bib. There were restless young men in droves; there was the atmosphere of adventure with prospects everywhere."

Everyone knew stories about prospectors who found a seam and followed it to fabulous wealth. Burnham resembled all the other dreamers hoping for a big strike. As an eighteen-year-old in Arizona he caught gold fever—his words—and never recovered. He chased bonanzas for the rest of his life, with just enough luck to keep his hopes burning.

In what was probably the latter half of 1880, he outfitted himself and rode into the mountains of central Arizona, "determined to wrest from them their hidden treasure."

———

The high country mocked his dreams and wore him out—the fate of most prospectors. By the spring of 1881 his clothes were rags, his boots busted. He was so skinny, as the saying went, that if he closed one eye he looked like a needle. He could hang his hat on his horse's jutting hip bones.

It was time to rejoin the world, recuperate, and make some cash. He heard about a new silver strike at Globe, eighty-five miles south, and decided to go where the fresh money was flowing. He rode down off the grand escarpment called the Mogollon Rim. "Others have ridden to the rock rim of the world and gazed into the depths below," he wrote, "climbing and delving into every cranny—to no end. My own venture cost me all I had made, and I came down into the warm valleys of Tonto Basin and Salt River to begin life anew."

That new life soon enmeshed him in the bloodiest feud in U.S. history.

CHAPTER FOUR

THE TONTO BASIN FEUD

THE ROUTE TOWARD Globe took Burnham into the Tonto Basin. This extensive bowl, fifty miles long and thirty wide, enclosed some of the roughest terrain in Arizona. The basin was flanked by mountain ranges and cut by dozens of creeks, gorges, and broken-rock canyons. Hostile Apaches often used it as a refuge. It was remote and even more sparsely populated than the rest of sparsely-populated Arizona.

The diary of a young woman named Angeline Mitchell Brown, who came to Tonto Basin in the late 1870s to teach, captures the flavor of life there at the time. Her school had walls made of brush that enclosed a patch of dirt, and no door. One day while teaching she felt something tugging at her skirts. It was a foot-long Gila monster that lived in a hole near her desk and liked to sun itself there every morning. They learned to tolerate each other. Whenever the venomous lizard got in the way, she picked it up by the tail and moved it. Sometimes she stroked its back with a pencil.

One night in the cabin where she was staying, a loud purring woke her. Through a chink in the wall, a cougar's paw was reaching for her. Twelve days later a band of Apaches in war paint rushed the cabin. The leader rode right in, but the low ceiling turned his dramatic entrance into a visual joke, so he backed out. Fourteen warriors and one boy stormed inside. They found Brown, two other women, and a baby. The oldest woman stepped forward and extended her hand. The Apaches, brandishing knives, pinched the women, pulled their hair, ripped earrings from their lobes. The women didn't make a sound. The Apache boy was ransacking the cabin. When he found Brown's precious photographs, she jumped up and grabbed them, and hit him in the face, an impetuosity she immediately regretted. Everything stopped. Torture and death seemed certain. Instead, in a bow to the women's bravery, the Apaches left.

Around this time, a family named Gordon tried to establish a ranch in the mountains on the basin's northern edge, but the bitter winters drove them into the valleys of the Tonto. (The family's first location is still called Gordon Canyon.) They tried again forty miles to the south, on the Salt River, where they built a primitive house and a few brush corrals for their cattle.

Burnham paused there one day on the way to Globe, to graze his scrawny horse. The Gordons had little, but the raggedy young stranger clearly had less. The family offered him a meal and a place to rest. "This hospitality and the consequent turning aside from my purpose forged the first link in a chain of events that for years I could not break," wrote Burnham. "I became a thread woven into a strange and intricate pattern—a pattern sometimes bright and cheerful, but never altogether free of the black warp of crime and the red woof of bloodshed which made up so much of the fabric of life in Arizona and northern Mexico in those days."

The bright cheerful bits stemmed from his deepening friendship with the Gordons. So did the crime and bloodshed. The family was about to be drawn into what became known as the Tonto Basin Feud, sometimes called the Pleasant Valley War. Burnham's code of friendship and justice evidently entangled him in the Gordons' predicament and endangered his life. Yet he was lucky. In the coming decade, many men in the basin would be killed in ambushes, gunfights, and lynchings.

The feud's origins were tangled and remain murky. Horse theft and cattle rustling played a part. So did animosity between cattlemen and sheep men. Friendships curdled because of greed and betrayal. Outside the basin, the money men in towns such as Payson, Prescott, Flagstaff, and Globe operated in the background, playing sides against one another to create opportunities for advancing their fortunes.

Many cowboys and drifters like Burnham were sucked into the feud, but its vortex was created by three families: the Grahams, the Blevinses, and the Tewksburys. All were shirttail ranchers trying to scratch a living in the most out-of-the-way fragment of the Tonto Basin, a verdant open valley tucked under the Mogollon Rim and hemmed in by mountains. The place was so isolated that settlers didn't penetrate there until the mid-1870s. They named it Pleasant Valley.

The fastest way for a small rancher to get bigger, or for a cowboy to supplement his meager pay, was rustling, either by outright theft or by branding other men's calves in the spring. The Grahams and Tewksburys began as friendly partners in crime, filching mostly from Jim Stinson, owner of the valley's largest cattle operation. But at some point the Grahams registered all the rebranded cattle under their name only, cutting out the Tewksburys.

This double-cross festered into a grudge. Stinson long suspected the Grahams and Tewksburys of stealing from him, and he shrewdly widened the rupture between them by hiring the Grahams to gather evidence of rustling against the Tewksburys. In an equally shrewd move, the Daggs brothers, who owned the Arizona Territory's biggest sheep operation, took advantage of the rift by hiring the Tewksburys to help them defy the basin's cattlemen and run sheep into the lush grass of Pleasant Valley.

The bitter emotions aroused by theft and betrayal were intensified by the cutthroat rivalry between cattlemen and sheep men for pasturage. On the Graham side, all of this was probably tinged with racial resentment of the Tewksburys as "half-breeds"—the mother of John D. Tewksbury's three adult sons was a Klamath Indian.

Throughout the early 1880s, the conflict escalated from legal counterclaims to rougher forms of hostility, mostly from the Graham/cattlemen faction. Someone killed a valuable sheepdog. Someone shot the coffeepot from a shepherd's hand. The cabin of a man associated with the sheep men was burned. A flock of prize male sheep was clubbed to death. Men on horseback, firing pistols, stampeded a herd of ewes over a cliff. In the surrounding towns, men in saloons traded threats.

Human blood spilled in February 1887. A Ute Indian hired to tend sheep in Pleasant Valley was found bullet-riddled and beheaded, perhaps to frustrate identification. Over the next few years, many more cold-blooded murders followed on each side. The famous Hatfield–McCoy feud claimed about a dozen lives. In the Tonto Basin War, at least thirty men died, with estimates up to fifty. The vendetta decimated the principal families and their associates, but also claimed innocent sheepherders, cowboys, and prospectors who wandered into its web. This feud, along with frequent rampages by Apaches and the rough justice in towns like Tombstone, helped convince the rest of the country that Arizona was too savage to deserve statehood. (Arizona was the last of the forty-eight contiguous states permitted into the Union, in February 1912.)

Among all the Grahams, Blevinses, and Tewksburys, only one male survived. In 1892 the last Tewksbury, Edwin, almost certainly murdered the last Graham, Tom, assassinating him from ambush with the help of an accomplice. Despite extensive evidence, including eyewitness identifications by several witnesses including Tom Graham, who took hours to die, neither Edwin nor his accomplice were convicted.

Despite the presence of sheriffs and judges on the Arizona frontier, justice was erratic. It could be as sudden as a bullet. Sometimes a town mob or an isolated band of cowboys turned matters over to Judge Lynch and sentenced a killer or rustler to the "jerk plan." In 1883, for example, during the robbery of a store in Bisbee, a gang fired indiscriminately into a crowd and killed five people. The five gunmen were caught, sentenced, and hung. A Bisbee dance hall owner named John Heith, who had planned the robbery but hadn't participated, also was arrested and sentenced to life in prison. Citizens from Bisbee considered that a lenient miscarriage of justice. They dragged Heith from the county jail in Tombstone and hanged him from a telegraph pole. No one in the mob wore masks, and everyone knew the men involved. This could have posed a problem for the coroner's jury charged with investigating the lynching. Tombstone's coroner, Dr. George Goodfellow, who had witnessed the execution, devised a solution: he ruled that the cause of death was "emphysema of the lungs" produced "by strangulation, self-inflicted or otherwise."

In the case of Edwin Tewksbury, justice proved not only blind but malleable to the point of farce. During his two trials for the murder of Tom Graham, Edwin benefited from alibis concocted for him by a parade of friendly witnesses. Equally crucial, Edwin had the advantage of a pricey defense team, probably paid for by the wealthy sheep barons, the Daggs brothers. In 1926 when an Arizona historical society wrote to P. P. Daggs asking for his memoirs, including his role in the feud, Daggs replied, "I know you would not be unkind enough to lure me into anything for which I would be captured and shot at sunrise. I have one consolation[—]the enemy will not do it. They are all sleeping in premature graves with their 'boots on.' I ought to know something about the 'Tonto War.' It cost me enough . . . ninety thousand dollars." Even forty years after the feud ended, Daggs tempered gloating with caution.

Volatile feelings lingered for decades in Tonto Basin. Zane Grey, writer of popular Western novels, was fascinated by the feud and started making research trips into the basin in 1918. He called it "the wildest, most rugged, roughest, and most remarkable country" he had ever seen, with inhabitants to match. He eventually bought a cabin on the Mogollon Rim and spent several months there every year. In the foreword to his novel about the feud, *To the Last Man* (1921), he remarked, "I never learned the truth of the cause of the Pleasant Valley War, or if I did hear it I had no means of recognizing it. All the given causes were plausible and convincing. Strange to state, there is still secrecy and reticence all over Tonto Basin as to the facts of this feud. Many descendants of those killed are living there now. But no one likes to talk about it."

During the feud and for decades afterward, each faction's supporters spun competing versions of events. The biases are apparent in most books written about it. From any perspective, the feud was ugly through and through.

———

The same year that P. P. Daggs responded to the historical society, *Scouting on Two Continents* appeared. In his account of the feud and his minor role in it, Burnham explained that he hid identities because emotions in Arizona were still raw. His rough draft, however, referred to the Gordons by name. This family consisted of "old man" William Gordon (then in his fifties), his rugged wife Betsy, five daughters, and a son, Tom, several years younger than Burnham.

After they befriended him, Burnham eventually went on toward Globe, a silver boomtown founded in 1873. Five years later there still wasn't a house made of lumber or a shingle roof. Everything was adobe, with roofs of dirt or grass. Around Globe, Burnham worked as a cowboy and mining camp hunter. From talk overheard in town, he gathered that large forces were about to collide. "I sensed the growing struggle among officials and politicians as to whether Arizona should be run by a few great cattle barons or by certain wealthy sheep men backed by allied interests in the towns."

Every few weeks he rode twenty miles or so to spend time with the Gordons on the Salt River. As a young drifter far from his kin, he clearly prized the warm sense of family they extended to him. He also valued old man Gordon's expertise as a marksman.

Gordon used an old black-powder buffalo rifle with a double trigger, heavy but deadly at long range. He taught Burnham how to compensate for light, shadows, and wind. Range could be gauged and corrected by shooting at something near the target that would make the hit visible, such as water or dust. If in doubt, instructed old Gordon, shoot low, since most misses go high. If you are lying flat on fairly level ground, don't shoot from the shoulder—that puts most of your bullets into the dirt or the sky. Instead, follow the example of the plainsmen—raise your gun a foot or so and shoot by hand. He learned that over-polishing a gun barrel turned it into a flashing heliograph saying "shoot me here." He learned the importance of keeping his bullets clean so they slipped easily from the cartridge belt when needed quickly.

Burnham applied these lessons by practicing with his own guns, a Winchester 1873 carbine and a Remington 1875 Army model revolver, both caliber .44–40. He modified the revolver's original sight by slotting it and soldering on half an Indian-head penny lengthwise down the seven-and-a-half-inch barrel. Intent on perfecting his marksmanship, he spent most of his money on thousands of cartridges, practicing until he was accurate and quick with both guns, using either hand, especially on snap shots from the hand, hip, and shoulder—the sort of quick instinctual shooting that could save his life in an ambush. He rode with his rifle balanced on the pommel of his saddle, "Arizona style," like the Apaches, and strengthened his wrists until he could raise and fire his rifle with one hand. He practiced snap shots not only in daylight but at night, to learn to feel the direction of a target by sound as well as shape. In the dark, if there was more time to shoot, it was best to stoop or lie, which highlighted the target against the skyline.

A snap shot from a revolver, he learned, often went awry beyond ten paces, but with practice was lethal at close range. "The one great advantage of the weapon is the possibility of instantaneous use," he later wrote. "It should be the aim of the scout to be able to draw and fire extremely quick—using only one continuous sweep of the hand until the bullet leaves the weapon." He could spin and put all his revolver's bullets within a small circle. "The master of the revolver need have no fear of any one man," he wrote. "The drunken bully or the giant pugilist is as much at his mercy as a child. A bullet in the instep will calm the most ferocious wife beater."

He practiced shooting while standing, lying, and running. He set five-gallon oil cans on the ground and did snap shots as he rode by or reined in. He spent even more time practicing from a galloping horse—moving toward the target, riding past it, or turning around to shoot while in flight, an important skill for discouraging pursuers. He learned to shoot Indian style, hooking one leg over his horse's back, then leaning over to fire from under its neck. To train his eye and reflexes, and incidentally to entertain others, he learned to shoot the water under a cork, lifting it and then hitting it in midair. "It can be done," he later instructed a friend, "by 3 months practice 10 trials a day."

All this practice soon found application.

——

The Gordons got pulled into the feud by debts, not passions. They owed money to people in Globe who favored the Tewksburys. These creditors sent an ultimatum: slaughter or scatter the other faction's livestock, or forfeit your herd to pay your debt. Old Gordon wanted neutrality and refused. His creditors immediately demanded cash, which they knew he didn't have. When old Gordon got word that his herd had been attached and deputies were coming to seize it, he decided to hide the cattle in the mountains.

Burnham heard of all this and rode to Salt River to help the family drive the cattle. He and young Tom Gordon rode point and flank with the main herd, followed by the daughters with the gentler cows and the dogs. Old Gordon rode the rear to cover their flight.

According to Burnham, two young deputies from Globe caught up to the daughters, which set the dogs barking. Burnham and Tom heard the commotion and rushed back. The deputies were demanding the daughters' cattle. Tom and Burnham said no. At this tense moment, one deputy dismounted. A dog bit him and he shot it. As everyone else drew their weapons, another shot echoed and the deputy fell dead. His outnumbered partner raised his hands.

At first no one realized who had fired the fatal shot. It was old Gordon, using his heavy buffalo rifle from 800 yards away. From that distance it was a lucky shot, the only lucky thing about it. "In that one act," wrote Burnham, "a whole family and their best friend crossed the Rubicon that divides the law-abiding citizen from those who live beyond." The killing forced the Gordons to choose sides in hopes of protecting themselves from the people who wanted their cattle—people allied with the Tewksburys. "In this Arizona trouble," wrote Burnham, "I found myself on the losing side"—the Graham side. According to Burnham, Gordon bought off the surviving deputy. In return for a portion of the herd, the deputy concocted a story for the authorities in Globe.

Burnham's involvement in the feud is unclear, as are his whereabouts and the sequence of his activities during the early 1880s. Nevertheless, certain documented events can help locate him and his movements during these blurry years.

The difficulties begin with his account of the feud. In *Scouting on Two Continents* he implied that he had been neck-deep in the bloodiest part of it. "Our friends were rapidly being killed off," he wrote, adding, "To my sorrow, I found that many of them deserved it." The Pleasant Valley vendetta evidently didn't become murderous until after the beheading of the sheepherder in 1887. That year and the next were the feud's most bloodstained. Yet during those two years, by Burnham's own accounts, he was mostly busy elsewhere in Arizona and California.

Still, his descriptions of the sinister atmosphere in Tonto Basin and his understanding of the issues carry the tang of authenticity and firsthand experience. He clearly was entangled in a feud and endangered by it. Animosities between cattlemen and sheep men had been simmering for years before the first recorded murder, not just in Pleasant Valley but in the wider arena of Tonto Basin. The Gordons' ranch, for instance, was about twenty-five miles south of Pleasant Valley. Burnham entitled his account "The Tonto Basin Feud," and never mentioned Pleasant Valley by name. Over the coming years, he undoubtedly discussed those violent days many times with his Arizona friends. Perhaps these conversations and Burnham's memory telescoped time and place. At any rate, the discrepancies and inaccuracies seem to stem from imperfect recall, not deceit, and his eyewitness account mirrors other reports.

After old Gordon killed the deputy, Burnham was occasionally required to give "personal service" to the feudists, a murky remark partly clarified by the next sentence: "At this time I used to practice incessantly with the pistol, both right and left hands, and especially from a galloping horse." Like everyone enmeshed in the feud, he felt like a hunted man.

> I moved warily and changed my name often. Throughout the Tonto feud, I kept one complete outfit in Prescott, where I not only had good clothes but loyal friends and a place I could safely disarm and rest. . . . I made use of all the craft and cunning I had learned among the Indians, as well as the methods employed by such bandits as Vasquez. In those days, every little detail of a man's equipment was observed and remembered by those whom he met, and, of course, his horse and brand were especially noted. I took care never to ride a horse from one district to another, but established a cache and a friend in each district. I found that I could travel long distances on foot and very swiftly. I had worked in mining camps and knew the lingo. I could drive ox teams well enough to get a job. At times, I was a prospector with burros. Again, I was a hunter of game on the Black Mesa. I learned by bitter experience to conceal whatever skill I had at arms. On more than one occasion, my boyish boasting had nearly cost me my life. The hardest things for me to disguise were my height and my eyes. Being young and slightly undersize, my best role was that of a tenderfoot from back East—a mere careless, harmless kid.

A photograph of Burnham from around this time partly confirms this physical description—he does look boyishly handsome, but neither careless nor harmless. He has a strong jaw, a cleft chin, and eyes whose intensity burns even in a faded black and white image. Everyone who met Burnham was struck by his eyes. "This quiet, unassuming gentleman would never pass unnoticed in a crowd did one but glimpse his eyes," wrote one observer, "blue eyes of startling keenness and brilliancy, eyes that see everything without seeming to see, eyes that at times are as cold and fierce as the steel of a drawn sword." Wrote another, with similar melodrama, "His eyes are of an amazing blue, and they fasten upon you when you come into his presence and never leave you, nor miss a shadow of your expression. They make you feel terribly naked."

His other distinguishing physical trait was his height. He stood about five feet four inches, short for a man even then. He weighed about 125 pounds. Yet he didn't seem slight, owing to an erect bearing, a deep chest and broad shoulders, and an air of alert energy. No one who looked closely would mistake him for a clueless tenderfoot.

So he tried not to give people a close look, staying on the move. For a time his head carried a bounty, and he often hid in the Pinal Mountains south of Globe. This life was stressful and solitary, but also forced him to hone survival skills that would save his life many times in years to come: observation, evasiveness, camouflage. He also learned about the consequences of taking sides in a conflict, even though that choice had been forced upon him. He found himself allied with people who were nearly strangers, whom he neither supported nor trusted, and whose actions he often deplored. Yet his fate was tied to theirs because of one rash act.

He knew good people on both sides whom the feud had turned into criminals, even murderers. "It was a harsh school of life—yet from this same belt of the West, Teddy's immortal Rough Riders were largely recruited. All that was really needed was a good cause and a good leader to transform outlaws into heroes." Whether a man became an outlaw or a hero depended on the leader, the cause, and the interpretation by others.

The feud also educated Burnham about the sordid side of politics, big and small, a view he never forgot. He realized that the feud and his role in it were merely pieces in a bigger contest between factions with money and political clout—real power, not firepower. "I had glimpses of the highest powers of government in that region," wrote Burnham, "and I saw that all of us were only pawns in the game." For the rest of his life he would be skeptical of big money and politics even while volunteering to be their pawn.

It made him feel helpless. "My life seemed no more than a twig of driftwood in a whirlpool." He often thought about California, where life seemed free and fair compared to the bloody anarchy of Arizona, "wherein stalk murderers, bandits, and all the grim underworld, which, once entered, grips a man in bonds that at first seem light as cobwebs but later have the cruel strength of steel." He was sometimes alarmed, sometimes roused, by the allure of that—"the swank and power that goes with supreme indifference to death." Of these years, he later told the journalist Richard Harding Davis, "The trouble was I had no moral anchors; the old ones father had given me were gone, and the time for acquiring new ones had not arrived."

———

He was walking this edge when he got an offer that nudged him closer to a moral abyss. The nudger was a young Kansan he had met on an Indian raid, likely in response to the Apache rampage during the summer of 1881. In late August that year, a Western Apache medicine man on Cibecue Creek, about thirty miles east of Pleasant Valley, began promising the return of olden times. This would happen, he said, through powerful medicine made from the pollen of tule cattails and a new dance that would resurrect dead warriors, who would help drive whites from the country. As his followers grew, so did white anxiety.

The army sent troopers from Fort Apache to take the man into custody. In a tense encounter at his camp, the medicine man submitted, but his followers, including some Apaches employed by the army as scouts, attacked the soldiers and killed eight. In the skirmish, the soldiers killed the medicine man. Bands of angry Apaches left the nearby San Carlos reservation and made a series of ferocious strikes. They killed three more soldiers, then murdered and mutilated four civilians near Fort Apache. They also raided a ranch in Pleasant Valley, killing two men and running off seventy-five horses. They shot many cattle in the valley and slaughtered sixteen pure-bred Morgan horses owned by the Tewksburys.

The army responded with numerous patrols augmented by local guides. This was likely Burnham's first action as a scout, and perhaps the first time he met Crook's famous scouts, Archie McIntosh and Al Sieber. By the end of September 1881 most Apaches had returned to the reservation. Others, including Geronimo, fled to Mexico and would soon be heard from again. A handful of "broncos"—Apaches who refused to surrender—continued to roam the mountains near Tonto Basin, keeping the region in a state of fear.

The young Kansan who had been Burnham's companion came to him in Globe with a proposition. For months the Kansan had been working as a night herder for a big mining outfit, protecting their cattle, at great risk, from rustlers and bronco Apaches. He had a sweetheart back home whom he hoped to marry, so he forced himself to save money by asking the outfit to hold his wages. The mining company, like many others, turned out to be a stock swindle. His wages disappeared into the bank accounts of a few pillars of the local community.

He wanted revenge and cash. He planned to start by stealing the super-intendent's personal horses and cattle, and then to rustle other small herds nearby. He already had a scheme to offload the beef. Someone from a gang led by Curly Bill Brocius, the leader of a notorious hive of rustlers and outlaws down near Tombstone, had offered cash for any cattle with brands from north of Globe and Phoenix, which would be unknown in Tombstone. The Kansan figured he could rake in a thousand dollars in three weeks, enough to marry his sweetheart. All he needed was a partner—Burnham.

It sounded easy. It almost sounded justifiable. Burnham, too, was tired of feeling like a pawn and a fugitive with empty pockets. Why not take something back for himself? Men were already hoping to kill him for something he didn't do. If he was branded a desperado, why fret about a few more misdeeds? His thoughts agitated him. "Up to this time," he wrote, "we had been adventurers but not criminals. Our decisions had been made, not by our minds, but by our environment and the quick blood of youth. But this was different. We must decide as men." He agreed to meet his friend the next day with a decision.

He couldn't sleep, so he rode into the pine-covered Pinal Mountains to think. For the rest of the night he swerved between the romantic and financial temptations of joining his friend and the arguments against it. Like many adventurous young men, he was excited by the idea of doing something daring and terrible. He thought about the dashing Tiburcio Vásquez and his bleak fate. He thought about his mother, and the dour relative who had predicted a bad end for him. He brooded about the girl in Iowa who saw something fine beneath his boyish pranks. He remembered his dreams of Africa.

When the sun rose he was still undecided. He rode into Globe. The stagecoach from Camp Bowie had just arrived with the mail. Like everyone in town, Burnham hoped for a letter. His always arrived addressed to the editor of the *Arizona Silver Belt*, Globe's newspaper. The editor knew Burnham's real name and received mail for him. Burnham didn't identify this man in *Scouting on Two Continents*, but he was "Judge" Aaron H. Hackney. Then in his sixties, Hackney was one of Globe's most respected citizens.

He had become another of Burnham's father figures. Burnham probably knew him through family newspaper connections. For a few years in the 1870s, Burnham's uncle Josiah Russell had been editor of the *Clinton Herald* in Iowa, and his uncle Edward Russell was the longtime editor of the *Davenport Gazette*. One or both of these men likely wrote to Hackney and asked him to keep tabs on their wayward nephew and report his activities. Hackney took an avuncular interest in the young drifter and evidently wrote to the uncles about the feud.

There was a letter for Burnham from Iowa—not from his mother or his sweetheart Blanche, but from Josiah, "the puritanical uncle of the town by the big river." The letter was brief and sharp. "Duty before all," it said. "Remember you come of the wrong stock to make a villain." These words, wrote Burnham many decades later, "went through me like knives." The letter's stern simplicity woke him up. He saw that vengeance solved nothing and perpetuated itself, and that he was becoming a disgrace to his ancestors. "I realized that I was in the wrong and had been for a long time, without knowing it."

He tried to convince his Kansan friend to abandon the plan, but failed. The young man ended up joining the Brocius gang. According to Burnham, he amassed far more than a thousand dollars but didn't get back to Kansas and his sweetheart. Within two years the outlaw life killed him.

Burnham confided his troubles to Hackney. The old editor advised him to leave Tonto Basin for a while and to shun contact with people there. He gave him names of some friends in the south. Shaken, hoping for another clean start, Burnham left Globe for the wild silver camp called Tombstone.

CHAPTER FIVE

TOMBSTONE

W HEN BURNHAM REACHED Tombstone in 1881, the town was two years old and notorious. "Six thousand population," noted James B. Hume, chief detective for Wells Fargo, a job that often took him to Tombstone. "Five thousand of them are bad—one thousand of them known outlaws." An exaggeration, but Tombstone certainly was swarming with gunmen, gamblers, smugglers, outlaws, con men, and "soiled doves" who roistered in the town's 110 saloons, fourteen gambling parlors, numerous dance halls, and brothels catering to all budgets.

Yet by 1881 it also was home to merchants, doctors, lawyers, and ministers who could spend leisure hours at the ice cream parlor, the bowling alley, the opera house, several dramatic societies, some fine restaurants, or four churches. Visitors or newly rich prospectors could luxuriate at the Grand Hotel, which featured thick carpets, elegant chandeliers, oil paintings, and walnut furniture with silk cushions. Guests ate from delicate china, or perhaps walked to the Maison Doree for quail on toast. From the hotel's roof they could look down into the shafts of several mines, which gaped throughout the town.

In short, Tombstone reflected the yin and yang of Western boomtowns. Allen Street, the main thoroughfare, neatly divided the upright from the red-light. Everybody in Tombstone had been lured there by the silver streaming from the richest strike in Arizona.

It had started with a scruffy dreamer named Ed Schieffelin. As a prospector he had a perfect record—absolute failure. His flops mapped the West: Oregon, Idaho's Salmon River, Nevada, up and down California, Great Salt Lake, southern Nevada, then Idaho again. He tried his luck in the Grand Canyon but lost his boat, equipment, and a companion, who drowned. He tried again in Nevada, went back to Oregon, then had a go in San Bernardino. He took another crack at the Grand Canyon. Same result. Everywhere, zilch. None of it tarnished his faith that a big strike was just ahead. Between failures he worked as a mule skinner to grubstake his next bust.

In 1876 an acquaintance in Arizona described him in words that applied to many dream-haunted men roaming the West with a burro and a pickaxe. Schieffelin, said the man, was

> about the queerest specimen of human flesh I ever saw. He was 6 feet 2 inches and had black hair that hung several inches below his shoulder and a beard that had not been trimmed or combed for so long a time that it was a mass of unkempt knots and mats. He wore clothing pieced and patched from deerskins, corduroy and flannel, and his hat was originally a slouch hat that had been pieced with rabbit skin until very little of the original felt remained. I have never known a prospector more confident of finding a big mining proposition than he was, yet he told me that he has prospected a good part of eleven years with no results, while he had a frightfully tough time of it. He was then 27 [actually 29] but looked like 40.

The following year Schieffelin drifted down to Fort Huachuca, about seventy-five miles south of Tucson near the Mexican border. The region was remote and empty. Most people avoided it because Apaches often killed those who didn't. In previous years, about seventeen miners with more hope than fear had been slain. Nevertheless, Schieffelin decided to prospect in the Huachuca Mountains. Soldiers at the fort reportedly warned him that the only thing he would find in that desert was his tombstone.

He had his usual luck, which brought his usual response: he decided to try again, a bit to the northeast. He moved into an isolated, abandoned hut called Brunckow's cabin, notorious because most of its occupants seemed to end up murdered.

In August 1877 his luck started to change. In a dry wash on a high mesa called Goose Flats, he found what prospectors call "float"—loose rocks containing precious minerals. Float occurs when geological forces such as wind, rain, and flood break rocks from a mineral vein and carry them off. Float is evidence of ore somewhere in the vicinity. It indicates that erosion has exposed part of a vein. Schieffelin's float showed hints of silver. In Tucson he filed a claim and wryly named it Tombstone.

He had the float assayed to see whether the silver content made mining worthwhile. It did. In fact the assayer was so enthusiastic he became Schieffelin's partner, along with Schieffelin's brother Al. They returned to the claim on Goose Flats in February 1878. First they had to backtrack the float to its source, which could be miles away. A miner might dig dozens of worthless holes looking for the vein. Even if he found it, it might be negligible or quickly peter out.

The partners' first efforts were disappointing. Schieffelin, of course, remained optimistic. For once he was right. They tapped a strong vein, then others. They didn't yet know it, but they had found the richest lode of silver in Arizona. Estimates of the value of the silver bullion mined near Tombstone during its boomtown decade vary from $40 million to $85 million, equivalent today to somewhere between one and two billion dollars.

In those first days their method was simple: one man descended into the shaft to break rock, another man hauled up the bucket. The mine was far from anywhere, so they agreed that if Apaches raided, whoever was above ground should run for his life; the man in the shaft could be buried later. They named the first mines Lucky Cuss and Toughnut, followed by Good Enough, Contention Ledge, and Owl's Last Hoot. (The names of

Western mining claims are irresistible. A few examples: Murderer's Bar, Squabbletown, Poor Man's Creek, Henpeck Flat, Gouge Eye, Liars Flat, Git Up and Git, Last Chance, Whisky Gulch, Grab-All, Humbug Creek, Bloody Bend, Mad Mule Gulch, Devil's Retreat, Hoodoo Bar, Cut Throat, Bloody Run.)

The Schieffelins' Tombstone claims became so bountiful they had to hire men to mine them. They built a stamp mill to crush ore and a cache dam to wash it. Before long they were making tens of thousands of dollars every month.

Schieffelin was quickly bored by the dull routines of processing ore and piling up money. His passion, like Burnham's, was for the prospect, the alluring possibility, not the drab reality of the steady thing. Besides, to a man accustomed to solitude, booming Tombstone was starting to feel crowded. In November 1879, after a year and a half there, he left to search for gold and silver in Colorado and New Mexico. When he returned in February 1880, he and his brother Al sold their two-thirds of the Tombstone mines for $600,000.

In two years Schieffelin had traded a lifetime of failure for a fortune. Al used part of his pile to build the Schieffelin Hall opera house, which opened in June 1881 and seated 450. Ed Schieffelin, financially set for life, left to go prospecting. He died of a heart attack at age fifty in 1897 while panning for gold in Oregon. His will requested that he be buried near Tombstone, where his faith had been rewarded, "in the dress of a prospector, my old pick and canteen with me." This was done, and tourists can visit his grave.

———

Within months of the Schieffelins' strike, word got out and miners poured in, followed by all the professions eager to profit from the sudden wealth circulating in a boomtown. Goose Flats, once an empty stretch of arid mesa populated mostly by mesquite and jackrabbits, sprouted tents and shacks, then homes and adobe buildings.

The population kept jumping: 100 in March 1879; 2,000 in February 1880; 7,000 in 1881; double that in 1885. Many inhabitants were miners, often immigrants from Cornwall, Ireland, and Germany. Riffraff and ruffians from Dodge City, Abilene, and Deadwood drained into Tombstone. Gamblers, prostitutes, con men, and whiskey peddlers arrived to siphon off the miners' money. Rustlers, smugglers, and stagecoach robbers turned up, drawn by opportunity. The certainty of trouble attracted gunmen such as the Earp brothers and Bat Masterson, who had worked as peace officers in those other wild places and now offered their pacifying services to Tombstone, when they weren't gambling. Disputes flared up not only with rustlers and bandits such as the Clantons, Johnny Ringo, and Curly Bill Brocius, but also with part of the town's establishment, including the sheriff, John H. Behan, who had a soft spot for outlaws.

In any case, law enforcement was relaxed. As one writer put it, "Shooting from behind or shooting an unarmed man in theory brought legal vengeance, and frequently did so. Anybody else who got into serious trouble for killing a man just didn't have any friends. There was apparently no limit to tolerance, as long as the slain man was armed and received his bullets in front." The population also grew steadily on Boot Hill, the cemetery outside of town.

With all the shooting and fighting, doctors did thriving business in Tombstone. Dr. George E. Goodfellow—the coroner who watched John Heith get lynched and then pronounced him dead from emphysema—had so much opportunity to treat gunshot wounds that he became the country's foremost specialist in them and published many papers about techniques he developed.

A droll reporter named William H. Bishop visited Tombstone for *Harper's* magazine in late 1881, soon after Burnham arrived. The town's "leading diseases," wrote Bishop, were "whiskey and cold lead." The two were linked, he noted: "What with the leisure that seems to prevail, the constant drinking and gambling at the saloons, and the universal practice of carrying deadly weapons." Depending on the venue, the liquor served varied from imported wines to tonsil-scorching potions laced with soap, chemicals, red chilis, and other alarming additives. Fluids sold as whiskey might be grain alcohol cut with water and dyed with tobacco or burnt sugar. Slang terms for these firewaters suggest their effects—tangle-leg, churn-brain, tarantula juice, Taos lightning, white mule (for the kick), and forty-rod (for its power to kill at that distance). Some Tombstone saloons offered a new keg beer brewed in Colorado by a Prussian immigrant who had Americanized his name from Kuhrs to Coors.

The quantity and duration of boozing in places like Tombstone was prodigious. It often started with a pick-me-up before breakfast and proceeded steadily into the night. According to Wyatt Earp, Doc Holliday drank two to three quarts of whiskey a day. The diary of George Hand, a Tucson saloon owner during this period, brims with entries like this one for July 5, 1875: "Got tight again today. Pearson and I had a fight. Davis hit him in the head with a bar pitcher and he ran out in the street hollering 'murder.' Lawyer Clark is tight. Everyone is tight." Hand's diary also details the consequences of nonstop drinking: fights, shootings, wife-beatings, murders, horrible delirium tremens, madness, suicide. Men like Burnham who didn't drink were considered abnormal.

Tombstone also was famous for its "houses of joy." The town licensed them for a fee. At the top were fancy parlor houses such as those managed by the beautiful Frenchwomen Blonde Marie and Madame Moustache. Their courtesans wore ball gowns amid gilt mirrors and oil paintings; gentlemanly decorum was required. At the bottom were the squalid cribs of doorway doxies. The large territory in between was filled by "hog ranches" run by hard-shell women such as Rowdy Kate or Crazy Horse Lil, and hurdy-gurdy houses where the molls charged a dollar a dance and extra for extra.

Some of these women, like some of the men they solicited, were degraded and doomed. Others were tough risk-takers and dreamers who braved the trip to Tombstone and serviced the filthy half-civilized men there in hopes of making a better life. Some succeeded, saving money until they could open a restaurant, boardinghouse, or some other business. But for most, as for most of the men, their dreams turned to ash.

Tombstone's most popular emporium, famous all over the West, was the Bird Cage Theatre. It opened in December 1881, and for the next eight years it never closed. The Bird Cage was an all-in-one entertainment center. It offered liquor, gambling, an orchestra, song-and-dance girls in skimpy attire, touring singers and comics, bawdy skits, and risqué "theatricals" featuring female thespians lightly constrained by clothing. The downstairs poker game, with a thousand-dollar buy-in, ran for years without stopping. The emporium took its name from fourteen "cages" upstairs—curtained rooms with beds—where the saloon's celebrated lovelies withdrew with their customers.

———

This was the "wild and romantic camp" that Burnham rode into in late summer or early fall of 1881, sometime before the gunfight at the O.K. Corral on October 26 ("The Earp Clanton feud was in full swing," wrote Burnham, though he never mentions the famous gunfight). He was carrying a letter of introduction from the editor in Globe to a man who turned out to be a gambler, not an occupation commonly held up as an exemplar for wayward youth.

But the old editor knew what he was doing. The gambler, wrote Burnham, was "of the old type," a solid professional who relied on skill and preferred a clean game, and thus despised people who tried to rig outcomes or take shortcuts, including "all stage robbers, rustlers, claim jumpers, smugglers, feudists, and criminals in general" (a sizable portion of Tombstone's population). This upright gamester tried to convince Burnham that decent hardworking people, not just criminals, could prosper. He also channeled Burnham's skill with firearms toward law and order by getting him a job as a night guard at one of the Schieffelin mines. "The owners needed quick and nervy men to keep off claim jumpers," wrote Burnham, "and I could make worthy use of the unusual strength and endurance inherited from my ancestors."

But his old friends in the Tonto Basin pulled at him. He disregarded the old editor's advice and wrote to the Gordons for news of the feud. Back came a teary plea from one of the daughters to come quickly; her sweetheart was in a jam. After riding 200 miles, Burnham found that the sweetheart had been replaced by another and the crisis was over. When he stopped in on the editor in Globe, the old man berated him as weak and silly for reentering harm's way. He ordered him back to Tombstone, a safe place by comparison. Burnham, embarrassed by his lingering foolishness, turned back south.

While riding through the saguaros and mesquite of the desert above Tucson, he caught up to a slow buckboard. Its owner was walking, a sign of jaded horses. As Burnham began to overtake the wagon, the man moved to put it between them, then casually picked up a rifle. Burnham stayed parallel 200 yards off and decided to forgo the usual greeting between travelers in a lonesome place. The man, after studying him a bit, waved him over.

Up close the stranger resembled Abraham Lincoln. In the buckboard lay another man, gunshot. They were brothers. Burnham offered to hitch his horse to their wagon to help pull it up hills and through stretches of sand. En route Burnham heard their story. The wounded brother was wanted in Nevada for killing a man over a woman. There was a bounty on his head and lawmen were in pursuit. The walking man, Burnham learned later, was "the most noted and successful smuggler along the Arizona frontier"—no small distinction in a region crawling with such hustlers.

His name was Neil McLeod. He lived on the outskirts of Tombstone. Behind his house, a corral with high adobe walls opened onto a deep arroyo. Mule trains from Sonora came up the arroyo at night and filled the corral with goods lacking a customs stamp. The Mexican government charged heavy tariffs on certain products in great demand across the border—

liquor, tobacco, blankets, jewelry. By dodging the tariffs, smugglers such as McLeod could sell the goods for a high profit in Arizona. To satisfy Mexican wants, he also smuggled merchandise in the opposite direction.

McLeod differed from the ruck of Arizona's two-bit smugglers. His operation stretched from Mexico City to San Francisco. He protected himself by keeping layers of secrecy between him and the men he directed, and he never accompanied his pack trains. He bought silent partnerships in stores throughout the territory so he could unload his illegal goods with no questions. He also washed his profits by diversifying into legitimate businesses such as mines, livery stables, and stagecoach services. In his spare time he liked to enter prizefights.

McLeod became another of Burnham's mentors. The smuggler had developed ingenious tactics to communicate with his network and to baffle pursuit by lawmen in two countries, skills that soon saved Burnham's life.

When he and McLeod reached Tombstone, someone warned Burnham that two men from Globe were in town to kill him. One of them hoped to avoid prison by stopping Burnham from testifying in a matter "concerning the sale of a certain stolen brand," probably a crime stemming from the feud. The other man was motivated by "insane jealousy." Burnham is silent on why, but Gordon's five daughters come to mind. He decided to take refuge in the Dripping Springs Mountains, about 150 miles north of Tombstone. Both of his enemies, Burnham knew, were able trackers, "hard-riding and relentless." He wasn't sure he could reach the mountains before they caught him.

McLeod devised a scheme. First, to get a few hours head start, McLeod told Burnham to make open inquiries around town about the route he intended to make, and furtive inquiries about a different route. Burnham's enemies would hear about both, and would assume that Burnham was too young and inexperienced to use misdirection as a tactic. McLeod told him to leave at night so that when his pursuers heard he was gone, they would take the wrong route and wouldn't be able to double back and pick up his track until daylight.

McLeod furnished Burnham with an excellent horse to ride and a poor unshod one to lead. He said that the unshod one, if turned loose, would head for its home corral in Tucson. Lastly, he gave Burnham detailed instructions to be followed exactly.

Burnham rode north through the Dragoon Mountains until daybreak. Then, as instructed, he found a gravelly ridge where he could feed and rest the horses for a couple of hours. During this break he removed the shoes from the good horse and put them on the poor one. Then he filled a piece of canvas with hunks of cactus, tied this bundle to the poor horse's tail, and whacked its rump. Pricked, the horse leaped about and then took off in the direction of Tucson. Eventually it would slow to a walk until it reached its corral.

Next, still following McLeod's instructions, Burnham mounted the newly unshod horse and spurred it over the ridge into a sandy wash. He galloped for a mile, farther than his enemies would bother to track the seemingly abandoned unshod horse. From his pack Burnham took another set of horseshoes supplied by McLeod, distinctly different from the first set, and shod his horse to keep it from going lame on the journey ahead.

"Do all this," McLeod had told him, "so it will look as if you had been surprised by Indians just as you saddled up after resting and your barefoot horse had bolted while you had barely been able to head your own horse, plunging with fear, toward Tucson. Be sure to pick a gravelly point so there will not be left a discernible change in the shape of the barefoot tracks, and yet a clear tale of all that happens to the shod horse."

Burnham later learned that his pursuers followed the bait all the way to Tucson. Meanwhile, he made his way to Dripping Springs and then on to Globe, where he again visited the old editor and told him about the men hoping to kill him. The editor, disgusted as always by the senselessness of the feud, wanted to broker a truce that would release Burnham from the vendetta. "This was not easy to accomplish," wrote Burnham, "for I was bullheaded and vengeful. I had been hunted to the point where fear was dead and the lust to meet and finish my foes grew stronger every hour." Nevertheless, the editor managed the truce. Burnham could exhale, but he didn't fully trust his enemies or himself to keep the peace. "The settlement finally effected gave me a still deeper view of the pit around whose crumbling edge I daily walked."

He turned back toward Tombstone.

———

While the gambler and the old editor were prodding Burnham toward law and order, McLeod began paying him to flout them. Burnham started carrying coded messages into Mexico to McLeod's network of smugglers and crooked officials, in the region encompassing Nogales, Guaymas, and the Sierra Madre. Burnham did so without question, on missions he usually didn't understand, to serve a man he admired. It was a pattern he would later follow as a military scout. "He did not ask me to do anything that would get me in wrong with the law," wrote Burnham, "but eventually it would have tied me to a group of smugglers and gunrunners operating between El Paso and Los Angeles."

The risks from soldiers and lawmen in both countries were considerable, but these foes were far less frightening than the Apaches who haunted the region. Bands led by Chatto, Juh, Geronimo, and Cochise's son Naiche had fled the San Carlos reservation in October 1881 and joined the old warrior Nana in the Sierra Madre region of Mexico.

McLeod no doubt paid well, and the clandestine adventure appealed to young Burnham. So did the skills McLeod could teach him about undetectable methods of communication. Letters, he told Burnham, were a poor way to send delicate information. "I never write anything that couldn't be published in the *Tombstone Epitaph* the next morning," he said. "And quite a lot of news is sent out by way of that funny paper every day"—in coded messages.

McLeod also sent dispatches via shotgun shells, each one carrying different-sized shot and a few inconspicuous marks that "conveyed a whole chapter of instructions to ships at Guaymas." Several crude, seemingly haphazard pencil strokes on a certain tankhouse or post office box were instructions for McLeod's partners. Paper dollars or pesos came and went with imperceptible perforations made by needles. Some domestic animals, such as that cactus-pricked horse, were homing devices carrying correspondence. McLeod never gave Burnham the keys to these ciphers, which protected both the messenger and the secrets.

One day McLeod told Burnham to show up at dusk for a ten-day ride. McLeod's provisions for him were characteristically odd, his instructions typically cryptic. He again furnished Burnham with a dubious horse, bony and nondescript. Its saddle was shabby but comfortable, with reins made of rope. Take no visible firearms, McLeod told Burnham, then handed him a sawed-off Colt revolver to hide in his boot or under his arm. "You must not have an outfit worth following," said McLeod, "but in spite of looks, your horse is grain-fed and very tough."

He also gave Burnham a matchbox made from two empty cartridges of different calibers fitted snugly together. Inside were common wooden sulphur matches. But don't use them, said McLeod. Ride into Sonora and camp on the hill called Cabeza Borago. Dig a hole six inches deep and bury the matchbox. At sundown build a fire on top of it using long-burning mesquite. Leave the fire but position yourself so that you can watch it and the surrounding hills. Do this each night, for up to five nights, until you see an answering fire on another peak.

Two nights passed without a signal. On the third, a fire blazed from an adjacent mountain. "My message had been delivered," wrote Burnham, "and I knew that each little match would be taken from the shell—by whom I knew not—and put under a strong magnifying glass, and every needle-point and mark on it interpreted in a code of which I knew nothing."

He left for Tombstone that night and rode until after daylight. Before resting he followed his usual precautions. He hid his horse in a thicket that had grama grass for forage, then concealed his saddle, boots, and food nearby so that if his horse got stolen, he wouldn't be completely stranded. He put on light knee-high moccasins like those worn by Apaches. Carrying his gun, canteen, binoculars, and some dried food, he climbed half a mile to the top of a stony ridge. He found a flat ledge with enough brush to screen him, where he could also overlook the mesquite plain—a safe place for sleeping.

When he woke, he scanned the landscape with his binoculars, ate some jerky, slept again. He woke around noon with a vague sense of unease. He was reassured by the small lizards panting on the rocks next to him, motionless and serene. He scanned the plain again for the dust of movement, but saw none. Relieved, he drank from his canteen, then froze. Something had faintly scraped farther along the rock ledge. His first thought: Apache. The Indian probably had seen his trail and was about to fire. Burnham fought the urge to run. Minutes passed.

Finally he heard a muffled clink. This clarified several things. The sound came from a cloth-covered metal canteen bumping a rock—a military canteen. The man was probably one of the Apaches who had left the reservation with Geronimo. He likely had a military rifle to go with his canteen.

When nothing happened for several more minutes, Burnham realized that the man was probably a scout who had picked this ridge for reasons similar to his own. Burnham knew the man would patiently watch the plain all day. If the scout didn't move, all Burnham had to do was sit motionless until dark and wait for him to leave.

The desert sun was baking the ridge. After a while Burnham heard another sound—light footsteps on gravel. The heat was pushing the Apache down the ledge toward Burnham's brushy shade. Burnham decided to climb up the rock and loop back toward the Apache's former position. The scout might see Burnham's sign on the ledge, but by then Burnham planned to be well down the other side of the ridge.

It worked—except that as he came over the ridge, he saw a group of resting Apaches. Worse, one of them saw him. As everyone including Burnham began yelling and shooting, he sprinted down the hill, through brush and boulders, and jumped off a drop into some mesquite bushes. The yelling had stopped, which was bad news. Silence meant that the Apaches were spreading out for the chase, trackers behind him, flankers on each side to prevent escape. As he scurried down the ridge, Burnham considered his poor options. If he tried to stay invisible in the brush on the ridge, the Apaches eventually would track him down. If he ran onto the plain, he would be visible, and if the Apaches had horses, they would run him down.

A slender possibility of escape appeared in front of him: a stock trail threading through a ravine clogged with cholla. "Many varieties of cactus can be endured, though painful," wrote Burnham, "but the cholla is impossible." Even for Apaches. They would have to drop their flankers and thread the cholla single file behind Burnham.

To most Westerners pursued by Apaches, this would not be much comfort. Unlike the Plains Indians, the mountain Apaches were just as happy on foot as mounted, and were even more lethal that way. Westerners were awed by the Apaches' endurance as runners—they could cover seventy miles a day and jog next to a horse until it collapsed. Braves had the deep chest that marks long-distance athletes. They trained by running up and down rugged hills with a mouthful of water that they did not swallow, to discipline their breath and themselves. Soldiers who chased them into box canyons were astonished by their ability to scamper straight up cliffs that looked insurmountable. General George Crook, who fought many campaigns against the Apaches and admired them, said, "the adult Apache is the embodiment of physical endurance—lean, well proportioned, medium-sized, with sinews like steel; insensible to hunger, fatigue, or physical pains." John Gregory Bourke, who served as Crook's officer in many Apache campaigns, wrote that there was "not one of them who was not able to travel forty or fifty miles a day over these gloomy precipices and along these gloomy canyons. In muscular development, lung and heart power, they were, without exception, the finest body of human beings I had ever looked upon."

These were the warriors chasing Burnham. He wrote of this moment, in a sentence as close as he ever came to boasting in print, "Again my legs took command—and no Apache could compete." Burnham, too, had trained himself to be an endurance runner. He had the same deep chest and lung capacity as the mountain Apaches. Once, in Globe, he had entered a 36-mile race over mountainous terrain. When several reservation Apaches entered, most contestants dropped out. Burnham won the race.

Today's contest had different stakes. Aside from the cholla, he had another advantage: "fear is a wonderful accelerator if it does not hold sway entirely or last too long." He ran all afternoon and into the darkness, "the godsend of the scout."

He outlasted his pursuers—or maybe they decided that killing one white man with nothing to plunder wasn't worth the extended effort. Apaches were the most pragmatic of warriors.

The walk from Fronteras to Tombstone was 100 miles. Sunburnt, in rags, Burnham reported to McLeod that the message had been delivered on Cabeza Borago. McLeod told him that Geronimo's band had been raiding in that area and several ranchers were dead.

In January 1882 word drifted north from Mexico that a raiding party of Apaches led by Geronimo, Naiche, and Chatto had left Sonora for Arizona. They were headed for the San Carlos reservation to recruit more Apaches and spread greater mayhem. The U.S. Cavalry tried to intercept them at the Mexican border, but failed. Apaches loose in Arizona always meant bloodshed. The army needed extra scouts to track and fight them. Burnham had gotten a taste of it in 1881 during the hostilities sparked by the death of the Apache medicine man on Cibecue Creek, and he was eager for more. He had been training for years to become a scout, and had closely studied his ideal, the Apaches. He was ready.

CHAPTER 6

THE TIGERS OF
THE HUMAN SPECIES

AFTER CALIFORNIA'S GOLD rush, after the rise and decline of Virginia City, Leadville, Deadwood, Abilene, and Dodge City, after Custer and Little Bighorn, after Quannah Parker and the Staked Plains War, the last act on the last frontier in the continental United States took place in Arizona. Isolation and harsh terrain partly explain this historical lag, but the other big reason that Arizona stayed unsettled, in every sense, was the Apaches. They terrified people, including other Indians.

A splintered group of related nomadic tribes, the Apaches were avid raiders and merciless killers, sometimes of rival bands of Apaches. Their geographical sway was out of all proportion to their modest numbers. Their ferocity and speed meant that fifty braves could spread terror over several hundred square miles. By the 1830s the Apaches had so decimated and frightened Sonora, Chihuahua, southern Arizona, and southern New Mexico that more than a hundred settlements had been abandoned. People took refuge in bigger towns, where garrisoned soldiers offered some protection. Sonora and Chihuahua began paying bounties for Apache scalps. It was said that the Apaches let a few ranchers survive solely to supply horses and meat in future raids.

In the 1850s and 1860s, after the Mexican–American War, Anglos began trickling into Arizona in search of grassland or precious metals. The Apaches treated them like everyone else: prey. The Indians' depredations, combined with the inhospitable landscape, led General William Tecumseh Sherman, commander of the U.S. Army, to complain, "We had one war with Mexico to take Arizona, and we should have another to make her take it back."

The brutalities on both sides were extreme. Apaches or Anglos would do something horrific, triggering terrible reprisals. Both sides massacred women and children. Occasionally an Apache or Anglo would attempt to make peace, but some betrayal or misunderstanding or fresh atrocity would set the blood flowing again.

Apaches inspired terror for good reason. They were as harsh and piti-less as the landscape they roamed. For non-Apaches, the worst imaginable fate was to be taken alive by them. Captured children and young women were occasionally integrated into the tribe, but men were doomed to tor-ments. Captives often were turned over to Apache women whose male rela-tives had recently been killed. Many accounts suggest that these women were even more sadistically inventive than the men. Burnham once watched some Apache women skin a young fawn alive for entertainment, a tech-nique also used on human captives, and he mentions watching Apache children stick thorns into the eyes of captured doves, "much to the amuse-ment" of their nearby mothers.

The Apaches excelled at torture and often prolonged it. In March 1873, for instance, a group of Tonto Apaches were waiting near Wickenburg to pillage the Arizona–California stage when three white men happened by. The Indians killed the first two quickly but reserved the third, a twenty-one-year-old named George Taylor, for their amusement. Taylor was found stripped, bound, and pierced with 150 sharpened wooden slivers, all in non-vital areas to protract his suffering. When his wounds had bled for a while but he was still alive, the Apaches lit the splinters. Another example from 1885: during one of Geronimo's outbreaks, buzzards led some soldiers to the remains of a prospector. The Apaches had cut off his soles, then staked him over an anthill. They cut into his side just deeply enough to let the ants in. Sometimes captives were hung by the heels so their heads could roast over a slow fire. Even freshly buried corpses weren't safe. The Apaches sometimes dug them up, cut out the heart, and mutilated the rest.

Such incidents understandably aroused outrage and hysteria. The settlers screamed for better protection from the distant U.S. government. By 1869 the army had established thirteen forts in the territory without curbing the Apaches' ravages. Arizonans wanted permission to form militias against them.

Instead, influenced by religious leaders and liberal thinkers in the East, President Ulysses S. Grant announced his new "Peace Policy" toward Indians, an about-face from the previous de facto policy of pursuit and extermination. A Board of Indian Commissioners, chiefly philanthropists and humanitarians, was appointed to advise on Indian matters. They favored civilizing Indians by distributing beef, flour, and clothing on reservations. This strategy of patience infuriated the inhabitants of Arizona, who were in immediate fear for their lives. Experience told them that the Apaches would see this policy as softness, an invitation to kill with impunity.

Nevertheless, the policy proved a modest success at Camp Grant, an army post at the confluence of the Gila and San Pedro rivers, seventy miles north of Tucson. In early 1871 a large group of Pinal and Aravaipa Apaches surrendered there and began peacefully farming. But other Apaches—especially the Chiricahuas, Tontos, Western, and White Mountain Apaches, all incorrigibly belligerent—continued their murderous, thieving ways, slaughtering miners, ranchers, and travelers, and running off livestock.

To most people in Arizona, all Apaches were untrustworthy and equally deserving of extermination. The sedentary group at Camp Grant made an easy target. Enraged by Grant's Peace Policy, two of Tucson's leading citizens, an Anglo named William S. Oury and a Mexican named

Jesús Maria Elias, plotted vengeance. They gathered a mob of 140 men—ninety-two Papago Indians (traditional enemies of the Apaches), forty-two Mexicans, and six Anglos. (Most of Tucson's Anglos, despite whiskey-fueled vows to kill Apaches, were suddenly otherwise engaged when it came time to saddle up.)

On the morning of April 30, 1871, the vigilantes descended upon the Indians around Camp Grant. In less than thirty minutes the mob slaughtered more than 140 Apaches living under the protection of the United States flag. Of the murdered, all but eight or so were women and children. The victims were clubbed, shot, chopped, and brained. Twenty-seven or twenty-eight children were taken captive, most of them given to the Papagos to be sold into slavery in Mexico (six eventually were recovered). Oury crowed that the raid had eradicated "about 144 of the most bloodthirsty devils that ever disgraced mother earth." For this act of valor he was lionized in Arizona.

Much of the country, however, was appalled. President Grant called the raid "purely murder." He warned the governor of the territory that unless the offenders were brought to justice, he would declare martial law in Arizona. So about one hundred men, including Oury and Elias, were indicted for murder. The trial was held in Tucson's adobe courthouse in December 1871. After hearing evidence for five days, the jury deliberated for nineteen minutes and declared everyone not guilty. The event became known to history as the Camp Grant massacre.

The Apaches responded to it by seeking blood vengeance on anyone they encountered. "I know that a book could be written regarding the black night of despair, unrelieved by the glint of one kindly star, in which all that pertained to that Territory was involved," wrote John G. Bourke, a young Army officer stationed in Arizona at the time.

I have in my possession copies of the Arizona newspapers of those years which are filled with accounts of Apache raids and murders and of counter-raids and counter-murders. No man's life was safe for a moment outside the half-dozen large towns, while in the smaller villages and ranchos sentinels were kept posted by day and packs of dogs were turned loose at night. All travel, even on the main roads, had to be done between sunset and sunrise; the terrorized ranchmen who endeavored to till a few acres of barley or corn in the bottoms did so with cocked revolvers on hip and loaded rifles slung to the plow-handles.

Two developments eventually wore down the Apaches. First, the discovery of gold and silver in Arizona drew a quickening stream of whites into the territory throughout the 1870s and 1880s, which led to louder calls for government protection. Second, in June 1871, in the aftermath of the Camp Grant massacre, President Grant's new military appointee arrived in Arizona: Lieutenant Colonel George R. Crook, the most relentless and perceptive Indian fighter in U.S. history. Crook was given the same mission that had battered the reputations of his predecessors: to conquer the Apaches and force them into peace. He had a plan that would soon anger the settlers.

For his first year and a half in Arizona, Crook was handcuffed by Grant's Peace Policy. An Indian commissioner named Vincent Colyer, an artist and humanitarian, arrived in September to evaluate conditions and establish reservations in Arizona, where none yet existed. Meanwhile, Crook was ordered to suspend military operations against the Indians.

Colyer was not welcomed. The settlers distrusted his motives, a suspicion he worsened by showing little interest in their opinions. The Arizona newspapers, in the style of the day, called him "a treacherous, black-hearted dog," among other colorful epithets. He met with Indians throughout the territory, including Apaches, and reported that many of them were sick, starving, and constantly endangered by the ranchers and prospectors overrunning their traditional lands. He set up half a dozen reservations near army posts and promised good treatment, food and clothing, and the protection of the U.S. Army to all Indians who moved to these reserved lands. Some bands of Apaches, tired of fighting and lured by free rations, reported to the reservations. Others scoffed at the offer. Why give up freedom for a few hunks of government beef when they could steal all the cattle and horses they wanted?

Even before Colyer left the territory in late 1871, a number of events undermined his peace mission. In November Apaches attacked a stage-coach near the small mining town of Wickenburg and massacred seven passengers. In December, the swift acquittal of the Camp Grant vigilantes encouraged the population's desire for violent retaliation.

The Apaches supplied frequent incentives. Within a year of Colyer's mission, they struck fifty times and murdered at least forty people while running off hundreds of cattle, sheep, and horses. Some Apaches who had moved onto reservations were treating them as refuges where they could be fed and protected between raids.

All this supported Crook's conviction that the Peace Policy alone would never tame the Apaches, because peace was an alien concept to them. Grant finally let him off the leash. He was ready. He had spent the previous year riding all over the territory and thinking about his enemy, whom he later called "the shrewdest and best fighters in the world," and the most fierce. They were, he said, "the tigers of the human species."

———

At first glance the Apaches hardly looked the part. A typical male stood five feet eight inches tall, thin and wiry, though with a deep chest. He didn't wear feathers or beaded shirts, opting for simple efficiency: a breechclout and tall moccasins to deflect thorns, perhaps a thin calico shirt. He wrapped a piece of flannel around his long, unkempt black hair. He might paint his face with dots and squiggles in red, black, or white, but never his body like the more theatrical Plains tribes. Aside from his weapons, he owned little. He didn't raise horses or livestock, preferring to steal them as needed.

Apache males devoted themselves from youth to perfecting the related skills of wilderness survival and warfare. Both required extreme fitness, deep knowledge of the landscape and everything in it, the ability to follow the faintest of trails without leaving one, and the training of all five senses for the dual purposes of self-preservation and annihilation of the enemy. They perfected their skills through hunting and war. They mastered battle tactics both improvised and strategic, and developed an almost unlimited capacity to endure hunger, thirst, fatigue, and pain. When on the move, Apache men carried little beyond weapons, relying on their ability to find food and water under any conditions. They could walk forty miles without eating or drinking. If provisioned, they could cover 120 miles by foot in two days. A single verb, "to scout," covered both raiding and warfare. To Burnham, Apaches were exemplars for scouts.

Crook often contrasted the Apache warrior with the U.S. soldier. Whereas a soldier followed orders mechanically, like a cog in a machine, every Apache warrior "is a general and knows exactly what to do under any circumstances," wrote Crook. The Apache is "an army in himself, waiting for orders from no superiors." Rank meant nothing to them. They would not follow a leader who wasn't in superb physical condition and who didn't demonstrate undisputed courage and judgment.

Apaches differed from most whites, and from many Indian tribes, in how they defined courage and judgment. Unlike U.S. soldiers or many Plains Indians, Apaches didn't charge fortified positions or ride circles around armed groups of enemies. They saw such actions as foolish bravado, not bravery. They would have admired Falstaff's trick of playing dead on the battlefield, agreeing with him that "The better part of valour is discretion; in the which better part I have saved my life."

Whites and soldiers often disparaged Apaches as primitive savages, by definition inferior to whites, and expressed disgust at their contemptible, sneaky tactics. Thoughtful opponents, however, including Crook, Bourke, and Burnham, admired them precisely because their tactics were militarily effective. Crook again:

In [Apache] combats it must be remembered that you rarely see an Indian; you see the puff of smoke and hear the whiz of his bullets, but the Indian is thoroughly hidden in the rocks, and even his exact hiding place can only be conjectured. The soldier, on the contrary, must expose himself, and exposure is fatal. A dozen Indians in the rocks can withstand the onset of a battalion of soldiers, and though they can be driven from their position at the cost of many lives in the attacking party, it only results in their attaining another position equally as strong as the first, or in their scattering like quail in the rocks, to appear at some point miles away, in front, on either flank, or in the rear, as may seem to them desirable.

The Apaches only fight with Regulars when they choose and when the advantages are all on their side. If pursued to their rocky strongholds, they send their families to some other point beyond the immediate reach of danger, while the bucks absolutely without impediments swarm your column, avoid or attack as their interests dictate, dispute every foot of your advance, harass your rear, and surround you on all sides. Under such conditions Regular troops are as helpless as a whale attacked by a school of swordfish.

In short, Apaches were superb guerrilla fighters. They aimed for maximum damage with minimal risk. To reach those ends, they were ruthless. To stay undetected by nearby enemies, they thought nothing of killing dogs that might bark or light-colored horses that might be visible in the dark. It was not unusual for Apaches to ride their horses to death and then butcher them for meat, or to kill them before vanishing into terrain where horses were useless. In remote places, to discourage pursuit, they might poison a waterhole with horses' entrails.

Each morning before moving on, they picked a rendezvous; if attacked, they would scatter and reunite there. To throw off pursuers, they often set decoy fires or burned the grass behind them to obscure their retreat. They sometimes waited for pursuers to get halfway down a long hill, then fired the brush below to trap their enemies in the up-rushing flames; horsemen in pursuit of Apaches learned to ride quickly down mountainsides.

They were masters of theft and ambush. These were meticulously planned, often after days of observation to discern weaknesses in the enemies' patterns of rest and movement. Most scouts, noted Burnham, would hold vigil for a day or two,

> but an Apache scout will lie on a rocky point for many days and make no trail or sign. His whole equipment consists of a gourd of water, a piece of dried meat or jerky, and a little mescal, mesquite beans, or a handful of parched corn meal. Every film of smoke, dust cloud, or glint of light on the desert below will be noted, as well as the flight of every bird and the movements of the few desert animals. Patience, patience, and then more patience! The Indian scout will make a little buried fire of smokeless dry twigs, warm up the ground all the afternoon, bury the embers under the earth, and then lie on the warm spot until toward morning, when it will have cooled again. Then he will make a tiny fire of two crossed sticks, wrap his blanket around him, if he has one, and doze and freeze by turns until the sun once more brings warmth and another day of silence and watching.

They were also masters of camouflage. Numerous accounts describe soldiers or settlers passing across flat featureless terrain where a lizard would feel exposed, and then being shocked when Apaches suddenly leaped up from slight dents in the landscape, shooting from feet away. They aimed first for the horses or mules, to hinder pursuit. If the initial blow didn't cripple the enemy, the Apaches fled to avoid casualties. To pull this off against travelers and soldiers already nervous about Apaches, the camouflage had to be perfect.

"They were clad in such a way as to disguise themselves as much as possible," wrote General Nelson A. Miles, who would replace Crook in the final Apache campaign in the late 1880s. "Masses of grass, bunches of weeds, twigs or small boughs were fastened under their hatbands very profusely, and also upon their shoulders and backs. Their clothing was trimmed in such a way that when lying upon the ground in a bunch of grass or at the head of a ravine, if they remained perfectly silent it was as impossible to discover them as if they had been a bird or a serpent. . . . An unsuspecting ranchman or miner going along a road or trail would pass within a few feet of these concealed Apaches, and the first intimation he would have of their presence would be a bullet through his heart or brain."

During the day they made small, nearly smokeless fires of dry wood. At night they hid fires in sheltered places, and sentries kept lookout from higher up. When traveling with women and children, scouts covered the front, rear, and flanks to avoid ambush. They waited for nightfall to cross open ground, and obscured their tracks by brushing them out, stepping on rocks, or walking on their toes. Everyone who fought Apaches marveled at their ability to fade into the landscape, leaving, wrote Crook, "no more trail than so many birds." If they did leave a perceptible trail, it was probably a ruse as they doubled back on the flanks to spring an ambush.

These were the formidable warriors Crook was supposed to subdue. All his predecessors had failed. He believed that the only way to defeat Apaches was to exhaust them through relentless pursuit, and to convince them that the alternative to peace was annihilation, a point of view that Crook knew the Apaches understood and respected. For his plan to work, he needed to track them to their hidden lairs and compel surrender or destruction. A handful of Arizona frontiersmen, such as Crook's chief of scouts Al Sieber, were skillful enough to track Apaches, but Crook also needed a force large enough to strike their *rancherias* (temporary encampments) as soon as they were found. Only one group combined the skills and ferocity necessary to execute his plan: the Apaches themselves. To track birds, Crook needed birds. To fight tigers, he would recruit tigers.

He sent Al Sieber to the Apache reservations to announce that the U.S. Army was hiring. Crook wanted "the wildest that I could get." He knew recruitment would be easy. Apache factions had always been happy to kill one another, and any male Apache would gladly abandon his corn hoe for the chance to stalk and destroy enemies in the mountains.

A couple of hundred warriors eagerly signed up to hunt down other Apaches.

——

Crook's first campaign using Indian scouts began in November 1872. Settlers in Arizona thought he had lost his mind. Territorial newspapers shouted that some of these new government employees had recently been raiders and murderers, and would surely betray the soldiers. Some of Crook's officers and military colleagues were insulted by the insinuation that numerous regiments in forts throughout Arizona could not tame a few bands of ragtag savages without help from the savages themselves. Did Crook really believe that West Point graduates and trained U.S. soldiers were the military inferiors of primitives in breechclouts?

Yes, he emphatically did. He planned a brief but arduous campaign. In November 1872 he and his troops, led by Apache scouts under Al Sieber and Archie McIntosh, began chasing renegade Apaches throughout central Arizona. Crook knew this pressure would push them into their usual safe haven, the Tonto Basin, where previous offensives had floundered.

He intended to turn this safe haven into a cage. Guided by his Apache scouts, he followed the renegades into the rugged snowy mountains and hounded them all winter. The fugitives soon realized they could not risk shooting game or building a fire because any unusual sound or sight or smell drew the Apache scouts. The renegades spent the winter months of late 1872 and early 1873 fleeing and fighting, starving and freezing, with no rest. Crook and his troops, Indian and regular army, got little rest as well, but were occasionally provisioned by mule trains.

The strategy was physically brutal for both sides. One military account described "the torture of a journey over the miles on miles of confused and jumbled masses of rocky mountain peaks," and complained that the relief at each day's ending was immediately pushed aside "by the prospect of the interminable, heart-breaking, rock-climbing struggle to begin again at daybreak." The soldiers constantly had to dismount and walk. "Cavalry in those regions were as useless as gunboats," wrote one officer. A soldier described looking up at another "jagged, peaked, rocky, gravelly, slippery trail, covered with sticking Spanish bayonet and cactus and barred by bushes that seem to take a catlike delight in clutching, with barbed thorns, every bone and joint."

But the strategy worked. The Apache scouts tracked the renegades wherever they tried to hide, then led most of the attacks. No band was too small to pursue. One command marched 1,200 miles in 142 days and killed an estimated 500 Indians. The remaining Apaches always scattered, but the constant attrition—four, eight, twelve deaths at a time—and the constant physical suffering eroded their resolve as well as their numbers.

By spring 1873 most of the surviving Apaches in the Tonto Basin were worn out. In April, groups began suing for peace. One leader, Delshay, said he and his band were surrendering because every rock had turned into a soldier, and the rocks themselves had seemed to soften and carry footprints that led the soldiers to his people, who could not sleep at night because every small noise alarmed them.

As soon as the Apaches began surrendering, Crook stopped the campaign. He told them that if they reported to the reservations, they would not be harmed and would be treated fairly—but if they left the reservation to raid, he would hunt them down and kill them. These were clear terms that the Apaches understood, from the relentless white warrior they now called "the Grey Fox."

The settlers were elated by Crook's success, but wanted him to finish the job through extermination. Crook brushed off the demand. By the end of April about 2,500 Apaches had reported to Camp Verde, and hundreds of others to reservations at Camp Apache and San Carlos. Crook soon had them digging irrigation ditches, planting corn and squash, and cutting hay to sell to the army. He outlawed tiswin, an alcoholic beverage made from the mescal cactus, and also the practice of slicing off the nose of an adulterous wife. His gamble with the Apache scouts had succeeded brilliantly. Ten of them received the Medal of Honor.

Within months, the peace crumbled. Crook's threat of annihilation wasn't enough to stifle some Apaches' deep-rooted predispositions toward complete freedom and belligerence. These were further provoked by putting traditionally antagonistic bands of Apaches together on the same reservation, and by the utter corruption of Indian Bureau agents, especially Dr. R. A. Wilbur at San Carlos. Wilbur cut the Indians' rations to the point of starvation. On May 27, 1873, disgruntled Apaches at San Carlos killed the commanding army officer and fled. By autumn, several other bands had left their reservations to raid and kill. The newspapers resumed howling.

Crook told his Apache scouts that he wanted the heads of the four main renegades. The scouts and the soldiers resumed their relentless pursuit in the mountains. By mid-1874 the renegade leaders had been hunted down and killed, and most bands had returned to the reservations. In August, when the newly appointed Indian agent entered San Carlos, he rode past a display of the rebels' heads.

The agent was John Clum, a twenty-two-year-old farm boy from New York with no experience of Indians. His appointment may have been arranged by "the Indian Ring," a network of corrupt contractors and officials who robbed the government and the Indians by shortchanging the reservations. If the Indian Ring thought this young greenhorn would be easy to manipulate, they were soon disabused.

Clum was energetic, curious, and intelligent, and he saw the same qualities in the Apaches. The key, he believed, was to channel their strengths away from violence. Like Crook, he treated them fairly and was clear about the consequences of misconduct. He began a program of building and farming. He helped the Apaches start a court to settle their own disputes, and appointed four of the most trustworthy as agency police. He introduced hygiene programs to prevent disease, and he blocked the parasitic suppliers who had been fattening on government contracts while cutting the Indians' rations. He also defended the Apaches against settlers who wanted them dead or expelled, and who considered Clum a mollycoddler. In these ways he earned the Apaches' trust.

All this was soon undermined by the federal government's new "removal policy." Despite objections by Crook, who had been transferred to the Great Plains to fight the Sioux, Apaches were forced to leave the reservations that had been promised to them, and to concentrate in one place. The policy was disastrous. It jammed hostile groups of Apaches together on the bleakest of the Arizona reservations, San Carlos. The population there swelled from 700 to 5,000. By the summer of 1877 Clum felt besieged by angry factions: Apaches, settlers, politicians, the army, the Indian Ring. In July, he resigned in frustration and disgust.

Two months later the tensions exploded into violence. Bands led by Victorio, Loco, and Geronimo bolted from San Carlos and rampaged through the region. These were the first of many agitations and outbreaks over the next decade, all traceable to the blunder of the removal policy, which added thousands of deaths and millions of dollars to the cost of peace in Arizona.

Burnham joined this cycle as a scout after the troubles at Cibecue Creek in the summer of 1881. In early 1882, after Apache warriors under Geronimo, Chatto, and Juh crossed into Arizona from Mexico, Burnham went to San Carlos and offered his skills to Albert D. Sterling, the reservation's chief of police.

CHAPTER SEVEN

HUNTING TIGERS
WITH TIGERS

THE PEOPLE OF Arizona knew the renegade Apaches were on their way because the leaders had sent messengers to San Carlos demanding that others join them on the warpath. Many Apaches at San Carlos were sick of war, and informants there told the authorities about the renegades' plans. The army tried to cut them off at the border but failed, so scouting patrols were increased throughout the region. Though everyone knew the renegades' destination, they raided and killed en route without being caught. Where would they strike next? The region was panicked. Al Sterling sent Burnham to scout for sign in the Apache Peaks, thirty-five miles northwest of San Carlos.

On April 18 the renegade Apaches cut the telegraph lines into the reservation. They hit quickly, killing Sterling and adding to their war party. In just a few weeks their sprce of plunder and murder claimed about fifty people—miners, freighters, and settlers, many of them horribly mutilated. At a ranch near the Gila River they tortured and killed five men, roasted one child alive, threw another into a thicket of needle-tipped cactus, and beat the brains out of the children's mother with a rock. Despite multiple army patrols led by Apache scouts, the renegades were hardly touched.

On July 7, another chief named Na-tio-tish riled up about sixty warriors among the White Mountain Apaches at San Carlos. They ambushed
and killed Sterling's successor as police chief, J. L. Colvig (nicknamed
"Cibicue Charley"), plus three Indian policemen, then broke northwest
toward the Tonto Basin. The next day they attacked the small mining town
of McMillenville, about ten miles above Globe. Most of the White Mountain band at San Carlos condemned Na-tio-tish and his renegades, and
offered to help hunt them down.

This raid close to Globe, when added to reports that nearly 700 Chiricahuas were haunting the region, pushed the area's residents close to hysteria. Globe filled up with frightened refugees. Women and children
crammed into the buildings. The men camped in corrals and open areas.
Eleven men, after filling up with whiskey, dubbed themselves the Globe
Rangers. They packed a further supply of high-proof courage and rode out
of town vowing to kill Indians. A day or two later, as they slept at a ranch
on the Salt River, the Apaches took a few shots at them and stole all their
horses. The rangers hiked back to Globe, sober.

This was the situation when Burnham rode into Globe early one morning after his long scout in the Apache Peaks. He was filthy, his clothes tattered. He was looking forward to a hot breakfast of beans, bacon, and
coffee, but a friend in the street told him to go straight to the man now in
charge of Globe's defense, Captain S. L. Burbridge. Burbridge had come to
Globe to supervise the construction of new copper smelters, but he evidently
had military experience.

A powerful, bearded man, he took in Burnham's dirty, ragged appearance and laughed in approval. It matched the stories he had been hearing
about the twenty-one-year-old. "I'm looking for a scout who is half jackrab-
bit and half wolf," said Burbridge, "and by the eternal blazes I believe you
are it." He gave Burnham a requisition to buy new clothes, supplies for a
ten-day scout, and new shoes for his horse. He told him to get some breakfast and report back in a couple of hours.

Burnham made a list of his purchases:

1 felt slouch hat

1 greenish brown woolen shirt

1 suit of light underwear

4 pairs of light sox

1 pair of Indian-made buckskin leggings

1 pair of hand-sewed light shoes, very best leather

1 pair of brown overalls, light weight

1 large red silk handkerchief, for signaling

2 small gray silk handkerchiefs

1 spool strong linen thread for night guard

1 small canvas water bag

He waterproofed the canvas bag by dipping it in melted tallow and beeswax. Unlike a metal canteen, this would pack flat when empty, and it could be filled with air to float his rifle and cartridge belt across rivers. He also bought two tanned, smoked doeskins, weighing about a pound each, to use at night against wind and cold; they were much lighter than a blanket. He packed fifty cartridges for his carbine and revolver, both .44–40 caliber. He removed the cleaning rod from the hole bored in the butt of the carbine, enlarged the hole, and filled it with a string pull-through cleaner and a small tin of Vaseline, some silk thread and a surgeon's needle for sewing a wound, and a small file and screwdriver for repairs. To eliminate glints from his gun barrel, he stretched a green hide from a deer's front leg over it, making tiny slits for the sights. For messages, he packed a stub of pencil and some paper.

Since he wouldn't be able to shoot game or light a fire, he bought a sack of dried venison, hammered it into fine powder, and mixed it with an equal amount of flour. He baked this nutritious mixture into dense loaves that went into his saddlebags. He also took some pinole (cornmeal) and pinoche (a confection made from sugar and corn). These minimal provisions left room in his pack for whatever he came across: nuts, dock leaves, mesquite beans, perhaps chunks of pitch to make smoke signals.

At the blacksmith's, he had his horse, Turk, reshod. He bought extra nails and a small hammer. He also carried some round pieces of bull hide, which could be nailed on if a shoe fell off or wore out. Arizona's granite and shale mountains were tough on horseshoes. He rolled up some gunny sacks and an old sheepskin, which he would tie over the horse's hooves and his shoes whenever he needed to cover tracks.

All this, he later wrote, was the drudgery required to prepare for a scout, so different from "the glamour and romance" found in storybooks.

There is an idea abroad that the usual mode of procedure for an Indian scout was, after eating a hearty breakfast, to saddle up his broncho and, equipped with an extra belt of ammunition, a rifle, two six-shooters, and possibly a spy glass and a canteen of water, gallop over the mountains until he ran across some Indian sign; then dismount, hide his horse, and with incredible stealth creep up on a large band of deaf Indians. He would probably pot a few of the fiercest, and might then be chased for a mile or two on foot. On reaching his horse, he would vault to his back without touching stirrup and ride gallantly away, still carrying all his equipment and no lighter than when he started, except for the lead in the bodies of the dead Indians.

Later that morning he reported back to Burbridge. The captain was worried that the Apaches might be massing near Globe for a surprise attack. Nobody knew where they were, and rumors were flying. He hadn't been able to get any information, he said, because many of the men in town were barroom Indian fighters and the others were too scared to get off their horses and nose around in the brush. He assigned Burnham to scout a wide semicircle, south beyond the Pinal Mountains, then north and west along Pinto Creek to the Salt River. Every inch of it was rugged. He told him not to return until he saw a smoke signal on a peak near Globe. If he found Apaches, said Burbridge, "put up three smokes anywhere within sight of town" and then run for it.

Burnham left Globe after dark and rode over the Pinals to Mineral Creek, arriving just before dawn. He hobbled Turk in a glade with grama grass and a spring, then secluded himself in the rocks to sleep for a few hours. After waking, he circled Turk for a half-mile, checking for tracks in case an Indian had followed him and was waiting in ambush near the horse. All clear. He breakfasted on a piece of jerky loaf and plotted his route. To stay as inconspicuous as possible, he decided to scout on foot. He packed four days' rations and cached his saddle, hanging it by a thong smeared with pine pitch to repel ants, high enough off the ground so coyotes couldn't gnaw it.

"It may seem rather terrifying to think of riding or even walking alone at night across an Apache-infested country," he later wrote, "but that is mostly tenderfoot jitters and was not actually dangerous. The Indians did not travel much at night except when pursued or when getting into position to attack. But daylight scouting against the Apache is quite different. To survive, it was well to feel at all times as though a great mountain lion were sniffing the trail and that you must conduct yourself so as to see him first."

To disrupt the contours of his face—a shape easily detected even from a distance—he drew a line in charcoal from his temples to his chin. He also put some grama grass in his hat band and on his shoulders. Then he began to climb. When the vegetation changed, he replaced the grama in his hat with oak twigs and also carried a small oak branch in front of him to muddle his body's outline.

He spent an exhausting day moving between high ridges and deep canyons, looking for sign. At sunset he made a bed of grass and leaves on a gravelly ridge where no one could trespass without sending pebbles clattering. He also set up his usual alarm system, stringing a length of strong linen thread between bushes and small stones around the hideout's perimeter, high enough off the ground to allow the passage of small creatures. Anything large, such as a human, would shake a bush or send stones clattering. A noise woke him at two o'clock: a bear shambling in the canyon below— reassuring, since it would have been spooked by the scent of Indians.

A bird's sleepy twitter woke him near dawn. He moved out while the shadows could hide him, carrying a pine branch as he climbed toward the dark firs on Pinal Peak. He came across some old Indian sign and spent cartridges, but nothing fresh. At the top he rested in the deep shade of a boulder and gazed south over the broken landscape of peaks, canyons, and deserts stretching to Mexico. Nothing was moving.

He scrambled down a side canyon toward a stream that led to the Gila River. At the bottom, where the side canyon met a larger one, he quickly filled his water bag in the creek, avoiding the sand and gravel so he didn't leave tracks, then moved into the cover of the bordering willows and scrub oaks where he could rest without being seen.

Minutes later an Apache appeared, riding down the main canyon. He was barely ten yards away. Burnham froze. Should he shoot? Was the Indian alone or part of a group? He heard the answer on the ridge above, where another Apache was riding a bay horse. When Burnham looked back at the main canyon, he saw a third warrior on a pony. He held his breath. They rode on, the soft thuds fading away. Silence returned. Fifteen minutes passed. No more Apaches appeared. That meant the three warriors were scouts, perhaps heading to a rendezvous on the eastern flank of the Pinals, where forage, water, and cover were plentiful—and just ten miles from Globe.

Burnham needed to see if the Apaches were massing there, but he also felt like running in the opposite direction. Two hours of daylight remained. He forced himself to climb the ridge to observe the horsemen and their bearing, but when he reached the top, they had disappeared. As he crossed to the next ridge for another look, a shot cracked above him, less than 100 yards away. The Apache on the bay rode up onto the ridge he had just left. The rider looked unconcerned, so Burnham assumed that the target was a deer. He was still undetected, but that would change as soon as one of the Indians crossed his trail on the ridge. He decided to get a head start down the gulch. Moments later he heard a cry and looked back. The Apache on the ridge had raised his rifle horizontally and was slowly turning it around and back. Burnham knew the signal: enemy sign.

He took off. A shrill yell told him that he had been seen, confirmed by a shot. But the Apaches soon gave up the chase, probably because the odds weren't high enough in their favor. Burnham knew this was caution, not cowardice. The Apaches would not risk a casualty to kill one lone but armed white man who would soon be hidden by darkness. But in case this apparent lack of interest was a trick, Burnham ran until nightfall, then slept in the mouth of an abandoned mine.

The next day, alert for ambush, he circled back to Turk, but found no sign nearby. He did the same to retrieve his saddle and provisions, then rode toward the eastern side of the Pinals to resume his scout. He crossed the trail of the three Apaches. He turned loose Turk, knowing he would return to the range near Mineral Creek and be easy to find there. For the next several days he scouted the canyons and bottoms. No sign of Apaches. He walked back to Mineral Springs, trailed down Turk, and headed north into the Pinto Creek drainage, "a wild, rough country, with brush, scrub oak, bear grass, and much loose rock"—terrible for daylight scouting because the sound of rolling pebbles and crunched gravel travels so far.

He had been reconnoitering for ten days and was out of food, but no smoke signal came from Globe. On the eleventh day, famished, he remembered a nearby smelter used by charcoal makers. Maybe in their rush to flee they had left some food in their cabin. He circled it. Every trail leading to it showed undisturbed insect tracks—all clear. Inside, he found flour and some rancid bacon hanging from the ceiling. The makings of a feast, but building a fire for fry bread and bacon would draw any Indians in the area. Ravenous, he did it anyway.

The moment he finished, his rational mind returned and warned him to get out fast. He was shoveling ashes over the fire with the frying pan when something blocked the light from the doorway. He turned to see three Indians pointing guns at him. "Hours on end old scouts had taught me caution," he later wrote, "and there I was trapped like a tenderfoot—all their teaching wasted. My appetite had conquered me. The penalty should have been death."

But he was lucky. They were friendly Apache scouts sent to bring him in, and had come to check out the cabin after seeing smoke there. A scout didn't get many second chances. Burnham was embarrassed. He had failed to live up to his mentors' standards—Apache standards.

He reported to Burbridge and then joined him and others in a rescue party to bring in the surviving settlers on Cherry Creek, which winds through Tonto Basin. During operations in the Pinal Mountains, Burnham's ability as a long-distance runner came into play. An officer wanted to send dispatches to a troop on the San Pedro River, twenty-two miles across hard terrain crawling with Indians. A cavalryman left on a horse, Burnham on foot. When the horseman arrived, Burnham had been there for hours. "A man who knows how to run has it all over a horse in rough country," wrote Burnham.

The 1882 campaign ended with the Battle of Big Dry Wash (sometimes called Battleground Ridge) on July 17, 1882, in the Mogollon Mountains above Tonto Basin. Burnham doesn't mention this event and must have been scouting elsewhere. Al Sieber and his Apache scouts, reinforced by U.S. troops, tracked down Na-tio-tish and his band and killed many of them. The survivors slipped back onto the reservation.

It was the last major battle between Apaches and U.S. troops in Arizona, though the troubles with Apaches were far from over. The Chiricahuas led by Chatto and Geronimo had retreated into Mexico, but everyone knew they would be back. In September Crook was recalled to Arizona to deal with them, and with the wreckage left by the recent raids.

Crook began by interviewing many Apaches, often at their rancherias. He wanted to hear their complaints and understand what had caused Cibecue and the outbreaks. Most Apaches had not supported the renegades and were relieved to see Crook. He had always been honest and fair, rewarding the peaceful and punishing the violent. What Crook heard, in story after story, enraged him. San Carlos had become, and remained, a powder keg, mostly because of white misbehavior. In early October he issued a general order reminding all officers and soldiers "that one of the fundamental principles of the military character is justice for all—Indians as well as white men." Anyone who violated this principle would be punished. He also called together all 400 chiefs at San Carlos and told them that he would assist all Indians who worked and kept the peace, but would show no mercy to any who chose the warpath.

Crook's report placed the blame squarely on the profiteers associated with the Indian Ring. They and their partners, the Indian agents, had been robbing the Apaches of their meager government rations and selling the clothing, blankets, and other goods intended for them to merchants in Globe and elsewhere. When the Indians' patches of corn, melons, and beans were half-grown, the agent had sent horsemen to trample them, thus forcing the Indians to buy overpriced food from him and his partners, the suppliers. The agent also threatened to kill any Apache chiefs who refused to sign away chunks of the reservation where prospectors, his partners, wanted to mine. Anyone who complained was put into irons. This agent, the reviled J. C. Tiffany, was appointed to San Carlos on the recommendation of the Dutch Reformed Church. Many of the Apaches had left the reservation because they were tired of starvation and mistreatment. Keeping the Indians riled up also assured the continued presence of the profiteers' other big customer, the army.

A federal grand jury investigated San Carlos. Their findings horrified them: "Fraud, peculation, conspiracy, larceny, plots, and counterplots seem to be the rule of action on this reservation. The grand jury little thought when they began this that they were about to open a Pandora's box of iniquities seldom surpassed in the annals of crime." They condemned Tiffany "and that class of reverend peculators who have cursed Arizona as Indian officials, and who have caused more misery and loss of life than all other causes combined." After reading this scathing report, Carl Schurz, the Secretary of the Interior, dismissed the entire Indian Office. He also fired Tiffany, who was never prosecuted.

In Globe, the *Arizona Silver Belt*, the newspaper of Burnham's old mentor Hackney, defended Tiffany. Burnham read the grand jury report and split from his mentor on this issue: "For such misdeeds, the prophets of old demanded of their people repentance in sackcloth and ashes and prayers for forgiveness." Many others in Arizona also were enraged by the reports from Crook and the grand jury—because they were soft on Apaches. This was reinforced by orders from Washington that the army was not to punish any Apaches, regardless of murderous past actions, as long as they were living peacefully on the reservation.

Bands of Apaches, mostly Chiricahuas, continued to leave the reservation and send flares of terror across the region. They tormented both sides of the border for five more years, in a rhythm that drove Crook and the people of Arizona mad. Crook's Apache scouts—also mostly Chiricahuas—would track them down. The renegades would swear peace and return briefly to the reservation before fleeing back to Mexico, raiding and killing along the way.

In March 1883, for example, Chatto stormed out of Mexico with twenty-six warriors. In six days they flashed across 400 miles and killed two dozen whites, stealing fresh horses as they went, always pursued but never caught. In May 1885 Geronimo and several other chiefs broke out of San Carlos with their warriors and families, about 135 people. By the first week in June they had murdered twenty whites and captured one girl alive, whom they hung from a meat hook spiked into her skull; when rescuers found her, she had not quite died.

The people of Arizona were disgusted that Easterners and the federal government counseled Christian mercy while Apaches killed their families and stole their property. "Massachusetts Has Tears for the Indian, Anathemas for the Whites," said a headline in the *Arizona Silver Belt*. In 1885

Tombstone sent a resolution to Washington, D.C., noting that Geronimo had been in custody four times for murderous renegade acts, most recently for killing twenty-eight citizens and three soldiers, wounding nine, and stealing an unknown number of horses and cattle. Yet the government always allowed Geronimo to return to the reservation unpunished, unlike any white man who committed similar crimes. The resolution asked that all Apaches be removed from Arizona before they killed more citizens (a status the Indians lacked).

Eventually, in September 1887, Geronimo and his small band of Chiricahuas surrendered for the last time at San Carlos. Most Apaches had long since stopped fighting or were fighting for the U.S. government, but the violent minority determined everyone's fate. Orders came from Washington to put every mountain and desert Apache on trains to the tropical state of Florida, where many would die. Those deported included the loyal scouts who had tracked down the renegades and made victory possible. One-dimensional bigotry had prevailed: all Apaches were alike; none could be trusted; all must go.

"There is no more disgraceful page in history of our relations with the American Indian," wrote John G. Bourke, who served with Crook throughout the Apache campaigns, "than that which conceals the treachery visited upon the Chiricahuas who had remained faithful to their allegiance to our people."

Crook too was angry. The Apaches who had kept their promise of peace and the scouts who had won the war all were treated like prisoners. "During the entire campaign," he wrote, "from first to last, without any exception, every successful encounter with the hostiles was due exclusively to the exertions of Indian scouts, and it is the unanimous testimony of officers commanding scout companies that the Chiricahuas were the most subordinate, energetic, untiring, and by odds the most efficient of their command." In bringing about the defeat of the hostile Apaches, he added, "the efforts of the troops in the field had little or nothing to do with it."

Burnham had tried to kill Apaches, as they had tried to kill him. He had been appalled by their cruelties and pleased by their defeat. But he had also studied them as masters of scouting, and he knew that something vital was lost when they no longer roamed the Southwest: ". . . admitting all that is worst in the Indian," he wrote, "there is still much that I admire: his unconquerable spirit, his love of freedom, his infinite patience and unflinching stoicism. They were, after all, a mere handful, fighting the world and holding themselves accountable only to the Great Spirit."

CHAPTER EIGHT

A MINE, A WEDDING,
A CHANGE OF PLANS

Burnham's service as a scout, along with the truce arranged by Judge Hackney with his Tonto Basin enemies, ended his fling with outlawry. "I began now to see life from another angle," he wrote. "Life worth living depended on property, and property on law, and these three factors were necessary to lift men from chaos and savagery."

Hackney suggested that Burnham's skills in eluding assassins and tracking Apaches would be valuable in more respectable pursuits. The old editor introduced him to lawmen in Globe who put him to work as a deputy. "The county taxes were hard to raise, the territory vast; trailing criminals was difficult and expensive," wrote Burnham. "By preliminary scouting, I could often save a posse of men from wasting their time—in fact, I could do most of their work." According to Burnham, as his value became apparent, he found work tracking fugitives for well-known sheriffs throughout Arizona: John Peter Gabriel of Florence, Robert "Bob" Paul of Tucson, William "Buckey" O'Neill of Prescott.

On one of these missions he was careless enough to let his horse get stolen by two Mexican thieves. This lapse in vigilance rankled. To atone to himself, he determined to track down the robbers. Their trail took him to Mexico, back to Tucson, then into the deserts south of Casa Grande. From there the thieves rode into and out of Mexico again. He lost the track for a while, but picked it up again at Weaver Station (a gold boom camp about sixty miles northwest of Phoenix) and followed it over the Apache Trail. The pursuit ended there, he wrote, with "a tragic capture in Tonto Creek." He didn't elaborate on the adjective, which implies fatality.

This sort of tenacity made him a natural hire for Wells Fargo, whose famous policy was never to stop pursuing anyone who committed a crime against it. Between 1870 and 1884, robbers attacked Wells Fargo stagecoaches hundreds of times, so the company's absolutist policy kept its detectives busy. The thieves were usually after Wells Fargo's iconic iron treasure boxes, painted green, which could hold up to 150 pounds of gold and silver bullion. At Wells Fargo, Burnham found another mentor in T. B. Thatcher, one of the bulldog assistants to Wells Fargo's main bulldog, chief detective James B. Hume. Thatcher sent Burnham "to distant points in California, mining camps and ranching counties, sometimes into towns, and into all the underworld life."

In between these assignments he rode on Wells Fargo stages out of Globe, protecting shipments of silver bullion. The job title was "shotgun messenger." The message was double-aught buckshot delivered from a sawed-off shotgun, a combination that could blow a window in a bandit. The work took nerve, since the robbers' first target was the messenger, who usually rode next to the driver. For that reason Burnham preferred to crouch in the rear boot, where he was small enough to fit. Because of the risks, the messenger was well paid. "He got a hundred and fifty dollars a month," noted one account, "and didn't have anything to do but kill or be killed." Others who rode shotgun for Wells Fargo included Wyatt Earp and Bret Harte.

After these stints in law enforcement, he decided to head into the desert with a few starry-eyed prospectors from Globe. Because of his skills, Burnham's main job was to position himself with a rifle in some hidden cleft, to guard against Apaches. They camped near Maricopa, twenty miles from Casa Grande, and began hunting for gold placers. These occur where gold has been eroded out of rocks and carried away in streams. The gold settles in the streambeds and banks, and sometimes accumulates in crannies or pockets called vugs (from the Cornish word for cave, *vooga*). In the desert Southwest, these streambeds are usually dry.

Finding gold was another form of tracking, of observing acutely and following geological signs to your target. Burnham and his companions looked for likely spots, especially quartz stained red by oxidized iron. Iron could indicate pyrite, often found with gold and silver. They winnowed surface gravels by tossing shovelfuls into the wind to get a residue of black sand and perhaps a few grains of gold. When they had accumulated large sacks of this sifted material, they loaded it onto pack animals and traveled to a water hole where they could pan it.

"We were always millionaires until the final clean-up," wrote Burnham, "when we generally found we had much black sand and little gold." They typically gleaned just enough to buy more supplies for another stint of shoveling under the desert sun, fueled by beans, flour, coffee, and salt pork, the prospector's characteristic round of drudgery and miserable food, made bearable by hopes about the next dig. Prospectors, wrote Burnham, were "dreamers of the desert" who have "a perennial optimism like the sublime faith experienced by those who have just joined the church or been converted to a new cult."

Burnham and another young romantic grew impatient with this slow pace toward wealth. They quit their crew, outfitted themselves in Tucson, and began chasing gold and good fortune. Those will-o'-the-wisps lured them through cactus, greasewood, and sagebrush in southwest Arizona, all the way to the salt marshes of the Gulf of California in northern Mexico. There, the horses died of thirst. "We saved ourselves," wrote Burnham, "by distilling salt water with the aid of a few ollas found in a deserted Indian camp." They started plodding north. Seventy miles or so later they stumbled into Yuma, "clad in such bits of rawhide and canvas as had withstood the thorns and cactus." In keeping with Western humor, their wretched emaciation made them the laughingstock of town. But bad luck and misery were never enough to discourage Burnham. Like Ed Schieffelin of Tombstone fame, he never abandoned the dream of a big strike, and would prospect off and on for the rest of his life.

After the debacle in Mexico, he vowed to give up glitter-eyed speculation, at least for a while, and to find work that paid cold cash. His destination was the Bradshaw Mountains, 100 miles north, where several silver mines were booming. The biggest and richest was the Tip Top, so he looked for work there first. The superintendent, Charles Jefferson Clark (grandson of the great explorer William Clark), told him that "only the best single-jack miners could break rock in the Tip-Top mine, for the vein was narrow and harder than flint to drill." A single-jack miner worked alone, using one hand to hit a steel chisel with a four-pound sledge and the other to rotate the chisel quickly between blows, in a constant exhausting rhythm. It was done in tight spaces underground, by the light of a candle that put a dull glint on top of the chisel so the miner had a target for his swing.

Burnham probably wasn't disappointed to be rejected for this dreary labor. Clark asked if he could shoot. "I demonstrated," wrote Burnham. Clark immediately offered him ten cents a pound for fresh venison to feed the miners. Burnham jumped at it. He had roamed the district and knew that deer abounded on nearby Black Mesa and in Bloody Basin. Before long he had to hire two Indians to haul his kills, marked with red flags, back to the mines. He baled the deer skins and slept on them in his small cabin in the mountains before selling them for twenty-five cents each to buy more cartridges.

In the spring of 1883 Burnham used part of his profits to take an overdue trip to Iowa. He visited his mother (his younger brother Howard was at school in Massachusetts). But the main reason for the trip was Blanche Blick, the Clinton schoolgirl who had listened to his dreams without laughing, and who had implicitly committed to him despite his wanderlust and poor prospects. She had been busy during the years of his absence, earning several teaching certificates while living with her parents. She was twenty-one, nearly a spinster, and he was twenty-two. He couldn't expect her to wait forever.

Burnham asked for her hand. Her father approved, with the provision that they couldn't marry until Burnham demonstrated an ability to support a wife, a trait hitherto undetectable. Burnham knew only one lawful, though improbable, path to financial independence. It led back into the desert, where hidden gold lay waiting. If he found enough of it, he could put a ring on Blanche's finger.

———

That fall he was back in Globe, where he teamed up with Richard Chilson. Three years older than Burnham, Dick Chilson came from a mining family and had lots of experience with a pick and chisel. Burnham bought a grubstake with his venison money. They decided to investigate the desert near an Arizona stagecoach station at Casa Grande. A married couple named Fryer ran a hotel and livery there. Burnham had met them while chasing the Mexican horse thieves, and they had excited him with tales about the area's potential riches.

People who knew Mrs. Fryer's history might have been surprised to find her in a remote Arizona burg—or perhaps not, since hard times and dreams had pushed people to reinvent themselves all over the country. Mrs. Fryer started life as Harriet Wood, born in New Orleans in 1833. She grew up to be tall and striking, more handsome than pretty. She moved to New York and became an actress under the stage name Pauline Cushman. During the Civil War she did theatrical tours. In 1863 in Louisville, at that time controlled by Union forces, Confederate sympathizers paid her to toast their president, Jefferson Davis, after her performance. She got fired for it, which advanced her plan. Beforehand, she had informed the Union commander of the offer and volunteered to use it as an opening to spy for the federal government.

The toast made her popular among Confederates. She headed farther south. In Tennessee, charmed officers gave this attractive actress tours of their fortifications and dropped chatty hints about their strategies. She took notes and made drawings. When she tried to leave for the North, she was searched and the documents were found hidden in her shoes. She was sentenced to hang. A providential attack by Union forces saved her; the retreating Confederates left her behind. General James A. Garfield (later president) awarded Cushman the honorary rank of brevet major, and President Lincoln praised her service to the Union.

Always opportunistic, she began touring and lecturing as "Miss Major" Pauline Cushman. P. T. Barnum scooped her up for his traveling show, dressing her in the uniform of a Union officer. By 1868 her commercial appeal had waned. She was alone and broke, but still resourceful, which led to her arrest as a pickpocket. In 1872, like other desperate people seeking better times, Cushman went west. She spent a few years around San Francisco, sometimes performing with an Irish comedian. In 1879 she married a man even taller than she, Jeremiah Fryer (her third husband), and went with him to the coach station at Casa Grande. That's where Burnham met her. He always called her Major Pauline.

Like most Arizonans, the Fryers were intensely interested in the possibility of a big strike. Prospectors who passed through Casa Grande left behind plenty of glowing rumors. When Burnham and Dick Chilson stopped there in autumn of 1883, the Fryers filled the young prospectors' ears with the newest enticing gossip, stoking their gold fever.

"We traced minute particles of float, fine as dust," wrote Burnham, "and worked for weeks in the burning sun, using magnifying glasses." Chilson's brother joined them. They carried water in canteens so they could immediately test promising gravels and float rock, crushing them and then swirling the grit with water in a horn spoon. They followed this tedious, laborious procedure for several months over hundreds of desert miles. Nothing.

Around Christmas, their luck changed. Dick Chilson wrote to his father:

I have struck four feet of gold ore that will go for $1,000 to the ton. I took out $300 worth of gold dust with my pocket knife. I have got two

25-pound boxes of gold dust worth about $3,000. I have got nuggets of gold, pure gold, as large as a bird's eggs. I sunk nine feet on the ledge and took out ten tons before I noticed the gold, and therefore blasted away several thousand dollars. I have $5,000 in sight.... There are clusters of gold as a big as dollars sticking through the ledge. There has been a sale made of one mine near me for $3,000,000; and another sold four miles from me for $20,000. I declined $16,000 for mine.

They named their mine the Christmas Gift. Mines were proving out all over the area, and that lowball offer of $16,000 soon shot up. Since none of the partners had the patience to develop the mine, and since the vein could peter out tomorrow, in January 1884 they accepted an offer of $90,000, equivalent to about $2 million today. (Over the next few years, the mine would yield about $200,000 worth of gold.)

Burnham's share would more than appease Blanche's father. To further demonstrate his sensibleness, in February he went to Pasadena and bought a twenty-acre orange grove, a symbol since boyhood of California's verdant promise. He knew nothing about oranges and had no interest in agriculture, but the grove made him a bona fide landowner with a rooted occupation, just the credentials to satisfy a fiancée's father.

He returned to Iowa in triumph. On March 2, 1884, he and Blanche were married. The day was rainy, but as the ceremony began, shafts of sunlight broke through, which Blanche took as a blessing on the union. They returned immediately to the orange grove. Burnham used the Christmas Gift money to bring his mother and brother to Pasadena; they probably were pleased to escape the charity of Burnham's uncles. He also gave his mother's parents a small pension to ease their old age. Throughout his life, whenever he had money, Burnham was generous with it, especially to members of his and Blanche's family, whom he called their tribe.

Installed in his orange grove with his new wife, the wandering scout seemed ready to set aside his dreams of adventure and settle into husbandry.

It didn't work. He could outrun Apaches and track thieves for hundreds of miles, but oranges stumped him. "I believe it takes more gray matter to outwit the vagaries of an orange tree and coax it into productivity," he wrote, "than is required for a railway president, governor of a state, or manager of a life-insurance company." He figured each orange cost him twenty-five cents to grow and sold for less than a penny. Almost immediately, "the mountains and the desert began calling again, and in the dim distance returned my lifelong vision of Africa."

He went to Mesa, Arizona, to talk to a Mormon engineer named George M. Sirrine whom he knew from his travels. Mormons had settled Mesa, registering it as a town in 1878. Burnham had been impressed by their ability to grow crops in the desert thanks to a system of irrigation canals built by Sirrine, who had reconstructed channels and gradients dug ten centuries earlier by the Hohokam Indians.

By 1883 Mesa had 300 people and was growing. So was nearby Phoenix. Sirrine told Burnham that the increasing need for water made a dam on the Salt River inevitable. Burnham, always prospecting, bought some land and water rights, and began studying irrigation. He also bought a small interest in the Mesa Canal Company. Blanche and Howard, bored by oranges, soon joined him. Blanche began teaching school. But waiting for water rights to bear fruit was as dull as watching oranges ripen.

Things were briefly enlivened by a ricochet from Tonto Basin days. Burnham heard that a friend from his side of the feud had killed someone from the other side in a gunfight. The friend was now in jail awaiting trial, but some townspeople wanted to hang him straightaway. This bloodlust was being further lashed toward violence by the dead man's lover, a beautiful woman and "a wonderful firebrand," wrote Burnham, "who knew well how to stir up excitement in a frontier community." She wanted his friend's head, so Burnham called her Salome.

He rode across the desert to the town. The citizens clearly were on the verge of fusing into a mob eager for what Burnham called "a necktie party." The endangered man had four other friends in town, including a tough ex-sheriff from Nevada who had a hotel room directly across from the jail. This became the allies' meeting place. In preparation, they slit the hotel room's cloth ceiling and hid an arsenal in the rafters. They also removed the window sash and several adobe bricks to create a wider line of fire toward the jail. It so happened that Burnham and the town's sheriff had ridden together as boys in California. Burnham told him that if a mob tried to take the prisoner, the sheriff could expect a fusillade from the hotel.

The next evening, the mob marched to the jail and called out the sheriff. Burnham's group took up their positions. The sheriff opened the thick wooden door and said he would shoot the first man who tried to walk through it. The crowd could overrun him easily, he added, but he wanted them to know that all four ringleaders were now in the gun sights of men who would kill them at the first shot.

There was a pause. Was the sheriff bluffing, or would some of them get perforated? That possibility took some air out of the mob's bloodlust. They seemed poised between a nudge one way or the other. Salome tried to provide it, shrieking, "What are you all waiting for?"

"Waiting for you to kiss the sheriff!" yelled one of the men in the hotel room, in a tone that mocked her as a Jezebel. Some in the mob laughed, a crack in their resolve, which the sheriff began crowbarring with all the reasons the townspeople shouldn't reject law and order. A few people called out that maybe he was right. Within moments the mob's will wavered and broke. People silently stalked off. Burnham turned from the hotel window and slumped to the floor, his gun across his knees.

———

During his first year in Pasadena, while trying to grow oranges, Burnham got reacquainted with his brother Howard. They hadn't seen each other in six years. At fourteen, Howard was nine years younger. He arrived in California ill from a severely injured leg. Doctors in Los Angeles said he wouldn't recover unless the leg was amputated four inches below the knee. Howard held Burnham's hand as doctors chloroformed him and sawed it off. One of the surgeons gave him six months to live. This began to seem optimistic after Howard contracted tuberculosis, which had killed his father.

But Howard showed the grit that marked him for the rest of his life. He quickly adapted to his wooden leg (it later came in handy as a hiding place when he worked as a spy in Germany during World War I). During the months of convalescence, Burnham taught him the rudiments of frontier life: riding, shooting, some scoutcraft, the art of the horn spoon. Howard was an eager, determined student, and learned to shoot well with either hand.

At sixteen, Howard left to look for gold in deserts "from the Panamints in Death Valley to Lower California," sometimes teaming up with old prospectors who could teach him how to spot promising ground or hunt down pockets. Whenever he collected a little gold, he stored it in a quill from a roadrunner's wing. Like his brother, Howard was a voracious reader, and his pack was always heavy with books about geology, metallurgy, and mining as well as history and military strategy.

———

Meanwhile, Burnham sold his land and water investments in Mesa. The engineer Sirrine was doubtless right that Phoenix's thirst would require a dam, but Burnham didn't have the patience to wait. (The Theodore Roosevelt Dam would be dedicated by its namesake in March 1911. The reservoir it created, Lake Roosevelt, put the southern portion of the Tonto Basin under water.)

Blanche was pregnant. They returned to the orange grove, but the place again made Burnham restive. He reconnected with some friends from Texas and Arizona. They decided "to take a whirl for fortune in the Northwest." They prospected for gold in Idaho, Washington, and Canada.

Burnham learned about icy rivers, deep snow, and sled dogs, lessons he would use in the Klondike. He and his partners didn't hit a big lode, but did discover a vein of silver that paid out modestly for a number of years.

When he returned to Pasadena several months later, in the fall of 1886, Blanche presented him with his new son, Roderick, born on August 22. (Burnham would be elsewhere for the births of all his children.) Roderick's arrival motivated him to take another stab at agriculture and domesticity. "I had recurring fits of aberration in which I persuaded myself that I could run an orange grove at a profit," he wrote. "It was not long, however, before I was seized with another attack of mining fever."

By early winter he was gone again, this time prospecting in the San Jacinto Mountains, west of Palm Springs. He and a partner found "a thread of gold in quartz," and with great expectations opened a mine. Howard joined them, as did a young man named William Kettner, later a four-term Democratic congressman from San Diego. But the golden thread soon broke, and by spring of 1887 Burnham was back in Pasadena with his exasperating oranges. Pasadena was growing. He began selling lots from the grove, holding the mortgages himself.

Blanche acutely missed her large family. By the fall of 1887 she and Burnham had persuaded her parents and eight siblings to move to California, where gold may have been elusive but dreams and schemes abounded. Eight Blicks plus the Burnhams were eligible to claim government land. "All were land hungry," wrote Burnham. "Like thousands of others, we all took up desert claims, timber claims, homesteads, homestead preemptions, and various other opportunities of securing the right to starve without let or hindrance." The closest homestead plots were in Antelope Valley, 100 miles away over the San Gabriel Mountains. Together, the Burnham–Blick clan marked off several thousand acres and built cabins to legalize their claims.

That fall, in the midst of this land speculation, Howard showed up, wrote Burnham, "and again infected me with the virus of mine hunting." The source of infection was an old prospector with Howard named Jack Guesford. Guesford repeated his tale to Burnham: in the mid-1860s he and two companions had been prospecting into Death Valley when they hit a lode of rich galena, the main mineral in lead ore. Lead ore often meant silver. Guesford was sure he had found his bonanza. But on the very day they found the galena, before they could load their burros with ore for assaying, Piute Indians had attacked and chased them off. Now, twenty-five years later, Guesford hoped to find his lost lode. Howard was eager to help him search. They just needed financing.

Fabled lost mines had been a staple of Western gossip and dreams since conquistadores sought the Seven Cities of Cibola. Whenever old chimeras evaporated, new ones appeared. The West was vast enough to accommodate anything imaginable, and sometimes reality matched imagination. Everyone knew the stories about prospectors who discovered fabulous ledges but had to abandon them because of Indians or thirst or hunger; about miners who loaded their burros with rich ore from some new discovery but got killed by Indians or thirst or a cougar or thieves before anyone knew the lode's exact location. Some of these mines became so famous they entered legend—the Peg-Leg, the Tayopa, the Adams Diggings, the Lost Dutchman—all stupendously rich, all poised for rediscovery. Thousands of miners searched for them over the decades, and still do.

Burnham certainly knew these tales and, given his recurring virus, would have been susceptible to them despite his skepticism about an old prospector's burnished memory. He grubstaked Howard and Guesford. They left for the desert mountains beyond Owens Lake.

Two months later, they were back. After a couple of days to regain his bearings, Guesford had tracked his memories to the very pile of galena he and his companions had dug out on the morning when Piutes drove them away. The ore he and Howard brought back assayed modestly for silver, but it was enough to bring on the delirium. In the spring of 1889 Burnham, Howard, and Guesford provisioned themselves to go develop the lost mine. Blanche, tired of staying home, came too, as did their two-and-a-half-year-old son. "Roderick was big enough to walk," noted Burnham, "therefore big enough to ride."

They left their horses in the settlement of Independence because horses couldn't survive at the mine's location in the Mojave Desert. The site was accessible only by a thin trail over dry mountains. At the mining camp, Guesford and Burnham dynamited the deposit to open a shaft. Howard kept them supplied with water, hauling it with burros from many miles away. The usual optimism of mining camps reigned. "For several weeks," wrote Burnham, "we were millionaires."

Then the bottom fell out of everything. After three months of work, the silver vein vanished, demonstrating the adage, "Many a good mine was ruined by working it." The land boom also went bust. All the acreage in Antelope Valley was next to worthless, as were the mortgages for the lots in the orange grove. Burnham and his family returned there "to see if the financial blizzard had blown away every crumb of my life savings. . . . we found the same sun shining as of old and the same acres still in place. Everything that had happened was in men's minds. . . . Most of us had been claiming equities we had never earned, although we made a great outcry when our paper profits vanished. There was hardly a soul of us who had not lost a million."

Perhaps Burnham developed his resilience by riding the boom-and-bust rhythm of mining. Throughout his life, he alternately made money or speculative fortunes and then lost much of them to financial panics or slippery partners. Then he would start anew, ever optimistic.

As usual, Burnham couldn't rest in Pasadena. He almost immediately bought a fifty-acre ranch near Fullerton, California, and took Blanche and Rod there to live. But ranching also paled quickly, and by fall he and Howard were prospecting in Hassayampa, Arizona, with Blanche and Rod settled in nearby Mesa. Hassayampa didn't pan out. By the spring of 1890 the Burnhams were back in Pasadena. Blanche and Rod stayed there while Burnham spent much of the next two years away, "hunting lost mines and opening up prospects from Colorado to Mexico, with occasional backslidings to ranching."

The long weeks on the road led to many letters between the couple.

Burnham didn't save Blanche's, but she saved some of his. They depict a driven man. He traveled all over the West, by horse and train, looking for potentially profitable mines. He slept in everything from fine city hotels to mining camps, and talked to prospectors, mining engineers, sellers, potential buyers. He took the train to Pittsburgh, Philadelphia, and New York to meet possible investors or to propose himself as a mining scout working on commission.

The letters bubble with prospects, with golden rings just beyond his fingertips. "If I had time," he wrote from Denver in May 1890, "could stay here and catch onto something and make money." But that would take patience, and he was rushing to the next possibility. The acceleration of modern life amazed him—Chicago the day before yesterday, he wrote to Blanche, Pittsburgh yesterday, St. Louis today, Kansas City tomorrow, with Denver soon after, then Salt Lake and home to Los Angeles. Less than twenty years earlier, a locomotive in Minnesota had astonished him. Now the vast spaces of the West were being tamed and cinched tight by rails and telegraph wires, making it harder to breathe.

The letters also showed a man deeply in love with his wife. In August 1890, from a hotel in Denver, he wrote to Blanche that someone was playing beautifully on the piano in the parlor, which put him in a wistful mood. "You shall be in my arms in thought tonight my dear," he wrote. "But why say that, for you are in my thoughts all the time anyway, except when on mining business and then I am dead to all the world. Your lover as ever, Fred."

Two days later, still in Denver, he was walking to the assayer's to look up a treatment for zinc ores. He paused at a shop window just short of the office to admire a photograph of Colorado sandstones. As he stood there, the front wall of the assay office blew out, knocking down a horse and lifting Burnham off his feet. Fire engulfed the building. Two more tremendous explosions followed, probably from the assayer's chemicals. If he hadn't paused, he would have been inside. "Is it not strange what trivial things turn the course of life?" he wrote to Blanche. "But my race is not yet run and it was not to be that I should die that way and time."

One of Burnham's investments was the Alvord Mine. It was northeast of Barstow, on one of the bleak isolated mountains that jut from the sagebrush flats of the Mojave Desert. Burnham and a revolving crew lived at this austere camp, sledgehammering hard rock to find gold. The rocks they broke varied widely in color: dark chocolate, milk chocolate marbled with blue quartz, red-and-black that rang like iron, glittering white quartz. The camp was more than thirty miles from the nearest railroad. Everything, including water, had to be hauled in from miles away.

Yet many strange characters found the place, looking for work or refuge. One night a red-headed giant appeared out of the desert, singing in a rich baritone. From his gunnysack he pulled a square-headed eight-pound sledge, twice the usual weight. His only other possession was a violin, which he played nimbly. Such characters "eddied in on the whirl-winds or floated in from nowhere on a moonbeam," wrote Burnham in a passage deleted from his memoir. "Indians, smugglers, miners, writers—even a poet, or missionary and several criminals, hiding from deputies. There was always time to study these people, and from all much of interest could be gleaned, because the contacts are so much closer than in cut and dried city life."

The rough ore from Alvord had to be hauled for crushing and refining to a mill at Camp Cady, about ten miles away. To fix this inconvenience, Burnham built a mill at the mine. In September 1891, right after they melted out their first bar of gold bullion, the mill burned down and "one snug little fortune went up in smoke."

This and other frustrations depleted Burnham's finances and aggravated his restlessness. He was still supporting his mother. Blanche's parents and siblings partly depended on him as well. Perhaps better opportunities awaited elsewhere. Blanche had absolute faith in him and would go anywhere. "My Darling B.B.," he wrote in late 1892,

> Your gem of a letter came to hand last eve. And the three little flowers
> fell in my hand still giving out their faint and delightful odor. I cred-

ited young Roderick with gathering them and that he had not forgotten me yet.

The letter though short breathed such sentiments as for a little time all the plans and schemes of the world faded away as mists in the morning and my heart went out to you unclouded by a shadow and with the confidence that only long years together can beget. And I felt you worthy of all that is best in me—and doubly fortified to meet whatever is in store in the future.

The West no longer felt like the future. The frontier was past, crisscrossed by railroads and telegraph wires. Homesteaders were draining in from all directions. The Indians were almost gone, either massacred as at Wounded Knee (1890) or shipped east to reservations. Territories that had been wild when Burnham came west were now judged tame enough to enter the Union: Washington, Montana, and the Dakotas in 1889, Idaho and Wyoming in 1890. (Arizona remained a territory until 1912.) Rowdy camps and boomtowns had become ghost towns or bland churchy places like the one he fled in Iowa. His mother's childhood friend, Buffalo Bill Cody, whose stories about the West had fired his imagination, had been transformed from a plainsman and Indian fighter into a gaudy entertainer. There was no demand for the scouting skills that Burnham respected above all things and had spent so long perfecting.

The tough prospectors, frontiersmen, and renegades who had ventured into the West's wild places were being replaced by a second wave with clean boots and soft hands. Since his early days in Globe, Burnham had resented the fat cats who used money and men like chess pieces in a rigged game. But paths of escape and opportunity had always been accessible. Now conglomerates, cattle barons, railroad tycoons, and ruthless big-money "rings," assisted by their corrupt political allies, were gobbling up land and banks, taking control of everything, hogging possibilities, leaving crumbs for everyone else. The egalitarianism of the trail and the camp was almost obsolete. The gap between rich and poor was widening, and so was the possibility of jumping over it. Democracy seemed to be slipping away.

Burnham became an ardent proponent of the ideas in Edward Bellamy's best-selling utopian novel *Looking Backward: 2000–1887* (1887), which decried the "beasts of prey" fattening from the era's brutal capitalism. Bellamy envisioned a future where private property was nationalized and socialism prevailed. Burnham approved the vision but doubted its likelihood.

The economy was spluttering. He wanted out, someplace where imagination and possibilities weren't yet hemmed in or already optioned by plutocrats. He and Blanche flirted with the idea of Patagonia. They got serious about prospecting in Panama, where malaria and yellow fever had recently defeated the first attempt to dig a canal. To prepare, he went to San Francisco in early 1892 to study mine engineering, and Blanche began learning Spanish (Burnham already spoke cowpen Spanish). In November they sold most of the orange grove, cutting the strings to what had been their home base for eight years. Next stop, Panama.

On a family timeline written by Burnham, the entry after the Panama plan is dated January 1, 1893: "Changed our minds and left for Africa."

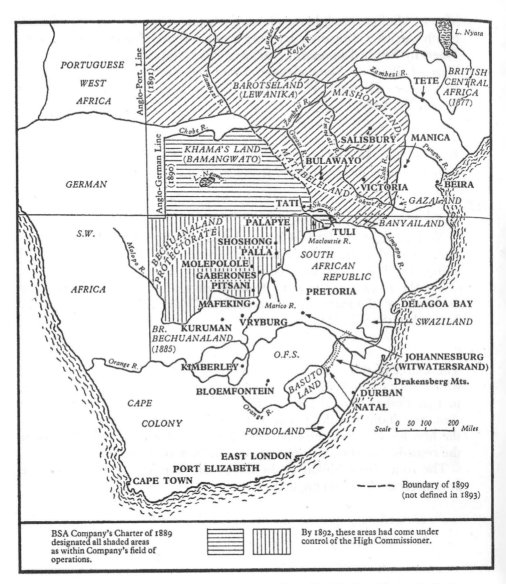

Southern Africa. (Reprinted with permission from *The Matabele War* by Stafford Glass (London: Longmans, Green and Co., 1968.)

CHAPTER NINE

TO AFRICA

Africa had been a reverie of Burnham's since boyhood. He never forgot the evenings in a Minnesota cabin when he listened to a girl reading by candlelight from a tale of adventure set in South Africa. Throughout his youth he devoured books about the continent, especially by explorers such as David Livingstone and Henry Morton Stanley, which kept his dreams of Africa glowing.

"After my marriage in 1884," he later wrote, "I believed that the beckoning spirits of Africa would fade away and no longer haunt me, but softly as the falling dew they kept returning . . . In the end I allowed myself to share with my wife the music they poured into my ears by night and often by day. Their magic won my wife completely, until in January, 1893, together we set out to make our dreams come true."

Several springs fed these dreams. Burnham was captivated by H. Rider Haggard's best-selling African adventure tales, particularly *King Solomon's Mines* (1885) and *Allan Quatermain* (1887). Quatermain, the hero of these exotic romances, is an educated Englishman and a sharpshooting outdoorsman who detests cities and prefers the rough life of Africa—a man after Burnham's own heart. (Quatermain was based on the British explorer and hunter Frederick Courteney Selous, whom Haggard met during his stint as a minor government official in South Africa from 1875 to 1882. Both Selous and Haggard would become Burnham's friends.) Haggard's tales also intensified Burnham's gold fever. *King Solomon's Mines* posed the intriguing notion that the biblical land of Ophir, whose gold and silver mines had enriched Solomon, could be rediscovered in the interior of southern Africa.

The connection to the lost mines of Solomon may have been fanciful, but the continent's mineral wealth was proving very real. By the time Burnham sailed from America, men had made millions by digging holes in the wilds of southern Africa. In the 1870s diamonds began tumbling from the mines of Kimberley. In 1886 came a big gold strike, 300 miles north in the Transvaal's Witwatersrand, soon world-famous as the Rand. Within a couple of years the boom camp there had turned into the roaring frontier town of Johannesburg.

Only a small group of men—it was always just a small group—had become rich from the Rand's gold. An even smaller group of these so-called Randlords had simply added golden wealth to fortunes already made from the diamond mines in Kimberley.

One of these latter men was Cecil Rhodes, founder and principal owner of the De Beers diamond cartel and principal owner of Consolidated Gold Fields in the Rand. He was also the chief funder and guiding force of the British South Africa Company (BSAC). In 1889 the British government awarded the BSAC an immense concession and virtual self-governance above the Limpopo River in southern Africa. The BSAC was Rhodes's primary tool for realizing his vast ambitions, what Burnham accurately called Rhodes's "colossal dream of empire."

Though one of the world's wealthiest men, Rhodes rarely made ostentatious display of it and had little interest in tracking his worth. Only unimaginative men were satisfied by personal gain. For Rhodes, wealth was merely the prerequisite for things of true value: power, influence, freedom from restrictions. He didn't crave these for small ends, but to shape countries, continents, perhaps the entire world, and to achieve immortal fame. He had the tremendous force made possible when fabulous wealth combines with monomania, utopian visions, and inexhaustible energy for turning dreams into reality.

In 1888, a year before the British government awarded the BSAC a concession, Rhodes made a deal with Lobengula, chief of the Ndebeles (at the time called Matabeles). The Ndebeles were the most powerful tribe between the Limpopo and the Zambezi. The agreement gave the BSAC the mineral rights to the eastern half of Lobengula's kingdom, Mashonaland, named after the people who occupied it, the subservient Mashonas (now called Shonas). In return Lobengula would receive £100 a month, 1,000 new rifles, 100,000 rounds of ammunition, and either a steamboat on the Zambezi or another £500. Burnham admired Rhodes for achieving his goal without shedding blood and keeping his word to Lobengula—at least at first.

Rhodes expected the mineral wealth in Mashonaland to match the strikes in Kimberley and the Rand. This new infusion of money would fund the next phase of his ambitions. His long-range plans were to expand the BSAC's reach on behalf of the Crown, first by taking over Mashonaland and Matabeleland, then by moving east to the Indian Ocean and north to Egypt, completing the dream of a corridor from "Cape to Cairo." He also expected the friction between the Boers and the British in southern Africa to end in a war that would absorb the Boer republics into the British Empire. In the long term he envisioned a United States of Southern Africa. In fact, he had a plan to hurry that along. He had come to South Africa from England as a young man because of a heart condition, and he suspected that his life would be short, which gave him a sense of urgency.

In 1890, within months of getting the royal concession, the BSAC funded a "pioneer column" that left Kimberley for Mashonaland. There were 380 men: 180 prospectors and 200 armed men to protect them from wild animals and warriors who didn't like Lobengula's agreement. The pioneers named their first permanent encampment Fort Victoria (now Masvingo in Zimbabwe). By September they had established a second camp 200 miles farther north, Fort Salisbury (now Harare). Each miner got a license to peg one alluvial claim of 150 square feet and ten quartz claims of 150 feet by 400 feet (for digging and tunneling). If a miner decided to work a claim, he had to form a company and give the BSAC a 50 percent share. Rhodes hoped this arrangement would refill the BSAC's coffers without adding to its expenses for the venture, which had already reached nearly £1 million.

In the first five months, 7,000 claims were pegged. Even Chief Loben-gula, who was now trying to repudiate his deal with the BSAC, sent some-one to stake gold claims for him. To persuade prospectors to endure the hardships and dangers of life in Mashonaland, the BSAC had assured them that the territory was littered and veined with gold.

But the pioneers found no alluvial gold waiting to be plucked. That left the arduous work of digging and tunneling, for uncertain reward. Instead of working their claims, many prospectors sold to syndicates. These had scant interest in hard investments such as labor costs and mining equip-ment, which had to be transported 800 miles from the nearest railhead at Kimberley. It was easier to float speculative stocks on the "Kaffir Circus," the London market for South African gold shares. Gold fever was running high because of the money pouring from the Rand. Anyone paying atten-tion knew that the BSAC was touting Mashonaland as the next Rand. Stock speculators, like prospectors, don't need much encouragement to imagine a big payoff. The stocks ran up and crashed, ran up and crashed, driven by rumors and dreams.

Burnham had been avidly following all this from California. Rhodes's new colony offered everything that enticed him: the chance to start over on a wild new frontier, the prospect of mineral wealth, and the opportunity to be part of a breathtaking plan to create a new country. That Mashonaland already had a ruler, landowners, and occupants were minor impediments, as they had been in the American West.

En route to Africa, riding the train across the upper American West, Burnham saw no bison but noticed "the remnants of the Cree tribe" hawking polished bison horns. The family stopped in Chicago to see the World's Fair (directed by architect Daniel Burnham, no relation). They no doubt paid special attention to the exhibits of villages imported from Africa, complete with bona fide savages. Burnham probably visited one of his boyhood idols, Buffalo Bill, and took in his Wild West show, with its bison, trick shooters, cavalrymen, and whooping Indians in feathered headdresses. The showbiz West was a blockbuster in Chicago, taking in about a million dollars.

Burnham attended the fair before Frederick Jackson Turner arrived to deliver a paper that would influence historians for a century, "The Significance of the Frontier in American History." Burnham would have nodded at Turner's premise that the American frontier had closed. The fair must have stimulated other thoughts about how quickly the future was burying the past: the spears in the African pavilion, the bows and arrows in the Wild West show, were a short walk from the building devoted to new weaponry made by the German armorer Fritz Krupp, including the biggest cannon ever made, a monster that fired a shell weighing 2,000 pounds.

Burnham never expected to return to the United States, so this farewell tour also included Washington, D.C. The place brought out his disgust with the Gilded Age traits that were propelling him away: political corruption, vested rights, squashed opportunities for anyone without money, dynastic wealth inherited rather than earned. In a vehement letter to his mother he wrote,

Great forces are gathered here strong enough to work wonders and miracles. But do they? Hardly, for so many are not in touch with the mass of people. *Abas* [down with] senators who buy their seats. *Abas* judges who are owned by R.R.s [railroads]. . . . But a better time is coming or a much worse time. Things are in change and the closing years of the 19th century will yet be a historical period. If the institutions of this civilization are not elastic enough, if the classes have served their purpose and will not bend, then we will make history in a sea of blood. Tis well. I can swim in that element for the animal in me is so strong that I am not troubled by that ghost of the many, *fear*. If the changes come in peace, that is well, for it answers to the secret desire of one's better nature. Only cast the die. I am anxious for it, if by force, then pity dies and mercy, mercy flees to the wilds. The location of great cities will be known only by the presence of a slag made up of iron, glass and brick well fluxed with human blood. That great strength and bulwark of the 19th century civilization, vested rights and inheritance, will be a prime factor in its complete undoing. But after all has been accomplished, when the old order of things have passed away as a dream of the night, will we rebuild on a better and truer basis? Being an optimist, I think *yes*.

———

Both sides of his family had roots in England, but Burnham had been brought up to despise Britain as a place to escape, a colonial oppressor. He was surprised to be moved by his ancestral home, despite London's dirty air and dreary weather. He felt his allegiances shifting. The idea of America's greatness, he wrote home, "is getting dim to me."

They took a train across Europe. Burnham loved Paris—"the only city I ever saw that I liked"—especially the Louvre and, for different reasons, the Bastille, "which showed to the world what an outraged people *can do*." As for the Alps, "we could carve a Switzerland out of California and have scenery to spare." Rome's Colosseum led him to muse that all great countries and civilizations rose from spilled blood. Naples disgusted him. At last, in Port Said, Egypt, they boarded the ship that would carry them through the Suez Canal, down the Red Sea to the Indian Ocean, and along the east coast of Africa. Five weeks, 6,000 miles. Then the real journey would begin.

The voyage introduced them to Africa and Africans. Two hundred Sudanese soldiers and their families inhabited the lower deck, and Africans thronged every port of call. The phosphorescent sea, the exotic vegetation, the striking variations among African peoples and their customs—all were strange and mysterious. Even the stars and the seasons were topsy-turvy, and the warm winds came from the north.

It all excited Burnham's love of adventure and novelty. "He is so happy and contented," wrote Blanche to her mother. "I am so glad that we came even if it never amounts to anything, for Fred's life ambition will have been gratified." Blanche herself was ambivalent. She already missed her close-knit family. In letters home, she urged them to come to Africa. Not long into the future, when Burnham's absences became almost constant, the theme of loneliness would grow stronger in her letters home.

She responded to Africans with more wariness than fascination. Like her husband, she assumed they belonged to an inferior race, but her views about them were simpler and harsher, tinged by discomfort and fear. "It does not take *any* stretch of imagination," she wrote to her family, "to believe that they are descendants of orangoutangs . . ."

The Burnhams' racial views, including casual use in their letters of the word "nigger," are reprehensible today. These views were typical of their era and were not uncommon among people admired by history. In the first chapter of *The Winning of the West*, for instance, entitled "The Spread of the English-Speaking Peoples," Theodore Roosevelt laid out the case for the inevitable triumph of the Anglo-Saxon race, not only over blacks but also over European peoples such as the Spanish and Portuguese who had foolishly mixed their blood with conquered natives instead of retaining racial purity. He believed strongly in "a square deal" for every citizen, and did more to achieve that than any president before him, but he also believed that blacks were generations behind whites in intellectual abilities.

Similarly, in 1901, after stints as an enthusiastic imperial soldier and correspondent in India, Sudan, and South Africa, whose natives he believed were fittingly "subject races," Winston Churchill noted, "The Aryan stock is bound to triumph." He likened conquered peoples to children in need of Anglo-Saxon care and discipline, a common trope. Woodrow Wilson was a racist and segregationist, yet was also, like Roosevelt, one of the most progressive politicians of his era.

Another striking example is Mahatma Gandhi. Revered for his nonviolent protests against imperialism and inequality in India, he first spent twenty-one years practicing law in South Africa, where he arrived the same year as the Burnhams. In South Africa he worked not only to improve the lot of Muslim Indians but to keep black Africans segregated and subjugated. He objected that Indians were often treated like native blacks—forced, for instance, to enter the post office through the door reserved for inferior races. "Kaffirs [blacks] are as a rule uncivilized . . ." he wrote, sounding exactly like a white Afrikaner or a British imperialist. "They are troublesome, very dirty and live like animals." He resented being equated with black people "whose sole ambition is to collect a number of cattle to buy a wife, and then pass his life in indolence and nakedness." He insisted that South Africa's emigrant Indians, like white Afrikaners, believed heartily in racial purity.

Such examples don't lessen the insidiousness of racism or excuse its handy rationale for imperial greed and oppression. The point is that the Burnhams, like others with similar views, didn't consider themselves malicious racist oppressors, but actors on the progressive side of history. That they were unable to transcend the racial attitudes of their era doesn't negate their struggles and achievements. They were blind to the contradictions and exclusions within their ideals, but when they mistook their prejudices for principles, they usually did so in the belief that they were advancing civilization, not merely themselves.

For instance, here is Burnham thirty years after he reached Africa, explaining why he so urgently wanted to go to there and attach his fate to that of Rhodes:

Rhodes had the courage of a lion. He hated bloodshed. He did not believe in lordship over subject races, but admitted that backward races should be guarded, conserved, developed. Scrupulous justice and unlimited mercy were shown in all his adjudications. He was never misled by slogans, nor did he believe that the Voice of the People is the Voice of God. He recognized too well the crimes that have been committed by popular vote, from the Crucifixion to the present day. He did believe that the civilization of the English-speaking world was to become the pivotal point around which all peaceful nations might safely rally. Under the administration of Rhodes, there were the fewest laws, the widest freedom, the least crime, and the truest justice I have ever seen in any part of the world.

Nearly every sentence of this can be attacked as untrue, uninformed, or self-serving. Yet that isn't the whole truth about the passage. Burnham's sincerity is clear. He isn't trying to conceal or rationalize. His pride in Rhodes, and by extension in himself, is apparent, and not all of it is wrong-headed. Rhodes could be admirably courageous. He did prefer negotiation to bloodshed—yet sometimes called for lots of blood. He did believe that the natives should be protected and developed—by lording over them. He also believed in justice and mercy for the natives, far more so than did the Germans, French, Portuguese, or Belgians—but only after the natives had submitted, and not equally for black and white. He certainly believed in the superiority of the English-speaking peoples—and to assure their position as guardians of world peace, he was willing to wage war. He also believed in "the widest freedom"—but only for whites, and not if that freedom interfered with what he considered best for everyone. By the light of historical hindsight, the passage self-destructs with contradictions, yet Burnham, a thoughtful man, was recording what he earnestly believed. To reduce it all to racist imperialism robs him and other progressive nineteenth-century whites of their flawed complexity and erases any hope of understanding our links to them, through their strengths as well as their prejudices.

—••—

At the port of Tanga, north of Zanzibar, Burnham watched blacks mana-
cled to each other by chains and neck irons unload a ship. He asked an
officer if the men were slaves. Oh no, the chains were simply a precaution to
keep the men from running off. "For an African or an Arab to do this
would be slavery," wrote Burnham to his uncle, "but for Germany or
England it is not. For my part I fail to see the fine distinction. No doubt my
mind is too much befogged by Yankee ideas yet." His Yankee ideas would
soon change, corrupted by the rationales of colonialism.

At the end of March 1893 the Burnhams debarked at Durban, a trim
British town whose pretty parks and shops reminded them of Pasadena.
Part of its charm, for Blanche, was that no natives except servants were
allowed to live within the town limits. Burnham noted with approval that
Durban remained affordable for newcomers because the town retained
ownership of the land, foiling speculators, one of his peeves about the
United States. Yet within a year he would be neck-deep in land speculation
on the frontier.

He set about outfitting the family for the trek inland: northwest for 400
miles by wagon road to Johannesburg, then 800 mostly trackless miles north
to Fort Salisbury in Mashonaland. The customary mode of long-distance
transportation in southern Africa was a heavy wagon pulled by eighteen
oxen. Because of the gold boom in Johannesburg, oxen and wagons were
exorbitantly expensive. Equally problematic, Burnham didn't know how to
handle the thirty-foot whip necessary to drive the huge ox-teams.

He applied Yankee ingenuity. He didn't understand oxen, but prospecting had taught him all about "desert canaries"—burros—which were
underappreciated in southern Africa and hence underpriced. They weren't
as strong as oxen, but they could cover more ground per day and needed less
forage. He bought four that had never been hitched to a wagon, for $15 each.

Next he searched Durban for an American buckboard. In a warehouse
loft he found the disassembled running gears of a "spider," a light Ameri-

can carriage made by Studebaker, a deal at $100. He hired a carpenter to make a slat wagon-bed and install a spring seat. He couldn't find breast-strap harnesses to fit the burros, so he bought leather hide, some tools and rivets, and made his own. Blanche bought supplies and packed them, along with her new Singer Jones sewing machine; she didn't intend to buy any dresses for five years. For their bed, she quilted a mattress filled with "coconut feathers" and sewed a cover for it from canvas. Meanwhile, Burnham had been breaking the burros to harness. Less than three weeks after arriving in Durban, they were ready to go.

Strangers snickered at their burros and light wagon. New acquaintances said they were crazy to head into the African veldt in that get-up. A woman urged Blanche not to go. "But she didn't know my wife," noted Burnham. To his uncle he wrote, "nothing can stop me till I reach the land of Ophir. . . . I will probably cast in my lot here. There is more room, a better chance, greater possibilities. . . . I am ready to tackle the frontiers again and help build a new empire . . ."

CHAPTER TEN

TO THE FRONTIER

THEY LEFT DURBAN on April 16, 1893. The country soon steepened. They had to walk and only made fifteen miles per day, but expected that to rise to twenty once the terrain flattened. At night they made fires from dried manure collected from the treeless landscape, and went to bed at dark. They began trekking each morning at seven, outspanned at eleven for three hours during the heat, then trekked again from two to seven. Six-year-old Roderick reveled in all of it—the burros, the anthills taller than he, the strange rocks and birds, the probability of lions and other marvelous wild creatures just beyond their campfire. Supper was sometimes cold, sometimes cooked—boiled potatoes, bacon and pan-fried bread, sometimes roasted ears of corn.

They spent the evenings planning and dreaming about the life ahead. They weren't clear about the British South Africa Company's rules for homesteading, but rumor said they could get 3,000 acres. After years in the arid Southwest, they pictured a green expanse with a stream that could be dammed for a pond. They didn't know much about the climate or landscape at Fort Salisbury, or whether it was in the fever belt. They weren't even sure of the settlement's exact location, but it was the capital of their imaginations.

The landscape en route to Johannesburg enamored them. "And only a handful of blacks to enjoy it all," wrote Burnham to his mother, adding that it was "a young paradise." Blanche wrote home, "In fact we are regaining our youth." The farther Burnham traveled into Africa, the more certain he became. "So there is no question of my *ever* returning from Africa farther than to Paris or Rome," he wrote.

They occasionally passed the isolated farms of Boers, with houses made of stone and iron. The stolid farmers looked amused or askance at the Burnhams' light wagon, and often warned them to turn back.

After about a month, they reached the boomtown of Johannesburg and camped outside it. Only seven years old, Johannesburg already had 40,000 inhabitants, plus thousands of black laborers on the gold reefs. The city swarmed with the usual collection of miners, gamblers, liquor merchants, speculators, prostitutes, and ruffians. The Burnhams marveled at its raucous energy and the inescapable thunder of giant stamp mills crushing ore.

"I have known nothing like this place in all the world," wrote Burnham. "Boer government, English capital, and black labour by hundreds of thousands under the management of American engineers, using their superior methods of mining, formed a combination that had never before been brought about." It was a volatile combination awaiting a spark. Burnham turned thirty-two there, "the happiest [birthday] of his life," wrote Blanche.

They reprovisioned and resumed the trek on May 26. They expected to cover the 800 miles to Fort Salisbury in two months. "How I hope that we shall like it," wrote Blanche, ". . . and if we are only successful you shall all come and we will end our days in the new Utopia in the heart of Africa."

In Pretoria they bought two more burros, a sawed-off shotgun, "and pounds of lead to keep the lions from eating up Roderick or the stock." They saw thousands of natives walking south to work in the gold mines of the Rand and the diamond mines of De Beers. A few days later they reached the bush veldt and could make fires with wood instead of dried manure. From here on Burnham's gun provided meat, at first mostly birds such as pigeons, partridges, and guinea fowl. He couldn't bear to shoot monkeys because they looked too human. All three Burnhams had enormous appetites from the rigors of walking. Blanche's letters described their recent menus: for breakfast, fried quail, fried pan bread, and coffee; for supper, birds filled with a mint-sage stuffing then roasted in the reflector oven, or pot pies ("Had one a few days ago made with a parrot, pigeon, and plover"). For dessert, pie, pudding, or cake. They missed California's fruits, especially grapes, peaches, and apricots.

Burnham assessed the country with his prospector's eye and saw signs of minerals everywhere, plus other opportunities of all kinds. He noticed that lumber was expensive, so he asked his uncle to send a catalogue of portable sawmills; owning one would bring a small fortune.

In mid-June they hooked up with twelve Boer wagons for mutual protection on "the lion road" that threaded the thorn and fever-tree country to the Limpopo (Crocodile) River. The men carried guns at the ready to shoot any lions or hyenas that attacked the livestock. Roderick was confined to the buckboard. At dusk they laagered the wagons in a protective circle and kept the fires burning all night.

Burnham studied the Boers, as he always did a new people. He admired them for daring to plunge into wild Africa and for proving that whites could thrive there. He noted their blind hatred of blacks, but approved their refusal to mix their blood with the natives', a mistake made by the Portuguese. Fiercely independent, the Boers resented any government interference and were "lovers of freedom and haters of British oppression and kings in general." Every Boer carved his own little cattle kingdom out of the wilderness—two or three thousand acres of high veldt for summer residence, six or seven thousand acres of bush veldt for winter. In between, he yoked a great team of oxen to a heavy house-wagon and took his family on a three-month hunting trek. In many ways the Boers' pioneer way of life reminded him of old days in the West, and strongly appealed to him. He sympathized with the Boers' suspicion of newcomers who threatened to spoil the frontier with towns, mines, railroads, rules.

On the other hand, Burnham saw that cheap black labor had made the Boers lazy. They were also illiterate, sluggish, and hidebound. "The English are slow enough especially the colonial English," he wrote to his uncle, "but they are lightning compared to the Boers." He foresaw that the Boers' ponderous refusal to budge would doom them. They would be washed away by the incoming tide of prospectors and go-getters. Like the Spanish and the Indians in America, the Boers had made a fatal mistake: they were "sleeping on the greatest gold field in the world and allowing to lay idle splendid veins of coal and other minerals." People sleeping in the path of progress, or doing anything else there, whether they were white, black, or red, were destined to get flattened. As Kipling wrote of the Boers in "The Voortrekker,"

He shall desire loneliness and his desire shall bring,
Hard on his heels, a thousand wheels, a People and a King.

To illustrate the Boer's "dread of innovation," Burnham mentioned a settler who told him to forget about crossing the Limpopo River for another two months. Puzzled, Burnham asked why. Because it can't be forded until then, said the Boer. Then I'll swim it, said Burnham. But what about your wagon? asked the Boer. I'll make a raft, said Burnham. But there's no timber within fifteen miles, said the Boer. So I'll go get it with a wagon, said Burnham, and then I'll turn my wagon's sideboard into a sweep and use my empty water casks as buoys for the running gears, "and cross I would."

By the end of June they were deep into the wilds and wouldn't pass another white man's home or a "winkle" (store) for 250 miles. Blanche complained that she constantly had to darn her dress because of thorn bushes. The natives no longer wore colorful miscellanies of cast-off white clothing; instead, wrote Burnham, "a string of beads and a patch of leather the size of an old stove lid (and that is not size enough) suffice for most of them."

The Limpopo River marked the boundary of Matabeleland and Mashonaland. The wagon train reached it in early July. Burnham shot into the water a few times, scattering the crocodiles so the burros could swim across. Everything and everyone else floated over to Lobengula's kingdom.

The wagon train paused for ten days to rest and provision itself with fresh meat. Burnham got his first close look at Boer marksmanship, which reflected much about them. Like the old buffalo hunters of the West, they excelled at deliberate long-range shooting. Some Boers, firing a rifle from a standing position without supports, could hit a hen's egg three times out of five at 100 yards, which Burnham considered a marvelous feat. They thought nothing of hitting standing prey at 200 yards, a skill that would devastate the British in the Boer War. Burnham, by contrast, had trained himself to be an expert at snap shooting, whether mounted or on foot, advantageous for hitting running prey in brushy country. In ten days of hunting he brought in a bigger bag than the party's two best Boer hunters combined, and could have done better with his old Winchester repeater; he was now using the heavier nine-pound Martini–Henry common in Africa.

They were less than 400 miles from Fort Salisbury, at the edge of what they hoped would be their promised land and final home, in the bosom of Rhodes's British South Africa Company. Burnham deeply admired Rhodes but had no illusions about his machinations. In a letter to his uncle, he astutely summarized the politics that Rhodes had exploited. The stakes were as vast as the area above the Limpopo River, now covered by Zimbabwe, Zambia, Malawi, and Mozambique—a territory bigger than California, Nevada, Utah, Arizona, New Mexico, and Colorado combined.

The southern portion belonged to Chief Lobengula of the Ndebeles. The Boers claimed part of it. So did Portugal, from its fragile perch on the Indian Ocean. Germany, entrenched directly west on the Atlantic coast, clearly had cross-continental ambitions. Britain didn't want any of them to have the area, but also didn't want the expense of possessing it. "In the struggle between financial economy and political greed," wrote Burnham, "the brilliant mind of Cecil Rhodes saw a great opportunity to satisfy British land hunger and still allow them to hold tight the purse strings of the imperial treasure."

To finesse all of the players, Rhodes envisioned a multi-part plan. First he finagled a royal concession for the British South Africa Company that covered part of the territory, "another of those liberal concessions which England often makes of other peoples' possessions to her own titled citizens," noted Burnham. This arrangement put the Boers and the Europeans on notice about Britain's imperial aims while leaving the financial risk and administrative responsibility to the BSAC. In return the BSAC got nearly free rein and the protection implied by the British flag.

Rhodes's second move was to make a deal with Chief Lobengula for mineral rights, which allowed peaceful entry into Mashonaland, the eastern part of Lobengula's kingdom. Burnham understood that Lobengula's days were numbered: "he inside of 2 years will have to do as thousands of other fierce chiefs have done, come under the Union Jack and the empire of the Matabele will be open for all white races." Meanwhile, by populating the concession with adventurous prospectors and settlers who had been drawn by generous offers of land and mineral rights, Rhodes not only avoided the expense of a large police force, he ensured that Britain would have to intercede to protect its citizens in the event of aggression by Lobengula, the Boers, or any other colonial power. "One can not but admire Rhodes," wrote Burnham, "yet [it] feels a little hostile to be under the government of what is practically a British syndicate."

——•——

The immediate hostilities, however, came from another quarter. On July 24, as the trekkers headed north, they met wagons coming from Fort Victoria, less than 100 miles ahead. They carried disturbing news. Lobengula's warriors had entered the settlement and, in front of the shocked settlers, had murdered 200 defenseless Shonas, including women and children, mutilating some by cutting off tongues and other body parts. A police force from Victoria had followed the Ndebeles and killed thirty of them. War seemed certain. Since Lobengula reportedly had 80,000 warriors (a gross exaggeration) to send against the concession's population of 3,000, some set-

tlers were clearing out. A number of wagons from the Burnhams' group
turned back.

The Burnhams never considered it. They had come too far. Burnham
wrote a will and sent it to his uncle. He relished the prospect of war. "We
are having exciting times," he wrote to his mother, "and I enjoy it." Blanche
made cartridge belts for herself and Roderick to carry. Because of her
familiarity with firearms, she wrote, "They count me as a man if any trouble comes, and it makes me quite proud."

The scraps of news brought by the retreating settlers were the upshot of
a knotty situation. Almost immediately after making the mineral deal with
the BSAC, Lobengula had developed seller's remorse. He tried to back out
in letters to Queen Victoria and other British officials, which were ignored,
yet he also accepted the BSAC's monthly stipend, rifles, and ammunition.
Lobengula, a regal man who stood six feet tall and weighed 300 pounds,
received visitors on his throne of elephant tusks and lion skins. By all
accounts he was intelligent and open to negotiation with whites. His tragedy was to understand his impossible quandary, caught between the white
colonials and the traditions of his own people.

The Ndebeles were an offshoot of the mighty Zulu tribe that had
fiercely resisted Boers and Brits in South Africa earlier in the century. After
those wars the Ndebeles had spread north, easily conquering the Shonas,
Karangas, and Makalagas, who became their subjects. Like the Apaches,
the Ndebeles had a warrior culture. Unlike the Apaches, they also had a
military structure. It was organized around *indunas* (commander-chiefs)
and their troops, who lived in stockaded regimental towns (kraals) around
Matabeleland. Lobengula's army totaled about 20,000 warriors. Males
trained rigorously for combat and liked to keep their spears wet with blood.
To satisfy that desire and to accrue wealth, the Ndebeles went raiding and
also collected tribute from subservient tribes. They did not have the disposition to accept trespassers or insubordinates of any color.

Lobengula understood that white trespassers were inevitable, and tried
to control both them and his warriors. In Lobengula's view, he had given

the BSAC only a license to dig mines, and only in Mashonaland. He believed he retained his ownership of the territory as well as his authority over the Shona people who lived there and tended his royal herds. If the Shonas disobeyed or refused to send tribute or stole his cattle, he regularly exercised his kingly right to punish them. His justice was not gentle. He unleashed his warriors, who wet their spears.

The white settlers didn't act like renters. They often referred to a boundary line between Matabeleland and Mashonaland, as if Lobengula didn't own it all. Nor did they limit themselves to digging mines. They built permanent towns and strung telegraph wires. They set up farms as if they owned the land. They hired Shonas as *their* workers.

Some Shonas began to believe that the whites would protect them from the Ndebeles' depredations. A few Shonas dared to stop sending tribute or to presume that they owned the royal cattle in their care. When Lobengula sent warriors to burn their kraals and kill them, or to bring them to his capital of Bulawayo for skinning alive, the whites acted as if the Ndebeles were the trespassers in their own kingdom. The warriors chafed at this arrogance.

In late June of 1893 Lobengula sent courteous messages to the leaders in Fort Salisbury and Fort Victoria informing them that he was sending an *impi* (regiment) to punish Shona cattle thieves near Fort Victoria. The warriors would not harm whites, said Lobengula, but he also reminded them that this matter was none of their business, and if the thieves sought refuge, they must be turned over.

News of the impi traveled before it. Frightened Shonas began crowding into Fort Victoria, hoping for protection. On July 9, before Lobengula's explanatory letter arrived, the Ndebele warriors entered the town, rattling their long shields and shaking their spears. The killing began. The warriors didn't touch the horrified whites. Eventually the impi withdrew.

In the following days, warriors burned nearby kraals and granaries, seizing cattle and killing Shonas. A Commission of Inquiry later determined that about 400 Shona men, women, and children had been massacred and often mutilated. Some of the cattle and property belonged to whites.

On July 17 the BSAC's administrator for Mashonaland reached Victoria from Salisbury. This was Dr. Leander Starr Jameson, Rhodes's most trusted associate. Doctor Jim, as he was called, found Victoria in uproar. Settlers from the region, including ninety women and children, had come to the fort for security. They were frightened and angry. Lobengula had kept the peace with whites, as promised, but his warriors were terrifying the region, and who knew when the spears would be turned on the settlers? Further, whenever the Ndebeles raided, the Shonas disappeared into the area's rocky kopjes (hills), leaving the settlers without laborers. They wanted retaliation and they wanted things resolved. Some threatened to leave.

Lobengula still preferred peace, because he knew it delayed the inevitable. Rhodes also preferred peace, because a war now would be financially inconvenient—the BSAC's coffers were empty. On the other hand, he needed to protect the settlers, and he had always intended to annex Matabeleland eventually. Though the timing wasn't perfect, this was an opportunity, and he rarely let those slip by. He instructed Jameson to use his judgment, but "if you do strike, strike hard." That suited Jameson's impetuous temperament.

On July 18 Jameson and fifty Ndebele commanders held an *indaba*, or conference, at the gates of the fort. Jameson gave them an ultimatum: start retreating toward the border of Matabeleland, thirty miles away, within one hour. Jameson waited two hours, then sent out Captain Lendy and fifty men, with instructions to drive the Ndebeles toward the border and, if they resisted or attacked, to shoot them. When Lendy caught up to the Ndebeles, they had barely moved and were burning Shona kraals. Lendy later reported to Jameson that the Ndebeles had fired first, but a subsequent investigation made clear that Lendy simply ordered his men to attack. They killed somewhere between ten and thirty warriors. The Ndebeles didn't fight back because their king had commanded them not to harm whites, and they knew how he dealt with disobedience.

Lobengula wrote outraged letters of protest to Jameson and British officials. In reply, Jameson asked for compensation for the settlers' property losses. Lobengula retorted that he must first recover his Shona slaves and cattle. He also expressed bafflement. What had he done wrong? His warriors had not harmed any whites. Why were the whites protecting slaves who belonged to him and stole from him? Lobengula didn't want war, but his wiles could no longer slow the momentum of events.

This was where matters stood on August 7 as the Burnhams, after four months of trekking, reached the gates of Fort Victoria.

———

Victoria was crowded. War hadn't been declared, but the place was wound tight with the expectation of it. A woman there later wrote about the Burnhams' arrival:

> We had been in Victoria only two days, when I was amazed at a peculiar equipage that came ambling into the town, drawn by mules. When the dust subsided, somebody told me that it was a real American buckboard, and that the driver was Frederick Burnham, the famous American Indian scout... It seemed incredible that Major Burnham, his wife and his little seven year old son could have made the trip across the veldt, through forests and over flooded rivers in so flimsy appearing a conveyance,—but there they were. They were a remarkable trio, the first American family I had known,—Major Burnham, with his strong, handsome tanned face, his alert gaze, and his quick, noiseless movements, reminded me of a leopard;—his wife was young, and very attractive, the most astonishingly practical person I had ever met. I could scarcely believe my eyes when in the midst of all the excitement and confusion, she insisted that Frederick unpack her sewing machine because she needed a new dress, and the boy simply had to have some shirts,—he had grown so fast that his arms were positively sticking out of his old ones. Thinking of the Kimberley women, and those I had known in Jo'burg, I suspected at first that she was posing, but her husband took her demands seriously enough to

delay his own urgent business, and in a few minutes she was serenely whirring away on lengths of gingham and denim, quite oblivious of the circle of black faces pressing close to witness the new "magic."

The fort offered no shade, no provisions, no feed for animals, so after two days the Burnhams headed east to find forage. They ended up camped at the ruins of Great Zimbabwe, a magnificent ancient citadel of labyrinthine stone walls and immense boulders that sprawls across 1,700 acres on a commanding hilltop. Europeans first heard of Great Zimbabwe when the German explorer Karl Mauch saw it in 1871. Mauch had been searching for the lost biblical city of Ophir, the supposed location of Solomon's mines, and he believed he had found it at Great Zimbabwe. He also believed it could not have been built by black Africans. In 1891 Rhodes financed a thorough investigation of the ruins by the archeologist James Theodore Bent (in a sense Bent was the first Rhodes Scholar, though Rhodes didn't establish the Oxford scholarships that carry his name until 1902). In *The Ruined Cities of Mashonaland* (1892), Bent speculated that the complex had been built by Phoenicians, a racial assumption typical of the era. (The complex was constructed from the eleventh century to the fourteenth century by ancestors of the Shona people who still populate Mashonaland.)

In his youth Burnham had been fascinated by the cliff dwellings in Arizona and New Mexico. At Great Zimbabwe he tried to imagine the people who had built such an astonishing structure entirely without mortar. Like his peers, he could not imagine them as black. Burnham knew that Great Zimbabwe had been a center for gold, and since a little stream ran through it, he tried his luck. In a few hours he panned out more than a hundred small, ancient gold beads and trinkets, all twenty-four-carat. He gave some to Blanche and sent a few to his mother. The beads affirmed his belief that this was a land of gold and treasure.

It would have to be, based on recent news from home. Soon after the Burnhams left for Africa, financial bubbles started popping all over the United States. The causes were bad high-risk loans to overextended railroad companies and other speculative ventures, a credit crunch, and a liquidity crisis caused by a run on gold. People rushed to withdraw money from banks, worsening the panic. Several railroads collapsed and hundreds of banks failed. Thousands of companies and farms went under. The unemployment rate spiked, as did hunger and homelessness. There were food riots. In New York City, the anarchist Emma Goldman was arrested for inciting a crowd by urging them to go to the "palaces of the rich" and demand work. If the rich wouldn't give work, she said, then demand bread, and if they wouldn't give bread, then take it. The Panic of 1893 was the worst financial disaster in U.S. history to date.

The Burnhams, living in a native hut outside Fort Victoria and expecting war at any moment, got word that their savings were gone. They still owned some property, but values were depressed and loans impossible. "Fearing things have gone wrong and my luck has changed," wrote Burnham to his uncle in September, "I shall take military service with the Chartered Co. and go into war."

CHAPTER ELEVEN

WAR IN MATABELELAND

THROUGHOUT AUGUST AND September of 1893, in preparation for war with Lobengula, Jameson had been recruiting volunteer fighters. The BSAC couldn't afford to pay salaries, but once Lobengula was erased, Matabeleland would be available for distribution, so the company lured volunteers with speculative incentives. During the war each man would receive a horse, a rifle, and rations when available. Survivors were promised 6,000 acres, fifteen mineral claims, five alluvial claims, and a share in half of the spoils, mostly Lobengula's cattle.

Jameson raised three columns of volunteers, in Salisbury, Victoria, and the Transvaal. He expected the British government to send a column as well, for a total of about 1,000 men. Burnham signed on as one of twenty scouts. This force would face 20,000 Ndebele warriors.

"It will be a hard and desperate service," wrote Burnham to his uncle, "but full of adventure and a chance to see unknown lands for which in spite of the long trek I still love to see more. In fact, I am infatuated with Africa. It is grand in size and life, is full of possibilities and not carried on in such a hammer and tongs way as in California."

He was sure he wouldn't die, and equally sure he could recoup his finances. He thought the war would last four months, and expected his reward of 6,000 acres to be worth a dollar an acre as soon as peace was declared. If necessary, he could make a good living with his rifle as a hunter. With his typical combination of hustle and democratic idealism, he added that he wanted to "help build a commonwealth where the cry of 'work or bread' should not be heard." He saw no contradiction between his proletarian politics and his intention to take Matabeleland from its natives.

As usual, he was astute about the politics behind the war. In England, the champions of native peoples such as the Aborigines' Protection Society were clamoring for the government to stop Rhodes and the BSAC. On the eve of war, in a sardonic letter to his mother, Burnham described what he called "the true situation" "for the benefit of your missionary friends," who evidently disapproved of events unfolding in the royal concession. To prevent other European nations from claiming this part of Africa, explained Burnham, Britain "gave it away to a company composed of her royal dukes, lords, &c. She gave an empire to which she had no shadow of claim and sanctioned the granting of a Royal Charter to perpetuate the power of the English nobility . . ." Lobengula had been compensated with lots of rifles and bullets "and other Christian tokens of sincere friendship." He went on:

> So the country is now owned by the Mashonas, claimed by King Lobengula in the hands of the Chartered Co, and supposed to be under the British government. Out of this muddle but one result can come—*war*—and as greed is at the bottom of all it would have been far more open and above board to have simply invaded the country at first and told King Lobengula, the Mashonas, and whites we take this because we want more empire and have the strength to uphold our claims. But that is not the way of England or English diplomacy. She has given her word to the whites to open up all central Africa that we may trade and settle in it. To the Mashonas she has said we will take you under the shadow of our wing and the Queen sheds tears as she says her evening prayers at the wrong the Matabeles have imposed upon you. . . . To the Matabeles she has said we only want to establish

friendly relations and be allowed to exchange courtesies and eventually mix the noble blood of your house with our own nobility and so
sail down the stream of time one lovely blended race of every shade
from brindle to sorrel and pinto. As to wanting your land, *impossible*,
did ever an Englishman rob a neighbor (unless very much weaker).

To the Christian nations she has said we claim only a little colony
at Cape Town and a few other small possessions, but of course we do
not expect you to interfere with our sphere of influence, which
includes all that unknown region north of the equator, also all the
known and unknown region south of the equator. All else we gener-
ously give as an Englishman always does . . . Under all this bombastic
talk of civilization remains the one fact that to the victor belongs the
spoils. Lobengula conquered by and holds his scepter by strength, and
by great strength will he be conquered and at this stage of the world's
evolution the Caucasian in spite of his gloss is a mighty fighting animal, and a little blood stirs him stronger than any race in the world.

He dismissed the fantasy of bringing peace to Matabeleland through
religious persuasion. In sixteen years, he pointed out, the missionaries had
made three converts, and were in despair at the savagery of the Ndebeles
and the Shonas. He also snorted at the hypocrisy of sugarcoating imperial
aggression with Christian rhetoric, as a minister in Victoria had recently
done by likening the volunteers to Crusaders spreading the Gospel. Far
more accurate, noted Burnham, was a cartoon drawn by a settler, showing
a cannon loaded with Bibles aimed at an Ndebele's head. "All these things
have been gone over with again and again in our Indian policy," wrote
Burnham, "and we are the same as the English in our greed and breaking
of treaties."

"To part of the world," he told his mother, "we will be Apostles of civilization; to some freebooters and land pirates; to the Matabeles murderers
and invaders; to the Mashonas what a lion is to a jackal, the giver of offal
and stray bones, hence welcomed not loved. To the historian in later years

we will but prove the continuity of evolution in the year 93–4. To the young and adventure hunting, and secretly that strain runs far into the life of many more men than one would at first believe, we will be considered lucky in falling upon stirring times."

Blanche had a different view, that of a young wife who didn't want to become a widow with a seven-year-old child on the African frontier. Her husband hadn't yet left, but she was already feeling lonely and anxious. "I tell him that if he gets through this alive," she wrote to her family, "he shall never go into another. Why *do* men love to fight."

In August and September, as Jameson and Rhodes schemed to persuade the British government into approving a war, Lobengula had been trying to avoid one. In mid-August he sent a delegation to Cape Town. They carried a letter for Queen Victoria, with instructions to visit England and plead their case. The British High Commissioner for the Cape Colony, Sir Henry Loch, delayed the delegation in Cape Town throughout September. Loch's main objection to grabbing Matabeleland was that Rhodes might control it instead of him and the British government. He tried to negotiate with the delegation to establish a border between Matabeleland and Mashonaland, and to end punitive raids against Shonas. The delegation rejected both suggestions as insulting to Lobengula's royal authority. On October 5 Loch sent them back to their capital, Bulawayo, and telegraphed Jameson that the BSAC could invade Matabeleland. The next day, Jameson ordered the Victoria and Salisbury columns to move toward Bulawayo. The other two columns would approach from the south.

In mid-October the Victoria and Salisbury columns rendezvoused at Iron Mine Hill, about 130 miles from Bulawayo. Around the same time, Lobengula learned he was at war. Major Patrick Forbes took command, though the administrator Jameson carried much influence. Combined, the columns included about 700 volunteer fighters, 150 natives who drove wagons or tended livestock, and about 900 Shonas. Some of the Shonas carried spears or muzzle-loaders, but they were camp followers, not fighters, who hoped to recapture stolen wives, children, and cattle.

In addition to rifles, the column had three small artillery pieces, a larger gun called a seven-pounder (because of the weight of its shells), and five Maxims, a new belt-fed machine gun that had never been tested in battle but could fire 600 rounds per minute, versus about six rounds per minute with a breech-loading Martini–Henry rifle. The Maxim's barrel was cooled by a water jacket; after several minutes of continuous firing, the water would boil.

The columns moved deeper into Matabeleland, "through as beautiful a land as ever an English army stole," wrote Burnham to his uncle. They were also looting grain and cattle from Ndebele kraals in their path. "We raid and burn and destroy everything as clean as Sherman's men did in Georgia," wrote Burnham. Lobengula had not yet organized his army.

The scouts ranged far in front. In the open country of the veldt, they were often visible to the gathering Ndebeles. The natives frequently laid traps for the scouts, which Burnham found crude and easy to detect compared to those of the Apaches. He also had the advantage of being mounted, which permitted quick escapes. He killed several Ndebeles in skirmishes and took souvenirs. Blanche, in a letter home in late October, mentions that Burnham tried to send her "two assegais, a shield and a pair of Matabele ears."

He kept his eye peeled not only for enemies but for opportunities. "This is a wonderful land in mineral," he wrote to Blanche, "hundreds of quartz veins and one ancient working I have already found. . . . I see a thousand chances to make money and I like the country fine."

On October 24, the army crossed the Shangani River. Each column formed its own laager in the usual way, arranging the ox-wagons in a square, with the livestock inside and the bigger guns positioned at the angles. The natives camped just outside the perimeter.

At four o'clock in the morning, a shot from the Shona camp startled the laagers. The Ndebeles had hoped to overrun the columns in the dark before an alarm could be given, but an alert Shona foiled that plan. Between 3,000 and 5,000 Ndebele warriors, including some of Lobengula's elite royal impis, attacked. In addition to the 1,000 Martini–Henrys supplied by the BSAC, the Ndebeles had a large collection of old muzzle-loaders. But their two main weapons were designed for close-quarter killing: the assegai, a fearsome stabbing spear about five feet long including a one-foot blade, and the knobkerrie, a short wooden club with a bulbous tip for crushing bones and skulls. They also carried oval shields made of thick bull-hide.

At daybreak they attacked again. Ndebles typically used the old Zulu formation of a crescent formed by two horns and a head. The horns consisted of fast-running young men who rushed along the enemy's flanks. The head consisted of stacked impis made up of older warriors who charged up the middle. The strategy was to surround, crush, and destroy the enemy.

Ndebeles were trained to be ferocious. They didn't attack with cries and whoops like American Indians, but chanted loudly to the beat of a war song while racketing their spears on their shields. Most warriors were over six feet tall and appeared even taller because of headdresses made of ostrich plumes. They wore the skins of lions and leopards. When thousands of these disciplined warriors stomped forward in tight formation, shaking the ground and making their eerie din before breaking into a running charge, it was nerve-racking and terrifying.

Because of the new Maxims, it was also calamitous. The machine guns shredded the compact blocks of warriors, mowing down each successive wave, causing the lines to waver and hesitate. The Ndebeles had never faced a weapon like the Maxim gun (nor had any other army). Many stopped to use their rifles, but they were poor marksmen, often overshooting because they believed that raising their gun sights improved accuracy. Still, if the Ndebeles had pressed on, they would have easily overpowered the whites and finished them with assegais and knobkerries. By eight o'clock the war's first battle was over. At least 600 Ndebele warriors lay dead. The column lost one white man and about sixty natives.

Jameson realized they might not be so lucky next time. The numbers were still overwhelmingly against the colonials. The countryside was swarming with thousands of Lobengula's warriors. If the columns got caught in rough wooded terrain, an ambush could engulf them, and their advantage of sweeping firepower would be lost. No road to Bulawayo existed here, so the columns were picking their way cross-country. They didn't know the territory ahead or even the precise location of Bulawayo. "Daylight scouting became extremely difficult," noted Burnham, "both on account of the roughness of the country and because of the harassing presence of the enemy. We were in country absolutely unknown to any of us; no man could even guess what the next hill or ridge might show."

Jameson entrusted Burnham and another scout named Robert Vavasseur with the mission of finding Bulawayo and an open route to it. Otherwise the columns were likely to be annihilated, and that would allow the Ndebeles to massacre the women and children left in Forts Victoria and Salisbury, protected only by a few old men and an antiquated Gatling gun from the American Civil War. If one of you gets wounded and can't ride, instructed Jameson, the other must abandon him and return to guide us to Lobengula's capital.

The two scouts left at daylight on October 28. They were immediately spotted by Ndebeles shadowing the wagon train. The two men spent the day edging west toward Bulawayo while playing cat-and-mouse with Ndebele patrols and people from the many kraals. At dark they took turns watching the horses and sleeping, then rode from midnight until daybreak. They were looking for a landmark near Bulawayo called Thabas Induna, "Mountain of the Chiefs," named for an event in recent Ndebele history. After a long absence from Bulawayo, Lobengula's father, Mzilikazi, had been presumed dead, so one of his chiefs assumed the throne. When Mzilikazi returned, he ordered this hasty usurper executed, along with his wives and his chiefs, on a nearby hill, known thereafter as Thabas Induna.

Burnham knew the story, and its dreadfulness led him to expect an imposing gloomy peak jutting from the grassland. But as he and Vavasseur rode along that morning with one eye on the spearmen flanking them, nothing on the horizon fit the description. They wondered if they had gone seriously off track. In one of their dashes away from an ambush, they surprised two old women carrying water jars on their heads. The frightened women calmed down when Vavasseur spoke to them in isiNdebele (the Ndebele language). He asked about the location of Thabas Induna. Right over there, said one, pointing toward a modest elongated hill that had been visible for an hour. And beyond that was Lobengula and his capital.

They rode toward it, constantly evading or spurring away from Ndebele pursuers. Cresting a rise, they saw Bulawayo. It was impressive. Behind a tall stockade, thousands of handsome woven huts were arranged in a deep circle around another stockaded circle—the compound of Lobengula and his many wives. Great storehouses held Lobengula's ivory, weapons, and other treasure. The smoke from a thousand fires hazed the air.

The scouts now knew the town's location and an open route to it. Inexperienced men would have rushed back to the wagon train, but they realized that without rest and forage, their horses would be too weak to carry them through the Ndebele lines. The men rode to a wide vlei (flat marshy lowland) where their horses could graze and they could see anyone approaching. Burnham slept first, for an hour. Vavasseur woke him with coffee and biltong (dried meat). Before napping himself, he said that the natives were running from kraal to kraal, forming a big circle around them. "He was enough of a fatalist to drop to sleep at once," wrote Burnham. He watched the Ndebeles gather in depressions and thickets until the circle was complete. When they began walking toward the scouts and shaking their shields, Burnham woke Vavasseur. It was time to go.

The Ndebeles expected them to head south, the easiest escape route, and had put most of their men and guns there. The line on the west was thin, since that direction took the scouts away from the colonial wagon train. Burnham and Vavasseur started south, then darted west, galloping through the line and into the darkness. They turned north, rested their horses by walking them, then shifted southeast. A sudden cold wind brought heavy mist that hid earth and sky, obliterating landmarks and direction. Vavasseur brought out a compass, but Burnham distrusted its reading. He never used a compass, relying on the Western Indian way of creating a mental map while traveling, "orientation by means of memory pictures." His mental map and

Vavasseur's compass pointed in opposite directions. They agreed to split up, and vanished in the mist. A few minutes later Burnham heard Vavasseur's soft "Coo-ee!" behind him. Vavasseur hardly knew Burnham, but after two days he trusted his American companion over his compass.

They hit the edge of a forest and heard voices—a large regiment of warriors, probably marching to attack the wagon train. The scouts rode parallel to them for an hour. Near midnight Burnham's horse abruptly stopped, snuffled, and dipped its head. Burnham, delighted by this message, dismounted and sniffed the ground. He found the odor of their own horses and saddles. This was the place where they had unsaddled and rested the first day. They were on the right track.

Within a few hours they found the wagon train. As they were reporting their findings to Forbes, scouts rushed in: a mass of warriors was quickly approaching. The columns hastily laagered on the red soil near the Bembezi River, about twenty miles east of Bulawayo. It was November 1.

After the rout at the Shangani River a week earlier, Lobengula sent his crack regiments, Imbizo and Ingubo (the latter his personal bodyguard), to stop the white army. These haughty warriors were disgusted that the other impis hadn't been able to eradicate a few white men. At Bembezi they told their fellow soldiers to watch how real warriors fought, and took their place in the "head" position among 6,000 others who attacked that day.

By all accounts, including Burnham's, the courage of these crack regiments was magnificent but suicidal. They charged into the mouths of the volunteers' rifles, artillery, and Maxims three times, the living climbing over the rising wall of the dead. "Nothing but death could stop many of them," wrote Burnham in a letter, "but under such a fire as we poured in a bird could not have lived long, and in a few moments the crack regiment was no more." Of Imbizo's 700 warriors, 500 died. Some survivors hung themselves in shame. A few years later Hilaire Belloc would summarize such carnage in a glib couplet:

Whatever happens, we have got
The Maxim Gun and they have not.

After Bembezi, Lobengula's days were numbered, though much bloody fighting was ahead, as well as an event that would make Burnham famous to most, infamous to a few.

———

On the morning of November 3, as the columns marched toward Thabas Induna, they were startled by a distant explosion followed by a black umbrella cloud in the direction of Bulawayo. Burnham was ordered to find out what had happened. He took two men, a colonial frontiersman named Harry Posselt and a twenty-two-year-old American friend from the Fort Victoria wagon train named Pete "Pearl" Ingram, who would figure in many of Burnham's later adventures.

They found the town deserted and in flames. Lobengula had ordered everything burned that he couldn't take, especially the storehouses of ivory, skins, and ammunition. The explosion had been his supply of gunpowder. The scouts found two white men sitting on the roof of a shed. James Fairbairn and William Usher had long been traders at Bulawayo under Lobengula's protection. When war broke out, some warriors wanted to kill them and take their goods, but Lobengula forbade it. He had promised his protection, and he sent a guard to uphold it. After hearing this, Burnham wrote in a letter, "Old Lobengula is, for a savage, not so bad as he might be."

On November 4 the wagon train entered the capital of the Ndebeles. But Jameson remained worried. The southern column of 400 men under Lieutenant-Colonel Hamilton James Goold-Adams, plus another 1,000 warriors under Lobengula's mortal enemy, Khama, king of the Bamangwato tribe, was supposed to meet the northern columns here. But Jameson had heard nothing from Goold-Adams since the campaign began. Had the southern column been wiped out? Lobengula still had thousands of warriors, now evidently heading northeast. Jameson could not hope to overtake the king and also protect the colonial towns unless Goold-Adams showed up.

It was imperative to find the column. It was equally important to inform Rhodes and the world—and the panicked stockholders on the Kaffir Exchange—about the fall of Bulawayo and the preservation, at least so far, of the BSAC. Goold-Adams and another Ndebele army were somewhere to the southwest. So was the nearest telegraph, at Tati, an outpost 130 miles away, over Mangwe Pass through the rugged Matopo Hills. On the same afternoon that the colonials occupied Bulawayo, Jameson sent off the man who had proven best at slipping through areas bristling with Ndebeles. Burnham chose Pearl Ingram to accompany him, plus a native who could ride and speak isiNdebele.

Fifty miles from Bulawayo, they reached Mangwe Pass. The scouts wound their way through the strange stacked outcrops of the Matopos, constantly evading Ndebele patrols. It was raining, which caused the hooves of their horses to soften and throw their worn shoes. The rocky terrain soon made the horses nearly lame, threatening the mission. In an abandoned hut, the scouts found several old Ndebele shields. Burnham, remembering an Indian improvisation, soaked the shields and then cut the softened bull-hide into moccasins that the scouts stretched over the horses' hooves.

They found the Goold-Adams column on the other side of the mountains and delivered Jameson's order to hurry. The scouts continued to Tati, covering the 130 miles from Bulawayo in thirty-eight hours. The telegraph transmitted the newsflash that Lobengula's capital was in the hands of the British South Africa Company. This report, Burnham noted wryly in a letter, would quadruple the value of the company's shares. He was also enthusiastic about his own prospects, ever more certain that opportunities abounded in Matabeleland.

He wrote to Blanche to arrange transportation for herself and Roderick from Fort Victoria to Bulawayo, where their African life would begin in a new frontier settlement. "All things will be explained when I hold you in my arms again," he promised, "for now I have tales to tell that would put Othello in the shade."

CHAPTER TWELVE

THE KING'S SPOOR

LOBENGULA HAD FLED his capital and his army was shredded, but he still had thousands of devoted warriors in scattered units. Matabeleland wouldn't belong to the white settlers until the king was captured or killed. He was reportedly traveling north toward the Zambezi River with a great herd of cattle and many regiments. Jameson sent a message to Lobengula: if he surrendered, he would be spared. Jameson added that he would wait until the messenger returned, plus two more days, but after that he would send pursuers. Lobengula replied that he was on his way to surrender, then immediately resumed flight.

Jameson wasn't fooled for long, but the colonials were short of ammunition and their horses were exhausted. Jameson and Forbes decided, perhaps because of economy, perhaps because of brash misjudgment, to cut the pursuit column to 158 men and two Maxims. Burnham and Ingram were among those chosen to go. They loaded provisions for ten days onto pack horses, took some slaughter oxen for meat, and left on November 25.

A number of men in the column acted as scouts, but by this point the most difficult assignments were given to the Americans, Burnham and Ingram, and to a Canadian named Robert Bain. Lobengula was traveling with seven heavy royal wagons whose tracks were easy to follow even among those made by his 50,000 head of cattle. But when the rains started, the cattle obliterated the wagon tracks and the trail sometimes went cold.

The spoor had been lost again when a native rumor reached the column that Lobengula's wagons had crossed a nearby river seven miles downstream. Major Alan Wilson, Forbes's second-in-command, sent Burnham to check the story. He took Jan Grootbaum with him. A Fengu native, Grootbaum appears in many histories of the era. Burnham often scouted with him and admired him. He compared Grootbaum to H. Rider Haggard's noble Zulu hero Umslopogaas, calling him "one of the pluckiest Negroes I have ever seen" and "the coolest and bravest black of all my African experience." Twice while tracking Lobengula, he and Grootbaum suddenly encountered bands of Ndebeles in the tall grass, and Grootbaum's quick thinking helped save their lives. Once, he immediately shouted in the Ndebeles' language that despite being with a white man, he was on their side, and they should run away because a troop of white men with guns was right behind them.

The native rumor about the river crossing proved true, and the column picked up the trail again. By December 2 they were near the Shangani River. Burnham, Ingram, and Bain reported to Forbes that many of Lobengula's impis were very close by. The volunteers were too tired to be alarmed. Their horses were exhausted; most could no longer gallop. The rains kept everyone wet and added to the misery of hauling the Maxims through sand, creeks, and heavy brush. The country ahead was dense with more acacia thorn and scrubby mopani trees. The ten days of provisions were almost gone. The column wanted a decisive confrontation or Lobengula's surrender.

Lobengula was ready to give up. His army had been decimated by the Maxims. Some of his regiments still wanted to fight, but others had started to desert with their families, weary of this sodden trek. He had been forced to abandon and burn several of his royal wagons. The rains had started and he was heading into fever country during fever season. Smallpox had broken out as well. More of his people would soon sicken or die.

On the morning of December 3, he and his entourage crossed the

Shangani. On the other side, he gave two messengers a bag containing 1,000 gold sovereigns. He told them to find the Forbes column and deliver the gold as a peace offering, with a simple message: I am conquered. The messengers took a route that they thought would intercept the front of the column. But the volunteers had been on the move that morning, too. They reached Lobengula's previous encampment on the banks of the Shangani while the fires were still warm. So when Lobengula's messengers emerged from the bush, the column had already gone by except for its tail end. The messengers' small miscalculation tilted events toward tragedy instead of diplomacy.

They delivered the gold and the offer of surrender to the only whites still in view, two men lagging at the rear, and then disappeared back into the bush. The recipients were William Daniel, thirty-one, and James Wilson, twenty-three, batmen who habitually dawdled behind the column. They opened the heavy bag. Simple greed did the rest. By the time anyone learned about the gold and Lobengula's offer of peace, the war was over, the king was dead, Forbes had been investigated for incompetence, and one of Rhodesia's foundational myths had taken deep root near the Shangani.

The warm campfires at the river confirmed that Lobengula wasn't far ahead. In his diary, Captain William Napier estimated that 1,500 people had stayed there the previous night. The king's trail led along the riverbank. The volunteers didn't yet know that Lobengula had crossed the Shangani two miles farther east. Forbes wanted to know the strength of Lobengula's force and to confirm reports by Burnham and other scouts that the Ndebeles seemed to be gathering again for another battle. Forbes ordered Burnham and Johan Colenbrander, a longtime colonial who often served as an interpreter, to nose ahead and capture an Ndebele for questioning, as Burnham had done several times during the march.

This was difficult in daylight, but the two scouts managed to seize a young Ndebele who was herding some of Lobengula's cattle. They brought him to Forbes, who sent Burnham back out to scout the flank. The prisoner turned out to be a relative of Lobengula's. He was "brave and crafty," wrote Burnham, "and he totally misled Major Forbes as to the positions of all impis and their ability to attack us." The interpreter Colenbrander, who had lived among the Ndebeles for years, warned Forbes that the youth was lying, but Forbes chose to believe that the Ndebele regiments had scattered and that Lobengula was protected by only 100 sick warriors.

By this point it was five o'clock. Forbes decided to rest the men and the horses. But Lobengula seemed tantalizingly close, so he sent Major Alan Wilson and nineteen men on a quick strike to try to capture or kill the king. If that proved impossible, ordered Forbes, Wilson should return before dark, in less than two hours. Wilson's patrol was leaving just as Burnham returned from his reconnoiter. Forbes ordered him to go with the patrol as a scout, along with Robert Bain. Burnham had been on horseback for most of the day, and his mount was worn out. Forbes said to take his horse, a strong young animal that had been resting all afternoon.

The patrol followed Lobengula's tracks along the river for two miles to a sandy drift, or ford, where two wagons had crossed. The Shangani was twenty feet wide there, but only six inches deep, with high steep banks. They crossed and stayed with the tracks, winding through the mopani and acacia thorn. After about five miles they came to the edge of an encampment of Ndebele warriors and their families. The camp seemed to go on forever, with thousands of people. Clearly, the captive boy had lied about the size of Lobengula's remaining army.

The sun was sinking. Instead of turning around, as both prudence and his orders dictated, Wilson consulted with his officers and made an impetuous but characteristic decision. He told two troopers whose horses were done in to return to Forbes with the message that the patrol had tracked Lobengula for six miles, across the river, and they hoped to capture him that night or the next morning. He asked Forbes to send reinforcements and a Maxim gun. These two riders made it back to camp about nine o'clock that night and delivered Wilson's message.

Then, on Wilson's order, the rest of the patrol spurred their horses and galloped right into the encampment. Captain Napier wrote in his diary, "The howling, shouting, and scurrying as we dashed through scherms [brush shelters] occupied by the King's guard and their family, boys milking, women and girls grinding their evening meal, must be left to one's imagination." Napier spoke isiNdebele, and as they galloped he kept shouting that they had not come to kill anyone but only to talk to the king. They rode through so many camps, past so many startled people, that Burnham later said they felt as if they were riding into the heart of the entire Ndebele nation. Behind them they could hear shouting and commotion as the warriors recovered from their shock at seeing this small group of white men passing among them.

Wilson hoped to find Lobengula's royal wagons, and suddenly there they were, two of them behind a rough brush enclosure. Napier shouted a greeting in isiNdebele, with many verbal curtsies and offers of peace. Silence. They pulled back the flap—empty.

From the dark all around they heard the cocking of rifles. Napier heard warriors asking their chiefs for permission to fire. He quickly told Wilson, who ordered the patrol to scatter and dash for some thick bush on the edge of the vlei. At that moment the skies opened and a tremendous thunderstorm began, the lightning illuminating their way. No shots had been fired.

The heavy rain turned the night inky, hiding them. But they couldn't stay where they were because the Ndebele would be able to hear the jangling of their horses' bits. They decided to work their way down the perimeter of the vlei, in the direction they had come. Progress was slow. They couldn't see, and the vlei was now marshy with small streams. They finally stopped in a thicket and dismounted.

Wilson discussed the situation with his officers. They agreed to sit tight while someone carried a message to Forbes. Wilson believed Lobengula would return to his wagons and could be taken the next day, if Forbes sent a large force and at least one Maxim before daylight. Forbes must do this without fail. Otherwise they would not only lose the king, the patrol would be trapped inside the Ndebele nation.

Because the message had to get through, Wilson sent three men, noted Napier, in case any two of them got "drowned, shot, or lost." The three were Napier, a trooper, and the scout Bain, who had the skills to backtrack the wagons in pitch darkness and avoid the roused Ndebeles. They left about eight o'clock. The heavy rain had obliterated the trail in spots, but Bain recovered it by feeling for the wagon ruts with his bare feet. As they crossed the Shangani, Napier saw that it was beginning to flood. They could hear a roar upstream. Their horses staggered into camp at 11:45. Bain fell off his mount, shivering with fever. Napier reported immediately to Forbes and delivered Wilson's urgent message.

CHAPTER THIRTEEN

THE SHANGANI PATROL

I N THE FIRST dash toward the king's wagons, the patrol lost contact with three troopers assigned to cover the rear. As soon as Napier and the others left, Wilson asked Burnham if he could backtrack to the wagons and look for the missing men. Burnham was game, but said success seemed doubtful because of the rain and extreme dark. He would need someone to lead his horse. Wilson volunteered; he wanted to see how Yankees worked.

Eyesight was useless. Burnham dropped to his knees and crawled until he found the curved imprint of a horseshoe. Then he backtracked, feeling with both hands for the previous print. Once he got the horse's stride and direction, the tracking went more quickly, and soon they were at the king's wagons again. It was quiet, the surrounding campfires dimmed by rain. There was no sign of the missing men. Wilson assumed they had gone into the vlei to await dawn. He had to risk calling them, and gave a loud "Coo-cc!" Burnham added a cowboy yell. They heard a distant reply from the vlei. The men called several more times, leading the stray troopers to them.

The weird yelling roused the Ndebeles, who began shouting as well. But they didn't investigate, Burnham learned after the war, because they were wary of a night attack. Burnham tracked back to the patrol, which now numbered sixteen. Wilson told everyone to get some rest, so they lay down in the mud and waited for the relief column from Forbes. Burnham had left the main camp quickly, without a coat, and was shivering in his wet shirt. Wilson threw his cape over both of them.

An hour later Wilson woke him and asked if he heard anything. Burnham put a billycan on the ground upside down as an amplifier and placed his ear to it, listening for vibrations made by tramping feet. Nothing. Wilson asked him to go out beyond the sounds of their horses and listen again. This time he heard faint sounds: brush being pushed aside, and many feet moving between the patrol's position and the Shangani. The Ndebele were cutting them off, he told Wilson, then went back to sleep.

Sometime before dawn Wilson woke him again and told him to venture toward the wagon track so he could intercept the relief force before it passed them. Burnham found the track and waited. Rain dripped from leaves. A dog occasionally barked in the encampment. Eventually he heard the faint plashing of hooves. He whistled and clapped sharply once, a signal used by him, Bain, and Ingram. A reply came. Silhouettes of mounted men emerged from the gray dawn.

Burnham was surprised to see Ingram in the lead instead of Bain. Burnham told Ingram to wait while he fetched Wilson and the patrol. When they returned, they saw in the growing light that Forbes had not sent the column, only another small patrol: twenty-one men (two others had gotten lost and returned to camp). And no Maxim. They were now thirty-seven men surrounded by thousands of Ndebele warriors. "All of us who had ridden through the great camps and spent the night in the bush," wrote Burnham, "knew then that the end had come."

——

Forbes had listened to Napier's message, which put him in a terrible dilemma. Wilson should have returned to camp before nightfall, as ordered. Yet Forbes trusted Wilson's judgment, and if Wilson believed he could capture the king, perhaps the risk was worth it. But along with Wilson's request to send troops and a Maxim, Napier had also delivered troubling new information. Forbes now knew the column was facing a big organized army of perhaps 3,000, not a few sickly warriors. The Shangani was running fast and was rising. Rain had turned the ground to muck. To attempt a night crossing of the river in such conditions, into the midst of a large force, would endanger the entire column. Splitting it was equally dangerous, since each half would be too small to withstand a serious assault. Captain Johannes Raaf vociferously advised against it.

Napier reminded Forbes that Wilson was risking everything by waiting for a Maxim and reinforcements. If those were not coming, Wilson needed to know so he could withdraw before daylight exposed the patrol to thousands of natives. Abandoning Wilson was unthinkable, yet Forbes was also reluctant to recall him, in case he really could capture the king and end the war.

Forbes decided to send another patrol to reinforce Wilson until the entire column could cross the river at daylight. He ordered Captain Henry Borrow and twenty-two men to saddle up. Napier expected to go, too, but was shivering with fever, so Forbes ordered him to rest. Bain was unconscious with fever. To replace him, Forbes sent Ingram, the only other man who could backtrack the trail in the dark. Each man took 100 rounds for his rifle, plus a revolver with twenty rounds. The patrol rode toward the Shangani at one o'clock. Near dawn, they found Burnham.

Wilson, Borrow, and the other officers were conferring. Burnham heard Captain William Judd say what they all knew: "This is the end." The question was how to reach it. They could die trying to cut their way out, or, as Wilson suggested, they could make another try for the king at his wagons, and either kill him or at least kill as many of his elite Imbizo regiment as possible. That was the ending they chose.

Watched by natives carrying spears and guns, the patrol rode across the vlei to the king's wagons, set back against the trees. "With the bravado of the doomed," wrote Burnham, "Wilson shouted to the king to surrender."

The wagons were still empty. Lobengula, believing that his offer of peace had been rejected, had left long before the Wilson patrol ever crossed the Shangani.

A troop of warriors stepped from behind the trees and opened fire. Two horses went down. Wilson shouted to cut the saddlebags to save the ammunition. The downed riders jumped on behind other horsemen, and the patrol retreated down the vlei to an immense anthill, twenty feet high and wide enough to protect their horses. But the Ndebeles soon outflanked them and poured in gunfire, disabling more horses and wounding a couple of men. Wilson ordered another retreat, into the trees where they had spent the night. When they reached the trees, the gunfire stopped. The Ndebeles knew they could take their time.

Wilson told the wounded and the unmounted to get into the center of the horsemen. In this formation the patrol slowly moved toward the Shangani to meet the main column and the Maxim, which they were certain were imminent. The Ndebeles let them proceed almost unmolested for about a mile. The reason became clear—a mass of warriors was waiting for them, blocking the path to the river.

The patrol paused. Wilson asked Burnham if he could get through to Forbes and tell him to hurry. Burnham said he didn't think it was possible, but he would try. Wilson assigned a trooper named William Gooding, whose horse wasn't as poor as the others, to accompany him. Burnham asked if Ingram could come as well. "We had done many things together," wrote Burnham, "and it seemed fitting that in this last fight we should also be together." Wilson immediately agreed, wrote Gooding afterward, figuring that three men improved the slim chance of breaching the wall of Ndebeles.

Burnham, Ingram, and Gooding rode toward the Shangani. Within 500 yards they ran into an impi approaching from the river. The warriors in front began firing. On the left was thick brush difficult for a horse to penetrate. On the right was open ground, the natural option for escaping on horseback. Some instinct told Burnham to avoid the right. He spurred his horse sharply left into the brush. Ingram's horse balked, but changed its mind after Ingram gave its jaw a vicious kick. Fifty yards away, the Ndebeles fired a volley, but overshot as usual. Shredded leaves rained around them. A hundred warriors raced after them into the thicket.

——

Forbes's column moved out that morning at 5:30, following the king's spoor along the Shangani. At 6:30, heavy gunfire erupted across the river. Napier knew it was Wilson. The gunfire stayed heavy until eight, then slackened.

At 9:30 a large force of Ndebeles attacked the column, forcing it into laager along the river. Napier heard sporadic shots from Wilson's direction until eleven, then nothing.

——

The counterintuitive turn into the thicket momentarily saved the three men. The approaching impi was the right horn of the formation advancing on the Wilson patrol. If Burnham had turned right, into the open vlei, the riders would have hit the central mass of warriors and been trapped by the flanking horns—as Wilson's patrol soon would be.

After putting some distance between them and their pursuers, Burnham and the riders slowed to rest their horses. Behind them they heard a shout. The warriors had picked up their trail. The riders reached a narrow vlei. Burnham decided to try a trick that wouldn't baffle Apaches but might work against the young warriors who ran the horn. The riders crossed the vlei, then made wide separate circles before coming back together to backtrack single file across the vlei. There, they separated and rode into the bush to hide in thickets where they could rest their blowing horses and watch the open ground.

The warriors raced by, down the vlei to where the jumble of tracks sent them milling in different directions. A crash of gunfire came from the direction of Wilson's patrol. The riders knew the main attack had started.

Eventually the warriors figured out the trail and began running back toward the hidden riders. Burnham's group remounted and retreated toward the sound of gunfire, then made a small loop and paused again. Their pursuers seemed to buy the ruse, assuming that their prey was returning to the patrol. The riders crossed the narrow vlei for the third time. Now they could hear the Maxims firing across the river and knew Forbes was under attack. That explained why the column hadn't relieved Wilson this morning. They wondered if the column was being wiped out as well.

They rode on to the Shangani and got a shock—it was now 200 yards wide and flowing fast. Their horses might be too exhausted to swim it, but staying on the bank meant certain death. They plunged in, holding their rifles and bandoliers above their heads. The current took them, but the horses managed to struggle to the other side. Atop the bank, they saw hundreds of Ndebeles watching them from the bush. They rode toward the sound of the Maxims, and when the Ndebeles began shooting, they asked their horses for one last gallop to enter the laager.

Burnham reported to Forbes. He told his commander that he feared the three of them were the only survivors of Wilson's patrol.

—–—

The battle continued throughout the afternoon. Sixteen horses were killed. By three o'clock, the troopers began seeing Ndebeles across the river wearing familiar uniforms—taken from Wilson's men. That evening Forbes sent up rockets to give any survivors the column's location. They could hear the Ndebeles singing and chanting in celebration.

Forbes needed to get word to Bulawayo that Lobengula remained free and that the column desperately needed food, ammunition, and reinforcements. It would be a hard ride of 100 miles. Three men were capable of slipping through the Ndebele forces. Bain was still down with fever. Burnham, after spending two days in the rain with no coat and no food, was shivering badly and had just vomited. Besides, Forbes wanted him as scout for the column. So Ingram would go. Because the ground was soggy and the horses exhausted, it was best to leave in the dark. Ingram took another man named Billy Lynch. They left during a thunderstorm on two gaunt horses that were also the column's best.

The next morning at nine o'clock, the column began a long retreat. They were moving east along the Shangani toward the place where it bends south. Their main food supply, slaughter oxen, was gone, as were most of their provisions. Their horses were worn out, forcing most men to walk. They had been soaked for days, and some men had malaria. The loss of the Wilson patrol—thirty-four men—was a terrible blow to morale. "The men are done up," wrote Napier in his diary. From across the river, the Ndebeles harassed them with gunfire throughout the day.

Perhaps these stresses led Forbes to make what Burnham called "a peculiar request." He wanted the scout to cross back over the river right then and look for signs of Wilson's squad. Burnham later wrote to his uncle:

In broad daylight to cross a swollen river in the face of a numerous enemy and on a weak horse in soft mud walk five miles up a narrow vlei thickly set on both sides with bush was absolute suicide. It was not likely that several thousand men who fought so determinedly on the 4th would allow a solitary horseman to ride among them in daylight on the fifth. In all the orders I have ever received in any campaigns against an enemy this was the most peculiar. But fully believing that a scout must go to his death at once if ordered—as the sacrifice of one may save many—and not knowing the reasons Forbes chose this time and place, I prepared to go. But told Maj. Forbes that I wanted it as an order and not a voluntary service. He was very angry. I did not volunteer. I said to him Make it an order Major, I never yet disobeyed one. He would not and the matter dropped.

As the retreat proceeded, the Ndebeles harassed them and attacked in force seven or eight times. The terrain often put the column into indefensible positions, perfect for annihilating the column with a large mass. But the Ndebeles, though a constant threat, no longer seemed organized. Their poor marksmanship also helped preserve the column; they wounded many but killed only one.

The column's other unrelenting foes were hunger and fatigue. The men marched for nine more days, much of it in heavy rain through rugged country—ravines, tall grass, dense thorn, rocky ridges and kopjes. The thorns tore their clothing into rags. The rain rotted the boots from their feet, which the rocks lacerated. They began wrapping canvas ammunition wallets and bits of tattered clothing around their feet. They slept on the wet ground, without blankets. The Maxims saved them many times when the Ndebeles attacked, so the heavy guns couldn't be abandoned; the men sometimes had to cut roads through the bush for the carriages.

Horses became too lame to walk and were shot. One night the column realized that their campground was a death trap. Warriors surrounded them on three sides. The fourth side was the wall of a ravine, so steep the Ndebeles left it unguarded. Yet it was the only path of escape. Burnham scouted a route up it and returned. The ravine had to be climbed in silence, so as a precaution the men killed all their dogs. They also uncoupled the Maxims from their carriages. Long after midnight Burnham led the scramble up the steep route. The men carried the Maxims and the wounded on their shoulders. That's where the guns rode for the rest of the march, as well as the heavy boxes of ammunition.

They were starving. Twice they stole some cattle and feasted, but during the last half of the march they had nothing but boiled grass and what was left of their emaciated horses. "Hide, sinew, and bones," wrote Burnham. The meat was so stringy and full of air bubbles that the men often threw it up. Burnham and Bain gladly accepted the portion no one else wanted, the head, having learned from the Indians that "the last bit of nourishment in a starving animal is in the brain."

Every night, Burnham scouted the route ahead. He kept himself awake by constantly splashing water in his face and pinching his eyelids. After Bain recovered from fever, he joined Burnham out front.

Dissatisfaction with Forbes's leadership grew so strong that Captain

Johannes Raaf, a Boer, virtually took command. The column's only hope was that Ingram and Lynch had somehow gotten through, and that a relief force was en route. On December 12 someone thought he saw a signal rocket, so the column sent up a reply. No response. Instead they fought another hour-and-a-half battle with the Ndebeles.

Then on December 14 they met two horsemen riding toward them. One was Frederick Courteney Selous, famous in Africa as an explorer and hunter, and greatly admired by Burnham. Selous said that Ingram and Lynch had made it to Bulawayo in four days. A relief force with food and medicine was just ahead, along with Rhodes and Jameson. Rather than wait, the ragged column marched the last few miles to Inyati, where they were met with cheers and a feast. They had been in action for twenty-three days on ten days' rations. That night they slept dry, gorged, and serene. Within a few days they had covered the forty miles to Bulawayo. After a medical inspection, Dr. Jameson pronounced Burnham the only man in the column still fit enough to walk forty more miles.

King Lobengula was in flight and his regiments were dispersing. Some pioneers had suffered or died, but the conquest of Matabeleland by a handful of settlers had been relatively quick and easy. On Christmas Day in Bulawayo, Rhodes announced that every soldier and officer who participated in the war would be awarded 6,000 acres, mineral rights to twenty acres, and an equal share in profits from the king's 250,000 cattle. "The key to a country as large as all Western Europe," wrote Burnham, "was now in our hands."

———

Blanche hadn't heard anything from her husband since he had left to chase Lobengula, expecting to be home in two weeks. In mid-December, she did hear of him from several men on leave in Victoria. They told her, "Dr. Jameson says that if there were ten Burnhams, Lobengula would have been captured weeks ago." Pleasing, but no salve for her worry and loneliness.

To celebrate New Year's Day 1894, many of Victoria's inhabitants rode in ox-wagons to picnic in a grove of towering fig trees. After lunch, during the running matches, they saw two horsemen approaching. "It's Burnham," said someone who recognized the scout's distinctive hat, a stiff-brimmed Stetson. Seven-year-old Roderick started running, shouting, "Papa! Papa!" Blanche followed, as she later wrote, "a *little* more sedately. . . . He has made a fine record and is more talked of I do believe than any man in the column, at least by the Victoria people. They never saw such scouting, such daring and such wonderful escapes."

But Burnham also confirmed to the picnickers that the rumors about Wilson and his thirty-three men were true. Many, including Burnham, blamed Forbes. The commander's decisions and everything about the campaign would soon be examined by a Court of Inquiry. In hindsight it was clear that sending a small patrol to help Wilson had merely increased the number of the slaughtered. But Captain Napier, Wilson's strongest advocate to Forbes on the night of that decision, defended Forbes in his diary. Wilson knew the risks he was taking, noted Napier, and Forbes was "quite right" not to risk the entire column to reinforce him. "Whatever may befall this action," he wrote, "no blame can ever attach itself to a single individual." The Court of Inquiry agreed. Forbes was exonerated, but his reputation never recovered. Burnham and Ingram won medals from the BSAC for their roles in the campaign, and were awarded extra mineral and land concessions for their exemplary services.

The two batmen were tried for stealing Lobengula's gold and for failing to tell Forbes about the peace offering. Testimony revealed that the men were heavy gamblers who had suddenly begun flashing lots of gold sovereigns, a rare form of currency in Matabeleland. Three Ndebeles testified, including the two who carried the gold. The batmen were found guilty and sentenced to fourteen years' hard labor.

In late January 1894 word arrived that Lobengula had died in the fever districts near the Zambezi River, perhaps of smallpox. The Ndebeles began drifting back into Matabeleland. Their indunas agreed to peace, surrendering their assegais and some of their guns. Rhodes and Jameson began planning large reservations for them in the north.

In late February 1894 some Ndebeles led a white trader to the place where the men of the Shangani Patrol spent their last hours. The trader saw a rough circle of remains where the men had crouched behind their dead horses. The Ndebeles told stories about the bravery of the white troopers, how they fought on despite many wounds, how they had killed ten times their number. In the weeks after the war, as more Ndebeles talked, such stories multiplied. To honor the patrol's courage, the Ndebeles had left the corpses unmutilated. More than one native said that near the end, just before running out of ammunition, the survivors stood up and sang. Folklore quickly turned the song into "God Save the Queen." The white trader buried the remains. Rhodes later had the bones exhumed and reburied at Great Zimbabwe. Later still he ordered them exhumed again and buried near his own gravesite, World's View, on a hill in the Matopos.

The last stand of the Shangani Patrol and the miraculous escape by three men made irresistible newspaper copy. The story was covered throughout the English-speaking world. *The Times* of London alone featured ten stories about the incident in the first three months of 1894.

The incident also brought Burnham his first fame as "the American scout," a tag he would carry for the rest of his life. Newspapers sought him out for stories about the Shangani Patrol. In early January 1894, he sent his own account to his uncle and asked him to forward a copy to the *San Francisco Examiner*, the brash newspaper owned by young William Randolph Hearst, who often published foreign correspondents. Burnham thought Hearst might pay $200 or so for a firsthand report about the Shangani Patrol, and might even want something once a month about Mashonaland. Burnham instructed his uncle to give the money to his mother in Pasadena, if anything came of it (nothing did). Burnham also sent an account to H. Rider Haggard, the writer of romantic adventures, not for publication but in case Haggard found anything useful in it for his upcoming story about the Shangani Patrol.

Like icons of the American West such as Davy Crockett at the Alamo and George Custer at Little Bighorn, Wilson and his thirty-three men almost instantly entered the realm of legend. They became heroes and martyrs for both imperial Britain and the nascent state of Rhodesia. The incident inspired at least two popular long-running dramas in London. For the settlers in Rhodesia, as the newly conquered territory was soon named, the story of brave whites surrounded by overwhelming numbers of threatening blacks became a keystone myth. It would resonate long beyond the racial turbulence of the next century and the name-change to Zimbabwe.

Burnham always spoke about Wilson and the members of the patrol with the greatest respect, and was proud of his association with it. But the attention he got because of it sowed the first seeds of resentment toward him among a small faction of British settlers, and later led to denunciations of him by a few Rhodesian historians as a lying coward. (See appendix.)

CHAPTER FOURTEEN

SPEARS INTO PEGS

O<small>N JANUARY 1,</small> 1894, the day he rode up to his picnicking family in Victoria, Burnham wrote home about the pleasures of returning to children's laughter and luxuries such as cake and butter. Whatever the coming year had in store, he added, "it cannot by any possibility prove as eventful a year as the one just past."

At the end of 1893, speculators and land-grabbers had flocked into Matabeleland, eager to snatch up the best gold reefs and farmland as soon as hostilities ended. They howled when Jameson declared that the volunteers who had fought in the war would have four months to roam Matabeleland and peg properties before any outsiders could file a claim.

Burnham and Ingram jumped to it. The promising reefs and ancient diggings they had noted while riding all over Matabeleland could now be claimed. To reach them all within four months, they needed horses, but because of the war, mounts were scarce and mostly worn out. Many others had died from African horse sickness, a disease that wasn't understood. But everyone did know that "salted" horses—horses that had been infected and had recovered—were unlikely to get sick again, so these precious animals cost double or triple the usual price. Burnham and Ingram paid $500 apiece for salted horses, and got busy. "For Ingram and me," wrote Burnham, "the year 1894 was one of fast, hard riding, and, when our mounts gave out, of swift marches." They pegged reefs and farms for themselves, and also hired themselves out, pegging more than a hundred farms for others.

They fixed their own biggest hopes on a place the Ndebeles called iKwelo ("the steep place"). They sunk the first pegs in what became the town of Gwelo (now Gweru). On a map, a straight line put it 100 miles northeast of Bulawayo, but because of the terrain it was 150 by wagon. They filed twenty-seven claims there and named it Scout's Reef.

Burnham returned to Victoria for Blanche and Roderick. On January 9 they left for Gwelo. The whole family began learning the Ndebele language, Roderick progressing quickly. En route they stopped at a Boer farm, where the bachelor owner joined them for dinner. "He had not sat at the table with a woman for six years," wrote Blanche. Many of the man's black workers stared, especially at Blanche's odd hair, having never seen a white woman.

They reached Scout's Reef on January 21. Ingram was there with Bob Bain and another white man, plus some black workers who were digging the mine. The Burnhams slept in one of the big wagons, the other men in tents. There was a thatched cook hut. A rough fence of thorn brush ringed it all to discourage predators. A similar fence protected their stock, twenty-six oxen (sixteen belonging to the BSAC), five horses, and three donkeys. They intended to add cows for milk and beef, as well as sheep, goats, and chickens. Their feed corn came from nearby kraals deserted by Ndebele regiments. The native workers had a hut down toward the mine.

Burnham left almost immediately to search for more work and other prospects, a pattern that wouldn't change for decades. He came and went during the next months as Blanche and Roderick settled into camp life. She learned to deal with the voracious white ants. A saddle left in a tent got eaten. To get at items inside, the ants gnawed through wood or mud-brick. She never put anything on the ground except iron. Everything had to stay in the wagons, and to keep the ants from collapsing them, the wheels had to be raised off the ground with stones. If the colonizing gluttony of the white ants became uncontrollable, you followed them to their hole, dug out their fat white queen, and squashed her. (Blanche missed the imperial metaphor.) Everything stayed damp from the constant summer rain.

In letters home Blanche alternated enthusiasm for their frontier life with plaints of loneliness because Burnham was usually gone and her family was so far away. She read and reread their letters, three months old by the time they arrived, and chided them if the stream of communication faltered. It rarely did. The Burnham–Blicks were prolific letter-writers.

Blanche also missed the company of women. She wouldn't see another female until they went to Bulawayo after more than three months at Scout's Reef. She did have plenty of male company, not only Ingram and Bain but nearby men drawn to their camp by the presence of a woman, especially one with Blanche's pleasing looks and warm nature. She had a gift for putting people at ease. A friend once wrote to Burnham about "Blanche's quiet voice and strong, restful personality. I never met another person who gave me such a distinct feeling of rest in their presence." She served these frontier bachelors from her London tea set and offered them biscuits, apologizing that she didn't have a proper biscuit jar. She must have made them think about home and wives-to-be.

On February 25 she wrote to Burnham's mother that she was thirty-two that day, and in five more days would have her tenth wedding anniversary. "In honor of my birthday," she wrote, "I put on my pretty pink dress trimmed with cream lace . . . and wore my hair waved as I did when first married. Fred liked it so much and does not want me to cut it again."

Blanche was a sturdy pioneer woman who could trek for months, bake in a reflector oven, and handle a rifle, yet also prattle about pretty dresses. She brought gowns from London and Paris to Africa as well as a sewing machine to make her own clothes. She often devoted long paragraphs to the state of her wardrobe and the details of home decor. She asked Burnham's mother to ship a tan ostrich feather left in California because she wanted it for hat trimming: "It will get crushed but I can curl it again. Please do not delay as I will need it."

She also wrote about her carved wooden jars, trays, and bowls, taken by Burnham from Lobengula's hut, and the gold beads from Great Zimbabwe. She asked her parents to send several specific schoolbooks for Roderick as soon as possible, since the books wouldn't arrive for four or five months. She also told them that she was pregnant with a baby due in late May or early June, conceived just before Burnham went to war with the Victoria column. Decent paper was still scarce, and she apologized that her letters were so hard to read, with writing on both sides of onionskin paper. Burnham called it "[water] closet paper" and advised recipients to put white cardboard underneath to improve the letters' readability.

In all her letters Blanche was a booster of Matabeleland, because she hoped to lure her family to Africa. So she didn't usually mention the hyenas and African wild dogs that came into camp, or the lions that killed oxen not far away, or the big crocodiles and surly hippos in the river, whose hides and skins began decorating their wagon.

She did mention that bands of Ndebeles were drifting back into the region. She wished Gwelo had a fort or at least a patrol, but neither existed for 100 miles in any direction. Lobengula seemed to be defeated, but that wasn't yet certain. Meanwhile, the men kept their guns oiled. "Well it is a strange exciting and somewhat dangerous life compared with life there," she continued, "but there is nothing like adapting yourself to circumstances."

Yet whenever possible, Blanche and the other settlers, like all conquerors, expected circumstances to adapt to them. "I wish there were no blacks in Africa," wrote Blanche. "It would be a beautiful country. No I have not overcome my fear of them entirely and there are so many in our camp now." When the white men were away or working on the reef, she kept a revolver handy. "I do not get at all nervous or afraid," she added, "but you know I always feel better and easier in my mind when I have a six shooter."

The blacks in camp included servants, mine workers, and mail runners. Gwelo was roughly halfway between Salisbury and Bulawayo. Burnham, always alert for ways to pick up a few dollars, struck a small deal with Jameson to make Scout's Reef a rest stop for the BSAC's runners between the towns. Burnham collected a fee for feeding and lodging three or four runners who stayed there every night.

Blanche saw the financial benefit but was ambivalent about its everyday price. She grumbled that the runners were Ndebeles accustomed to having slaves wait on them. They didn't even want to grind their own corn. Laziness, she complained, referring to men who ran 250 miles in each direction. The Burnhams also had nine natives working at the mine. When they got fever, Blanche dosed them with quinine and castor oil. One morning all but two had disappeared, just a few days after Burnham had taken pity on their shivering and given them blankets, two weeks earlier than agreed.

"Fred and I are too good to them," wrote Blanche, "and I expect we will be humbugged many a time." They wished they weren't temperamentally unable to follow the advice of their colonial neighbors. "All the old Afrikanders and old timers," wrote Blanche, "say the rougher you treat the blacks the better they are and the more respect they have for you. The old Boers are the best masters. Civilize and educate them and they are spoiled, think they are as good as white men and become saucy, cunning and thieving." She did like her servant Longboy, a Zulu around forty years old, who stayed with them, he told her, because they didn't yell at him and paid promptly. No one wanted workers who had been ruined by missionaries.

The Burnhams employed natives on the same terms as their neighbors. "Help is cheap in this country," wrote Blanche. Her personal boy, aged ten, was contracted by his father to stay with the Burnhams for a year in return for a cow and a calf. Two other workers fetched wood and water, cooked and did dishes, and washed the laundry. They were paid about ten shillings per month, plus room and board of bush meat, beef, and salt. The mine workers made ten shillings per month, and their board included cornmeal, rice, "Kaffir beans," meat, and coffee. The ox driver got £3 a month. The head man, Longboy, drew £10 per month.

The mines and farms of Matabeleland could not develop quickly without native labor. So the BSAC, like the Cape Colony and Natal, instituted a hut tax. It was paid to the BSAC, not to the British government, and could

be satisfied in currency or in contracted labor. Since few natives had currency, they essentially had to indenture themselves to whites for several
months a year.

Burnham had forsaken the United States partly because banks and
robber barons were bleeding the country and creating a gulf between economic classes. He arrived in Africa strongly opposed to cheap black labor,
complaining that it made white colonists lazy. He deplored the way Boers
treated blacks. (The Boers made the British and Americans feel relatively
virtuous about racial matters.) But after less than a month at Scout's Reef, as
his mine workers kept disappearing, Burnham began adapting to circumstances. A letter to his uncle illustrates the twisting rationalizations required
of colonists in southern Africa:

> And the one great stumbling block to this country is the presence of
> the nigger whose labor is to be had for a pinch of salt per day. True he
> only does a pinch of salt's work, but it enfeebles the white race just the
> same and servants are a curse to a strong race. Nevertheless I am
> already surrounding myself with them ... It is remarkable how
> quickly one's ideas of the black change after being among them.
> When they get saucy and clear out or do some act of a worthless race
> you mentally reason it out about thus. He did not object to being my
> servant, and practically slave, for any love of country pride or indepen-
> dence. Far from it. It was simply to run off from your work, to lounge
> around his own dirty kraal and force the women to slave for him
> without pay save sundry thrashings. So you say the lazy worthless
> wretch, he is fat and stout. I pay him what to him is a priceless luxury.
> He shall not desert me to beat even black women. I will gradually
> civilize the brute and incidentally he shall have my corn and get my
> wage. So you find yourself voting for the law that compels each black
> to work 3 months per year at a certain wage or pay a tax to the state,
> and your final views are diametrically opposite from those entertained
> when landing on these sunny shores.

Not everyone applauded the addition of Matabeleland to the British Empire. It was opposed by "Exeter Hall," the collective name given to various British religious and philanthropic groups such as the Aborigines' Protection Society and the Anti-Slavery Society. The most virulent critic was Henry Labouchere, editor and publisher of the anti-imperialist weekly *Truth*, and also a parliamentary leader of the "Little Englanders" who opposed British expansion. He excoriated Rhodes as a pirate and the British South Africa Company as "a ring of financing adventurers, who would violate every commandant of God and man, in order to send up the shares of their Company, or to make profits for themselves . . ." He accused the government of practicing imperialism by proxy for allowing a commercial enterprise to invade a foreign land under the British flag. Labouchere's hostility was ecumenical. In addition to imperialists, he also reviled Jews, foreigners, suffragettes, and homosexuals.

His criticisms of Rhodes and the British government, though sometimes overblown, held truth. Burnham sometimes said much the same things about the BSAC and British imperialism. But it stung Burnham that Labouchere also sprayed the settlers with his machine-gun rhetoric. "*Truth* stigmatized us as land pirates, hired assassins and murderers of the deepest dye," wrote Burnham soon after the Matabele War, "vile drunken loafers and everything else a subtle master of the English language can command." He would like to remind Labouchere, he said, that the men who fought the Ndebeles were not hired soldiers but pioneers who left their homes and livelihoods in Mashonaland to volunteer. He noted that these same horrible vandals had built hospitals and churches in the country they were creating. He wondered why Labouchere called the pioneers murderers while disregarding the savagery of Lobengula's men, who slaughtered the Shonas, including women and children, and cut out their tongues. Could it really be true, he asked, that 1,000 intrepid pioneers had suddenly, en masse, turned into "scavengers of the earth and plunderers of the innocent"?

"Can it be," he continued, "that the English colonist, noted the world over for carrying the solid virtues of his race into every clime, has in this instance carried unanimously only faults and vices?" The settlers had come looking for opportunity, not war. They were pioneers, not villains. But ultimately, wrote Burnham, Labouchere failed to see the bigger picture—that the volunteer soldiers who conquered Matabeleland were the instruments of history and fate: "They have taken this king's country as a result of the inevitable war that must always come between barbarism and civilization when the two come together."

Burnham's criticisms of Labouchere, like Labouchere's of Rhodes and the BSAC, also held truth. But like Labouchere's accusations, they were partial and ignored many things. During his first year in Africa, Burnham saw the BSAC and British policy clearly, as instruments of imperialism. But once the white settlers were attacked, and once he became a vested landowner, his perspective changed. He seemed to believe, at first, that he could be both independent and an integral part of the BSAC's plan to colonize Matabeleland. He criticized the BSAC as land-grabbers and imperialists without accepting responsibility for helping them do what he was criticizing. He thought he was adapting to circumstances, or sometimes bending circumstances to his will, but he was often bent by those circumstances himself.

By March 1894 the workers on Scout's Reef had dug three shafts. They unearthed enough "free gold"—loose crumbs and nuggets—to foster hopes of a big vein.

Burnham planned to be off prospecting for most of the winter, and Blanche didn't want to stay at Scout's Reef for so long without him. On April 1 the family packed their wagons and went to Bulawayo. En route they stopped at the battlefield at Bembezi, where Lobengula's finest regiments had been mowed down by Maxims. They camped amid the bones and skulls. Burnham searched in the tall grass to show his wife and son the remains of an Ndebele chief he had killed. Roderick played with the chief's skull and picked out some teeth, which Blanche sent home as souvenirs.

"All this may seem strange and unnatural," wrote Burnham in *Scouting on Two Continents*, "but perfectly normal children become accustomed to war as a common thing and will amuse themselves by very gruesome imitations, as we did in Minnesota by scalp dances and the like."

At Bulawayo, the new town was going up a few miles from Lobengula's burnt capital. The pegs that marked the lines and boundaries had been cut from spears surrendered by the Ndebeles. There were no houses yet—the first public sale of lots had been held in March—but the pegs outlined Rhodes's vision of a city whose boulevards would be shaded by fast-growing trees, and wide enough for a span of sixteen oxen to turn around. Rhodes and Jameson instituted zoning regulations. To discourage speculators and shack-builders, anyone who bought a lot was required to make £200 of improvements or forfeit the property. All houses had to be brick, with iron roofs. Rhodes, with blunt symbolism, would soon build Government House, his residence in Bulawayo, atop the ruins of Lobengula's royal kraal.

Jameson gave Burnham his pick of the lots reserved by the BSAC and charged him the base price of £30, another sign of the scout's standing. Burnham chose a corner lot not far from the square designated as the center of town. Blanche immediately began planning a four-room house. Burnham hired a carpenter to build it, since he expected to be gone for most of the next month. Meanwhile, they camped in their wagon. The colony's most important men often sat under the Burnhams' tarpaulin, talking to the American about business prospects. "Strange how well known he has become in such a short time," wrote Blanche. "His deeds of daring in the campaign have fairly made him, and we are doing *well* in this country."

A week after arriving in Bulawayo, Burnham was itchy to make some money. He took Blanche and Roderick to the farm of two male friends, five miles out of town, where they set up quarters in a cozy hut. There were no ants, but rats did scrabble around the floor and drop from the thatch roof. Roderick sometimes stayed up to throw a knobkerrie at them so Blanche could sleep. Burnham left for a week to peg farms at £10 per job. He came home for three days, left for two more weeks, came home for another three days, then was gone again. He was also pegging mines, and was more financially flush than he had been in years.

Blanche appreciated the income, but when her husband was away life felt dull and lonely. Her chatty letters to family about their great prospects always contained several sentences of lament. "It is a lonesome life out here," she wrote. "I shall be glad when we are settled in town if Fred has to be away so much. I ought to be getting used to it but I am not." She hoped Bulawayo would be more lively, once her house was ready.

Some of this was surely related to being more than eight months pregnant. Bulawayo had two doctors, Jameson and Dr. Hans Sauer, another confidant of Rhodes, so she wasn't worried about the delivery. But since Burnham was usually gone, she longed for the presence of another woman. She complained that she had seen only one woman in the last five months, a sixteen-year-old Boer bride who didn't speak English. If only her mother or her mother-in-law could be with her. "Oh why can't I get to you and *talk*," she wrote. "That is the hard thing." She was hoping for a girl, and hoping that a baby would lessen the loneliness she and Roderick felt during Burnham's absences.

Just before his thirty-third birthday on May 11, Burnham left again for three weeks. The baby was due in late May or early June. On May 31, less than twenty-four hours after Blanche and Roderick moved into the new house, the birth pangs began. Blanche lay on bedding supported by woven rawhide, held up by bedposts made of fifty-pound cases of dynamite. Both of the town's doctors were away, so her attendants were Roderick, not quite eight, and Andrew Main, the carpenter who built the house. Blanche later said that despite her own pain, she felt sorry for Main, a shy bachelor, whose face drained of color as the big moment approached and he fully understood his task. She could hear him pacing and murmuring, "My God! My God!"

Soon after, Burnham sent a telegram to his mother from Bulawayo: you are the grandmother of a healthy baby girl. He added, "I as usual was off." The baby was the first white child born in Bulawayo. Her eyes, like

her father's, were piercing blue. They eventually named her after the hero-
ine of the novel Blanche had been reading, H. Rider Haggard's *Nada the
Lily* (1892), the romantic tale of a beautiful South African Zulu woman
loved by Umslopogaas, son of the Zulu king Chaka. All of the book's characters were black. (In Haggard's most famous book, *King Solomon's Mines*,
Allan Quatermain refuses to use the word "nigger," noting that many Africans are more worthy of the title of "gentleman" than the Europeans who
live or travel in the country.)

The house in Bulawayo—just two rooms to start—had glass windows
and nice curtains, a cloth ceiling, and smooth mud walls (there was no
wallpaper in Matabeleland). The floorboards were salvaged from whiskey
cases, the main source of planks in Matabeleland, and were padded with
goatskins. A corner cupboard held china; dishes and books sat on shelves.
Most of the furniture was homemade. Above the fireplace hung battle
trophies—an Ndebele shield, assegai, and battle axe, as well as Lobengula's
knobkerrie made of white rhino horn.

Bulawayo was booming, with prices to match. Butter was a dollar a
pound, milk a dollar a gallon. Potatoes were so rare that a sack of them was
sold at auction in lots of five, netting the owner $215. The days rang with
the sounds of saws, hammers, and pickaxes, and red dust hung in the air.
Burnham made sure to be home for the auction of house lots in early
August. Each parcel was 100 feet by 140. On market square, where Burnham's house stood, lots sold for up to £1,000. Burnham bought five more
lots as investments. He used the cash from selling one of his two 6,000-acre
farms—he and Ingram were partners—for £1,500. He knew from booms
in the American West that this one couldn't last, but he wasn't worried.
Africa was vast. Another frontier was just a trek away.

Burnham's letters to Blanche's family, like hers, often urged them to
come to Africa and help shape a new country. His brother Howard had
already done so and was working as an assayer in Johannesburg. Burnham
sweetened the lure for the younger Blicks by offering to advance two of
them $500 each to cover the cost of transportation to Bulawayo. To Blanche's

joy, her nineteen-year-old brother John and twenty-four-year-old sister Grace accepted. Once they repaid the loans, Burnham would fund the immigration of more Blicks. Over here, he wrote to John, "any path is open to you and you can feel yourself more than a fly on a bull's horn in building up and uniting this great country . . ."

On August 10 he left with Ingram for a two-month prospecting trip into the tsetse-fly country near the Zambezi. The new baby kept Blanche busy, and the town's growing number of women offered more social opportunities, though many of the women, she wrote, "are of the shady sort." She enjoyed the heavy traffic of male visitors when Fred was home, but that dropped off during his absences, "for you know I am not a flirting woman." So she was doubly eager for her lively sister Grace to arrive, both for her companionship and because she would attract male visitors and handle all the flirting herself.

Burnham returned from the Zambezi two weeks earlier than expected. Three days later he left for business in Johannesburg. From there he wrote to his uncle that he was brimming with prospects and schemes. "If the country proves good," he wrote, "I must win." He added that he remained a firm believer in the socialist utopia imagined by Edward Bellamy, and hoped this new country would develop along those lines, "as soon as we can cut loose from the imperial leading strings, but the golden milk of the mother country is hard to refuse, however we will get weaned ere long."

He met John and Grace Blick in Johannesburg and put them on the carriage to Bulawayo. They brought Blanche a gust of youth and family. They all lived without privacy in the two-room house, soon to be four. John, with a teenager's relish of adventure, immediately took to Bulawayo's energy and promise. Burnham put him to work pegging claims with Ingram, and then left him in charge of the mining operation at Scout's Reef at a salary of $100 per month plus board.

Grace, bubbly and frank, also enjoyed the adventure and the big pool of attentive males. But unlike Blanche, she wasn't obliged to see Rhodesia through Burnham-tinted spectacles. "Oh I can tell you this is no paradise," she wrote not long after arriving. "I shall never spend all my life here by any means." Bulawayo was booming, all right—lots of excitement and bustle, houses sprouting everywhere, three newspapers, dances and socials where cavalier men spent eight dollars on a bottle of champagne. But it was also windy and dusty and raw, and she quickly tired of the monotonous food. "Not a potato since we came and no fruit and vegetables," she wrote to her parents. "You people are in clover and if I were you I'd remain there."

Both John and Grace were impressed by Burnham's reputation. "Fred is pretty hot stuff out here," wrote John. "He is known all over the country." Grace wrote, "He has the biggest men in the country asking his advice about things. He is very much liked here and is as full of business as ever. He is just the same dear old Fred though, always thinking of someone besides himself." John mentioned an old American miner who came to Bulawayo after completing a contract to dig 120 feet of tunnel. The miner was dead broke but the owner refused to pay until his partner returned from England at some unknown date. Burnham heard about it, changed his clothes, "and is going down to kill the boss if he don't pay up," wrote John. "Fred is one of the most *popular* men in Matabeleland."

Burnham and Ingram decided to go to London to try to float some mines while the boom was still on. Burnham also wanted investors for an irrigation proposal. They expected to be away for several months. Blanche, Grace, and the children would spend the time in Cape Town. After two months in Bulawayo, Grace was ready for a change. "Bulawayo is no heaven I can tell you," she wrote to her parents in late November, "and I am more glad than I can tell that we are going to leave it." Fred, she added, was gone as usual, pegging mines, including diamond claims for Rhodes and De Beers. In the last two months he had been home only two weeks. "Isn't that fine for [Blanche]? I wonder that she hasn't quite died of lonesomeness. I know I should have in her place."

Before leaving in mid-December, Burnham and Ingram decided to abandon Scout's Reef. The crumbs of free gold hadn't led anywhere.

CHAPTER FIFTEEN

CASHING IN

Bᴇ Y MID-DECEMBER THEY were in Cape Town. It reminded Blanche of Southern California. She loved the substantial homes, the shady avenues, the nice shops, the fresh fruit—things she missed. She wrote to Burnham that they should build a house here, this was a place where she and her parents could be happy.

Aboard ship, Burnham wrote to his uncle about his many prospects and schemes in London, but added that if none of them panned out, he wouldn't lose a wink of sleep, because he already had so much going on in Bulawayo. To stave off boredom, he was climbing ropes and pacing miles on deck every day. The salons and dark suits and dainty etiquette were a pleasant change, briefly, but he already missed the wilds of Africa. "I often wonder," he wrote, "if the swallow tails around me cover such savages as Mr. Ingram and self." He was more certain than ever that he belonged on the African frontier. "It is the arena of action and nation building," he wrote, "and is the only spot left over which hangs mystery and romance and unknown possibilities."

Blanche missed him at Christmas. They had been together for their first seven Christmases, but apart for the last four. At least this time, she wrote, she didn't have to worry that some Ndebele was sticking a spear in his ribs. She described Roderick playing on the floor with his new game, "The Chartered Forces in Matabeleland," iron figures of twelve Ndebeles and six whites on horseback, plus two Maxim guns.

A few days later she proposed that they build a family compound in Cape Town where all the Burnhams and Blicks could live. She missed him and the way things used to be. "Write me as much of your plans and schemes, dear, as you can find time, for I am beginning to realize more and more how very little we have been together during the last year and so little time for the long confidential talks that we used to have."

In London, investors were eager to throw money at Burnham. He also met one of his inspirations, H. Rider Haggard, who invited him as a guest for several days. The men became lifelong friends. In his memoir, Haggard wrote of Burnham, "Indeed taking him altogether I am not sure that when the circumstances of his up-bringing and life are considered, he is not the most remarkable man whom it has been my privilege to know."

Meanwhile, Blanche was feeling more and more blue. By the end of January they had been separated for seven weeks. She slept with his letters under her pillow. One night, writing to him, she left half a page blank. Grace told her to fill it up with a favorite song lyric, so she wrote, "Come, oh come my love to me," again and again, larger and larger, like a shout.

He was supposed to ship on February 16, but when that boat docked at Cape Town, Blanche and Roderick got a letter instead. It opened with apologies and yearning for her voice. He had been staring at a photograph of her from Arizona days and daydreaming. But the trip had been successful beyond his greatest hopes. He had sold three companies and was coming home with a sack of sovereigns. He would be delayed a week because he and Ingram were closing another deal.

It was a deal that could make him rich. He had come to London not just to float some mining claims but to float some ideas past Cecil Rhodes. They had met during the war and liked each other from the start, partly because each recognized a fellow gambling dreamer. In late January, after listening to Burnham's pitch, Rhodes had given him, Ingram, and Maurice

Gifford each the mineral rights to 100 square miles above the Zambezi River as a reward for their exceptional service in the war. (Gifford had come to southern Africa to manage the Bechuanaland Exploration Company after fighting in the Mahdist War in the Sudan and spending eleven years on the Canadian frontier.) Rhodes granted them the right to peg 6,000 acres of coal as well. They also could dig for antiquities of all sorts, with the stipulation that "all ancient ruins or buildings shall be preserved intact." Another explicit instruction: do not fight the natives unless absolutely necessary.

After awarding the grants, Rhodes suggested that the three men sell them to the Northern Territories (B.S.A.) Exploring Company, in which he happened to have an interest. The men did so for 42,500 shares each, with the value of a share estimated at £1 (in today's dollars, more than $6 million each.) On paper they were rich. Burnham and Ingram agreed to go prospecting beyond the Zambezi, with the company paying the expenses for the expeditions. If the company floated any gold properties discovered on the concessions, the company would take only 33 percent instead of the usual 50, "owing to the valuable services rendered" in the war.

The companies involved were interwoven, with Rhodes at the center spinning the web. He was the managing director of the British South Africa Company, and had interests in the Bechuanaland Exploration Company and the Northern Territories (B.S.A.) Exploring Company. Lord Edric Gifford (brother of Maurice) was a director of both the BSAC and the Bechuanaland Exploration Company. So was Sir Edmund Davis, who was also a director of the Northern Territories (B.S.A.) Exploring Company. The Bechuanaland Exploration Company managed the business of the Northern Territories company in southern Africa.

Rhodes was always thinking far beyond the present. To him, Bulawayo wasn't an isolated frontier town 600 miles from the nearest railhead, but the future hub of southern Rhodesia. To fund his visions, he needed fresh sources of income and raw materials. Gold was always welcome, but he also wanted minerals that fueled expansion, especially coal and copper.

He was brilliant at enlisting people who could help him achieve his ends. He recognized that, among the pioneers in Matabeleland, Burnham and Ingram not only had the pluck and savvy needed to go beyond the Zambezi and survive, they also were experienced prospectors who could judge mineral formations. If Burnham found rich coal fields in the north, Rhodes could raise capital to build a railroad to them. Railroads opened up a country for everything else, and locomotives ran on coal—all the way to Cairo, in Rhodes's master plan. The coal that powered locomotives got shoveled into fireboxes made of copper—copper, essential for electricity, telegraph wires, lighting: for civilization. And while Burnham was prospecting for coal and copper and gold, he could note the best route for a railroad across the Zambezi and into the north.

Rhodes and Burnham both saw an expedition beyond the Zambezi as a smart gamble. If they found minerals, they would get rich (richer, for Rhodes and his partners), and Africa would be pried farther open for white settlement. If Burnham found nothing, at least he would have had a memorable adventure, and Rhodes's companies would only be out some expenses.

———

In Bulawayo, word of the expedition got around. Burnham expected to be gone for five or six months. About a hundred men applied to go, but he stuck with family and trusted veterans—Ingram, John Blick, a few others. Two more of Blanche's brothers, Judd and Homer, were en route from California with another young family friend named A. Kingsley Macomber. These three would bring the total of white men to ten, plus about seventy natives, some armed.

In the north, Burnham would be chasing hints and rumors. A native had told him about a place south of the Zambezi where black rocks burned: coal, thought Burnham. Another tip arrived on the arm of a young woman, wife of an Ndebele who was digging a well at Burnham's house. Burnham, the observant prospector, noticed her bracelet: pure copper, not the usual alloyed brass. He asked where it came from. After multiple translations in different languages, he knew she was a Batoka from the north, captured by her Ndebele husband in a raiding party before the war. Her home was as many days march beyond the Zambezi as Bulawayo was from the river—about 250 miles. The red metal was mined by men in holes, she said, like her husband digging the well, which told Burnham there were workable veins.

So much to do before leaving. Real estate values had skyrocketed, so he sold their new house and hired someone to build another on one of his lots just outside town. Meanwhile, the family rented. He also worked out the last details of another deal with a man named James Doré. The BSAC (that is, Rhodes) had given Doré the right to peg ten farms of 6,000 acres each. In return Doré guaranteed to spend £10,000 improving the land. Doré hired Burnham to buy up farmland in the Insiza Valley, about forty-five miles southeast of Bulawayo, for Doré's "colonization scheme." He intended to dig irrigation canals and then sell or lease land to small farmers for growing fruit trees. (Rhodes laughed at him and said the territory's agricultural future was big cattle ranches.) Burnham would get 10 percent of the net from any profits, and he also expected to get the contract to dig the canals. He was getting rich with paper prospects.

Anticipating the construction job, Burnham urged Blanche's father, James, to come over and handle it. To prod him, Burnham sent the money for his passage, plus $750, a gift from son John, who had already paid off his and Grace's transportation loan. "Come out and get a rifle on your shoulder among the big game," wrote Burnham to James, whom he called father, "and grow young again while your children grow to be men." He added that James's daughter Grace was now wearing an opal and diamonds. She and Ingram were in love, which perfectly suited Burnham's devotion to clan, which he often called "our tribe."

A few days before going north, he wrote to his mother that the expedition was "laying a stepping stone in the stride of the northern march of the race." If it went well, he wanted her to come live in Cape Town. "B. and I will probably keep up our travels till we die," he said. He called himself a "rambler and a money maker," and said he would never live in the United States again.

———

They found the burning black rocks south of the Zambezi. It was first-rate bituminous coal, and the deep seams ran five to fifteen feet wide. They pegged forty miles of it. It would become known as the Wankie Coal Field (now Hwange), one of the world's largest.

Next, they needed to cross the Zambezi above Victoria Falls. The river was 600 yards wide. The naked ferrymen, streaked with red pigment, lounged by their dugouts. They demanded steep fees payable in great lengths of calico and wire. Burnham knew about this extortionate monopoly from his first trip to the Zambezi and had prepared for it. At the edge of the river, his men began unpacking thick rubber mattresses brought from England. The ferrymen watched in disbelief as the mattresses were inflated with a bellows, lashed into rafts with rope and bamboo poles, and launched. Ferry rates dropped immediately.

It took a week to get everything across. They killed a hippo for meat and used its grease on the pack ropes. They felt lucky not to lose a man or an animal to the hippos and crocodiles. Burnham felt lucky, period. He flourished in wild places. "The moon is now full all night and the river by night is a marvel of beauty," he wrote to Blanche on a scrap of paper, sent to Bulawayo by runner. "The beating of tom toms and the low soft music of the Kaffir piano, the gleam of fires through the reed huts and circles of naked savages make an impression not easily forgotten and on such a day as this I find my rewards for the long and dreary treks without water and endless thorn of the western route. . . . When I leave here I will be treading on new ground and what it may hold in store tis hard to say."

The river marked the border of Barotseland. In 1890 its king, Lewanika, had sold mineral and trading rights to the BSAC. Like his enemy Lobengula, Lewanika would soon regret the deal and appeal it to the Queen, with the same result. Lewanika's Lozi people had been missionaried, and a few evangelicals had a station not far north of the river. The results were mostly sartorial. Burnham noted that Lewanika's son wore tailor-made clothes, starched white shirts and collars, and a derby hat.

Beyond the Lozi were the Batoka and other tribes rarely visited by whites. Most worrisome were the Mashukulumbwe (or Ba-ila), whose plastered hair rose off their heads in a thin, curving horn three feet high. A few years earlier they had tried to murder Frederick Selous.

The group trekked north. Several times they passed killing fields littered with skulls and skeletons, remnants of previous Ndebele raids. They saw thousands of ancient gold workings. The old miners had worked the quartz veins by building fires along the ledges, then pouring cold water onto the hot rock to crack it off. They crushed the chunks of quartz in mortars to remove the gold. Each old working was a prospect. Burnham and his men panned gold in streams, found golden traces in quartz formations, pegged claims over hundreds of miles. They went almost to Katanga, in what is now northern Zambia, where they found copper and Mashukulumbwes, pegging one and escaping the other. The copper belt they marked turned out to belong to one of the world's richest deposits.

They fell asleep with their guns beneath them, listening to lions roar. Near the Zambezi, game had been plentiful—stembok, hartebeest, water buck, boar—but in the north it became scarce. The natives there were reduced to eating the roots of the blood lily, soaked in water for days to leach out the poison. The dry season had begun, so water was also scarce. They often drank from shallow slimy pools, staying alert for lurking crocodiles. By August they were back at the Zambezi near Victoria Falls. It inspired Burnham to one of the best descriptions in his letters:

> The broad blue river widens out for its great leap and numerous small rocky islands on which tall palms are waving break the monotony of a single sheet of water. The rock is black basalt all round the Falls for many miles and the contrasts of color between forest, reeds, rocks, and yellow grass is very vivid. The long purple ridge marking the

borders of the valley makes a picturesque setting for one of nature's wonders. The river plunges into a black chasm a little less than 400 ft. at one fall and then its two mile sheet of water is compressed between its narrow walls only a few hundred yards apart. If I was asked what impressed me the most of all the various sights, the awful roar, the circling clouds of spray and mist, the dancing rainbows, or gurgling whirlpools, I should say above all the sense of energy and irresistible force grows upon one. It gives one a faint gleam into what the building of a mountain range, the sinking of a continent, or the crash of a planet might be. Days might be spent here and pass as hours. By moonlight gaze on its banks of clouds like northern fields of snow, or in the somber darkness of the night sit on some projecting rock and hear such sound come out of this gash in mother earth as though it were a mortal wound and this the surging out of her heart's blood. One's own utter nothingness is brought home as no prayer book passage can bring it and one feels the same strange calm as when death is just upon you.

To explore more territory between the river and Bulawayo, they decided to split into three groups. Burnham's guide was a Bushman from the Kalahari Desert whose knowledge about the region's water holes dried up soon after leaving the river. At the last known water, Burnham told his twelve carriers to fill their calabashes and to ration the liquid carefully, since the next source could be several days away. That night they ran into a vast thorn belt growing out of soft sand. The big fishhook thorns lacerated the carriers' skin and shredded Burnham's clothing. Between the sand, the thorns, and the heat, the natives drank their water or poured it out to shed the weight. The next day at noon, when Burnham checked their supply, he was shocked to find not a drop among them. That left the water in his own canvas bag for all of them, but later that day a thorn tore it open and the sand drank the spill.

They marched that day and night without water, then into the furnace of another day. Always sand, thorn, rock, heat. The group began to break apart. Stopping meant death. Burnham's lips were swollen. When he touched his tongue and found it bone-dry, he knew he had less than twenty-four hours to live. His vision began to fail. He briefly lost consciousness. Doubtful that he could make it to the Gwai River, he carved last messages on his gunstock: "Aug. '95, a.m. No water. Boys exhausted. My mule dead. Am west of Guay, am going east. P.M. One boy finished. Aug. 10th. Boys going mad. I am suffering. The thorns will end all of us soon. B.B. [Blanche Burnham] Love, Roy [his pet name for Roderick] all."

They staggered on. Near evening he found damp sand in a thin watercourse. A few carriers dug frantically. The hole filled with sandy muddy liquid. At first they could barely drink because their tongues were too swollen. Burnham filled a calabash and backtracked to look for the missing. He found most, but several died. "Some were mad and all terribly torn and exhausted," he wrote to his mother. They pushed on to the river and found a kraal where his men could recuperate. Burnham continued to Bulawayo, walking forty-five miles the last day, August 14. "I am a little thin at this writing," he wrote to his mother four days later, "but otherwise in splendid health. You know I recover quickly from any hardship."

Ingram and Judd Blick also nearly died of thirst before reaching Bulawayo. At one point they tried to kill their remaining burro to drink its blood, but were too weak to cut its throat with a case knife.

The expedition pegged 400 square miles for gold and copper, plus 6,000 acres for coal.

While Burnham was away, a carpenter began building the family a new house on the outskirts of Bulawayo. Meanwhile Blanche lived with Grace and Nada in a rented house beset by ants and fleas. Roderick, now nine, had been sent to school in Germany under the care of Burnham's brother Howard, who was being treated for tuberculosis there. Blanche missed Roderick terribly. She wasn't happy when Howard wrote that he had gotten married before leaving South Africa, which meant that Roderick was living with an unknown woman. Blanche would have been furious to know that instead of overseeing Roderick in Germany, Howard had enrolled him at a school for boys in Paris run by monks. Roderick hated it there. Blanche got a letter from someone about Roderick crying once in the middle of the night, and when comforted he said, "Oh if I could only have my mother for five minutes." It broke Blanche's heart. She hoped Fred's endeavors were successful enough to allow her to see Roderick by Christmas.

As always, she missed her husband, and Grace missed Ingram. Letters from above the Zambezi had to be brought by runner and were infrequent, more than three weeks apart. Their social life remained robust. An opera singer from Cape Town, in Bulawayo to seek his fortune, visited several times a week to sing to Grace. One week they had thirty-five callers. They tsk-tsked the married women who flirted and rode and danced with young men while their husbands were away prospecting.

In midsummer Blanche, Grace, and Nada moved into the new house: three rooms, walls and roof of corrugated iron, shaded by many trees. Decorating was a welcome distraction while awaiting news from the men. Loneliness streaked Blanche's letters. When her husband was gone, the dream of Africa dimmed for her, but his enthusiasm always revived it. "We will always be wandering," she wrote to her mother.

Her father James reached Bulawayo soon after Burnham returned. He was sixty-two. Burnham had paid his way over partly for Blanche's sake and partly to give his father-in-law a sinecure as superintendent of construction for Doré's farms. It paid well and required no physical labor.

Bulawayo was about to hold another public auction of lots. Beforehand, investors offered to buy Burnham and Ingram's lots for 200 percent above the price paid a year earlier. The partners sold all their property, including the Burnhams' brand new house, with the expectation of buying more lots at the auction. Burnham's profit was $5,000. But the auction prices were so crazy that Burnham didn't bid. He began paying rent to the new owner of his house while he looked for land.

He knew the boom couldn't last. In *Scouting on Two Continents* he wrote:

> So for the next two months I turned into a regular money grubber and sold and cashed and bought and sold again—farms, mines, interests, stocks, etc. I never took my eyes off the glint of gold. It was hard work and exciting, but not calculated to bring out the best in a man. Business is a ferocious game, and while it goes on, all thoughts of things of real beauty and lasting value are forgotten. . . . This was the day of gold, and this my opportunity to gain it; so, although I hated the slavery it entailed, I did my best to gather it for the sake of my children and those dependent on me. It seems to me that, in one way or another, nine tenths of our proud race must bend the knee to the power of money.

James Blick saw Bulawayo with clear eyes. He wrote home that the place was a boomtown built on a real estate bubble. Most of the overpriced lots were bought by syndicates filled with BSAC shareholders, who bid up the prices to inflate the worth of their shares—essentially a pyramid scheme. He developed a similar view about the mining fever. A prospector would find a little color in some rock, file a claim, then sell to a syndicate that floated shares to rash optimists in England. Blick doubted that many of the mines would ever be worked, much less become bonanzas.

Like Grace, he was also amiably immune to Burnham's enthusiastic conviction that Rhodesia was the place of dreams. Too hot, too many thorns, too expensive, too primitive. Definitely not a country for his wife and family. He intended to collect his easy salary for a year, maybe two, and then hightail it back to a real paradise, California.

Through Grace and James, Blanche began seeing things through eyes other than her husband's. "You were wise in not coming," she wrote to her mother. "It is a good place in which to make money but it is not a homelike country and the people are not our people. . . . Your home is too lovely a one to give up."

James also noticed many preparations for war. Matabeleland's entire police force had been called to Bulawayo, and Jameson had bought more than a thousand horses. Everyone knew the BSAC and the British government wanted all of southern Africa. Everyone knew that Rhodes had some master plan. But who was the target so soon after defeating Lobengula? Khama, king of Bechuanaland in the west? The Boers in the Transvaal? Burnham and Ingram vowed they would not join an invasion of Bechuanaland.

————

In mid-October Grace and Ingram were married. At the end of the month they, along with Burnham, Blanche, and James Blick, left for a trip to London. Nada, seventeen months old, remained in Bulawayo; Blanche didn't want to subject her to the rigors of the journey. The group from Rhodesia was meeting Roderick, Howard, and Burnham's mother in London. Following the holiday, James would return to California; two months in Rhodesia had been enough. Roderick was going to California with Burnham's mother to attend school.

After nearly three years in Africa, Blanche was thrilled to be in refined, comfy London. She had Roderick again, as well as her father and Mrs. Burnham, whom she called her second mother. They took in the sights, ate out, went to the theater to see *The Prisoner of Zenda* and the wildly popular *The Sign of the Cross*. At Burnham's insistence, Blanche was having several dresses made, as was his mother. Burnham and Blanche spent a few days as guests of Rider Haggard. Everything seemed perfect.

In early January stunning news reached London from southern Africa. Jameson and 400 men, including most of Rhodesia's police force, had crossed the border of Transvaal to attack Johannesburg. Jameson had been expecting the British, Americans, and other foreigners there to rise up and help his militia overthrow the oppressive Boer regime. No one joined them. A large force of Boers rode out to meet Jameson's troop, picked off sixteen, and captured the rest.

In Johannesburg a number of men, including Rhodes's older brother Frank and the American engineer John Hays Hammond, were jailed for conspiracy and treason. At the center of the web, Rhodes went silent. On the Kaffir Circus, stocks plunged. And in Matabeleland and Mashonaland, the natives noted that almost the entire Rhodesian police force had gone missing.

CHAPTER SIXTEEN

WAR AGAIN

T HE RAID INTO the Transvaal was a massive miscalculation by all who plotted it: Rhodes, Jameson, conspirators in Johannesburg, and colonial officials in London and South Africa. It brought on the Second Matabele War and the Boer War, and also prepared the ground for World War I after Kaiser Wilhelm II of Germany sent a congratulatory telegram to the Transvaal's president, Paul Kruger, and later sent him military aid. Winston Churchill called the Jameson Raid the "event which seems to me when I look back over the map of life to be the fountain of all ill."

At the time, in Rhodes's view, the raid combined high purpose, business sense, and realpolitik. The Transvaal's fabulous riches—Kimberley's diamonds, the Rand's gold—had been developed by foreigners (called Uitlanders by the Boers), mostly British investors and American mining engineers. Natives worked the mines. The Uitlanders and their mines quickly became the Transvaal's major sources of income. By the 1890s the foreigners far outnumbered the Boers and owned more than half the land. The Transvaal government, concerned about losing control of their country, denied Uitlanders most rights. They couldn't vote or own a gun. They couldn't serve as jurors, so justice against Boers was almost impossible. Boer policemen were laws unto themselves. Only Boers were given contracts to supply crucial goods, another means of gouging Uitlanders. If Uitlanders tried to publish a newspaper that objected to any of this, the government shut it down. In response to every protest, the Transvaal's shrewd fundamentalist leader, Paul Kruger, merely shrugged.

To Rhodes and various British officials, including Colonial Secretary Joseph Chamberlain, all this was a clear injustice. It also offered an excuse, under the right conditions, to remove an impediment to capital while absorbing the Transvaal and the Orange Free State (the other Boer republic) into a united British South Africa.

So the plotting began. Guns were smuggled into Johannesburg as Jameson gathered men and materials in Bulawayo. By the last months of 1895, the BSAC's idle militia was draining the company's finances. So Jameson, impetuous as always, made his premature move, despite the cautions of Rhodes, John Hays Hammond, and the other conspirators in Johannesburg.

But Rhodes certainly was behind the plan to invade. Afterward, Jameson took all the responsibility, as instructed by Rhodes, who worried that the British government might yank his charter. That didn't happen, perhaps because Colonial Secretary Chamberlain couldn't risk exposing his own winking connection to the plot. Rhodes got blistered by an official inquiry and by critics such as Labouchere, but denied everything and wasn't charged. He was, however, forced to resign as prime minister of the Cape Colony. In Pretoria the jailed conspirators were sentenced to death, but Kruger decided that mercy could be purchased by the five ringleaders for £25,000 each. Rhodes paid the fines as well as other costs of the raid, for an immense total of £300,000.

—◦—

After Jameson arrived in London for his trial—Kruger had shipped the raiders home—Burnham had breakfast with him one morning. Burnham regretted that he hadn't been in Rhodesia to go on the raid, and blamed Jameson's predicament on "the cowards and curs who failed to come to his assistance." Jameson and some officers received sentences of between five and fifteen months but ended up serving less than half because public opinion had transformed Jameson's folly into valor. He was portrayed as a quixotic hero who rode resolutely toward glory despite the odds. The poet laureate, Alfred Austin, set a treacly verse about the raid to music, and a small sculpture of Jameson astride his horse became a popular gimcrack.

In London, Burnham was managing some legal affairs of his own. Doré had died suddenly, ending that stream of income. The Jameson Raid had sent South African stocks crashing. Almost overnight, Burnham and Ingram lost $10,000, a small fortune.

The Jameson Raid also prompted Burnham to write a rambling eighteen-page will and final instructions. War with the Boers seemed imminent, and this time the opponents would be sharp-shooting frontiersmen, not natives with spears. The document, sent to his Uncle Josiah, ranged widely across serious matters. After years of spiritual turmoil, he wrote, he was finally "at rest on religious belief," though "it has been reached by a tearing down process that was very severe." If young Americans asked Josiah what Burnham thought about emigrating to Africa, he said to tell them "That if they want to come to Africa to heap up a pile and go home again to live, that we can do our own blood sucking without help and I hope they will stay away. But any man who finds himself crowded and wants to help build up a new nation of Anglo Saxon people in this great Continent, come, he will find friends and plenty of work, rough and hard, maybe—for that is the proof of the man—if he won't work hard at home, we don't want his worthless carcass here. We want men not paupers—or Mamma's darlings. We want men who can plow and live hard, shoot straight and ride well—for them there is room."

He turned to Roderick. "I would fain shield him from the woes and failures I have passed through." He was comfortable entrusting his young son to Mother Burnham's enveloping love. But Roderick also needed "the other and more rugged virtues of true manhood," and to that end Burnham was sending detailed instructions. He wanted his son to know how to ride and shoot, swim and fish, sail and row. Roderick also should learn to dance, a request Burnham felt necessary to defend to his strict religious uncle: "Tis natural in all races in some form and I believe no harm comes of it in moderation." He wanted Roderick to learn responsibility by owning and caring for a horse, so he was including $15 to buy a little mustang, which his son should learn to ride bareback to improve his horsemanship. For its upkeep in feed and hay, Burnham was providing $10 a month, and Rod was to keep strict accounts that Josiah checked. Rod's allowance would be a dollar a month to start, and he needed to mark down every penny spent for candy, pencils, and stamps, for Josiah's auditing. "I will see but little of him till he is a man grown," he wrote, explaining these fatherly wishes, "and am anxious to hold a few threads between us that may influence him for good."

Then to business. He instructed Josiah not to sell the two farms in California, which weren't worth much but assured the family a place of refuge. Besides, he continued, Nada "may marry a worthless pup who would squander money, and she might have to raise vegetables for the family, and I might need to give [a farm] to her." He wanted the pesky orange trees cut down since they continued to drain money, most recently through the state's expensive demand to spray them for black scale. Burnham told Josiah to sell the other two houses he still owned in California, and to use the proceeds to buy a nice lot where a small home should be built for his mother and Roderick.

Despite recent losses, he had done well in Africa and was sending home more than $12,000 to be invested so that the interest supported his mother and Roderick, and also helped provide a small pension for Blanche's parents. When all this was done, he concluded, "I can draw a breath and know that my long struggle to place those that are dependent on me out of the clutches of poverty, is at last over."

He felt ready for the impending war that would unite South Africa. It struck him, once again, that every empire and religion seemed to require a baptism of blood. "It is the only cement that holds a people together," he wrote. "It took the blood of the Son of God to save the souls of men, and it constantly takes the blood of the bravest and finest of the sons of men to save the earthly kingdoms."

Yet when war came, he was as shocked as everyone else.

———

On March 20, 1896, some Ndebeles east of Bulawayo killed several native policemen. Within days blood was flowing all over Matabeleland as Ndebeles massacred isolated settlers and prospectors. Whites called it the Second Matabele War. Natives called it the First Chimurenga or the War of the Red Axe. The whites later learned that the revolt was supposed to start on March 28 with a simultaneous uprising throughout Matabeleland, with the goal of wiping out most colonials. The impatience of a few young warriors had spoiled this plot. Nevertheless, the revolt had been comprehensively planned under the noses of the settlers. The Ndebeles had stockpiled food, weapons, and ammunition. Yet even old hands such as Frederick Selous didn't see it coming—a measure of the settlers' obliviousness.

The easy victory in the first war, combined with the economic boom and racial arrogance, had blinded the settlers to the natives' seething discontent. Their grievances were many.

First, land. The BSAC claimed it all. Like the U.S. government in the American West, the company adopted a policy that sounded humane and high-minded but in reality called for sequestering natives on desolate reservations while saving the best land for settlers, miners, and powerful allies. Rhodes gave one friend, Sir John Willoughby, 600,000 acres (an area a bit smaller than Rhode Island). As in the American West, the white colonizers justified taking these lands because the natives were wasting them by merely living on them, and besides, the people were savages. The two reserves set aside for natives in northern Matabeleland were so arid and inhospitable that most Ndebeles and Shonas refused to move there. Instead, they became squatters on their former lands, many of which were owned by absentee white speculators.

Second, cattle. The culture and economy of the Ndebeles and Shonas were based on cattle. After Lobengula's defeat, the BSAC seized thousands of head, at least 200,000 according to one British official's estimate. The BSAC claimed ownership of all cattle belonging to Lobengula as part of the loot that had been promised to the volunteers. The BSAC also pledged to redistribute some of the royal cattle to the Ndebeles. But the separation of royal cattle from private cattle was done sloppily and corruptly, robbing many Ndebeles and Shonas of their only economic means. About 65,000 cattle were auctioned or distributed as loot. Another 20,000 were appropriated for "police rations." Only 41,000 were redistributed to Ndebeles, leaving at least 75,000 unaccounted for. Most of the cattle given to the Ndebeles went to chiefs and elders, leaving many young men with no cattle and no land, and hence no status. Two years earlier this volatile group had been elite warriors with assured futures. Now they were indentured laborers with no prospects.

They were indentured laborers because of the third major grievance, the hated hut tax, which forced natives to work for white miners and farmers. These laborers often ran off before their contract was up. In January 1896 John Blick described what happened after he reported several truants to the police: two native (Ndebele) policemen caught and returned two of them to Blick for judgment. "After all evidence was in," he wrote to his sister Kate, "I rose up and spake thus, 'Guilty, fetch um, tie um and give em ten.' The police then ran a rope through them, handcuffed them up through the crotch of a tree about two ft above the victim's head and then lashed his feet to the trunk of the tree and then stood off and laid on ten with a hearty good will."

Which brings up the fourth grievance: the police. They spent much of their time recruiting laborers, chasing runaways, or confiscating cattle. Most were young men handed considerable power, and they developed a reputation for bullying and brutality. In a country with few white females, some policemen inevitably used their power to abuse native women.

Then there were the native police. After the war, the BSAC trained some Ndebeles from Lobengula's crack regiments as policemen, including marksmanship with modern rifles. These men were equally detested by the natives, perhaps more so, for inflicting cruelties and depredations on their own people. The first victims killed in the revolt were native policemen. By that time, most natives had learned to flee at the sight of police of any color.

In early 1896 all these grievances were intensified by terrible drought and a plague of locusts. And then, from the north, came the scourge of rinderpest. In early March this contagious disease began annihilating Matabeleland's herds of cattle and oxen. To slow the spread of rinderpest, the BSAC ordered the shooting of any animal that showed symptoms. The Ndebeles, who had already lost most of their cattle to the BSAC, didn't understand the concept of a fatal invisible virus and thought the whites were killing healthy cattle to starve the natives.

And so plans for the revolt went from simmer to boil. Many of the leaders were sons, brothers, and nephews of Lobengula, as well as his old indunas. They were urged on by priests of the god Mlimo, who assured them that the whites would be driven from the land. The settlers had assumed that once the Ndebeles had been defeated, the matter was closed. But the tribe's longstanding belligerence had merely gone into hiding, where it had been sharpened by losses and humiliations.

The Burnhams heard about the revolt when they stepped ashore in Cape Town. In the first week, more than 140 men, women, and children had been slaughtered, often gruesomely. Many victims were the Burnhams' friends. The Burnhams and Ingrams departed immediately for the north. The husbands left their wives in Mafeking and continued toward Bulawayo, promising to send for them as soon as possible.

Like the other settlers, Burnham was stunned by the uprising. The whites saw the Ndebeles as docile and grateful. Many settlers had stopped carrying guns. The BSAC was so confident of the natives' loyalty that the company hadn't required them to turn in most of the 1,000 rifles given to

Lobengula, and had taught about 200 natives (150 Ndebeles and fifty Shonas) to use modern rifles for their jobs as policemen. Most of these policemen deserted to the rebels, taking the rifles that they now knew how to use, unlike the warriors in the first war.

"These brutes who were treated better under the white man than they ever knew have neither gratitude or pity," wrote Burnham to his mother while en route to Bulawayo, sounding like the Minnesota settlers who had been shocked by the Sioux uprising. Despite later reports and accounts about the abuses that led to the revolt, Burnham never abandoned his myopic view, perhaps because of the searing personal consequences of the war for him. Thirty years later, in *Scouting on Two Continents*, he still sounded baffled and outraged by the uprising. "Under the terms of peace made with the Matabele at the close of the first war," he wrote, "natives were given generous reservations of land; also certain allotments of cattle, seed, etc., and ample employment for all who were willing to work on the farms, in the mines, or for the Government. . . . Here were people given more liberty than they had ever known before; the slaves all freed, labour paid in coin, lands held in safety, and taxes lighter by far than those levied on any white man in the empire." All these blessings, he continued, were blown away by a whisper from Mlimo's priest, "the Mouthpiece of God."

———

At Palapye Burnham and Ingram bought horses, already scarce. For a mount worth $15 in the U.S., Burnham paid the war price of $600. The road to Bulawayo was littered with thousands of stinking carcasses—oxen and cattle killed by rinderpest. Some of the animals had dropped in their yokes, still attached to wagons that had been looted of goods. Bulawayo depended on supplies hauled by ox-train from the nearest railhead at Mafeking, 600 miles away. As the oxen died, so did Bulawayo's lifeline for supplies.

Burnham and Ingram reached Bulawayo in early April without incident, a surprise since by then about 10,000 Ndebele warriors had the town surrounded on three sides. Bulawayo was in laager (defensive encirclement). Settlers and natives had come in from the countryside—about 2,200 whites and 2,000 natives. Like the settlers in Minnesota, the people in Bulawayo were panicked and unprepared for war or siege. They had only 380 rifles for the 800 men able to fight. Of their eight machine guns, three were broken. So were two of their three seven-pounders. They could muster only 100 horses for a cavalry. Burnham helped build a series of small fortifications—mostly sandbags atop kopjes—on the road between Bulawayo and Mangwe Pass, to protect coaches and supply wagons.

In Bulawayo, the white women and children were staying in the market building, the town's biggest. Burnham helped fortify the laager. Wagons chained together encircled the central square, with sandbags between the wheels. The defenders broke all the empty bottles in town and spread the shards several inches thick in a wide band around the wagons. Barbed wire formed a third ring. Around all these defenses Ndebele campfires formed a fourth ring, visible every night.

If the Ndebeles attacked after dark, the defenders would ignite oil-soaked bundles of wood on the rooftops so that riflemen could see. A machine gun was positioned at each of the laager's corners. The defenders spread blasting gelatin between boards and positioned these crude bombs on the perimeter so they could be detonated by rifle shot or electric current. They dug a well inside the laager and built tanks to hold reserves. After hearing stories about Ndebele atrocities, they formed a plan to prevent women and children from falling into native hands: if the laager got over-run, each man was assigned to kill a family not his own. In the weeks after the revolt began, nine black men were charged with spying or looting, and were hung in Bulawayo. Photographs of them caused an outcry in England.

Conditions in the laager were so unpleasant that during the day many settlers stayed outside in their houses, returning to the market building only at night or when the alarm bell clanged. Rinderpest and the Ndebele blockade had cut off almost all supplies. The plague also wiped out cattle, eliminating the settlers' main sources of milk and fresh meat. Nada Burnham's two pet ostriches, like other domestic animals, ended in the stewpot. By May the defenders were reduced to drying and salting meat from diseased carcasses of livestock, whose stench pervaded the laager. Like the Shangani Patrol, the siege of Bulawayo pitted outnumbered whites against encircling hostile natives, and contributed to the emerging Rhodesian identity.

—-—

Burnham's brief letters to Blanche about conditions in Bulawayo made her wild to get there and see her little girl, now almost two. "If only I had her in my arms this minute," Blanche wrote to her mother. "I will *never* leave her in Africa alone again." She also learned that one of her brothers had slight wounds and another had narrowly escaped death at a cabin besieged by Ndebeles. If anything happened to them, she wrote to her mother, she would never forgive herself for urging them to come to Africa.

Most travel was prohibited, and space in the few stagecoaches was limited. In mid-April Burnham arranged a special pass for Blanche and Grace, but everyone in Mafeking strongly advised against the trip, so they let two coaches leave without them. But Blanche had been separated from Nada for six months, and the desire to see her finally outweighed the risk. She left Mafeking eight days after her first opportunity, an interval she would always regret.

The journey to Bulawayo took eleven days. Food and water were scarce. Putrefying livestock were inescapable. At Palapye, Grace left with Ingram for Bloemfontein, where he was going to buy horses and mules for the war. Blanche reached Bulawayo on May 13. The next day Burnham left with a patrol to meet a relief column coming from Salisbury with Rhodes.

Blanche's reunion with Nada was distressing. A few days earlier, the child had become seriously ill with a fever and a cough, perhaps the result of poor diet. She seldom opened her eyes but seemed to know Blanche and kissed her several times. Blanche expected her to be fine in a few days. Instead she worsened, leaving Blanche with the ifs of regret—if only she hadn't left Nada in Africa, or hadn't stayed so long in London, or hadn't delayed her departure for Bulawayo. "How I wish she could have been well until two or three days after I came," wrote Blanche to Roderick on May 18, "so I could have seen all the cute little ways they tell me about."

On May 19 the Blicks in Pasadena got a telegram from Bulawayo: "Nada died today." Burnham was away and out of reach. So were Blanche's brothers, John and Judd. Grace and Roderick were elsewhere. For ten days Blanche was nearly alone in her grief before Burnham returned from patrol and learned about their child's death. Two days later he wrote to Roderick to break the news. Nada often kissed your photograph, he wrote. He wished Roderick could be with them to comfort his mother, but the war made that unwise. He signed the letter, "With unbounded love for you my dear boy." A week later Blanche sent her son a wistful, loving letter. She mentioned that there were still bits of biscuit on Roderick's photo, left by Nada's daily kisses. "Our little war baby," she wrote, "born just at the close of one war and buried in the middle of another."

Rider Haggard sent a letter of condolence. Burnham's reply was aggrieved but restrained, with one exception: "You know the tempest that is raging in my soul," he wrote. "I am hit awful hard, but for Africa and the Empire I will fight on."

———

Many children in Bulawayo died because of the siege, but the settlers were far more enraged by the Ndebeles' atrocities in the countryside. During April and May, as patrols ventured out of the laagered townships, they came upon horrifying scenes from the revolt's early days: women and girls naked and violated, children pinned to the ground with assegais or brained by knobkerries, men slit open with their toenails pulled out. Most victims had been taken by surprise.

These savageries ignited a bloodlust that often surprised even those who felt it. Frederick Selous had spent decades hunting and exploring in south-central Africa, and knew the region and its peoples better than most white men. By all accounts he was modest, thoughtful, and evenhanded as well as brave. (Rider Haggard modeled his character Allan Quatermain on Selous.) At the first reports of the uprising, Selous immediately grasped the timing and motivation—the police were away so the Ndebeles saw a chance to recover their seized land and cattle. Unlike Burnham, he also granted that, from the Ndebeles' perspective, the attempt to overthrow white rule and reclaim property was understandable. He was, he later wrote, "inclined to judge the Kafirs very leniently," though of course the revolt would have to be quelled.

Then he saw what the Ndebeles had done to their victims, especially to women and children. A fury for revenge rushed through him. "I don't defend such feelings nor deny that they are vile and brutal when viewed from a high moral standpoint," he wrote in his classic personal account of the uprising, *Sunshine and Storm in Rhodesia*,

> only I would say to the highly moral critic, Be charitable if you have not yourself lived through similar experiences; be not too harsh in your judgment of your fellow-man, for you probably know not your own nature, nor are you capable of analysing passions which can only be understood by a European who has lived through a native uprising, in which women and children of their race have been barbarously murdered by savages; by beings whom, in their hearts, they despise; as rightly or wrongly they consider that they belong to a lower type of the human family than themselves. . . . the murder of white women and children, by natives, seems to the colonist not merely a crime but a sacrilege, and calls forth all the latent ferocity of the more civilised race.

Like Burnham, Selous was agitated that the settlers were condemned by critics such as Henry Labouchere, who insisted, from a safe distance, that the poor natives be treated humanely, as if they had not slaughtered whites without mercy. Selous returned to the subject over and over in his book, trying to explain the rage felt by whites, to explain why in skirmishes they chased down and killed as many Ndebele warriors as they could find, including the wounded. In *Scouting on Two Continents*, Burnham put it succinctly: "There were scenes pathetic enough to melt a heart of stone, and others so awful in their shocking cruelty that the blood surged with the craving for vengeance."

———

Within a month of the first murders, the settlers knew this war would be different. Thanks to training, many of the Ndebeles were now better marksmen. They also had adjusted their military strategy, using their overwhelming numbers to surround all four white settlements in Matabeleland: Gwelo, Mangwe, and Belingwe in addition to Bulawayo. Better to starve out the whites and to attack smaller patrols away from the forts, they realized, than to charge into the mouths of Maxim guns.

The strategy worked for a while. The settlers' patrols lost men. Conditions in the settlements deteriorated. But ultimately the Ndebeles' new patience was a mistake. Time was not on their side, immediately or historically. With their greater numbers, if they had attacked the laagers in April, they almost certainly could have overwhelmed them despite the Maxims. But in mid-May two relief columns arrived in Bulawayo—from the south, 800 regulars sent by the British government, and from the north, another 150 volunteers from Salisbury, including Rhodes. At the end of May, Major General Frederick Carrington arrived to take command. The besieged people of Bulawayo relaxed a little.

On the evening of June 5, during a routine patrol, Burnham and a companion detected a force of more than 1,000 Ndebeles close to the town, clearly planning to attack. After eluding capture, Burnham reported the force to Carrington, who sent out a troop of 250 cavalry, including Burnham, now eager to avenge Nada. The next morning the last major battle of the Matabeleland uprising was fought at the Umguza River outside Bulawayo. The Ndebeles retreated in a rout, with more than 200 killed. The settlers lost one man. Burnham told Blanche that he killed three natives, then later returned to the battlefield and helped finish off twenty-five wounded.

"It all sounds awful," wrote Blanche to Roderick that evening, "but when the men think of the women and children who were brutally murdered they could do anything and then think of all the deaths that have been caused there by people leaving to go into the laager. Our dear little Nada. I could kill the black beasts myself."

After June 6 about 10,000 Ndebeles took refuge in the granite kopjes of the Matopo Hills, a warren of caves, clefts, and huge boulders, terrain almost impossible to conquer. In a reverse, white patrols began destroying native granaries to starve out the insurgents. The war was far from over, but the momentum had shifted.

Then on June 17, while most of Mashonaland's policemen were in Matabeleland fighting the Ndebeles, the Shonas began massacring whites in Mashonaland. About 120 were murdered in the first few days, with the usual atrocities. To the settlers, this uprising was even more shocking. Weren't the Shonas grateful for being freed from Ndebele taxes and oppression? Weren't the Shonas servile by temperament and happy to be under white protection? The settlers couldn't conceive that the answer to these questions was no. Not a single Shona warned the whites that an uprising was brewing. Salisbury went into laager. It was Bulawayo's turn to send relief.

A day or two after the news from Mashonaland, Bonar Armstrong, a young native commissioner from Mangwe in the Matopos, came to Bulawayo to propose a risky mission that he believed would help end the war: the capture or assassination of "the mouthpiece of God," the high priest of the deity called the Mlimo.

CHAPTER SEVENTEEN

THE MOUTHPIECE OF GOD

BECAUSE THEY WERE blind to the real causes of the Ndebele uprising, the settlers blamed agitators, especially the natives' religious leaders. The whites knew little about the Ndebeles' religious beliefs, but understood that priests, often termed witch doctors, served a deity called the Mlimo (or M'Limo or Umlimo). Foremost among these men, explained Selous in *Sunshine and Storm in Rhodesia*, was a high priest also referred to as the Mlimo—not because he was the real deity, but because the Mlimo spoke through him at the main temple, a secret cave in the Matopos not far from Mangwe. This man's influence had alarmed the settlers during the first war and they had tried to capture him, without success.

Some colonists, including Selous, believed that Ndebele military leaders had fomented the uprising by exploiting the natives' faith in the pronouncements of the Mlimo's priests. Most settlers simply blamed the man they called the Mlimo. He reportedly urged the Ndebeles to rid the land of whites, and promised that the god's magic would turn the whites' bullets into water.

When native commissioner Bonar Armstrong told Lord Grey (the Administrator), General Carrington, and Burnham that he knew where to find the Mlimo's secret cave, they immediately recognized it as vital military intelligence. Armstrong had learned the cave's location from a disaffected Zulu married to an Ndebele woman. The Zulu said a big *indaba* (meeting) would be held near the cave in the coming week, and the priest of the Mlimo would be conducting a ceremony. Though skeptical of the information, Carrington couldn't afford to dismiss it. He approved the mission under the charge of his gregarious chief of staff, Lieutenant-Colonel Robert Baden-Powell.

Baden-Powell and Burnham had just returned from a three-day scout into the Matopos. "Burnham a most delightful companion on such a trip," wrote Baden-Powell in his book about the uprising, "amusing, interesting, and most instructive. Having seen service against the Red Indians, he brings quite a new experience to bear on the scouting work here. And, while he talks away, there's not a thing escapes his quick roving eye, whether it is on the horizon or at his feet."

Baden-Powell was fascinated by Burnham's expertise at scouting and woodcraft, and he picked the American's brain. After stints in India and Zululand, Baden-Powell had become convinced that scouts were crucial to military success, yet they were largely disregarded by Britain's military establishment, as was woodcraft. He also worried, like many Victorians, that the urbanization of Britain was eroding masculine values and skills learned through an outdoor life: self-sufficiency, resourcefulness, knowledge of nature, physical and mental toughness—skills also needed by the military scout. Baden-Powell wanted to preserve these things, and he had vague ideas about teaching them to boys. He mentioned this notion to Burnham, who enthusiastically endorsed it.

Baden-Powell had arrived in Rhodesia wearing the British officer's pith helmet and red blazer, invitations to enemy marksmen. He soon adopted Burnham's distinctive stiff-brimmed brown Stetson and neckerchief, which would become emblems of Baden-Powell's creation, the Boy Scouts. (In 1911, Burnham's brother Howard wrote about watching the newly-crowned King George V review 30,000 Boy Scouts: "it made me feel quite queer to see your hat on every one of those boys' heads and I recalled the one you took to Rhodesia which introduced the idea to B.P. and is now transmitted to these 30,000 boys.") Baden-Powell's motto for the Boy Scouts also may have been inspired by Burnham: "Be Prepared." Though the two men spent only a month together in Rhodesia, they became lifelong friends and correspondents.

The day after the meeting about the Mlimo's cave, Baden-Powell got scratched from the mission. General Carrington needed him to check into the movements of Ndebele regiments near Bembezi. The general told Burnham and Armstrong that he wouldn't order them to go because it was too risky. Both men immediately volunteered. Carrington gave them their final instructions: "Capture the M'Limo if you can. Kill him if you must. Do not let him escape."

"There was small need for that last injunction," wrote Burnham in *Scouting on Two Continents*. "Constantly before my enraged vision rose the picture of my wife vainly holding to her breast our dying Nada." He went to say goodbye to Blanche. Neither of them expected him to return, yet she didn't ask him not to go, knowing it would be futile.

On June 20 he left for Mangwe with Armstrong. "The blackness into which I rode was no darker than the thoughts that ebbed and flowed through my mind during that night . . . Many gruesome pictures of tragedies to settlers at the hands of the natives rose before me. . . . And now, by a strange turn of fate, I was setting out in the hope that I might meet the artist who had inspired all those horrors."

The next night they left Mangwe on a preliminary scout. Using the Zulu's description, they failed to find the mountain with the cave. They tried again in daylight. The landscape mixed high granite kopjes, mesas, and flatlands covered with scrub trees, thorn bushes, and tall grass, all of it laced with trails. They proceeded slowly. Armstrong held the horses in a thicket or in tall grass while Burnham looked for a route to the next hiding place. Then he returned for Armstrong and the horses, and they repeated the procedure. They screened themselves with branches or bunches of grass as they moved through different terrains, and brushed out their tracks when crossing a trail.

Finally they saw it, swelling from the countryside like a blister: a huge oblong dome of dark granite, 600 or 700 feet high and perhaps three-quarters of a mile long. Most of it was naked stone, though big boulders littered a few places, and grasses and scrub sprouted from crevices. After more slow progress, they found the cave's entrance about halfway up the mountain, hidden amidst a jumble of boulders and brush. At the mountain's base, a ceremonial space had been flattened by thousands of dancing feet. Beyond that stood a hundred thatched huts. To get into the cave undetected while the priest was there seemed impossible.

That night they met with the Zulu informant outside Mangwe; he didn't want to be seen talking to whites. Armstrong had been born and raised in Zululand, and knew the people and the language. In Burnham's opinion, Armstrong "could extract more truth from a native than any man I ever knew." The Zulu said the Mlimo's priest was performing a ceremony the next afternoon to immunize a regiment of warriors against the settlers' bullets. Beforehand, the priest would speak with the god in the cave, which only he was allowed to enter.

If the Zulu was correct and telling the truth, Burnham and Armstrong needed to be inside the cave when the priest arrived, to make sure they got the right man. They planned to kill him there and thus undermine two of his claims—that he could turn bullets into water and that anyone except the priest who entered the temple would be struck dead.

On June 23 they left Mangwe before dawn. They retraced the route scouted the day before, using the same cautions. They hid the horses in high grass as close to the mountain as possible, and tied the animals' heads high to eliminate jingling harnesses. Camouflaged with grass to break up their profiles, they crept up the mountain. A breeze stirred the vegetation, helping to disguise their movements. They were often in full view of goatherds and women carrying vessels of beer to the huts for the upcoming feast. After two hours, they slipped into the cave and hid in its cool shadows.

Burnham at age 20 in Arizona.

Burnham's revolver, a Remington Model 1875, caliber .44-40, with grips made of hippo ivory. Used in Arizona, southern Africa, East Africa, and Mexico. *(Courtesy of the Burnham family.)*

Burnham with scouts during the First Matabele War, 1893. Burnham is
kneeling, second from the right, with Robert Bain to his right and
Pete Ingram standing at far left.

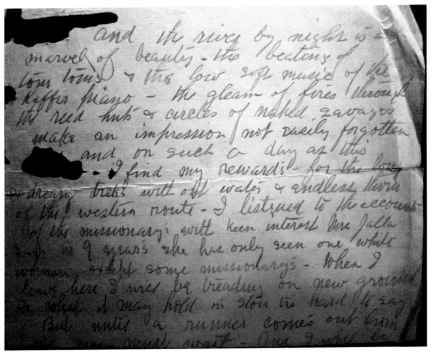

Note from Burnham to Blanche written during the Zambezi expedition of 1895.
(Frederick Russell Burnham Papers (MS 115), Manuscripts and Archives, Yale University
Library. Courtesy of the Burnham family.)

Blanche Blick Burnham in
Bulawayo in 1896.

Bulawayo in laager, 1896.
(From the collection of Rob Burrett, used with permission.)

Fort Mangwe, 1896.
(From the collection of Rob Burrett, used with permission.)

Illustration from *The Graphic*, a London newspaper, of Burnham and Armstrong
escaping after killing the Mlimo. *(Courtesy of the Burnham family.)*

Burnham in 1900,
prior to leaving London
for the Boer War.

Skagway, 1897.
(University of Washington Libraries, Special Collections, Hegg 36.)

Burnham in late 1901 after
receiving the DSO.

Sketch by Roderick Burnham of the Burnhams'
houses in the Hollywood Hills. Frederick's is on the right.
*(Frederick Russell Burnham Papers (MS 115), Manuscripts and Archives,
Yale University Library. Courtesy of the Burnham family.)*

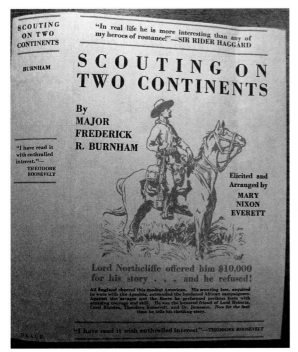

Dust cover of *Scouting on Two Continents* (1934 edition), with sketch of Burnham done by Robert Baden-Powell during the Second Matabele War. *(Frederick Russell Burnham Papers (MS 115), Manuscripts and Archives, Yale University Library. Courtesy of the Burnham family.)*

Burnham and Blanche at La Cuesta, their California ranch near Sequoia National Park, c. 1920. *(Courtesy of the Burnham family.)*

Burnham in 1941 on his 80th birthday, with Boy Scouts
in Carlsbad Caverns, New Mexico.

Burnham family gravesite in Three Rivers, California.
(Photo by Steve Kemper.)

Some time later they saw a man walking up the crooked path toward the cave, stopping occasionally to dance and pray. Burnham was surprised to see that he wasn't an Ndebele but a Makalaga, a tribe indigenous to Matabeleland long before the arrival of the conquering Ndebeles. The man was about sixty years old but vigorous, with short white hair and skin more mahogany than black. He wore none of the animal skins and charms typical of a witch doctor.

He stepped into the mouth of the cave. "Here was the author of all our woes," wrote Burnham of this moment. "Because of him, my little daughter was dead and the bones of hundreds of brave men and good women were scattered on the veldt by hyenas." Armstrong's information had gotten them there, so Burnham offered the young native commissioner the honor of killing the Mlimo's high priest. "You do it," whispered Armstrong. Burnham raised his Lee–Metford rifle and put a .303 bullet under the man's heart.

The cave amplified the shot, which boomed down the mountain. Some startled Ndebeles began running away. Burnham later learned that this strong amplification was key to the high priest's power—the cave turned his pronouncements into the thunderous voice of the god.

Burnham and Armstrong fled down the mountain toward their horses. The main obstacle to escape was the regiment of warriors awaiting the ceremony, half a mile away. To create confusion and a smokescreen, Burnham and Armstrong set fire to some huts. Within minutes the Ndebeles recovered from their shock and gave chase. For two hours, according to Burnham in *Scouting on Two Continents*, they "had a long hard ride and a running fight over rough ground" before crossing the Shashani River.

—•—

The news that the man called the Mlimo had been killed by the American scout Burnham flashed through Rhodesia and eventually around the world. Burnham wrote a report for Lord Grey on June 26. Most of the colony's leaders and settlers, including Burnham, assumed that the assassination would cripple the rebellion. On June 27 the *Bulawayo Chronicle* noted, "If the right one be killed it should go far to damp the spirit of the natives, for it was this gentleman who was at the bottom of the rebellion, and who led the natives on by promising them the most wonderful things . . ."

But doubts quickly surfaced, mostly about whether Burnham had killed the right man. Did the chief prophet of the Mlimo really live at Njelele, in a district where the natives had not revolted? Wouldn't the chief prophet be protected by many regiments?

In the first week of July, Sir Richard Martin, deputy commissioner of South Africa, was dispatched to make inquiries for the government. Rhodes was in disgrace because of the Jameson Raid, and Martin wasn't averse to further embarrassing the British South Africa Company. Lord Grey asked Burnham to submit a more detailed report, which he did on July 8. A number of settlers who had lived in the Mangwe area for many years—among them Commander Van Rooyen, Hans Lee, and a missionary named Father Prestage who lived among the natives of the district—confirmed to Deputy Commissioner Martin that they as well as natives in the area believed that the man killed in the cave at Njelele was the oracle of the Mlimo. A native named Banko also corroborated this and added that he should know, since the dead man was his brother, Jobani. Martin concluded that Burnham had indeed shot the chief prophet of the Mlimo.

The British South Africa Company awarded Burnham a gold watch but ignored Armstrong, perhaps because he had thorny relations with the administration over several matters. Moody and headstrong, Armstrong also had ignored the chain of command when reporting his information about the Mlimo, bypassing the chief native commissioner, Herbert J. Taylor, due to mutual dislike. Worse, he had gone to Bulawayo despite Taylor's specific order to stay in Mangwe. Taylor's enmity would cost Armstrong, and Burnham as well.

Meanwhile, doubts about the Mlimo incident persisted. That offended Armstrong, who insisted on another thorough investigation. The BSAC appointed Judge Watermeyer, who spent several months collecting testimony and evidence. Watermeyer's report has been lost, but it evidently confirmed the official story, since neither Lord Grey, General Carrington, nor any other official ever suggested otherwise by word or action, nor were Burnham and Armstrong censured or reprimanded. If the report had suggested that the two men duped Lord Grey and Carrington, it's doubtful that Burnham and Lord Grey would have remained lifelong friends, and even more doubtful that a few years later Carrington would have recommended Burnham to Lord Roberts as Chief of Scouts for the Boer War. Further, after Watermeyer's inquiry, the BSAC finally sent Armstrong a gold watch, which implies exoneration—though Armstrong returned it, probably piqued by its lateness. But doubts about the episode never died and led to accusations that Burnham and Armstrong had concocted a hoax. (See appendix.)

Eleven days after the assassination of the Mlimo's oracle, the Bulawayo Field Force was disbanded because of the arrival of the Matabele Relief Force. Some men joined other companies, some packed it in. Selous departed for England to write *Sunshine and Storm in Rhodesia*. Burnham also had plans. A week after the disbandment, on July 11, he and Blanche left Rhodesia for Britain and Pasadena. Burnham's Rhodesian critics sometimes suggest that he was running away, an accusation they never aim at their hero Selous. But family letters make clear that Burnham considered the trip a hiatus and still expected to settle permanently in Rhodesia.

The Burnhams went home because Blanche needed to get away from the place that had killed her daughter and constantly threatened to make her a widow. She needed to embrace her remaining child and see her mother. In a letter announcing their surprise visit, Blanche regretted that they couldn't bring their "African lily," and added, "Sometimes I just *hate* the country but I must not let myself do that for Fred's sake." That Burnham agreed to leave Rhodesia during wartime suggests how worried he was about her.

They arrived in London on August 16, spent a few days there, then continued to New York and on west. When they got to Pasadena in October, they had been away for three years and ten months. On November 15 the *San Francisco Chronicle* ran a page one story about the Burnhams and *The Wizard*, Rider Haggard's new book dedicated to Nada. (He dedicated two other books to her as well: *Elissa: The Doom of Zimbabwe*, and *Black Heart and White Heart: A Zulu Idyll*. All carry the same dedication: "To the memory of the child Nada Burnham, 'who bound all to her' and, while her father cut his way through the hordes of the Ingobo Regiment, perished of the hardships of war at Bulawayo on 19th May, 1896, I dedicate these tales—and more particularly the last, that of a Faith which triumphed over savagery and death.") The article noted that the Burnhams had returned to Pasadena "partly with the hope that the change of scene would benefit Mrs. Burnham who is heart-broken over her little daughter's tragic death. The family expects to return to south Africa next January." This is confirmed by a letter Burnham wrote to Blanche while away on a business trip during this time. He mentioned his hopes of striking some deals when they returned to London, and then added, "For I tell you B. life is getting more and more worthless and ere long will not be worth living at all. You and Africa are still my Gods and none can step between."

——

In Rhodesia, during the month after Burnham killed the Mlimo's priest, the war intensified. Major battles in the Mambo Hills and in the Matopos proved that the Ndebeles remained fierce and determined. About 10,000 of them were hiding in the rugged kopjes and labyrinthine caves of the Matapos. General Carrington foresaw a lengthy war of attrition there. To the east, the Shona rebellion had opened another front. Carrington told Rhodes he would need 2,500 more imperial troops, 2,000 more carriers, teams of engineers to blast the natives from their caves, and more artillery. Such an expansion also would require thousands more horses, mules, and oxen, plus food for men and animals, not to mention rifles, ammunition, tents, blankets, and other necessities of war.

The tab for all this would fall on the British South Africa Company as a condition of its charter. The company was already reeling from expenditures caused by the Jameson Raid and the Ndebele uprising. A long war on two fronts would bankrupt the BSAC and also install thousands of British troops in Rhodesia, increasing the imperial government's control over the territory. But refusing the troops would prolong hostilities and endanger the settlers, who were demanding protection.

To Rhodes, all these choices were bad. In a burst of genius and courage, he conceived another possibility: he would try to end the war by talking directly to the indunas. He knew the tactic would anger the British government—he had no authority to negotiate—and also the settlers, who wanted the Ndebeles punished if not exterminated. But Rhodes saw that if he succeeded, he would end the bloodshed, save the BSAC, and preserve the company's control over Rhodesia. He suspected that the Ndebeles were tired of fighting and hiding, and probably were hungry since so many of their granaries had been destroyed.

He approached the indunas through intermediaries. The chiefs agreed to talk if he came into the Matopos with no more than half a dozen men, unarmed. Too dangerous, warned his associates, probably an ambush. Rhodes hadn't become one of the world's wealthiest men by ducking big risks. On the afternoon of August 21, 1896, he rode into the hills with several interpreters, white and black, and also, shrewdly, a journalist named Vere Stent who had been critical of the BSAC. Most of Rhodes's associates didn't expect him to return. As the group reached the designated place, the kopjes above them filled with Ndebele warriors. Rhodes's companions didn't want to dismount, wrote Stent in his account, but Rhodes insisted, as a sign of trust. He sat down on the remains of a giant anthill, a natural throne. The indunas appeared. "Yes, yes, there they are," said Rhodes with a huge smile. "This is one of those moments in life that make it worth living."

The indunas gave Rhodes an earful. Somabhulana, the Ndebele spokesman, detailed many grievances: how the native policemen violated Ndebele
girls and insulted elders, how the white policemen brutalized Ndebeles and
took their cattle, how a native commissioner had stopped a wedding ceremony and claimed first rights to the bride. These injuries seemed to surprise
and disturb Rhodes. But still, he asked, why had the Ndebeles killed and
violated white women and children? The white tax collectors had started it,
replied Somabhulana, by murdering four Ndebele women who wouldn't
reveal their hidden cattle. Johan Colenbrander, one of the interpreters, confirmed the incident. "You came, you conquered," said Somabhulana. "The
strongest takes the land. We accepted your rule. We lived under you. But not
as dogs! If we are to be dogs it is better to be dead."

Rhodes was moved. He promised to abolish the native police force,
reform the administration, and investigate the seizure of cattle. To avert
starvation among the Ndebeles, he pledged to send loads of mealies (corn).
He also promised the chiefs that if they made peace, they would not be
punished. The indaba lasted four hours. Rhodes was elated that peace
seemed at hand.

When the British deputy commissioner, Sir Richard Martin (the same
man who had looked into the Mlimo episode), heard about the indaba, he
was furious at Rhodes's usurpation of his authority. Rhodes asked him to
the second indaba on August 28, but Martin insisted on bringing an armed
escort and was disinvited. Martin wanted unconditional surrender and
criminal trials. Colonial Secretary Chamberlain told him that the government couldn't afford to appear more punitive than the BSAC. He instructed
Martin to offer advice but to let Rhodes negotiate.

On September 21, after two more indabas, most Ndebeles surrendered.
Rhodes kept his promises, for a while. He disbanded the native police force
and appointed a strong deputy to reform administrative practices. He tried
to stay alert to native concerns by holding more indabas. He realized that it
had been a mistake to disregard the Ndebele leaders after the first war, so
this time he honored their authority by offering some of them salaried posi-

tions as district heads—which incidentally coopted them into the BSAC administration. He also allowed the Ndebele leaders to return to their original landholdings for two years while a permanent solution was designed. Speculators were angered when he ruled that any whites who hadn't yet pegged their allotment of land must wait until the land issue was settled. He also decided to enforce the BSAC's original stipulation that landowners must improve their holdings or lose them.

The reforms were sincere but temporary. When the two-year reprieve for Ndebele landowners expired, they again lost their property. Nor did the BSAC ever repossess and redistribute the huge idle holdings of absentee syndicates and influential London friends—land whose seizure had initially been justified because the natives weren't fully using it.

The settlers watched Rhodes's negotiations and reforms with growing rage. For them the war's cost in blood and grief had been steep. Of the 450 whites killed, more than 80 percent were settlers, as were about 70 percent of the nearly 200 wounded. (At least ten times as many natives died.) About 10 percent of Rhodesia's white population had been wiped out, a substantial loss.

Like the pioneers in Minnesota and Arizona, the settlers in Rhodesia wanted vengeance as much as peace. Instead they watched Rhodes and the BSAC reward the commanders who had brought suffering and death to their families and friends. Like the pioneers in Minnesota and Arizona, they were sure that coddling would bring more atrocities. This resentful fear hardened into the siege-mentality racism that plagued Rhodesia for generations.

Burnham, too, wanted the Ndebeles exterminated, a desire thwarted by Rhodes's policy of appeasement. Years later, in an essay entitled "An American Viewpoint of the Greatness of Cecil John Rhodes," evidently never published, Burnham noted that this was one of many times when, because of Rhodes, "I had to enlarge my view points on important matters."

[The Ndebeles] had attacked us so unjustly and killed our women and children so mercilessly that we, their fathers and neighbors, were

seeing red worse than some of the present nations of Europe. It was
Rhodes who took his life in his hands to save these people by going
unarmed into their bloody power. There is nothing finer in all history. Yet while we foamed and raged at the time he was right and
above all just.

After five months in California, the Burnhams started back for Africa.
During their pause in New York City, a gregarious police commissioner
insisted that Burnham be his guest at the Boone and Crockett Club. Though
only thirty-nine, the commissioner already had considerable reputations as
an author, reformer, and outdoorsman. Born an eastern aristocrat, he had
gone west and turned himself into a tough Dakota rancher. (Early on, he
instructed a cowboy to round up a steer by saying, "Hasten forward quickly
there.") As an appointee to the U.S. Civil Rights Commission he had
chopped away at the spoils system, and as a New York police commissioner
he had waded into the city's deep corruption with a sharp muck rake.

The prospect of meeting this dynamo made Burnham pace up and
down the street beforehand. But Commissioner Theodore Roosevelt was
equally impressed by his guest's reputation and was eager to hear about
African hunting, Frederick Selous, Rhodes and Rhodesia, and the problematic Boers. Burnham thought Rhodes would find a way to prevent war
with them, but Roosevelt said it was inevitable, as was a war between the
United States and Spain over Cuba. The lunch began a lifelong friendship.

By mid-May the Burnhams were back in Africa. They stopped in
Kimberley to see Rhodes, then went on to Bulawayo. The Ndebeles were
peaceful, but the Shonas were still at war in the east and wouldn't surrender until late 1897. The Burnhams began building another house outside of
town. In letters home, Burnham described the fast growth of Bulawayo and
Gwelo. Prospectors were poised to rush north of the Zambezi, he wrote,
and the coming of the railroad later that year would connect Bulawayo to
the outside world and accelerate progress. The war had delayed all this, but

perhaps soon he would realize a fortune from his shares in the rich concessions up north.

Blanche, by contrast, noticed that everything, including food, was scarce and expensive, and that fever had killed many people. Nada's shadow still darkened the place. They had arrived in town on the anniversary of her death. A few days later Blanche wrote to Burnham's mother, "Coming to Bulawayo brought it all back so vividly to my mind. I cannot write more." She already missed Roderick, and since Burnham was soon gone for weeks at a stretch, making up for lost time, loneliness quickly descended.

That autumn, a few weeks before the railroad linked Bulawayo with Cape Town, Burnham was still imagining their future in Rhodesia. "Just think," he wrote to his mother, "when I touched Africa only in 93 Bulawayo was in hands of Loben and only a few white men had ever set foot in the country and in four years we have fought two wars, endured a pestilence, built a city, and hundreds of miles of R.R." Meanwhile, Blanche was writing that she hoped her husband would only be absent a week on his newest trip, because "it is *very lonely* when he is away now that Grace has gone." When Burnham looked at Rhodesia, he saw how much had been achieved and the rewards to come. Blanche, despite her desire to support her husband's dream, saw loss, with loneliness ahead. Something had to give.

In typical fashion, they changed direction abruptly. On January 4, 1898, Burnham bought a prospecting license in Bulawayo. Three weeks later they were headed for California again. En route they stopped in London, where some of the investors in Burnham's African ventures formed a syndicate to fund his newest gamble. As he explained in a letter to his mother, "We have a dose of Klondyke fever and have a strong desire to lose 30 or 40 toes and fingers in the arctic circle."

Even his dream of Africa couldn't withstand gold fever. Blanche was no doubt enthusiastic to leave Bulawayo for the white North. They were joining the gold rush.

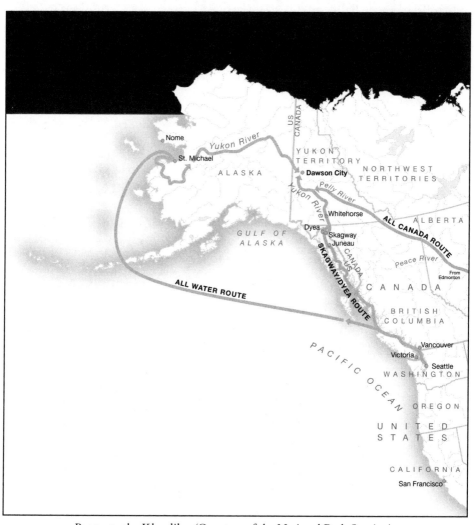

Routes to the Klondike. (Courtesy of the National Park Service.)

CHAPTER EIGHTEEN

THE KLONDIKE

The change wasn't as sudden as it must have seemed to the Burnhams' parents. Gold had been discovered in the Yukon in late summer of 1896, but by the time the ecstatic early prospectors had dug out the first fortunes, the rivers were frozen and no one could leave. The outside world didn't learn about the strike until July 1897, when the new tycoons disembarked in Seattle lugging bags heavy with gold dust and nuggets worth at least $1.14 million.

Their tales of a fabulous strike in the far north set off a worldwide rush. During the next year, about 100,000 stampeders, as they were called, left for the promise of the Yukon. Most of them couldn't tell a mining pan from a pie pan, and were clueless about subzero temperatures. But practicalities withered in the heat of gold fever. Experience wouldn't be necessary in a place where the ground was sprinkled with nuggets. The classifieds filled up with homes and businesses for sale by owners headed north. Women ran ads offering to accompany the men going. A sociologist and advocate for women's rights named Charlotte Smith hatched a scheme to take 4,000 single women out of New England's factories and ship them to a better life as wives in the Yukon. Clairvoyants offered to visualize the location of gold. Other labor-saving devices included an x-ray machine for detecting veins and gophers trained to tunnel through frozen ground.

When news of the strike reached Rhodesia, Pete Ingram caught the fever and took off for the Yukon. Burnham, ever susceptible, soon followed with Blanche and her brothers John and Judd. By the time they got to Pasadena on March 5, 1898, Blanche knew she wouldn't be able to go north with them—she was pregnant. The men left on March 28.

The quickest, easiest, and therefore most expensive way to reach the gold fields was the all-water route from Seattle to St. Michael, at the mouth of the Yukon River, a trip of 3,000 miles. From there, stampeders could hire a smaller boat to go up the Yukon another 1,400 miles to Dawson. In the summer of 1897 the price of a ticket to St. Michael jumped from $150 to $1,000, and scalpers got $1,500. In addition to being expensive, the all-water route was frozen for most of the year.

Most stampeders, including Burnham's group, took a boat 1,200 miles to Dyea or Skagway, mudflat hamlets far up the Lynn Canal in the Alaska panhandle. Hundreds of vessels along the Pacific coast, including some that hadn't been seaworthy for years, began ferrying passengers north. Dyea and Skagway didn't have docks, so boats disgorged thousands of stampeders and their equipment on the shoreline flats. Everyone scrambled to move their kit onto land before high tide.

Beyond their waterfronts, the towns were swarming with enterprise and crime. Before the gold strike, Skagway had been a tiny isolated smudge. In 1897 it sprouted 12,000 tents and a hundred new buildings. By the time Burnham arrived in 1898, it was the biggest town in Alaska, with 15,000 to 20,000 people. Its muddy rutted streets were lined with tents and rickety buildings advertising businesses aimed at stampeders. Saloons and gambling parlors predominated, often nothing more than a big tent with a plank bar and some crude tables for poker. There were brothels, stores, and services for packing and transport. Pawnshops sold the equipment of people who had given up and gone home with broken dreams. Moneylenders offered fresh hope in exchange for exorbitant collateral.

Skagway's lawlessness impressed everyone who arrived. Much of the crime was organized by Jefferson Randolph "Soapy" Smith, whose gang numbered 200. Soapy's men met every boat and helpfully steered newcomers to establishments where they could be bilked or robbed. Soapy's welcoming crew impersonated sweet clergymen, kindly old sourdoughs, and flattering newspaper reporters, who feigned interest in newcomers to learn the size of their poke. The plumpest pigeons became the targets of bunco artists and gamblers who skinned them using poker and three-card monte. Others were directed to bogus packing companies that stole their equipment. People who wanted to wire their relatives because they were homesick or had just been robbed were sent to Soapy's telegraph office, where the operator took their money and tapped out their urgent messages, which never left the room—Skagway didn't have telegraph service. Yet replies always arrived, always sent collect. Soapy reigned for about a year before vigilantes got fed up and shot him in July 1898.

Many stampeders who reached Skagway ran out of money or nerve there, and retreated south. Those who continued from Dyea or Skagway had to slog all their food and equipment over the mountains through Chilkoot Pass or White Pass to the lakes at the Yukon's headwaters. Most stampeders, about 22,000, used Chilkoot. At 3,500 feet, it was 600 feet higher than White Pass, but the route was ten miles shorter and didn't require pack animals, which were rare and expensive.

Because the gold fields were remote and hard to supply, the people who had wintered there the previous year had almost starved, and scurvy was common. (The disease took writer Jack London's health and teeth that winter, but the gold rush gave him the material for *White Fang, The Call of the Wild*, and Klondike stories such as "To Build a Fire.") Consequently, the Canadian government required anyone entering Yukon Territory in 1898 to bring a year's worth of food, about 1,150 pounds. Equipment increased the total weight to nearly a ton per person. It all had to be carried, pulled, or pushed over the mountains. This was done over several weeks in about thirty slow trips, sixty-five pounds at a time, single file in heavy traffic.

From a distance, the stampeders looked like an unbroken line of black ants toiling up a white slope. Avalanches sometimes washed out part of the line.

Burnham's group, all accomplished horsemen, took pack animals forty-five miles over White Pass. Some men who had money but no experience with pack animals also took this route. The trail sometimes narrowed to two feet wide. Poorly packed horses bumped the cliff wall and tumbled onto the rocks below. The narrowness caused bottlenecks and long pauses during which thoughtless men left their horses standing, fully loaded. Many collapsed from exhaustion or from sores rubbed by excessive or imbalanced loads. In spring and summer, overburdened horses sank up to their tails in the route's bogs, and no amount of whipping could budge them. The living walked across dead and dying horses, whose bones littered the entire route, most notoriously at Dead Horse Gulch. The Northwest Mounted Police estimated that White Pass became a graveyard for at least 3,000 horses and mules during the rush. Burnham, meticulous about his mounts, must have been disgusted.

At the end of the route stood a cabin where Mounties made sure incomers were hauling a year's rations. They also collected customs fees on anything bought in the United States. A few miles later, the routes from Chilkoot and White merged at the headwater lakes of the Yukon River. When Burnham's party got there around May 20, tents were strung for sixty miles along Lakes Lindemann, Bennett, and Tagish.

More than 30,000 stampeders were waiting for the ice to break. The forests near the lakes had been turned to stubble, partly for fuel. All along the lakes, men were pushing and pulling whipsaws through green timber, sawing boards to build boats to carry them 500 miles north, down the lakes to the river that led to Dawson. Burnham and the Blicks built their vessel from cedar boards hauled from Seattle, then caulked the seams with oakum and pitch. They parked it with the fleet along the shore, also jammed with mountains of goods. Awaiting the thaw, stampeders could visit tents offering whiskey, poker, haircuts, hot baths, fresh bread, and religion.

The Spanish–American War had broken out while Burnham was en route. An invitation to join Theodore Roosevelt's Rough Riders reached him and gave him a touch of war fever. But at Lake Bennett, with the ice about to melt, gold fever was stronger.

On May 29 the rotting ice cracked and began to move. Eight hundred boats of all descriptions, including Burnham's, were launched into the floes. The race was on. Boats made of green spruce boards had been shrinking during the wait and immediately leaked. Boatmen rowed, poled, and hoisted homemade sails made of blankets or clothing. Two women caught the wind by sewing together their voluminous undergarments and stringing them between two oars.

Within two days the ice was gone and so were all 7,100 boats, rushing north. Every boat carried prospectors, though many had no intention of touching a pickaxe. Two boats carried disassembled printing presses that would soon publish the rival *Klondike Nugget* and *Midnight Sun*. One carried a disassembled piano destined for a music hall. Others were loaded with eggs, live chickens, candy, lemons, tinned milk, and a dairy cow (the owner would soon be selling fresh milk for $30 a gallon). One man was hauling a load of cats and kittens; he later sold them to lonely miners for an ounce of gold each. Others boats were filled with gamblers, sharpers, entertainers, prostitutes, lawyers, merchants, and speculators who planned to excavate their bonanzas from the credulous and the newly flush.

Boats got jammed in floes, swamped by rough water, splintered by rocks. Those that made it through the boulder-strewn torrents of Miles Canyon and White Horse Rapids washed up in Dawson, a boomtown erected on top of a bog. To make room for the stampeders, the Canadian government had pushed the nearby Hän people downstream into a reserve. In 1896 Dawson's population had been 500. Two years later it was somewhere between 30,000 and 40,000. Those who had arrived before the rush called themselves sourdoughs. Newcomers like Burnham were cheechakos. The hill overlooking Dawson turned white with tents. Others lived on their boats, nosed together along the shore for more than a mile.

—·—

Burnham and the Blicks were among the first of thousands to arrive that June. The town was so starved for news that when Burnham gave the gold commissioner an old copy of the *Seattle Post-Intelligencer*, he read it out loud to a crowd, even the ads. Some of the arriving cheechakos knew the town was ravenous for outside goods and would pay almost anything for eggs, fruit, and other luxuries. "In the brief space of a few days," wrote reporter Tappan Adley in his lively firsthand account, *The Klondike Stampede* (1900), "there seemed to be nothing that could not be purchased in Dawson, from fresh grapes to an opera-glass, from a safety-pin to an ice-cream freezer."

Dawson also had been preparing for the rush of stampeders. "At Dawson buildings of every description sprang up like mushrooms in a night, from the black, reeking bog," wrote Adley. "Many of them were substantial logs and lumber, but the greater part, both large and small, were mere coverings, intended to last only through the summer."

Of the 100,000 stampeders who had started for the Yukon after the news broke in July 1897, about 30,000 raced into Dawson the following summer. Most were shocked by what they found. In a place saturated with gold but lacking almost everything else, prices were stratospheric. Newcomers hoping to open a store or business faced costs of between $10,000 and $20,000 for a lot in town. That lot probably faced an unpaved street turned into knee-deep muck by the spring thaw. Dawson was built on a bog and didn't have sewers, so the lowest parts of town flooded in spring, leaving behind the waste of thousands of people and more thousands of sled dogs. This effluent often ended up in the creeks and rivers, which led that summer to epidemics of dysentery and typhoid. Men rubbed clay on their faces to reduce torments from clouds of mosquitoes and biting flies. The mosquitoes caused malaria, though people didn't yet understand the connection.

Burnham had seen it all before. The place was another boomtown—

half-built, half-crazy, electric with dreams, hazardous with sharks. On the main streets, saloons, dance halls, and gambling houses stood shoulder to shoulder. Some were simple tents, with a bar of rough boards and whiskey to match. A few finer establishments had wooden walls and charged admission, fifty cents or a dollar, which entitled the customer to one drink or one cigar.

Burnham knew one of Dawson's most striking entrepreneurs, Belinda Mulrooney. She had arrived in 1897 and quickly opened a restaurant, then a roadhouse in the gold fields. In the summer of 1898 she opened the town's swankiest hotel, the Fairview, offering thirty rooms with carpeting, wallpaper, lace curtains, and electricity.

Mulrooney aside, many of Dawson's women earned their money in the usual boomtown professions, from entertainers to high-priced courtesans to crib hookers. Some of their pungent names survive: Spanish Dolores, Limejuice Lil, Diamond-Tooth Gertie. Somewhere in between were the hostesses and dance hall tootsies, who made about $120 a week, with bonuses for persuading customers to buy champagne at $60 a bottle. All were experts at trimming a flush miner or gambler. Some wore belts made of gold nuggets—tips from their admirers. Bar tabs were paid in pinches of gold dust. Barmen kept their hands moist and their fingernails long, and after extracting payment from a miner's poke ran their hands through their hair, which could be washed out and panned later. They also were adroit at spilling a few flakes on or behind the bar, a dividend they could wipe up.

Despite being awash in alcohol and vice, Dawson stayed peaceable, unlike Skagway. The difference was the presence of the Canadian Mounties under their exacting superintendent, Colonel Sam Steele. Steele let the town run rough, but within tolerable channels. "You could do anything except destroy life or property," wrote Burnham. ". . . Like Rhodesia, it was a land of the greatest personal liberty, yet the strictest observance of law." Saloons and other pleasure palaces were required to close at midnight on

Saturday and stay closed until 12:01 a.m. Monday morning. Sunday labor of any kind was banned. Anyone caught lifting a finger paid a fine or was sentenced to chop firewood for the Mounties. During the frenzied year of 1898, when Dawson's population swelled to 30,000 and some tents held sacks of gold, there wasn't a single murder and thievery was rare.

The worst shock for the newcomers that summer was that they had arrived too late. Land along the best gold creeks—Bonanza, Eldorado, Hunker, and Dominion—had been claimed by the first prospectors of 1896 and by the handful who made it to the Yukon before the freeze in 1897. Well-capitalized cheechakos such as Burnham could buy options on some of these claims, and he immediately spent about $50,000 on several plots along Eldorado Creek.

But most newcomers had sunk everything they had into reaching Dawson. They dreamed of gathering gold nuggets like shelled corn, and instead faced high expenses for everything, including the costs of digging and operating a claim. Some, disheartened, sold their equipment and turned around for home. Others began probing unproven creeks. Every rumor and stray nugget set off a small stampede. Some men gave up their own dreams to work at rich claims for the going rate of $15 per day, paid in gold.

After the best creeks were pegged out, a few miners started sinking test shafts in the hillsides, or benches, above the gold creeks. People laughed at these fools until their theory paid off. They were looking for old streambeds, indicated by a stratum of white gravel. If they found it, they started digging, because that's where geology deposited Klondike gold. Some of these "bench claims" turned into bonanzas, particularly around Gold Hill, Cheechako Hill, and French Hill.

The Klondike was laced with thick veins of gold, but they were hard to find and hard to mine. Even during the brief summer, anything more than six feet below the surface was locked in permafrost. Prospectors solved this by building a fire in the shaft and hauling out the thawed earth, again and again, summer and winter, down to the bedrock at anywhere from five to twenty-five feet deep. On the positive side, the permafrost saved them the labor of shoring up the shafts. In the cold months, pay dirt couldn't be processed because it immediately froze at the surface, so a massive gravel dump accumulated at the mouth of every mine, awaiting the spring thaw.

When the creeks began running and the dumps softened, miners shunted water down a flume into a cascade of sluice boxes that separated out the heavier gold. On the hillside benches, which usually lacked running water, miners divided dirt from gold by using rockers, which resembled a baby's cradle with a sieved bottom, or with long toms, a bigger version of a rocker. "All day long," wrote Tappan Adley, "was heard the *swish, swish* of hundreds of rockers." And much of the night as well, since people stayed up with the sun, twenty hours a day.

With the last $50,000 of his syndicate's capital, Burnham bought a "proved" bench claim on French Hill that had yielded $32,000 in thirty-seven days. He and his partners dug laterals and found more white gravel. In the next month they washed out nuggets and dust worth about $29,000.

On July 12, after just five weeks in Dawson, Burnham and a partner named Burke left for London to report to the syndicate. Judd and John Blick stayed to dig the claims. Burnham and Burke were carrying 104 pounds of gold, including one twelve-ounce nugget. It was the first Klondike gold to reach England. Burnham told Lord Gifford, the head of the syndicate, that the Klondike was the richest gold field he had ever seen. He was confident he could make money there for the investors. But to capture real wealth, he recommended that they capitalize a bigger company and bring in hydraulic dredgers to scour the creek bottoms.

Gifford was intrigued, but it was a dicey, expensive proposition in a remote wilderness. Gifford arranged for Burnham to make his pitch to the Rothschilds, the London banking family that had funded, among other projects, Rhodes's British South Africa Company. Spilled on the bankers' table, the Klondike gold was an impressive sight. The Rothschilds looked, listened, and a few days later declined: too risky. Once again Burnham felt a fortune slipping from his hands. In less than two years a railway from Skagway to Whitehorse would ease the transport of heavy equipment, and most Klondike gold would be processed through hydraulic dredging and steam machines.

In October, before returning to the Yukon, Burnham stopped in Pasadena. Blanche presented him with his new son Bruce, born on September 5. In a story about Burnham's Yukon experiences, the *Los Angeles Evening Express* reported that his interests in Rhodesia were "still considerable," and he planned to return there after the Klondike played out.

When Burnham went north again in early December, Blanche accompanied him to Skagway, probably to get a look at their newest possible home. She expected to see him off to Dawson and return to Pasadena, but when they boarded the boat in Tacoma Burnham was ill, and by the time they reached Skagway four or five days later, he was almost debilitated. The cause wasn't clear, but the symptoms were weakness, swelling, and extreme fatigue. A doctor in Skagway promised to cure him if he stayed in bed for ten days. "Lying in bed is no easy task for a man of Fred's disposition," wrote Blanche in a letter home, explaining why she had already been gone for three weeks.

Skagway suited her. She liked the way the mountains came right down to the sea, and their majesty when winter sunlight washed them from ten o'clock to two o'clock before darkness fell again. She didn't even mind the four big sled dogs chained next door, whose howling kept them "well supplied with music."

But she was anxious to return to baby Bruce. As soon as Burnham could get up, she went home. He stayed in Skagway impatiently recuperating so he could sled the 500-mile winter trail to Dawson. On January 10, 1899, he wrote to Blanche from the Golden North Hotel that the temperature in Skagway was three below zero and the town was paralyzed by a heavy blizzard that dimmed the weak sun. No mail had come in or gone out for a week. Still ailing, he missed Blanche intensely, and didn't expect to see her again until summer. The miserable darkness matched his state of mind and triggered an atypical letter full of agonized doubt, love, and clumsy syntax:

> It seems an age already since I last held you in my arms. What in the world it will seem six months hence I don't know. . . . I am getting better but very slowly and sometimes feel blue. I have such a dread of physical breakdown. I fear the Klondike will not turn out well so I will lose my money and my strength. But the worst bridge I cross is that with the physical break will give way that iron will and determination and in its place a soft and vacillating nature will rule and if it does with the violent evils and passions with which I am loaded, I will surely do something that you will despise so the end of all will be— sans money sans strength of body and mind—and worst of all sans your love—and high respect—pity will not take its place nor love of former perfections. The memory of every day from the time you arrived in Tacoma to the day you sailed on the Cottage City will be with me til I die.
>
> In fact that is what made me build the third bridge because such perfect confidence and love can not last forever according to everything taught or read so I have figured how it would be destroyed . . . [by] some act of my own which after all is the only way deep sorrow can ever come. The evils done us hurt but soon heal it is the evils we do that make open wounds for ever. . . . I send Roderick a long letter. I hope he will understand the spirit in which it is written for I do not confess sins to many and never without deep purpose and reason. Tis generally best to bury them deeply.
>
> Yours with love forever, Fred

This was the nadir. Five days later he estimated that within two weeks he would be fit enough to start for Dawson. His optimism was returning with his energy. His money-making instincts were sparking as well. He started looking for real estate bargains in Skagway because the place "seems to be on the boom." He bought a log cabin, ten feet by fourteen, for $225. He expected it to be worth $1,000 to $2,000 within five years, and meanwhile it was renting for $10 a month. He registered it in Blanche's name in case he didn't make it to Dawson. "I want you all the time," he wrote to her, "and want this to be my last long absence." He was worried about his investments in the gold fields: "I hope French Hill will not play me false."

To work himself back into shape, he took long walks through the snow on successive days: ten miles, then fifteen, then twenty. He bought a small sled and two St. Bernards to pull it. He made moccasins for the dogs' paws, to prevent ice balls from forming between their pads and laming them. He bought fur robes, a light silk tent, and rice and bacon for himself and the dogs. He left on January 29.

———

Deep snows and subzero temperatures made the 500-mile trip from Skagway to Dawson grueling and dangerous. Because of the gold strike, crude roadhouses had sprung up along part of the route, offering occasional relief. Burnham used his own bedding in the roadhouses to avoid infestation with lice or bedbugs, but knew he was only delaying the inevitable, "as there are some awful dirty brutes come along once in a while and one such can infect every bunk house along the line." The cleanest place he stayed was on the marge of Lake Laberge, at a hotel owned by an Indian who served him on solid silver and then tootled church music on a harmonica.

Whenever Burnham passed a musher headed in the opposite direction, they exchanged packets of letters to be passed along. Burnham's letters told Blanche that he dreamed of her every night. "And every mile I travel inland I shall register a fresh vow never to leave you for so long again," he wrote, "if you will just be to me as during the last month we were together. Tis better than gold and may be better than war."

He was traveling in temperatures 25 degrees below zero but was appropriately dressed and hardly felt the cold, except on his partially exposed face. Cheechakos naively grew beards for warmth; sourdoughs stayed clean-shaven, because beards were magnets for frost, which also accumulated on eyebrows and eyelashes. Dog-freighters knew it was time to take shelter when the bottle of mercury tied to their sled froze solid, a sign the temperature was at least 40 below.

Aside from a lame knee, he was getting stronger, but remained cautious. At Whitehorse Rapids the snow was piling up so fast that he laid over a day to wait for some other musher to break trail, perhaps someone with a team of malamutes. "They look like great hairy hyenas, sullen and fierce," wrote Burnham, "but they run all day—and fight all night." Malamutes could cover the trip to Dawson in twelve days, half the time he expected to need. Still, he was pleased with his St. Bernards. He began averaging more than thirty miles a day in the faint winter light, which disappeared at three o'clock. Twenty-four days after leaving Skagway, he sledded into Dawson.

A couple of his claims were worthless. The others weren't jackpots either—the gold was too patchy, but patches added up. Judd Blick had taken out one pan of pay dirt worth $300. Burnham also had hopes for the Hunker Creek claim, since the prospectors just above them had struck good color. Burnham's group was finding just enough gold to ease his mind about the syndicate's investors.

Burnham was living with the Blicks above Eldorado Creek in a place they called Camp Content, about seventeen miles south of Dawson. Their two-room log cabin stood among fifty others. It had two stoves ventilated by pipes through the roof. The men had splurged on the luxury of a four-paned window, despite the outrageous price of nine dollars. Because glass was so expensive, many cabins let in light through stacked clear bottles or white flour sacks. Candles and lamp oil were pricey, too, so most cabins were lit by a "bitch," made by sticking a wick into a can of bacon grease. The platform beds consisted of spruce-bough mattresses, heavy blankets or fur robes, and pillows made by stuffing clothes into flour sacks.

The drawback of a cozy, well-chinked cabin was heavy condensation, which rose and formed thick ice on the ceiling. This dripped off every morning when the stove got stoked, keeping everything damp. Icicles, inside and out, were handy to make drinking water, which had to be melted from snow or ice. Most meals featured coffee, bacon, boiled beans, and pancakes or bread. "Bacon we chopped off with an axe," wrote Tappan Adley, "salt was as hard as a grindstone, and the ice rang like flint-glass."

It was a harsh place in winter, but not without moments of beauty. "It is a great sight," wrote Burnham to Blanche, "to look down Eldorado Creek and see a thousand fires keeping a blue cloud ever suspended over the tiers and tiers of mines and cabins. It seems warm and cheerful compared to a blizzard on the stretches of the great lonesome river. Little white snakes glide over the frozen snow, legions of them. They twine about your feet and hide there, their scales are minute crystals that make a hissing, crinkling sound."

By the summer of 1899 Dawson had fine hotels and restaurants, movie theaters, two banks, three hospitals, electricity, steam heat, and other civilized amenities. But the town was a hothouse bloom that quickly withered. The previous winter there had been a big new strike near Nome, Alaska. During the summer of 1899, thousands of people had stampeded out of Dawson, deserting the new for the newer. By 1902 Dawson's population had dwindled to 5,000, and by 1920 to less than 1,000. But during those three glittering years, 1897 to 1899, miners dug at least $29 million worth of gold from the Klondike.

—•—

In early July 1899 Burnham was back in Skagway, where he got a surprising letter from Lord Gifford, dated April 28. Gifford was a principal in the Klondike syndicate and was also a director of the Northern Territories (B.S.A.) Exploring Company (NTE), for whom Burnham and Ingram had taken the exploratory trip north of the Zambezi that had nearly killed them. They had pegged miles of gold and coal, and Burnham also brought back evidence of an extensive copper field that he strongly recommended should be further explored. In the normal colonial way of things, the NTE would have used Burnham's report to raise capital and build a railroad so these riches could be exploited. Burnham would have become wealthy from his shares. Those possibilities got squashed, first by the uproar over the Jameson Raid and then by the Second Matabele War. The value of south African stocks sank, as did the possibility of raising capital.

Now Lord Gifford had written to Burnham to say that another expedition had confirmed his report of vast copper deposits near the Kafue River. These were so promising that the company was changing its focus and even its name, to the Northern Copper (B.S.A.) Company. Burnham felt gratified that the investors' faith in him might finally pay off. Even better, reports about the copper field had raised the value of the company's stock. Gifford, following Burnham's standing instructions, had sold 3,500 of the American's shares. The profit came to about $15,000. This windfall energized Burnham. He wrote to Blanche that they no longer had to be apart so much, and told her to pack for Skagway.

Over the next five days he was an entrepreneurial whirlwind. He rented a four-room frame house for his family. He bought a 200-foot waterfall to drive the hydroelectric plant he intended to build to sell power to the growing town. In between these transactions he hustled around the region to examine promising quartz reefs, often a sign of gold, and he bought a 25 percent interest in six of them. He also had his eye on the telephone company and was about to buy several lots on the best streets for $300 each. Blanche's hard-luck sister Madge, recovering from a bad marriage, had been helping Burnham and her brothers in Dawson, and had come to Skagway with Burnham. To give her a chance at financial independence, Burnham bought her a lot and a store. She was so excited, he wrote, she was "flying around like a headless chicken." After describing all these deals to Blanche, he added that he was closing a $125,000 bond that night "on 17 locations for a big copper silver scheme."

"So you see I am out of my slough of despond," he wrote. "N.T.E. saved me. . . . Hurry up, bring all the plunder you want. Bring the kids, bring Mother, and don't forget to come yourself."

Blanche and the boys soon arrived at their newest home. By September the family had moved into a new house with two stories, the first plastered residence in Skagway, bragged Blanche. She contentedly began furnishing it. As always, she was excited to start over in a semi-raw place. "I like the country and hope that Fred will do well here," she wrote in a happy, chatty letter to her parents. "The place seems to suit him. Plenty to do."

At the end of it she mentioned running into their friend Terry Laing from Bulawayo, who had fought in the Matabele wars and had been in Dawson with Burnham. Laing was headed back to southern Africa "to see if he can do anything in the Boer war that he is sure is coming off." Content with their new life in the north, that storm cloud seemed too far away to touch them.

———

On October 11, 1899, after the collapse of talks that had no chance of succeeding, the Boer republics of the Transvaal and the Orange Free State declared war on Great Britain. Though expected, the news dismayed Blanche and agitated her husband.

On December 21 Blanche wrote to her parents that a two-day blizzard had left snowdrifts higher than thirteen-year-old Roderick's head. "Fred gave us an awful fright yesterday," she added. "He said that he was going to Africa. I know that he *wants* to go but it seems as though I could not bear it to have him go and leave us. The English are having serious reverses and it makes him restless."

Three days later Blanche sent her parents another letter. "We were all as quiet and contented as could be and planning our prospecting trip next summer," she wrote. But then the latest papers arrived carrying news about all the British calamities in South Africa. "Fred said he was going to Africa and talked about it all that P.M. and evening," continued Blanche. "I thought I could not stand it and he gave it up the next morning." Not for long: ". . . but after supper that evening Fred told me that he was getting too restless and could not stand it here any longer and that he thought it was best for us all to go to London." Burnham intended to find a way to join the fighting. They began settling their affairs in Skagway.

Meanwhile, British officers in London were thinking about Burnham. On December 15 General Sir Redvers Buller was replaced as commander-in-chief of British forces in South Africa by Field Marshal Frederick Sleigh Roberts, Lord Roberts. The terrible British setbacks in the first months of the war had been caused partly by poor intelligence. Lord Roberts intended to fix that. Major-General Frederick Carrington, commander of British forces during the Second Matabele War, mentioned to Roberts that his best scout in Rhodesia had been an American named Burnham, now reportedly somewhere in the Yukon. On December 28 Roberts sent off a cablegram that he hoped would find the American.

On the morning of January 4, 1900, the steamer *City of Seattle* docked at Skagway and the purser dropped the mail at the post office. When Burnham fetched his, he found the cablegram from Roberts. He rushed home and told Blanche to pack a few things. The *City of Seattle* was leaving in two and a half hours and they were going to be on it. Lord Roberts had offered him a commission on his staff as Chief of Scouts.

CHAPTER NINETEEN

CHIEF OF SCOUTS

THREE MONTHS AFTER the world powers made half-hearted pledges of peace at the Hague Conference of 1899, Britain had provoked the Boer republics into war. The British expected a cakewalk. The country's newspapers sneered at their opponents, ignorant farmers led by a shabby hayseed with an unkempt beard and ever-present pipe—Paul Kruger, a fundamentalist Bible-thumper who thought the earth was flat. It was ludicrous. A handful of rubes in a backwoods country with no standing army were daring to challenge the imperial might of Great Britain. Surely the rustics would be smashed in time to give the Queen a Christmas present of all South Africa. The Boers' terrible oppression of the natives would inexorably give way to the benevolent discipline of British civilization.

The rustics soon shredded these vanities of empire. Unlike Britain's recent foes in Africa and India, the Boers were not poorly armed natives who obligingly attacked in dense ranks for easy slaughter. Daft old Kruger had been stockpiling supplies and munitions for years, and he had organized the burghers into commando units that could be mobilized in days to create an army of 50,000.

In the first two months of the war, despite being overwhelmingly outnumbered and outfinanced, the Boers outmaneuvered, outgeneraled, and outfought the British Army, leaving it dazed and bloodied. Instead of marching nobly into battle as soldiers were supposed to, the Boers laid ambushes, struck suddenly, melted away. They set up deadly fields of fire from camouflaged positions and used their marksmanship, honed by life on the veldt, to slice up any British regiments ordered to march splendidly into them. Like the Apaches, another outnumbered people, the Boers relied on mobility, surprise, improvisation, invisibility, and knowledge of the terrain. They always chose survival over a glorious death.

All this flummoxed the British Army. In mid-December, instead of mopping up the last of the Boers as most Britons had expected, the army suffered three successive defeats during what became known as Black Week. At Stormberg the army was routed and 600 men were taken prisoner. At Magersfontein the British scouts studied the plain ahead and failed to notice, less than a mile away, the trap set by the Boers: twelve miles of breastworks and trenches dug into the plain, camouflaged with grasses and acacias, where lines of marksmen waited invisibly. When the British forces entered the killing field, a thunderous fusillade cut them down. More than 200 British soldiers were killed and another 700 were wounded, compared to Boer losses of 90 killed and 190 wounded.

The third blot of Black Week happened at Colenso, where 143 British soldiers died, 750 were wounded, and 240 were captured, compared to Boer losses of six killed and twenty-one wounded. Further, the towns of Mafeking, Ladysmith, and Kimberley (with Rhodes inside) were under siege, and British forces had been unable to relieve them. Rhodes was threatening to save his diamond city by surrendering to the Boers.

The British Army and public were shocked. In addition to the heavy casualties, 2,000 of Her Majesty's invincible troops had surrendered to a militia of ragged yokels in slouch hats whose officers wore old black claw-hammer coats and semi-top-hats. Many of these casualties and embarrassments could have been prevented, or at least reduced. Whether through arrogance or lack of trained scouts, British commanders often failed to gather intelligence or do basic reconnaissance, funneling their troops directly into the Boers' waiting guns. And then, instead of withdrawing, commanders ordered the troops to march into the guns again, manifesting what the war's best historian later called "one of the great traditions of the British army: courage matched only by stupidity."

A few days after Black Week, the army appointed one of its most experienced generals commander-in-chief in South Africa: Lord Roberts. He had spent most of his career in India but also had fought tough campaigns in Afghanistan and Abyssinia. Sixty-seven years old and five feet two inches tall, he was affectionately referred to as Bobs, and was popular with his troops and the British public. By the time of the Boer War, Rudyard Kipling had already written two poems about him. Roberts's eagerness to take over the army in South Africa went beyond the military. His only son had been killed in the disaster at Colenso.

To avert blunders and defeat the Boers, Roberts knew he needed accurate military intelligence about his enemies' numbers, positions, supplies, weaponry, and movements. The Boers were mobile guerrillas, so the necessary information could only be obtained by scouting deep into their territory. This required skills that had been disappearing from Britain as the country's rural population fell, skills that the British Army had long ignored as déclassé. Baden-Powell's insistence on the importance of scouts was considered eccentric.

Then came the early fiascos of the Boer War. The rural aristocracy began raising companies of irregulars from the countryside, men who could ride and shoot and live outdoors. In Scotland, for instance, Lord Lovat (Simon Joseph Fraser) enlisted stalkers and ghillies from estates in the Highlands, forming a regiment called the Lovat Scouts. Desperation cast the net wide. Some men signed up as scouts because of the dashing image, but couldn't track a horse across wet sand. "The cry for scouts of renown in the South African Campaign has gone forth far and wide," announced one newspaper after Black Week. "The Maoris have been talked about, Canadian half-breeds have been requisitioned, and to America Lord Roberts has cabled for Mr. F. R. Burnham, who has immediately set sail in answer to the summons."

———

It's a measure of both Burnham's reputation and the British Army's need that Lord Roberts gave an American an officer's commission and named him Chief of Scouts. Burnham left Blanche and the children in London and sailed for Cape Town on the SS *Scott*. The ship was crowded with British officers bound for the war. Burnham wrote to Blanche that two of the most interesting people on board were a striking newlywed couple, Richard Harding Davis, the dashing war correspondent, and his lovely tomboyish wife, the painter Cecil Clark Davis.

Burnham likewise impressed Davis. In his popular *Real Soldiers of Fortune* (1906), Davis wrote that every night during the seventeen-day trip between Southampton and Cape Town, a group of skeptical officers convened in the stateroom to shoot questions at the famous American scout and test his supposed uncanny woodcraft. Burnham's inquisitors, noted Davis, were hardened soldiers who "had either held command in border fights in India or the Sudan or had hunted big game, and the questions each asked were the outcome of his own experience and observation." How to tell, they asked, if a column of dust was made by cavalry or trek wagons? How to tell from a horse's tracks whether it was galloping or trotting, and how to make a fire without becoming a target? A faker, wrote Davis, would have been exposed immediately. "And what made us most admire Burnham was that when he did not know he at once said so."

Burnham amazed them. "The knowledge he gathers from inanimate objects and dumb animals seems little less than miraculous," wrote Davis. "And when you ask him how he knows these things he always gives you a reason founded on some fact or habit of nature that shows him to be a naturalist, mineralogist, geologist, and botanist, and not merely a seventh son of a seventh son." Within two nights, added Davis, Burnham "had us so absolutely at his mercy that we would have followed him anywhere; anything he chose to tell us, we would have accepted."

In his letters to Blanche, Burnham didn't mention these nightly jousts-turned-seminars. Instead, he entertained her with descriptions of a shapely widow in her mid-thirties, worth £200,000, who had a gaggle of older men responding to her every whim, fanning her and fetching her ices, "trot trot trot all day long."

As they approached Cape Town, his excitement grew. "The blood is stirring in my veins," he wrote to Blanche. He was too hyped up even to play chess. We're nearly there, he wrote a few days later, "and I tingle to my fingertips." He signed his letter, "Your wandering erratic demented but ever loving hubby." He claimed to regret the necessity of war but rushed jubilantly toward it, with a peculiar confidence in his survival. Blanche tried to share that faith. "How such a peace loving woman came to have such a warlike husband is more than I can make out," she wrote to him, "and she poor fool is proud of him too."

He arrived in Cape Town on the morning of February 13 and left that afternoon for the front, to join Lord Roberts and his chief of staff, General Herbert (Lord) Kitchener. Lionized for his campaigns in Egypt and Sudan, the six-foot-two Kitchener shaded five-foot-two "Bobs." Burnham reached headquarters soon after British forces relieved Kimberley on February 15. The town had been under siege for 124 days, and its recapture lifted morale on the front and in Britain.

The next target was the old Boer general Piet Cronje, whose retreat toward Bloemfontein, capital of the Orange Free State, had been halted by shelling from the pursuing British Army. Cronje had taken his column of 4,000 people, including fifty women, with their animals and covered wagons, into the bed of the Modder River. It was a placid stream lined with willows and tamarisks that wound through a plain near Paardeberg. While Cronje pretended to consider the British demand for surrender, the Boers dug themselves into the Modder's overhanging banks and dry lateral arroyos. Then Cronje defied the British to come get them.

This played straight into the blunt-minded arrogance of Lord Kitchener, momentarily in command because Roberts was ill. Kitchener had learned nothing from the carnage of Black Week. On February 18 he bombarded the Boers from 120 pieces of artillery. Not a sound came from the Boer lines. Kitchener assumed they were either dead or stunned to the point of surrender. Against the advice of other officers, he ordered a mass frontal attack across 1,000 yards of flat treeless plain. At first there was silence from the Modder. Then the British lines stepped into rifle range and the Boers' Mausers shredded them from invisible positions. Kitchener's response: regroup and do it again.

The British suffered 1,270 casualties that day: more than 300 killed, nearly 1,000 wounded or missing. It came to be called Bloody Sunday, the worst single day of the war for the British. Kitchener's report to Roberts described the day as a success. Others saw things more clearly. "Everywhere there was a terrible monotony about the experiences of the various regiments, which learned once again the grim lessons of Colenso and Modder River," wrote Arthur Conan Doyle, who served as a volunteer doctor during this phase of the war. "We surely did not need to prove once more what had already been so amply proved, that bravery can be of no avail against concealed riflemen well entrenched, and that the more hardy is the attack the heavier must be the repulse."

Roberts, perhaps alarmed by his chief of staff's cavalier dismissal of heavy casualties, rallied from his illness and returned to his command the next day. The British had 35,000 men and heavy artillery surrounding Cronje's 4,000. Instead of suicidal frontal assaults, Roberts decided on patient attrition. On February 20 he ordered an almost ceaseless bombardment of the Boer position. "It seemed that every living thing in the river bed must perish," wrote Burnham to his uncle that week. The shelling splintered all of Cronje's wagons and killed thousands of his horses and oxen, whose rotting carcasses began fouling the river and the air. "Still they held out," wrote Burnham. "We could not understand it." Every time the British sent an infantry probe, the silent riverbank erupted with gunfire.

Meanwhile it rained often, adding to the misery. The British had no tents. Burnham considered himself lucky to have a blanket. They were also on half rations (dry biscuits). They drew their water from the Modder, where dead swollen horses and oxen floated. Typhoid fever broke out, killing some and sickening thousands. A letter to Burnham's Uncle Josiah offered a glimpse of conditions: "as I write, the wailing of the pipes tells of another last patrol. The miles of twinkling lights, the endless stream of convoys, the never ceasing boom of cannon goes on night after night. And I ride through this fringe of hell out into the darkness among the enemy who are hovering round our cordon trying to break it and free their general. This hour that I write I should be asleep as it rains a great deal and I get almost none at all."

He was behind enemy lines almost every night. At one point he was asked to discover conditions inside the Boer camp. How many of their supply wagons survived the barrage? How many men remained alive and in what condition? Were they starving? Would another full attack be catastrophic for them, or for the British?

Though Burnham had crept close to the Boers' trenches several times in the dark, he couldn't get near enough to answer Roberts's questions. He remembered a story about one of his military ancestors. This man had gathered intelligence about the Confederate batteries on Island Number Ten in the Mississippi by floating past them in a hollow log. Burnham adapted the ploy to suit the Modder, clotted with dead livestock. He built a rough box and stretched a fresh cowhide over it. He added a crossbar to hang onto and a few slits for peepholes. It wouldn't fool anyone during daylight but might pass muster at night. He wouldn't have to worry about crocodiles; the bombardment had pushed them elsewhere. As Burnham launched into the darkness, above the Boer camp, a native who had come with him said, "Good-bye, Baas. I think dem Boers shoot you sure."

The current took him. The river was twenty feet wide and six to ten feet deep, red with mud. He felt claustrophobic inside the dark box. A bump from a carcass made him shudder. Eventually, he heard men speaking Afrikaans and drifted within a few feet of Boers cooking, eating, talking. Cronje's men lined two and a half miles of the river. After floating for two hours, Burnham swam to shore.

For all his risk, he had learned almost nothing of value. He resisted the desire to look good to his commanding officers by feeding them information in which he had little confidence. He later learned that his waterline perspective had kept him from seeing all the men entrenched in the lateral arroyos, so any estimate of the Boer force would have been seriously deficient. "That night's work showed with what care a general must sift and discount the reports of his scouts," wrote Burnham.

A number of years later Robert Baden-Powell asked Burnham to critique one of his books about scouting. Burnham made only one suggestion: emphasize that a scout must develop the nerve to admit to his commander when he has failed. It's tempting, wrote Burnham, to whitewash failures and substitute assumptions for facts. But if a commander bases a decision on faulty information, men may die. Better to tell the truth, wrote Burnham, even when it reflects poorly on oneself. Such honesty will earn the commander's trust, so that if he gets conflicting information from several scouts or insistent "experts," he will confidently act upon the intelligence of the scout he trusts most.

By February 27 the Boers on the Modder had had enough. They weren't broken by the incessant pounding, terrible though that was, but by the overwhelming stench from heaps of rotting carcasses, with the attendant swarming flies. Even the vultures were too sated to eat. Cronje and more than 4,000 people surrendered. Their casualties had been light. As a student of military strategy, Burnham wanted to know why. He visited the abandoned trench works and saw that the Boers had dug small pits about five feet deep into the bank. The pits were only eighteen inches wide at the top, three feet at the bottom. A man crouching in one of these cocoons would be impossible to kill by bombardment except by a direct hit. The Boer marksmen didn't even have to show their heads to sweep the plain with salvos. They just lifted their rifles parallel to the ground and fired. It was a new sort of warfare that would be brought to horrifying perfection in World War I.

———

The Boers' toughness and self-reliance, their drive to carve farms from the wilderness, reminded Burnham of American frontiersmen, Mormons in particular. He compared their long-range marksmanship to that of the old buffalo hunters. He admired much about them and credited them with teaching him valuable lessons in African woodcraft. He sympathized with their desire to preserve a pioneer way of life. "Once a taste for that life gets into a man's blood," he wrote in *Scouting on Two Continents*, "it is hard to shake it off, and I, for one, would not willingly exchange it for the most magnificent residence to be found in the West End of London."

Burnham also respected the Boers' audacity at defending their territory against the might of the British Empire. In this he agreed with much of the world, including most Americans, who saw the conflict as David versus Goliath. The Boer cause drew volunteers not only from the United States but from Germany, Ireland, Russia, and elsewhere. Canadians and Australians rallied to the Union Jack.

People in the United States followed the war closely. Newspapers sent correspondents, most of them pro-Boer like their readers. During the war and afterward, several states in the U.S. offered free land to Boers who didn't want to live under British rule. Just before Burnham left for South Africa, his best childhood friend, Arthur Bent, wrote that he was pulling for the Boers. Pasadena was so pro-Boer that Blanche instructed relatives there not to read Burnham's letters to anyone outside the family. Burnham's first cousin, the muckraking journalist Charles Edward Russell—who later ran as the Socialist candidate for governor of New York, U.S. senator, and mayor of New York City, and who helped found the National Association for the Advancement of Colored People (NAACP)—wrote a number of caustic articles and poems in support of the Boers. He thoughtfully mailed copies to Blanche, who refused to forward them to her husband at the front.

The Burnham family scrapbook features a line drawing of Burnham from an unidentified newspaper; an anonymous critic has scrawled alongside his face, "A dam [sic] pity the Boers didn't get your measly carcass."

Burnham understood the appeal of the Boers' way of life and their armed resistance. But he also had seen the Boers up close and knew their world was doomed—and not just because they were outnumbered. Their willful ignorance and isolation, and their brutal repression of black Africans, couldn't be sustained. The nineteenth century was over. The Boers would be swept aside by the future, which belonged to stronger powers such as Britain and the United States.

Burnham also knew that despite the Boers' military advantages—their marksmanship and woodcraft, their skills with livestock, and their ability to travel across the veldt at night—they had crippling military flaws. Like the Apaches, every Boer was a general who resisted authority. He was required to report to his commando unit but didn't have to fight. If a Boer disagreed with an order or thought it too dangerous, he didn't have to obey it and could initiate a different tactic or simply withdraw. If a commander ordered him to burn his wagons or crops to keep them from falling into British hands, he often refused. Soldiers constantly went AWOL to check on their farms or to rest. Burnham believed the Boers' lack of organizational discipline and their reluctance to sacrifice property for the war effort would eventually sink them.

———

Almost every night Burnham made a foray deep behind Boer lines, usually alone, probing for the edges of the Boer picket lines and looking for troop movements that might reveal plans. The terrain reminded him of the country east of the Rocky Mountains—plains, rocky kopjes, rolling treeless hills cut by steep canyons and arroyos.

Lord Roberts asked him to check out a rumor that Boers were massing at Petrusburg, about twenty miles east of Paarderberg. Petrusburg lay between the army and Bloemfontein, capital of the Orange Free State and

Roberts's next objective. Burnham found the Boer picket line when a dark figure jumped in front of him and shouted, "Hands up!" Burnham threw himself backward off his horse as the Boer fired. His mount galloped off, drawing fire from two more pickets. Burnham lay still in the dark, about twenty feet from the Boers. He could hear them asking each other where he was, then they withdrew. He had a long walk back to Paardeberg, with nothing to report.

Roberts told him to try again the next night. This time Burnham took along a mounted native. He tried to avoid roads, where he might run into Boer patrols. That meant cutting across country, literally. The region was laced with barbed wire fences, typically with three strands. "Almost impossible to move in enemy lines without clippers," wrote Burnham, "and the British had none for months. We sometimes charged through, killing the scouts' horses and injuring good men for life." He occasionally borrowed cutters. Otherwise he chopped the fences with a hatchet or broke them by hand. The Boers often posted mounted pickets along the wire fences. These men leaned their heads against a post so that when a wire was touched or cut, they immediately felt the vibration. Burnham used a similar tactic to help make up for the army's lack of scouts. In encampments, he strung wire between bayonets; anyone approaching would cause the wire to vibrate and sing. On most nights Burnham also swam many streams. He avoided the regular "drifts" or fords where pickets waited, often riding miles to find a place where a cut in the steep banks allowed entry. It was tedious, solitary, dangerous work.

On the second foray, Burnham and the native cut fences as they crept toward Petrusburg. They suddenly found themselves in front of a large farmhouse. When Burnham sharply turned his horse's head to steer clear of it, he ran right into another barbed wire fence. The horse panicked and began plunging. The saddle twisted under its belly, throwing Burnham inside the fence near the farmhouse. The noise roused twenty Boers, who streamed from the house with guns. The native, "with splendid presence of mind," galloped alongside Burnham's horse, grabbed the reins, and took off as the Boers shouted at him. After a while, Burnham crawled through the fence into the countryside, expecting another long walk home, but was delighted when the native responded to their prearranged signal. The stirrups had been torn from Burnham's saddle. He remounted and they continued toward Petrusburg.

Within half a mile, Boer pickets challenged them, then fired at their fleeing figures. The scouts cut two more fences, but dawn was approaching and Petrusburg was still miles away. They had to return to Paardeberg again.

"It is always a most humiliating moment in the career of a scout when he is obliged to report to his commander and acknowledge that he has turned back from his objective and is defeated," wrote Burnham. "In this instance, my whole scheme had resulted in utter failure." Roberts and his staff asked him to try again later that day. The native companion wanted no part of another mission, so Burnham left alone, before sunset to give himself extra time.

Soon after crossing the Boer line, a solitary horseman appeared. He rode almost parallel with Burnham while gradually lessening the gap between them. The two men occasionally studied each other with binoculars. Because the terrain was so open, rival scouts often monitored each other during daylight. It was a peculiar game that Burnham often enjoyed. But this man's tactics and deliberation made him uneasy. When the Boer was 800 yards away, he dismounted and prepared to shoot. Burnham galloped out of range, but the Boer quickly followed.

Burnham had seen that his stalker had a better horse, so he began looking for defensive ground. He made for a big anthill. The Boer saw the plan, dismounted, and began firing from a prone position. Bullets thudded and whistled around Burnham, much too close. From behind the anthill he could see the Boer's horse standing on the veldt, but not the prone shooter. From the placement of the bullets, Burnham realized that the man intended to leave him on foot by shooting his horse, only partly protected by the anthill. Burnham reluctantly decided to use the same tactic. On his third or fourth shot, the Boer's exposed horse tumbled. Burnham galloped off. He later learned that this man was Daniel Theron, the Boers' best scout, who entered enemy lines as often as Burnham did. Burnham called him the Boer he most wanted to meet after the war. Theron was killed in September 1900.

With an hour of daylight left, three more Boer scouts spotted Burnham and spread out to flank him. Again Burnham turned and galloped, with them in pursuit. He used every rise and curve to shield himself from their gunfire, occasionally turning in the saddle to shoot back. Richard Harding Davis once asked him if he really could hit someone in that situation. "Well," said Burnham, "maybe not to hit him, but I can come near enough to make him decide my pony's so much faster than his that it really isn't worth while to follow me."

Darkness, the scout's friend, finally descended, but Burnham had lost most of the ground gained earlier toward Petrusburg. He decided to try a long detour to the south, which took most of the night. Near dawn he rested himself and his horse in a brushy arroyo, determined to try for Petrusburg again that night.

Four hours later he heard voices and the creak of wagons. It was a Boer commando of forty horsemen and four wagons, moving toward a farmhouse a mile away. They laagered there. A few hours later two native boys from the column ventured into Burnham's arroyo to play. They stopped short when they saw his horse, then began jogging back to the farmhouse. Burnham quickly saddled up and rode off.

He came across an abandoned farmhouse, intending to stay until dark, but within minutes several Boers driving cattle came over a hill and made for the house, so he had to flee again. Everywhere he turned, there were Boers and barbed wire fences. Cresting another hill, he saw a Boer riding with two natives. The man assumed Burnham was a countryman and pulled up to let the stranger join him. Instead, Burnham veered off. The Boer, now suspicious, sent one of the natives galloping over to identify the stranger and report back. When the native reached him, Burnham casually covered him with his rifle and told him that if he turned his head or tried to run, he would be shot. They rode side by side, always slanting away. The native told Burnham that the white man was Daniel Theron, and that the commando at the farmhouse was Theron's celebrated unit of scouts. Burnham kept the native close for an hour, then released him.

These encounters had nudged him farther from his goal. He was going to fail again. "Mental depression and physical exhaustion seized me at this time," he wrote. He turned onto a road, glum, eyes downcast. His powers of observation, crucial for survival behind enemy lines, had flagged. He almost rode right into a troop of Boers driving some horses and cattle. They had already seen him but assumed he was a countryman, an error they would correct if he got much closer.

Burnham's instincts fired. He swerved and began riding slowly in a circle, studying the ground, sometimes pausing or backing up, always edging farther from the road. A couple of Boers shouted at him, but he ignored them, hoping they would think he was intent on tracking a lost horse and had no time for cordiality. It worked. That evening he returned safely to the British lines, but once again without the intelligence Roberts wanted.

Later, after the fall of the Boer capital of Pretoria, the British Head of Intelligence told Burnham that a dozen scouts had been sent to investigate Petrusburg and none had reached it. That was some consolation.

Yet successes outnumbered failures. His skills astounded his superiors. Richard Harding Davis:

Indeed, than Burnham no man of my acquaintance to my knowledge has devoted himself to his life's work more earnestly, more honestly, and with such single-mindedness of purpose. To him scouting is as exact a study as is the piano to Paderewski, with the result that to-day what the Pole is to other pianists, the American is to all other "trackers," woodmen, and scouts. He reads "the face of Nature" as you read your morning paper. To him a movement of his horse's ears is as plain

a warning as the "Go SLOW" of an automobile sign; and he so saves
from ambush an entire troop. . . . Like the horned cattle, he can tell by
the smell of it in the air the near presence of water, and where, glaring
in the sun, you can see only a bare kopje, he distinguishes the muzzle
of a pompom, the crown of a Boer sombrero, the levelled barrel of a
Mauser. He is the Sherlock Holmes of all out-of-doors. . . .

In South Africa he would say to the officers: "There are a dozen
Boers five miles ahead of us riding Basuto ponies at a trot, and leading
five others. If we hurry we should be able to sight them in an hour." At
first the officers would smile, but not after a half-hour's gallop, when
they would see ahead of them a dozen Boers leading five ponies. In the
early days of Salem, Burnham would have been burned as a witch.

Burnham rejected the idea that there was anything magical or romantic about his skills. "In the literature of the West," he wrote in *Scouting on
Two Continents*, "the hero, bad man, or sheriff is usually endowed by high
Heaven with superhuman powers and has not found it necessary to go
through long dreary months and years of training, like ordinary mortals;
but I have never, in my experience, met either savage or white man whose
natural traits without careful development would have made him
distinguished."

Once, Roberts got conflicting reports about the number of Boers gathered on a certain hill (from 300 to 3,000), and also about how many heavy
guns they had and the guns' positions. These numbers and positions could
reveal the enemy's plans and weaknesses, allowing a commander to plan an
offensive or a defense. Burnham went through the Boer lines that night and
found the tracks of the dragged guns. Because it was dark, he felt the tracks
with his fingers and learned that the Boers had four guns, two heavy and
two light. He followed the tracks and located a camp of 2,000 men, clearly
the Boers' main force. Then he returned and reported it all to headquarters.

Again and again he penetrated the Boer lines, eluded their patrols and
pickets, and returned with actionable intelligence. He was as well-known to

the Boers as Theron was to the British. His reputation and constant infil-trations peeved the enemy. They made his capture or killing a priority. "To overcome the keen wits of hundreds of able men alert to prevent the acqui-sition of just the particular knowledge which the scout is after," wrote Burnham, "is the joy of the game and compensates for days and nights of strenuous effort and physical hardship."

CHAPTER TWENTY

BEHIND ENEMY LINES

IT TOOK NEARLY a month for a letter to travel from the front lines to London. By the time Blanche heard from her husband, the news in his letters was old and she had no idea what had happened since. He often assured her that he was barely in danger. She tried to believe him. (His letters to his Uncle Josiah and others told a different story.) She studied the papers every day, especially the lists of casualties. She and Roderick tracked the army's campaigns on a large map of South Africa.

"They are having *real* battles out there now and *what* is Fred doing?" she wrote to Burnham's mother in late February 1900. "How anxiously I read the lists—no one knows. 130 in today's list. War is a cruel thing between civilized nations. I wish Lord Roberts had not sent for Fred. I know and appreciate the honor and am very *very* proud of him but it is *Fred* I want."

Bloemfontein fell on March 13 without a fight. Even better, the Boers had left warehouses, granaries, and pantries intact. For men who had been living on half-rations, Bloemfontein was a cornucopia. Burnham and several others settled into the abandoned house of the State Secretary. They raided the larder for a meal of turkey with trimmings and fresh bread, served on silver dishes, with wine in crystal glasses. Other luxuries: a roof and feather beds, though Burnham didn't get to spend much time in his.

In the previous month the British had captured Cronje's militia, relieved Kimberley and Ladysmith, and occupied the capital of the Orange Free State. Lord Roberts wrote to the Queen that victory was near. Burnham shared the general optimism. In late March, writing on rice endpapers torn from a book in the State Secretary's library (paper was scarce), he told Blanche he expected the war to be over by May.

Meanwhile, he was spending most nights behind the lines, trying to intercept Boer dispatch riders or observe troop movements and artillery placements. On the afternoon of March 30 he was ordered to investigate a rumor that Boer troops were massing in the country between Bloemfontein and the hamlet of Thaba 'Nchu, forty miles east in the foothills bordering Basutoland (now Lesotho). If true, the Boers probably were targeting the 1,700 British soldiers under General Robert Broadwood moving west toward Bloemfontein. Burnham couldn't take his favorite horse because it was exhausted after being ridden 800 miles. Horses, like wire clippers, were scarce. He picked "two sorry nags" from the Remount Department and left that night for territory all new to him.

Before dawn he was near Sanna's Post (Sannaspos), twenty-five miles east of Bloemfontein. In the graying light he saw the shapes of a farmhouse and a stone kraal. A door slammed. Beyond the buildings, a dark tree line marked a streambed, now mostly dry. He surmised this was Korn Spruit (a spruit is a small stream). He smelled a camp in that direction, and heard the soft click of stirrups. He hid his horses and crept toward the spruit. It was still too dark to see into the streambed, but the noises and smells told Burnham it was full of Boers, particularly around the drift (ford). Their presence there puzzled him.

He decided to skirt the spruit and find another place to cross, then to hide in the Bloemfontein Waterworks, whose tower darkened a sliver of sky in the distance. As he retrieved his horses, artillery fire began in the east, where Broadwood's army was positioned. Another puzzlement.

Then the sun popped up and everything became clear. Hundreds of Boer horsemen were waiting beneath the high banks of the spruit. During the night they had ridden around and behind Broadwood's troops. The Boers' artillery barrage was now pushing Broadwood west, straight into the spruit ambush. This stratagem had been designed by the brilliant Boer general Christiaan de Wet.

Burnham felt helpless. He was on a hill in full view of Boer scouts on each side of him, 400 yards away. His clothing resembled theirs, and for the moment they assumed he was one of them. He was also in plain sight of the oncoming British wagons now nearing the drift. He could save himself by riding off, but the idea was impossible.

He pulled out a red silk handkerchief, two feet square, that he carried for signaling, and began waving it frantically. "But there was not a single British scout to observe my warning," he wrote, "and no advance guard appeared in front of the oncoming transport wagons." Another failure of basic reconnaissance. If any of the British noticed Burnham, they paid no attention, but the Boers soon did. Several came galloping over. Burnham knew his nag couldn't outrun anything. He surrendered. They seized his horses and guns and took him to the stone kraal.

Through chinks in the wall, he watched the disaster of Sanna's Post unfold exactly as de Wet had planned. As the British wagons rolled into the drift, the Boers pointed their Mausers and demanded surrender. Resistance would have been suicidal. The captured men and wagons were directed right and left into the dry streambed. No shots had been fired. Then a troop of cavalry rode up to the drift to see why the spruit seemed to be swallowing the wagons. Ordered to surrender, the cavalry officer barked a command to wheel and retreat. Burnham watched in horror as a salvo cut down the officer and many of the horsemen. Then real firing began, sweeping the exposed plain where the British forces marched.

Burnham began thinking about escape. He tied a shoelace tightly around his leg below the knee to remind him to limp. Then he knotted his red handkerchief around his knee as if he was wounded. When the British retreated and the battle finally ended, the Boers took Burnham, limping badly, down to the other *verdomte rooineks*—damned rednecks—detained in the spruit. The Boers had captured 428 men, 117 wagons, and seven artillery guns, while killing or wounding about 160. They also destroyed the waterworks, which led to epidemics of typhoid, dysentery, and cholera in Bloemfontein that killed several thousand more. (Burnham saw 1,100 men of the Guards Brigade buried in a common grave.) The Boers' casualties were three killed and five wounded.

Burnham was directed onto one of the wagons carrying the injured. By ten o'clock that morning the column was on the move. They were headed for Winburg, where the prisoners would be put on trains for the notorious Pretoria jail. The prospect made Burnham shudder. They traveled until four o'clock, rested until dark, then resumed. The terrain was so flat and treeless, and the guards so vigilant, that Burnham saw no chance to escape.

The following morning, a Boer officer stared at Burnham and approached for a closer look. I know you from Rhodesia, he said. You're the American scout Burnham. Burnham told the man he was mistaken, that he was a mapmaker snagged in the mess at Korn Spruit. The officer didn't believe him and sent for someone from the Boer Intelligence Department to question the prisoner. If this was the famous scout, it would be a coup.

The intelligence officer had been educated in Britain and considered himself astute about the differences between mapmakers and American frontiersmen. Burnham discerned from the man's questions that the Boers had accurate information about his physical characteristics, but also expected him to be a coarse half-savage from the Wild West. This stereotype, which Burnham detested and often mocked, for once worked in his favor. Playing to his interrogator's biases, he turned the conversation to the African explorations of Richard Burton and John Hanning Speke, followed by reflections on some fine points of Christian doctrine. He sprinkled in verses of poetry, perhaps from his cherished Kipling or Burns. He may have casually referred, as he often did in his writings, to Caesar's Tenth Legion, the *Iliad* and the *Odyssey*, and historical events from the days of Sparta to the present. The intelligence officer concluded that this educated, well-spoken gentleman could not possibly be the barbarous American scout.

In *Real Soldiers of Fortune*, Richard Harding Davis described the gap between Burnham and the dime-novel stereotype: "Personally, Burnham is as unlike the scout of fiction, and of the Wild West Show, as it is possible for a man to be. He possesses no flowing locks, his talk is not of 'greasers,' 'grizzly b'ars,' or 'pesky redskins.' In fact, because he is more widely and more thoroughly informed, he is much better educated than many who have passed through one of the 'Big Three' universities, and his English is as conventional as though he had been brought up on the borders of Boston Common, rather than on the borders of civilization."

Burnham's initial accuser remained suspicious. He assigned a Bushman to watch the prisoner closely. The native walked next to Burnham's wagon tirelessly, all day and into the evening, barely leaving room for a shadow, much less an opening for escape. As the night march proceeded, Burnham grew more desperate. They were approaching Winburg. The next stop would be Pretoria jail. Better to die than be confined in a cell, he thought. He was perched on the front corner of the last wagon, alert for any lapse in the Bushman's vigilance. Dawn would break in an hour. The guards, prisoners, and drivers all were nodding with exhaustion.

The Bushman walked forward to say something to the driver. An opening. Burnham dropped to the wagon's disselboom between the oxen, then slipped onto the ground. An ox kicked at him and then the wagon passed over. He rolled a few times and lay still on the edge of the road. The rear guard, half asleep, thudded by him. He crawled into a field, then stood and ran. He had twenty minutes to hide before daylight.

The plain was flat and bare, with a few scattered kopjes. He ran toward one. Nearing it, he saw a small Boer farm with a kraal. Dogs began to bark, which stopped him. Dawn was breaking. Not far from the farmhouse was a small field, newly plowed. He ran into it and lay in one of the shallow furrows. He covered most of his face with his dust-colored hat, but much of his body was exposed. He lay without a quiver.

The furrow was about 150 yards from the road, which bustled all day with Boer horsemen and wagons. He didn't dare shift position or lift his hat. Instead, to avoid cramping, he systematically tensed and relaxed every muscle. The day was sweltering, and by afternoon he felt addled from lack of water. He began to obsess about the ear of boiled corn in his breast pocket, convinced that it was jutting up like a beacon. The sun seemed frozen in the sky, but its rays finally slanted. He made himself wait for full dark before rising. After stretching the kinks from muscles stiffened by twelve hours of immobility, he started running.

Two miles later he found a small stream and drank like a camel. He was grateful now for the ear of boiled corn. He saved the biscuit in his pocket for later. He found a sheltered spot near a kopje and slept most of the day. That night he started back toward Bloemfontein, hiding during the day and traveling in the dark to skirt Boer pickets. It took him three days to slip through seventy miles of Boer territory. He reached a British outpost near Bloemfontein at four a.m. At eight he reported to Lord Roberts, relaying what he had learned about Boer numbers and movements.

———

To Blanche he wrote, "Again I write you, after one of those strange escapes with which my life seems dotted." He also described the escape to his mother and added, "I would have been a Major General if I had had the education. I have the natural instinct of military position even on a big scale as I now see it. Where the firing line is 25 miles in length I can grasp it all. But in my own little field of scouting I am still far ahead of any other living man. I do not write such stuff as this to any one but you, not even to B.B. So destroy it at once." (She didn't.)

After the debacle of Sanna's Post, the army made sure the war correspondents heard about Burnham's capture and escape. The London papers were filled with it, a bit of good news. "You have created quite a stir my darling," wrote Blanche. But she added that his confidence about the war's imminent ending was wrong. "*Eleven weeks* day after tomorrow since you left, and it will be that many and maybe more the way things look now."

He kept sending assurances that he took few risks and avoided battlefields. "So when you hear of great battles and charges I am only an interested spectator and not in the thick of it." His idea of low-risk behavior, such as riding around in the dark behind enemy lines while pickets shot at him, struck Blanche as peculiar. In a letter to her at the end of April he wrote, "I am not going to be in any more fights. I am to go into the enemy's country and send news back, so the worst that can happen is my capture. So don't worry, my fighting time is over." If this calmed her for a moment, the rest of the letter probably did not. He had just led twenty-five men on a raid into Boer territory. They captured 2,000 sheep, 40 horses, and 300 cattle, and, though chased, did not lose a man, but did get routed by a hive of bees. Milton Prior, a well-known war correspondent, wrote and illustrated a story about the episode.

But he was weary of these low-risk escapades. The army had been idling in Bloemfontein for six weeks while the command worked on logistics for the next phase. Burnham was impatient to push north and finish things.

On May 3 Lord Roberts launched what he expected to be the war's final offensive, toward Johannesburg and Pretoria. His combined force included 58,000 troops and multiple thousands of horses, mules, and oxen to haul the supplies required by a vast army on the march. Opposing them were about 15,000 Boer irregulars.

On May 7 Burnham was given the mission of cutting a railroad behind the Boer forces to impede the transportation of supplies as they retreated. The Boers were using the same tactic, blowing up every bridge and culvert ahead of the advancing British. Most of the rivers in South Africa were too small for navigation, so bridges and railroads were crucial to move troops, guns, and supplies. Both sides devoted special units to quick repair of these damaged lifelines.

Burnham left on foot with two native carriers. They took eighteen pounds of explosives and rations for ten days, mostly biscuits, chocolate, and condensed soup. Burnham set a hard pace, an "Indian jog trot" that covered nearly forty miles before dawn. During the day they hid in native huts. The next night they passed through many pickets and three commandos. Burnham noted their numbers, armaments, and movements. They hoped to stay the next night at a farm owned by an Englishman, but found it occupied by a trigger-happy Boer, and then were chased by pickets. Burnham and the natives evidently got separated. Boers were buzzing around the countryside like disturbed bees. The cause, Burnham suspected, was an imminent clash with the British Army.

Near daylight, he began to hear gunfire. The bare plain offered no place to hide, so he approached a group of huts. An alarmed old woman there tried to shoo him off before the Boers saw him. They would punish her by burning her huts, taking her goat and chicken, and perhaps killing her. He calmed her with two sovereigns in exchange for letting him wait out the day in one of her storage huts. She brought him a dish of goat's milk and shut the door from the outside by leaning a pole against it.

The gunfire intensified and got closer. Burnham poked a hole in the mud wall and watched the battle of Zand River from the Boers' vantage. As the morning passed and they began to retreat, several of them chose the old woman's huts as a resting place. They ordered her to kill her goat and cook it for them, then sat leaning against the storage hut. A commandant rode up and told the woman to open the hut so he could eat in the shade. She bustled around the door, making noise to warn Burnham. His eyes had long since adjusted to the dim light, and he had noticed several sheepskins and sacks near one wall. He quickly backed farther into the dark and pulled them over him, crouching with his knees against his chest.

Daylight fell into the hut. The commandant and two officers entered and sat inside eating and discussing their next moves, a few feet away from the inert scout in sheep's clothing. This time he only needed to hold the pose for an hour or so before they finished and rode off. At dark he crept back to the British lines with the information he had gleaned.

The British had advanced so quickly that Burnham's original railway target was obsolete. Instead, he was ordered to report to Major Alymer Gould Hunter-Weston, Royal Engineer, for a mission to blow up the railroad fifty miles above Kroonstad, now the center of the Boers' concentrated forces. Hunter-Weston asked for volunteers, warning that the Boers would be expecting them, so capture or death was likely. Two hundred men stepped forward. Hunter-Weston chose fifty cavalrymen and eight sappers. The plan was to burst through the picket lines in the dark, and when the Boers responded, the cavalry would fight, creating a diversion that allowed Burnham, Hunter-Weston, and the sappers to slip into the night toward the railway, with Burnham leading them past other pickets.

The diversion worked as planned. By four a.m. Burnham's group was fifteen miles behind the lines and within a quarter mile of the railroad. But the Boers had stationed a commando just at the place the British wanted to blow up. A road busy with patrols and convoys ran in front of a farmhouse where some of the commandos were asleep. Others were scattered along the road. Their horses were in an adjacent pasture, enclosed by a barbed wire fence. To minimize the risk of casualties, Burnham and Hunter-Weston decided to blow the railroad themselves. They cut the fence and walked their horses into the pasture among the commando's herd. On the other side, they snipped the wires and exited toward the railroad. There Burnham covered the fuse with his hat and Hunter-Weston lit it.

As they hurried back the way they had come, an explosion shook the air. Startled Boers began dashing about, but chaos and darkness helped the two men reach their patrol and take off. After a morning filled with pursuits and evasions—one man wounded, one horse killed, telegraph wires cut, seven prisoners captured—they reached the British lines about eleven o'clock. "This happened on my thirty-ninth birthday," wrote Burnham, "so we called it a party."

Hunter-Weston recommended Burnham for captain. "I have brought your excellent service to the notice of General French," he wrote, "and have told him what a pleasure it is to have to do with a man who like yourself combines caution of counsel with boldness and quick decision in action."

The Boers quickly repaired the railroad, so the exploit had minimal impact on the war, but the cheeky dash of it made great newspaper copy. Once again Burnham's exploits were splashed across the London papers and picked up in the United States. On May 14, Blanche wrote to him that he was "making a great stir in the papers again." The *Daily Telegraph* had devoted two columns that morning to Bennett Burleigh's interview with him about the escape after Sanna's Post. The *Daily Mail*, the *Star*, the *Sun*, and the *St James's Gazette* all were carrying stories that day about the blown-up railroad bridge, calling it "a very daring deed." There was also a large sketch of him in that week's *Black and White*, a popular illustrated weekly, that showed him riding through some amazed Boers to warn Broadwood's convoy about the ambush at Korn Spruit (which he didn't do). By the time Blanche continued her letter three days later, several other papers had run the railroad story. "I am prouder than ever of you," she wrote, "but your work is *very dangerous* not withstanding all you tell me." The campaign seemed to be climaxing, she added, "So don't let anything happen to you now."

She didn't mention her depression of the previous two weeks, caused by his prolonged absence and her anxieties about him. "I had the blues so deeply tinged that it amounted to genuine black agony," she wrote to Burnham's mother. "I could not help it. I felt so discouraged. Usually I try to keep in good spirits for the boys' sake, for where mamma is blue life is not very cheerful and I must think of my boys."

Her mood, and the mood of the whole country, was lifted a few days later when cables brought news that Mafeking had been relieved on May 17 after a siege of 217 days. Mafeking's commander, Burnham's friend Robert Baden-Powell, had become a household name as all of Britain followed his stubborn, jaunty, and often ingenious resistance. The nation celebrated for nearly a week. Blanche and Roderick went to the Crystal Palace to watch fireworks, wave ribbons, and blow trumpets. Roderick shouted until he was hoarse. The delirium was so strong that the next morning Blanche made sure all her husband's civilian clothes were in good order, as if he might walk through the door. Later in the day, after reading in the papers that the war might continue for another two months, "I returned to my sober senses," she wrote, "and for a short time went to the other extreme."

She didn't get her usual letter from Burnham that week, which she depended on for peace of mind.

———

Toward the end of May, when the British were closing in on Johannesburg, Lord Roberts wanted to cut the railroad between that gold-mining city and the Boers' capital of Pretoria. The goal was to prevent the evacuation of rolling stock filled with critical supplies that could help extend the war. Burnham was given the mission. He was told not to blow the railroad until the attack on Johannesburg began, so that the Boers wouldn't have time to destroy the cars and goods. To accompany him, Burnham chose the toughest native scout. The target was about 100 miles from the British lines, and they might have to survive many days on meager rations before the attack started.

The flat, treeless landscape was teeming with Boer troops, so the two scouts traveled only at night. By day they paid a few coins to hide in native huts and perhaps buy some eggs or a tough old hen. After skirting the dust and lights of Johannesburg, they reached their destination, the barren country north of the Rand. To hide during the day, they curled themselves into abandoned aardvark holes, exiting at night to stretch and to drink at a nearby spruit. Their food ran out.

After two aardvark days and nights, they finally heard the boom of artillery from the south. They popped from their holes, placed their explosives, and blew up the railway above a small station called Zurfontein, about twenty miles south of Pretoria. They took refuge in a maize field. This became their home and commissary for four days. Grinding at the raw corn made Burnham's jaws so sore he could hardly talk. While waiting for the British forces to reach them, they cut the railroad at another place hard to repair, on a curve between two culverts, then retreated to their maize field. When the Boers fixed the break, the scouts blew it again.

It was time to leave before their luck ran out. The Boers still controlled the area between them and Johannesburg. They set off south, toward the British lines, and as day broke they hid in a large plantation of blue gum trees. Not long after, a Boer commando rode into the plantation and set up camp, walking through the grove to pick up dead wood for fuel. Burnham and the native obscured their profiles with branches of blue gum, creeping into vacant parts of the plantation ahead of the foraging Boers.

The day was highly stressful. The scouts were also hungry and terribly thirsty. When night finally came, the native fell to pieces. He was terrified the Boers would catch them and flog him to death. Boers treated white prisoners of war decently but habitually killed any natives caught helping the British. Burnham advised him to crawl into the veldt alone, so that if he got stopped, he could say he lived in Johannesburg and was trying to get home. Burnham took him through the Boer lines, then they separated.

The countryside toward Johannesburg was thick with Boer pickets. Burnham spent that night and part of the next day crawling, listening, evading. When he reached British lines late that morning, he had been gone for eleven days. After reporting to Lord Roberts, he slept for fourteen hours. When he got up, he learned that his railroad blasts had enabled the British to capture a dozen engines and 200 cars filled with supplies worth hundreds of thousands of dollars.

—•—

For the British, the next prize was Pretoria, the Boer capital, forty miles north of Johannesburg. The Boers' supply lines in the south had been cut off. The last uncut artery was the 400-mile railroad between Pretoria and

Lourenço Marques, a port on the Indian Ocean in Portuguese East Africa. Supplies from Lourenço Marques, especially munitions from Germany, helped the Boer army keep fighting. Lord Roberts also wanted to stop the Boers from evacuating supplies and artillery out of Pretoria, and he worried that the Boers would use the railroad to transport several thousand sickly British prisoners from Pretoria to fever country farther east.

On the evening of June 1, 1900, Burnham led 200 men under Major Hunter-Weston on a raid to blow up some of the railway's bridges, curves, and culverts east of Pretoria. The area was thick with Boers, and by dawn it was clear that the raiders not only couldn't reach the railroad but were in danger of being wiped out by overwhelming numbers. They retreated, fighting constant rearguard actions, and were lucky to get back with only twenty casualties.

As Burnham and the others were escaping with their lives, Blanche was writing to him that yesterday would have been Nada's sixth birthday. "Six years ago this very evening," she continued, "you came home and saw your little daughter. How I hate war when I think what it has cost us."

—•—

For Lord Roberts, cutting the railroad between Pretoria and Lourenço Marques remained a priority. On June 2, the day after the failed first attempt, Burnham was ordered to undertake the mission alone. To improve the chances of getting through, Hunter-Weston led a diversionary raid to the west while Burnham rode east on his favorite Basuto pony, Stembok. He carried twenty-five pounds of guncotton in his pack and a map of every curve, culvert, and bridge on the railway.

At dusk he met a troop of twenty cavalrymen en route to the rail station at Irene, which lay in his general direction. The commander asked him to scout ahead for them. "I very much disliked delaying my special mission," wrote Burnham, but the Lancers didn't have a scout or even a native guide, so he felt he couldn't refuse.

Sometime in the middle of the night they approached a small rise covered with tall grass. To Burnham it looked like a prime spot for a Boer outpost, so he stopped the troop to investigate. Typically he would have dismounted and reconnoitered on foot, "but so much time of the precious darkness had been wasted that I decided to chance it by working along on my mount."

All remained quiet as he neared the summit. Then twenty Boers jumped up from the grass, rifles leveled, and yelled at him to surrender. He shouted, "Frints!" (friends), which froze the Boers for an instant. At the same time, he jerked the reins and slid sideways on Stembok, Indian style, putting the horse between him and the Boers as he galloped away. They fired. The British cavalrymen answered with a volley. A half moon gave the Boers enough light to follow Stembok's profile, so Burnham dashed toward a patch of burnt ground that he thought would swallow their shape. When he reached the dark spot, 400 yards from the Boers, he felt safe enough to slow Stembok and sit upright.

Despite the British counter-volleys, one Boer marksman had stayed focused on the fleeing horseman. One of his bullets found Stembok. "My last vision of my good Stembok was his silhouette against the sky, legs in air, directly over me."

When Burnham awoke, the moon was setting. That told him he had been unconscious for about two hours. The night was silent. He remembered Stembok rearing and falling on top of him. Excruciating pain hit him. He thought his back was broken. His frightened impulse was to summon help, even Boer help, by shouting or lighting a fire. No one would blame you, whispered his pain. You've done what you can. Give up.

"But in the instant the terrible pain slackened," he wrote, "another voice spoke, in the simple words of bygone ancestors who did the right thing in the right way without any heroics whatever." The temptation to surrender waned, "but the lesson of that night has never been forgotten—not to judge too harshly what a man may do under intense physical pain suddenly inflicted."

The pack filled with explosives was still on his back. He stood and began to stumble in the direction of his target. He found he could lessen the pain by pressing hard on his abdomen with both hands. When dawn streaked the sky, he needed a place to hide. The veldt offered no cover. About a mile in front of him was a small marsh with a farmhouse at each side. Horses grazing nearby told him that both farmhouses were occupied by commandos. Just ahead stood a native's small stone kraal, about three feet high. He crawled inside and lay against the wall.

All morning he heard Boers passing. Waves of pain assaulted him again, and the impulse returned to cry out for help. He passed out. Awake again, he had a spell of intense nausea, then vomited a great deal of blood. That seemed to relieve him a little and also calmed him, because he now felt sure he was going to die. He scrawled a note to Blanche. He hoped the British would advance quickly enough to find him before the Boers did, so he didn't die a prisoner. He slept most of the day. When he woke, he felt a bit stronger.

At dusk he watched the Boers post pickets. They left a gap at the marsh, assuming that no one would try to cross there. So that became his plan. As soon as darkness fell, he waded in. The water was cold but never rose above his waist. He was helped, too, by the Boers' practice of gathering each evening for a religious service. From both farmhouses came the sound of commandos chanting psalms.

Just before two o'clock he heard a train whistle and saw the lights of a distillery, the marker for his target. At the railroad track he set his charge of guncotton, lit the fuse, and crawled off into a grassy dent in the landscape. The explosion stirred the Boers at the distillery, but they didn't send out a search party, evidently assuming that the saboteur was long gone. A repair crew immediately went to work, and by four o'clock they were finished.

Burnham had another charge of guncotton. When everything was quiet again, he crawled back to the railroad. He lit the fuse on another bomb, then crept into a better hiding place, another plantation of blue gum trees. The second explosion woke the Boers in an angry mood. They knew their enemy was still nearby, and they saddled up. Day was breaking. Burnham watched them spread out and begin to search the area. They were clearly country Afrikaners, expert at beating the veldt to flush prey.

Combing the area on horseback yielded nothing. The commander ordered them to burn the grass. Nothing. Burnham watched them turn their attention to the last possibility—the blue gum plantation. He knew they would search it, and if by some miracle they didn't find him, they would raze it.

At the plantation's margin, a small spruit was fringed by a strip of green grass about a foot high. At the edge of this strip grew a stunted gum tree about four feet tall, with spindly branches. Burnham judged the green grass his only hope of escaping a fire, as the green corn had saved him in Minnesota. The spindly tree seemed his best hope of eluding detection, because it so obviously could not hide a man and might get less attention.

To break up the outline of his body, he stuffed grass into his hat brim and through his pack's shoulder straps. Then he wrapped himself around the thin trunk of the gum tree and lay motionless on his side. Several times, Boers rode right past his little tree. The commander, more and more irate, ordered the grove burnt. Then the Boers dismounted and walked along the rows of smoking trees, passing close by Burnham's tiny oasis. And then they were gone.

The rest of the day was a torment of pain and disturbed sleep. The night passed the same way, with the addition of intense cold. He had no blanket. The next day dragged, but he could hear big guns booming to the west, a sign that Pretoria was under attack. He later learned that cutting the railroad had allowed the British to capture five engines and several hundred cars filled with supplies bound out of Pretoria.

He waited for the arrival of British forces, but none came. Darkness fell again. He hadn't eaten anything for three days. Hunger and pain made him too weak to walk. He knew he wouldn't survive another day's wait. He cut up the guncotton bag, wrapped the canvas around his hands, and began crawling toward Pretoria.

The whispering voice of surrender returned. He resisted it by vowing to pull himself to a bush fifty yards away, then another, and another. Eventually he heard the calls of British pickets. He later calculated it had taken him five hours to crawl three miles.

He cried out. Once the picket realized it wasn't a ruse, Burnham was rushed to the field hospital and into surgery. A large abdominal muscle had ruptured and a blood vessel had burst in his stomach. He should not have survived three days on the veldt, much less been capable of staggering several miles to a railroad, blowing it up twice, and crawling several more miles to safety.

He showed his usual amazing powers of recuperation by being up and about within a week, but the doctors forbade him to ride or do anything strenuous for several months. For him the war was over. He was being invalided to London. He had penetrated the Boer lines more than one hundred times, far more than any other scout.

"It is a source of satisfaction to me," he wrote to his Uncle Josiah from the hospital, "to know I can beat the Boer at his own game and in his own country. They boasted they would have this Yankee in Pretoria inside a week as a prisoner."

While Burnham was away, Lord Roberts had promoted him to captain. After the heroics of the last mission, Roberts promoted him to major. He also sent a note that Burnham later called his most precious possession. It said in part, "I doubt if any other man in the force could have successfully carried out the perilous enterprises in which you have from time to time been engaged, demanding as they did the training of a lifetime, combined with exceptional courage, caution, and powers of endurance."

Soon after, Roberts awarded Burnham £2,000 "in recognition of the valuable services you rendered while attached to the F.I.D. [Field Intelligence Department] out here, more especially with regard to the large amount of rolling stock captured at Johannesburg, mainly through your exertions."

CHAPTER TWENTY-ONE

CELEBRITY AND HINTERLANDS

B Y JUNE 13 Blanche hadn't heard from her husband for almost a month and was getting anxious. She didn't yet know that he had nearly died. Burnham sent her several letters from the hospital in Pretoria, but they wouldn't arrive until early July. For some reason, perhaps the expense, perhaps a reluctance to alarm her, he didn't cable. A week later, still in the dark about her husband's injury, Blanche read another newspaper account about his exploits in the war. "I am fearful that after living such an exciting life," she wrote to him, "you will not be able to settle down to humdrum existence with your wife and boys but will want to go to China or to the West Coast [of Africa]." This proved prophetic.

Blanche finally heard about his injury on June 26, when Burnham cabled her. He told her it wasn't serious and that he would soon board a ship for home, even if he had to sleep on a couch and borrow a room to change clothes. He left Cape Town on July 4 on the *Dunottar Castle*. A fellow passenger named Major A. W. A. Pollock later wrote, "Burnham, the American scout, was on board, as well as other celebrities." These included

The Gold Coast Colony, Ashanti, and the Northern Territories. (Reprinted by permission of the University of Wisconsin Press from *The End of Slavery in Africa*, edited by Suzanne Miers and Richard Roberts, © 1988 by the Board of Regents of the University of Wisconsin System.)

generals, aristocrats, the mayor of recently-relieved Mafeking, and a young war correspondent named Winston Churchill.

Burnham and Churchill knew each other slightly from the war, but on the eighteen-day voyage to Southampton they deepened their acquaintance by discussing their mutual interests: explorers, military history and battle strategies, and the details about how each had escaped from the Boers (Churchill had broken out of Pretoria jail). Churchill questioned Burnham closely about his youth among Indians. They were also tablemates, and among their small group some topics were off-limits. Burnham wrote to his uncle that they had agreed on the following fines: "Anyone talking about the war, $1.25; about Pom Poms, $1.75; about armored trains, $5.75; about Boers, $7.25; about scouting, death; criticism of the war and explaining how it should have been conducted, penalty death by torture."

But scouting never left Burnham's mind. He had started making notes to write a technical manual about it (never published). The impetus was his experience in South Africa, where he had been appalled by the cost of the British army's incompetence. He wrote a long letter to Baden-Powell on the subject during the voyage. "I saw things every day that would make an angel weep, the C in C [commander-in-chief, Lord Roberts] asking for information of this or that column and no man knew where it was or where the enemy were. I saw whole troops of men calling themselves scouts that did not know enough to pound sand in a rat hole—and yet it was the only stuff the C in C could get." Because of poor scouting, many British soldiers had died needlessly in ambushes or night attacks or foolish charges.

Burnham asked Baden-Powell to use his new renown from Mafeking to convince the British military to form a capable scouting corps. War was becoming more lethal, with powerful long-range rifles and artillery that could lob devastating shells several miles. To save lives and fight effectively, it was more important than ever to scout troop movements and gun placements. And the next war, predicted Burnham, wouldn't be a minor conflict like the one in South Africa, where an outnumbered enemy could be overwhelmed by throwing more and more troops into battle. (Like others, Burnham foresaw a brutal showdown between Britain and Germany.)

"It will all depend upon the man behind the gun," wrote Burnham. "He will need brains." To find the best men for scouting, continued Burnham, "They should be put through a severe test physically and tried mentally to see if they could stand all night in a drizzly storm watching a path to catch an enemy's dispatch, and do this night after night on ½ rations. Some fellows start strong for the adventure, but shy of the drudgery in obscurity. Their enthusiasm dies as the sun goes down." If Baden-Powell would take on this vital task, Burnham offered to help in any way he could.

The *Dunottar Castle* docked at Southampton on July 20. For the time being, Burnham basked in the love of his family. He was especially joyful to renew acquaintance with Bruce, now two.

London society swept him up as a war hero and celebrity. Burnham's background as a Westerner and scout was deeply appealing to the public, yet he was also expected to conduct himself like a Victorian gentleman who knew literary allusions and the correct fork. "Since his return, several months ago," reported the London periodical *Mainly About People*, "he and Mrs. Burnham have been feted all over England, and have been guests at country houses without number, whilst endless dinners, receptions, and luncheon parties have been given in their honour in town." Lords invited Burnham to join them for partridge shooting. Even Queen Victoria requested his presence, but took ill and had to cancel. Blanche saved the embossed menu from one honorary dinner at the Savoy Hotel on July 18. Among the nine Francophile courses were Truite-Salmonée au Champagne en Gelée, Chapon de Paris Albufera, Selle d'Agneau à la Broche, Corbeille de Friandises, and Savoury à la Bayeldi. It was a long way from raw corn gnawed in an aardvark hole.

The invitation he most appreciated came from the dons of Oxford University. He hesitated to accept, afraid he would be out of his intellectual depth. But the visit over several days delighted both sides as they shared knowledge about botany, mineralogy, animal behavior, and other subjects that Burnham and the dons, for very different reasons, had studied closely.

The Boer War was the first media-saturated conflict, with seventy correspondents sending dispatches and illustrations to feed the public's appetite. Newspapers also had discovered the profits in creating and covering celebrities. Likewise, companies had started using famous soldiers, actresses, and athletes to sell their products. In its series on heroes of the Boer War, Ogden's Cigarettes issued two "cigarette cards" featuring photographs of Burnham, an odd pairing since Burnham avoided tobacco to preserve his sense of smell. Newspapers reported Burnham's activities and whereabouts, quoted his views on scouting and the Boer War, retold his adventures. To keep track, Burnham subscribed to a clipping service. Four months after his return, the scrapbook held 130 stories. Typical was one that covered his honorary appearance at the Anglo-African Writers Club, where the chairman read aloud Lord Roberts's letter praising him and added, "any one of Major Burnham's adventures would provide an ordinary man with conversation for the rest of his life."

Rider Haggard gave Burnham's name to Lady Jeune, wife of Sir Francis Jeune, a prominent judge and member of the Queen's Privy Council. "Lady J is fond of the celebrities who chance to shine in the season's sky," wrote Haggard to Burnham. "She knows everyone and might be useful." Soon the Burnhams were weekending at the Jeunes' estate, Arlington Manor. "I wonder if you would know your Freddy and B.B.," wrote Blanche to her mother on the Manor's stationery, "if you could see us sweeping down to dinner in this grand old place with my lords and my ladies and a few Sirs thrown in." Mid-letter, she switched from ink to pencil because her fingers were getting black, "and that will never do here."

Blanche was surprised to find herself enjoying this swirl, at first, but the relentless stream of invitations and visitors—two to five callers every day—grew tiresome. And expensive. Sweeping down to dinner and receiving visitors required frequent new dresses, and Blanche wasn't sure how long they could afford their new English life. Neither was Burnham. In October he wrote to his mother that he and Blanche were tearing around the countryside visiting lots of fancy people, which might bankrupt him in six months since the overhead of every visit was about $100. Too bad the tariffs are so high, he added, or he would send her Blanche's old gowns, since Blanche could only wear them a few times.

Throughout Burnham's war service in South Africa, his letters often contained paragraphs about money, stocks, and business affairs. "I will have to get out and hustle again after this war for $ again," he wrote to his mother, "as I will be a long way behind." He felt pleased that no matter what happened in the war and afterward, he had given several Blicks a financial head start and had saved enough to educate his children.

But the value of his African investments had plummeted after the war's early debacles, and during the first months of 1900 the news from the Klondike was bad. John and Judd Blick were still there, working on Burnham's syndicate mines, but the claims had proven disappointing. Burnham hated to fail the Blicks and his investors. Blanche soothed him. "What is not in the ground cannot come out and everyone knows that," she wrote. With the gold rush over, Burnham also worried that the Skagway store he had bought for Madge Blick wouldn't support her, and he would have to move her family back to Pasadena, where jobs were scarce. Blanche brushed aside these concerns while he was in South Africa and told him to focus on staying alive, not on money, because he had proven many times that he could always make more.

———

After several months of honors, celebrity, and recuperation—he was once again able to tear a deck of cards in half—Burnham was restless with drawing-room life. He needed action and income. In December Blanche wrote to Burnham's mother that he had been asked to lead several expeditions in the spring but hadn't yet picked one. "He was offered something *very* good to go to the gold fields of Ashanti [now in Ghana]," she added, "but I said *No*, I will never consent for him to go to that fever hole for any amount of money. The word Ashanti has a perfect horror for me. What would I care for money if Fred died of fever? Not much. No Ashanti." For her, the only worse possibility was a return to combat in South Africa, where the Boers were refusing to surrender.

Two months later Blanche wrote to Burnham's mother that he was leaving in ten days for Ashanti. "It all came up and was arranged in one day," she wrote. "I *was* astonished. I have *never* wanted him to go to the West Coast, but he thinks that is the only and the best thing to do." Burnham had signed a partnership agreement with a group of investors calling themselves the Wa Syndicate. Wa was the most remote outpost in the Northern Territories, also known as the Hinterlands, in Britain's Gold Coast Colony. Wa was also Burnham's destination. Once again he was going to look for gold.

—·—

Burnham and John Blick left from Liverpool on February 13, 1901. The trip out was spiced by tales from a prospector who had been to Patagonia, which rekindled Burnham's desire to try his hand there. He wrote to Blanche complaining that he couldn't find a challenging chess match on board. He drew a picture of the ship for Bruce, who loved boats and water.

After rounding the bulge of Africa into the Gulf of Guinea, they stopped at several places. European ships had been calling along this coast for hundreds of years, and these ports had been centers of the massive transatlantic slave trade. Burnham was struck by the difference between the natives here and in Rhodesia. The Guinea Coast natives spoke English with Cockney or Yankee accents, dressed "to the nines," wore glasses, "and if you call him a nigger he has you arrested and found for insulting him."

The voyage's most memorable event occurred on this leg, a concert of the natives' plaintive songs and chants. Some people didn't like it, wrote Burnham, but "it just held me spellbound and put me in that strange mood it always does and that I can't understand or express. . . . There is not in London anything that can move me in the same way as this."

The syndicate had deposited £5,000 for his use in a British bank in Cape Coast, a former slaving depot on the Gold Coast. The money was for expenses, including the purchase of concessions from inland kings and chiefs. Burnham hoped he hadn't come too late. Gold had been discovered in the Gold Coast Colony—or rather, discovered by Europeans, since Ghana had been the primary source of gold in northern Africa for centuries. Mining companies and speculators had started crowding into the country.

To foil the worst of them, the British government had passed the Gold Coast Concessions Ordinance of 1900. It reflected the government's usual high-mindedness about protecting the natives, de jure if not de facto. It stipulated that no individual could own a concession larger than five square miles or total concessions of more than twenty square miles. Further, no concession would be recognized unless the commissioner and commandant of the Northern Territories both reported that the affected natives understood the agreement, and that it was reasonable. Syndicates were a legal way around the size limitations. Burnham had power of attorney for twenty-nine investors, allowing him to buy up to 580 square miles of claims.

He wasn't working for a salary. Always a prospector at heart, he preferred to gamble on the possibility of a big strike. For his services, the syndicate agreed to cover all his expenses, including first-class travel accommodations to and from West Africa, and to give him 20 percent of the net profit from the sale of any concessions he bought for the syndicate. If he found rich deposits of gold, that 20 percent could be worth a fortune—that is, if the chiefs would sell the concessions, and if the government approved the terms, and if the gold could be extracted by native labor at reasonable expense, and if the government would build a railroad or allow one to be built so that transport to and from the Hinterlands became feasible, and if fever or the region's sometimes belligerent tribes didn't kill everyone and shut down the whole thing. As usual, Burnham didn't allow these foreboding ifs to cloud his optimism.

First, he needed to find 100 carriers for the overland trek to the Hinterlands. They were scarce and everything was expensive because a minor gold rush had been on for six weeks, with hundreds of men in the country to buy concessions. He was also pestered by social invitations, "but it is all booze booze booze. Every five minutes the fools drink and yet each swears they don't drink anything at all."

Burnham entrusted the recruitment of carriers, and much else, to the Honorable J. H. Cheetham. Burnham described him as "a well-educated negro owning large property in Cape Coast and acting as shipping agent for several companies." Cheetham also owned warehouses where the expedition's goods could be stored, which might be useful in the future. For the investors, Burnham listed Cheetham's other bona fides: he was a lawyer, a thirty-degree Mason, a member of the Royal Geographical Society, and a consul for Belgium. He had ten wives and drank a bottle and a half of whiskey a day, but never boasted or raised his voice, and he read heavy books such as Thomas Carlyle's *The French Revolution*. He could be reached at any time by cable. A good man to have in Africa.

Just three days after disembarking at Cape Coast, Burnham left for the interior—a new record, he was told. "I am like a whirlwind among these slumbering officials," he wrote to Blanche. To buy supplies and concessions along the way, he was carrying British money weighing 150 pounds.

Heading north from the coast, Burnham was entranced by the landscape. Forests of mahogany and cotton trees towered nearly 200 feet, with orchids, ferns, and other botanical surprises filling the shade underneath. He sometimes walked for hours without seeing the sun. They rose at four o'clock for coffee, bread, bananas, pineapples, and coconut milk. Then they trekked for six or eight hours, with short breaks, before stopping to eat and overhaul the packs and write letters. By seven or eight o'clock they were under their mosquito nets. The bugs weren't bad but there was "fever galore."

He remained enraptured by African drums. Their power and his reaction mystified and discomfited him. "The land of the Ashanti is the home of the throbbing drum," he wrote in *Taking Chances*.

We rose, we ate, we marched, we danced, we slept, we fought, and we died to its interminable tom-tom. Its low booming was as persistent as the beat of a man's heart, and its crashing roar of war made the native hearers foam at the mouth and their eyes turn red with fury. Some white men find the reverberation of the drums unbearable. Others are indifferent to it, but there are many over whom it seems to weave strange spells or patterns of excited imagination. When the trees of the forest tower inky-black at night and the dance fires leap high; when hundreds of glossy, sinewy naked savages bound in rhythm to the pulsating sounds pouring rapidly from a dozen great drums, an uncanny feeling steals over the white man—a feeling that the experience is not new to him. But where? When? I know this madness, for I have been part of it. The blood ebbs and flows to the beat of the drums. The whole black earth and sky seem to move in rhythm with that reverberating pulse-beat. Time is not. Then the sudden light of dawn dims the fires. The drums cease, the dancers glide away, and with an agonized sigh of relief the white man comes out of the strange enchantment and tiptoes to his tent to lie down for an hour's sleep before the heat of day comes on.

Within a few days Burnham convened a meeting of the carriers, about half of whom were women. He and Blick had noticed that the strongest men were putting the heaviest packs on the women, many of whom were also carrying children. Burnham ordered it stopped. This ignited four hours of yelling, stomping, and threats to leave, much of it from the women. Nevertheless, the packs were redistributed. Burnham required lighter loads than other white men, but the women still carried about 55 pounds on their heads and often an infant on their backs, plus a few pounds of their own food. The men carried 80 to 100 pounds. They did this for six to eight hours each day, for fifteen to twenty miles. For eleven weeks of work, most of the carriers were paid a bit more than £4.

Throughout the expedition there was often some minor complaint from the carriers or squabbling among them. Religion had spoiled them, wrote Burnham. "They are a truculent band of devils, half missionaried so they are not afraid of the white man." He preferred Muslims—"more fierce but not such liars and thieves." Neither he nor Blick ever responded to the carriers with anger, he wrote, since that was pointless and minor frictions were an expected part of travel in Africa. Several carriers told him there were lots of gold workings in the Hinterlands, and silver as well.

—••—

The landscape changed. The trees thinned and shortened, the fever waned. Bananas and pineapples gave way to rice and sweet potatoes. Burnham was eager to get farther north, away from the government stations where, he complained, "it is always a big chin chin and dinner, and I hate dinners," especially since the table always disappeared beneath bottles.

On March 14 they reached Kumasi, 130 miles from the coast. This important town had been the capital of the Ashanti Empire until Britain conquered it in 1874. But the Ashantis were fierce warriors who had not been fully defeated. Britain's most recent conflict with them had broken out almost exactly a year before Burnham's arrival. The garrison at Kumasi—native troops, mostly Muslim Hausas, led by a few British officers—had been besieged for nearly four months before relief arrived.

This was the so-called War of the Golden Stool, sparked when the arrogant colonial governor, Sir Frederick Hodgson, traveled to Kumasi and assembled the Ashanti chiefs to demand that they turn over the Golden Stool, the solid-gold throne of their king. The British had captured the king several years earlier, along with much of the golden royal treasure, but the throne had been hidden away. Hodgson wanted it as a sign of the Ashantis' subservience. He declared to the assembled chiefs that he represented the greatest power on earth, and commanded them to fetch the golden throne so he didn't have to sit on an ordinary chair. Instead, the outraged Ashantis fetched their weapons.

Burnham described the Ashantis as the cleanest natives he had ever seen. They bathed every day, cleaned their clothes every other day, washed their dishes after each meal, and maintained a latrine for sanitation. He added, "but a more bloodthirsty lot does not live under the canopy of heaven," an impressive ranking considering Burnham's experience. The Ashantis had once controlled a vast region, enriching themselves through gold and brutal slave raids. Burnham visited their fetish grove in Kumasi, where great mounds of skulls and bones testified about the slaves tortured and sacrificed there for entertainment.

Burnham scouted for gold near Kumasi and found a promising reef that he traced for two miles. It had been easy to find because it was pitted with old workings dug by natives looking for "shed gold," eroded from the reef by the little streams that ran down it and deposited golden bits not far from the surface. He bought some concessions on the reef after negotiating with the king of Bekwai, who could not be tempted with trinkets. The king bedecked himself with gold jewelry and luxurious robes, sprinkled himself with Florida Water cologne, and was fond of champagne. Burnham cabled the syndicate that the Ashanti country was rich and the company likely would have "a little gold empire."

He couldn't wait to leave for Wa in the far north. White prospectors hadn't yet reached it, so it was still possible to buy big concessions there, though no one knew if there were concessions worth buying. He and Blick bought horses in Kumasi. Burnham's had a fetish bag hidden in its foretop for protection.

They stopped in Kintampo, 110 miles above Kumasi. The landscape reminded him of Mashonaland. The people were no longer Ashanti. The region was ruled by the king of Banda. Burnham bought a concession of fifty square miles from him for a fee of £50 per year until the property was worked, whereupon the fee would rise to £300. He bought another concession of 200 square miles farther north, inside the big curve of the Black Volta River at a place called Wasipe, where he traced a gold reef for twelve miles. As before, the old workings showed him where to look. The Banda people were used to mining and "would furnish a good supply of labor if properly treated," he wrote to the investors. To Blanche he wrote, "I feel that if we find nothing more our expedition is a howling success, and *we* are the pioneers in all the hinterland and ought to reap some reward for it."

But rumors about even richer fields kept him moving north. The whole country was abandoned because of the depredations years earlier by Samori Ture, an Islamic warlord who once had a kingdom in what is now Guinea. When the French claimed his territory, Ture fought them for a dozen years. To elude them he adopted a scorched-earth strategy, devastating the landscapes he moved through and taking slaves to replenish his army. He was finally captured in 1898. Burnham's party walked over the bones of hundreds of his victims. "When he finished a country," wrote Burnham, "a locust would starve in it."

They stopped in Bole, 100 miles beyond Kintampo. At this remote outpost, they found one British officer commanding a small troop of native soldiers. The officer was delighted. He hadn't seen a white man for four months or a white woman for sixteen. "Poor devil," wrote Burnham. To cheer him, Burnham asked their cook to make a special dinner: soup, fish, roasted birds, fried yams, bread, jam, and tea. Wrote Burnham,

These young fellows will be found two or three in a station stuck away in a corner of the wilderness and ruling a half dozen tribes of wild savage people with a handful of house troops. Sometimes a solitary Lieutenant and 20 men live for months on a station cut off from supplies of all kinds, no mails, no luxuries. Native chop for food and [shea butter] oil for light. Some antiquated magazines and almanacs for literature. But they are holding down a stake on the Empire's boundary so that some day the man of commerce can slowly develop the resources of the country, and then the Lieutenant will be shifted deeper into the wilds.

On April 20 they finally reached Wa, more than 400 miles from the coast. The trip had taken nearly seven weeks. Wa was the Gold Coast Colony's outermost station. Three white officers and 100 native soldiers, mostly Hausas, held it for King and Empire. (King Edward VII had succeeded his mother, Queen Victoria, who died in January 1901.) After the usual official niceties, Burnham invaded France.

French West Africa began fifteen miles to the west, across the Black Volta River. A native had told Burnham about a vast gold field there, which no whites had prospected. He found it easily. There were thousands of pits, old and recent. He traced the reefs back across the river into British territory, his excitement growing with each mile. The French side was richer, but the British side was the richest he had seen in the Gold Coast Colony, with reefs running four to twenty feet thick. He pegged 200 square miles of it along twenty miles of the Volta. "Lord but I would like to see you right now," he wrote to Blanche. "I am so full of schemes I shall burst."

It was the wildest country he had ever trekked. Most of the native people, the Dagara (or Dagaaba), didn't wear clothes, though the women donned a loincloth after marriage. They were farmers, he noted, strong workers who would make good miners. Until Burnham's party arrived, most of them had never seen a white man, French or otherwise, nor a horse or a gun, though they had heard rumors of such marvels. They used bows and arrows with poisoned tips. They were friendly at the moment, but Burnham's habit was to anticipate conflict, so he ran tests and made measurements like a military anthropologist.

The Dagara's unfeathered arrows, he reported, had expertly-made iron points, but the bows were short and weak, with bamboo strings. At fifty yards, the bows couldn't drive an arrow through a pigskin legging or three folds of tent canvas. But the Dagara could shoot their arrows "with wonderful rapidity," relying on quantity rather than power or accuracy. Their poison, on the other hand, was deadly, even from a scratch. The Dagara knew an antidote, and Burnham recommended that the syndicate and the army discover it before any conflict arose.

When attacked, the Dagara retreated into their compounds made of "swish," a blend of mud and mortar. It hardened like concrete and was impenetrable by bullets. The compounds had no doors and could be entered only from the roof. Attackers without artillery would have to get close enough to use dynamite or battering rams while Dagara bowman on the roofs showered them with poisoned arrows. Therefore, advised Burnham, soldiers fighting the Dagara should wear leather or three-ply canvas from their breasts to their knees. Officers should wear helmets and tunics fronted with "wire cloth."

After a week or so in the environs of Wa, Burnham and Blick started for home. They suspected that the Volta was navigable for most of its length. If so, steamships could get to within twenty miles of the syndicate's claims, and short railroad spurs to the river would cover the rest, allowing the company to do away with "all this head-carrying business." John Blick was going down the river to test the theory, while Burnham went overland. (Blick traveled 500 miles down the Volta. The chief hazards were hippopotamuses. He saw at least 400 and had to kill six that attacked.)

"I shall be very very glad to see BB's face again," wrote Burnham to his mother while aboard the ship to England, "and each time I go off for so long, I think what a fool I am, but the spirit of unrest I must have suckled with the milk of your breast, so I wander and rove and do things that no other living man can do."

During her husband's absence, Blanche had wearied of socializing and the demands of fashion. She wrote to his mother that she hoped Burnham would take her to the desert. "I am getting *tired* of civilization." (A couple of months later, she was pushing for Patagonia.) She also hoped the expedition would generate enough income to keep Fred home awhile and out of unhealthy places.

———

Burnham reached London in early July, after five months away. Many papers covered his return, running stories about his latest adventure and his thoughts on the gold prospects in West Africa. "It will become one of the very greatest goldfields in the world," was a representative quote. A story in the *Daily Mail*, later picked up by the *New York Times*, was headlined "New Eldorado—Major Burnham's Discoveries in West Africa—Famous Scout's Story." The syndicate's investors must have rubbed their hands at such coverage, which could only increase the value of their concessions.

On December 17, King Edward VII made Burnham a member of the Distinguished Service Order (DSO), Britain's second highest military honor after the Victoria Cross. The king also granted an exception that allowed him to retain his rank of major in the British Army without giving up his U.S. citizenship. The ceremony took place in the hallowed setting of St. James's Palace. Burnham had to kneel, and he worried that his sword would hit the floor because he was so short. In *Scouting on Two Continents*, he wrote, "I realized at that moment why it is men so cheerfully die for the Empire . . . There was no desire now in my heart to boast or strut. I felt of no more importance than a grain of sand on the shore of the mighty sea."

The honor made Blanche proud, but she was probably even more pleased that her husband remained in London. "Thank fortune that I am not going to be a widow this winter," she wrote to her mother. She worried that he would get the urge to return to South Africa, which remained an ugly bog. More than two years after the war began, 200,000 British troops sent to South Africa had been unable to defeat the surviving 20,000 *bittereinders* (bitter enders), who persisted in small guerrilla groups that struck and disappeared. The British public was war-weary.

Lord Roberts had been succeeded in December 1900 by Lord Kitchener, who once called Boers "uncivilized Afrikander savages with a thin white veneer." Kitchener resolved to end the war by any means. He instituted a scorched earth policy, burning every Boer farm and killing or seizing all livestock. He also herded all Boer women and children—eventually 160,000 of them—into about eighty internment centers that became known as "concentration camps," another of the Boer War's gifts to the twentieth century. An additional 130,000 natives also were interned. Malnutrition and disease in these camps killed 28,000 Boer civilians, 22,000 of them children, and at least 14,000 black Africans.

Even Burnham no longer seemed keen on this war. In late 1901 and early 1902 he stayed busy exercising his mind at his chess club, seeing old friends such as the Rider Haggards, and monitoring the many dormant investments that formed a map of his wanderings in the United States, Rhodesia, the Klondike, Alaska, and Africa's Gold Coast.

But he was soon agitated by the old restlessness. "Can't stand London high life another minute," he wrote to his mother in February 1902. "Things are too comfortable and easy. Everything I can think of, every-thing I used to want—friends, fame, health, leisure, and some money, a good family—I have them all. Yet I cannot stand it and must be off into some wilderness. And strange to say B[lanche] is just wild to go with me." He began looking for something adventurous and potentially profitable.

In March came news that Cecil Rhodes had died in Rhodesia at age forty-eight. Burnham later said that from that moment on, his devotion to Africa began to wane. But he and Africa had one more episode together.

The Boer War finally ended in late May 1902. The cost to Britain had been severe: £200 million, more than 22,000 dead, more than 75,000 sent home wounded or ill. To keep the peace, the British government urged the Boers to join in the reconstruction and governance of the expanded colony. The "white man's war" changed little for the colony's black Africans. They went back to work in white men's mines and on white men's farms, with no new rights and no promise of a vote.

Just as the war was ending, Burnham was stepping back onto the con-tinent, this time in British East Africa.

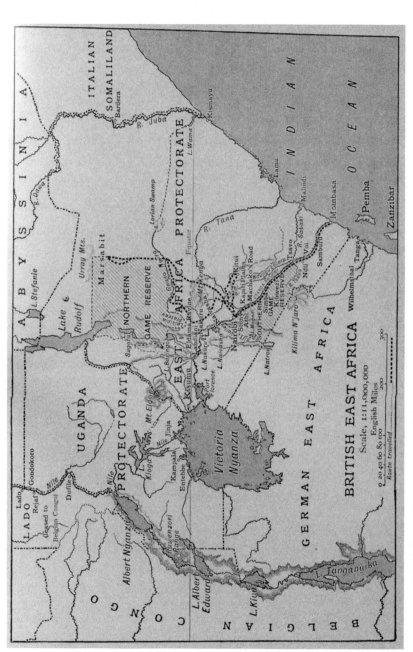

British East Africa. (Courtesy of the Watkinson Library, Trinity College, Hartford, Connecticut.)

CHAPTER TWENTY-TWO

BRITISH EAST AFRICA

Burnham disembarked at Mombasa, Kenya, on May 27, 1902. A
new company, the East Africa Syndicate, had hired him to explore the British East Africa Protectorate (now Kenya) for minerals and desirable agricultural land. He agreed to organize four expeditions that would stake
claims of 500 square miles each. In exchange he would get 20 percent of any
profits from the claims, plus expenses and a hefty salary of £150 per month.
His contract called for him to work "entirely at his own risk and peril."
This deal was sweeter than the one with the Wa Syndicate, since it put cash
in his pocket every month no matter what he found.

Burnham considered the Protectorate another example of enlightened
British imperialism. A few brave souls had endured hardship, famine, and
bloodshed to plant civilization in a savage place. They had abolished slavery
and made relative peace with the tribes. Few people, wrote Burnham,
understood the adversities of pioneering, and far fewer had the guts for it.
He was eager to explore the Protectorate's unvisited regions. "This was an
opportunity to weave another thread into the rich tapestry of white dominion in Africa."

The first threads were woven in 1888 when Her Majesty's government
gave responsibility for East Africa to the Imperial British East Africa Com-

pany (IBEAC), a chartered enterprise like Rhodes's British South Africa Company. As in southern Africa, the charter was awarded to relieve the government of the financial burdens and political entanglements of administering another colony. But debts and quarrels soon dragged the company into bankruptcy. It dissolved in July 1895. The British government assumed responsibility and renamed the territory the East Africa Protectorate. To investors and speculators, that meant the colony was open for business, and the scramble began.

During the two years he spent there, Burnham hired between 500 and 1,000 native askaris and porters for his expeditions. He also recruited twenty tough, experienced white men: hunters, explorers, ex-soldiers, assayers, surveyors, mining engineers, and two gentleman adventurers. They came from Britain, Canada, New Zealand, and the United States. He chose them for their temperament and character as well, because he needed to trust them. The syndicate expected him to explore a vast region: north to Abyssinia (now Ethiopia), south to German East Africa (now Tanzania), and west beyond Lake Victoria. To cover more territory more quickly, he sent off expeditions in different directions. "Anybody can stir up trouble with the natives," wrote Burnham, "but judgment, self-control, and justice are essential qualities in a leader who is to enter alien lands and break a trail which the next white explorer can follow without risk of being robbed or attacked." His rule was to aim for peace but be ready for conflict.

The toll of blood began before the expeditions even launched. First, the porters got bubonic plague and had to be quarantined. The horses and mules brought from Italy died beneath swarms of ticks. Leopards ate all the dogs. A crocodile ate one of the servants. Nevertheless, Burnham loved Nairobi and the abundant wildlife just beyond its borders: ostriches, hartebeests, thousands of zebras, countless gazelles. He wrote to Blanche that she would love it there and should come back with him on the next trip. He was bubbling with "lovely schemes": a farm, a cattle ranch, a coal mine, a hunting safari on the savannah. As always he longed for her and sighed about the wanderlust that pushed him away.

In mid-June the expeditions were cleared to begin. Burnham traveled west. He spent twenty-five hours on a small steamer crossing Lake Victoria to Entebbe, arriving during the festivities to honor King Edward VII's coronation. He left Entebbe on July 1 with twenty-five paddlers in three canoes, heading for the north coast of Lake Victoria and Kampala. He was chasing a rumor of coal.

———

That rumor, like most Burnham pursued in East Africa, was a chimera. During the first year, one of his exploratory teams found a sprinkling of gold on the eastern shore of Lake Victoria, but nothing worth exploiting. No silver or diamonds. No copper. But in July of 1902 he heard of something just as good.

There are at least three versions of the story, two by Burnham. They sometimes overlap, sometimes contradict. In *Taking Chances* he wrote that in Zanzibar an explorer and scientist (identified in the rough draft as Sir John Willoughby, an old acquaintance from Rhodesia) told him of native reports about a lake in the Great Rift Valley made of "snow that did not melt in the sun." A caravan sent by the sultan of Zanzibar had returned with some of this snow, which Willoughby had analyzed. It was almost pure carbonate of soda (also called soda ash and sodium carbonate). This valuable mineral was used in glass-making, dying, degreasing, water softening, and many other industrial processes.

In the Protectorate, Burnham heard similar rumors about a white lake somewhere near the border with German East Africa. But no one seemed to know the lake's precise location or size. The rumors reminded Burnham of Western stories about lost mines—catnip for him. He put the lake on his list of possibilities. According to *Taking Chances*, two Australian prospectors named Duncan and Welsh happened into Burnham's camp just before he left for Lake Victoria. (Typically, he misspells their names, which were Thomas Deacon and John Walsh). He hired them to search for the lost white lake. They prowled the southern end of the Great Rift Valley, where natives vaguely acknowledged the lake's existence but refused to guide them there. Eventually the two prospectors tracked the spoor by following small white crystals that had spilled from the sultan's caravan. At last they stood at the lake, as big and white as the tales described. They were exhausted and parched. The last leg had required a journey of seventy miles in searing heat without water. They turned around without exploring further, and eventually reported to Burnham.

He told a similar but less dramatic version to Blanche in late June 1902, and repeated it in his report to the syndicate in September 1903. "Last night an old Rhodesian prospector came to see me," he wrote to Blanche. "He has found a great soda lake 50 miles from Nairobi, soda carb by the million tons. It may be possible to utilize it but can't say. It is in a healthy country and a RR could be built to it for $100,000." His report to the syndicate said that "prospectors" had told him about the lake. These contemporary versions are more trustworthy than the reminiscence in *Taking Chances*. The prospectors were no doubt Deacon and Walsh, both of whom registered claims on the lake at some point. Burnham certainly knew both men. Perhaps they found the lake in the dramatic way that Burnham described in *Taking Chances*, perhaps not.

A third version accuses Burnham and the East Africa Syndicate of falsely taking credit for discovering the lake after hearing about it from Deacon and Walsh, whose claims the syndicate bought out. But this doesn't substantially contradict either of Burnham's versions. He was always scrupulous about crediting others, and in *Taking Chances* he praised Deacon and Walsh for finding the soda lake after much hardship. Burnham also was always fair to the explorers and prospectors he hired, and paid them well. As a prospector himself, he understood Deacon and Walsh's entitlement to an interest in the soda lake, whether they discovered it while on his payroll or not. It's not surprising that, like most prospectors, they soon sold their interests and moved on.

In any case, it's undisputed that Deacon and Walsh's discovery stirred Burnham to set off for the lake in the summer of 1902. To avoid the baking heat of the Rift Valley, his team traveled mostly after sunset. One night they crested a ridge. "The brilliant moon shed a flood of light into a black basin of basalt," wrote Burnham, "and in its depths glittered the snowy M'gardi, a great gleaming white gem cupped in Africa's black palm." The lake's eerie beauty transfixed him. So did its potential profitability. "The long hidden treasure lay at last at my feet, more valuable than the richest gold reef in the world, for this wealth, unlike gold, continues in the making."

Lake Magadi sat at the bottom of a deep desert basin similar to Death Valley. Warm springs continuously recharged the lake with liquefied soda. Intense heat evaporated the moisture, leaving a thick crust of soda that was constantly replenished. The lake was twenty miles long and two miles wide. John Blick returned the following year and sampled forty million tons of soda from a small portion of the lake. The mineral was nearly pure. At $15 dollars per ton, those forty million tons were worth about $600 million. Once again Burnham was certain he had found his bonanza. To tap it, the syndicate just needed to build sixty miles of railroad from Nairobi.

Burnham left East Africa in late August for London. Aside from the soda lake, he didn't have much good news for the syndicate. He had started to believe that East Africa's real wealth lay in its fertile highlands, where Europeans could farm and stay healthy. If he was right, the land itself, not the minerals hidden in it, would be the best investment. Good agricultural land always drew settlers. Before he left, he bought several thousand acres himself and hired a local planter to experiment with coffee, tea, cotton, Indian corn, castor beans, many European vegetables, and even his old nemesis, orange trees. Most of these experiments turned out well and helped to encourage future settlement.

In London the investors were displeased to see him back after only three months, but he had promised to join Blanche and the boys in Pasadena for a family visit. This domestic excuse didn't appease the syndicate. They revised his contract to specify that his monthly salary would be paid only when he was in East Africa. Some of the Wa investors were unhappy as well, because the Ashanti claims weren't yet proving out. He wasn't worried. "We will make money out of it bye and bye," he wrote to Blanche. On the positive side, the soda lake intrigued the syndicate, and they had been coming to conclusions similar to Burnham's about buying land for agriculture. A number of the main directors wanted Burnham to peg a concession of 5,000 square miles, which the company would lease to fifty settler families.

He would be busy when he returned to East Africa, but first he was going home. On September 10 he left for a short visit to the United States and Pasadena.

In October, on the way back east, Burnham stopped at Salt Lake to learn about the processing of lake minerals. He also stopped at the White House for a long chat with Theodore Roosevelt, now president after the assassination of William McKinley the previous September. By Christmas he was back in East Africa, this time with Blanche and Bruce. Roderick remained at school in London. Burnham wanted Rod to end up at Sandhurst, Britain's West Point, leading to a career in the British Army, an idea that dismayed Blanche. The plan reflected Burnham's ongoing expectation of living outside the United States.

As he busied himself and his teams with expeditions into remote parts of the Protectorate, Blanche began adjusting to colonial life in Nairobi. They lived in a house with a large veranda on the syndicate's forty-three-acre compound near town. Every resident (many lived in tents) had at least two armed guards at night, partly because of thieves but mostly because of animals from the surrounding plains—lions, rhinos, and especially the brazen hyenas.

The contrast between the place's wild fringes and British conventionalities often entertained Blanche. She wrote to Burnham's mother about watching two men in starched white shirt-fronts walk into a tent to dine. The British colonials dressed formally every night for dinner, and amused

Blanche by insisting they would do so even if they were supping alone on the veldt. Such contrasts were everywhere—flower shows and rhinos, formal luncheons and painted natives.

One evening Blanche and Bruce were in a rickshaw on their way to dinner when they ran into a war party of Maasai en route to punish an enemy tribe. The warriors wore feather headdresses, and their bodies were slick with castor oil and red clay. They carried shields and their alarming spears, with blades four feet long. The rickshaw man excitedly launched them down a hill. He lost control, and as the rickshaw capsized, Blanche put her arm around Bruce's head. The rough ground tore off a section of her skin. On top of that, she complained, "one of my prettiest muslin blouses ruined."

She wrote home that they had been socializing a lot in the syndicate's camp, receiving visitors, giving and attending dinner parties. "Rather swagger ones where we will all be in evening dress," she wrote. "I am getting use out of my evening gowns. Danced through the chiffon ruffles of my lace dress the other evening but I can mend it."

Like all colonials, she had plenty of servants. They were Muslims, since "missionaried" natives were spoiled. Her house servant was a forty-year-old Somali eunuch. He spoke English and dressed in pure white trousers and a long overshirt, accented with a wide sash of red or yellow, with a matching turban. Her Goanese cook was occasionally drunk by the end of dinner, sometimes earlier, but was too talented to let go.

Blanche took her turn hosting dinners, making do with a mix of silver, china, and enamel plates. When short of glasses, she drank out of Bruce's little silver mug. Four natives served from side tables, two carried food from the kitchen, and two more washed dishes for reuse with the next course. She proudly described one of her menus in a letter: pre-dinner drinks (champagne and whiskey-and-soda, though she stuck to water), caviar on toast, soup, fried oysters, mutton cutlets with green peas, venison cutlets with mushrooms, roast venison, red currant jelly, potatoes, and cauliflower.

For dessert, plum pudding and sherry sauce, then lemon cling peaches ("tinned but awfully good"), and finally fresh fruit, sweets, coffee, and cigarettes.

They were frequently reminded that starched shirt-fronts and multi-course dinners couldn't turn this place into London. One night gunshots woke them. Burnham was outside with his revolver before Blanche got out of bed, but within a minute she was at the window with a rifle. It turned out to be some men chasing thieves. Everyone was on edge because of con-stant rumors of a Maasai uprising, and at a meeting the next day the camp discussed what to do in case of attack. They decided that all the whites would gather at the Burnhams', and planned accordingly. "My bedroom looks like an arsenal," noted Blanche. She added, "I do hope it is not our fate to be massacred."

After four months of colonial conventionalities, swagger dinners, pests, and menacing rumors, Blanche was weary of life in Nairobi. "If Fred was not here I would not want to stay a single day," she wrote. "It is not real pioneering yet we have many dangers and terrible society." Her brother John Blick noticed the change in her. "She is really getting tired of this country," he wrote to their sister Kate. "I don't mean this country in partic-ular, but of traveling around. She wants to settle down."

But not quite yet. In late April, when Burnham left on an expedition to the soda lake, she and Bruce went to live at 7,000 feet in a big grass house in the lovely highlands sixty miles north of Nairobi. She took only the Goanese cook and two servants, some cots, and safari clothes (no gowns). Her spirits immediately improved. Their camp, at a place called Naivasha, was simple, the landscape beautiful, the conventionalities absent. Leopards occasionally prowled through camp, but they could learn to live with those. Burnham visited between expeditions.

———

He and his teams had been poking into every corner of the Protectorate. The conditions were always arduous and often dangerous. Depending on the terrain, porters carrying head-loads of fifty-five pounds could cover only six to fifteen miles per day. When possible, the expeditions lived off game, but the standard fare was rice, with some flour and sugar for the whites. Sometimes they had good Abyssinian coffee. Some of the syndicate's investors had suggested that Burnham cut expenses by feeding the natives on cheap cornmeal, but he rejected the idea as a false economy. Rice ensured him of getting the best carriers. The expeditions were also physically draining and could be wrecked by poor nutrition. His porters repaid good treatment, he wrote, with patience and hard work.

Hazards were plentiful enough without worrying about unhealthy food. At the soda lake, a man was eaten by a lion. Another died from a snake bite. A man was seriously injured when a rhino tossed him. One night a sleeping man had his face torn off by a hyena. Two porters who strayed from the safari were killed and eaten by cannibals, despite the safe-passage Burnham had negotiated with the cannibals' chief. Burnham felt that if he did nothing, the cannibals would declare open season on his men, but if he killed any natives in retaliation, the British government would likely boot the syndicate from the Protectorate. So he marched to the cannibals' village and arrested the chief for breaking the agreement. He demanded recompense and called for a trial that afternoon.

The chief turned out to be the Clarence Darrow of cannibals. The criminal party, he argued, was Burnham, who had negligently let his porters wander off into the high grass, thereby placing themselves "on par with a bunch of bananas." Therefore, reasoned the chief, he was the party who deserved compensation, since Burnham had not only broken the agreement, he had humiliated the chief with a false accusation. The chief graciously offered to forgive Burnham and reinstate the original agreement in return for one of Burnham's rifles. Burnham, outwitted and amused, finessed this dilemma by offering to release the chief from arrest and to make him a member of an exalted secret society called the Order of the Buffalo, whose pricey initiation fee would be waived. Both sides were happy with the plea bargain.

The worst predators were tropical diseases. The expeditions passed through districts where sleeping sickness killed people so quickly that some corpses had bananas in their mouths. The vultures and hyenas could hardly move, gorged. For three days Burnham's group never escaped the stench of death, and the disease also exacted its toll from Burnham's men. So did blackwater fever. "Half my white men were wiped out within two years," wrote Burnham in *Taking Chances*, "by fever, hardship, or accident—or invalided home, permanently disabled. About half my blacks succumbed to fevers and disasters of one kind or another."

He didn't mention that fever had rocked him as well. In July 1903 Blanche wrote to her parents that Fred was at Naivasha recovering, and was very thin. (He had weighed 143 pounds before leaving for East Africa.) She was sure, she continued, that after this and his experiences in West Africa "he will never go to the tropics again and I am *so* glad. He has made so many of these awful trips in his life and he cannot expect to keep it up forever and still keep his health. But it takes a hard jolt to make him realize it."

—•—

While searching for minerals, Burnham studied the tribes he traveled through. He believed natives should be allowed to keep land and cattle and to maintain their social customs and laws, because that was the best way to keep peace. The three main tribes of East Africa's interior were the Kikuyu, the Wakamba (or Kamba), and the Maasai. He recorded details about their weapons, temperaments, social structures, and amusements. He was especially intrigued by the most warlike of the three, the Maasai. "Many peculiar customs practiced by the Masai and neighboring tribes are of deep interest to the anthropologist and doubtless have meanings not comprehended by the white explorer passing through their country. I have read many flippant references to various practices of the natives, but it is my conviction that the observers did not understand their true significance." He saw that two scourges had ravaged Maasai culture—rinderpest, which decimated their cattle-centered way of life, and white settlers, who forbade the tribe from raiding their neighbors and ended the tradition of military training for young men. As this disappeared, so did the tribe's devotion to discipline and self-sacrifice. "The purity of their blood," wrote Burnham, "can no longer be protected."

Unlike many people of his era, Burnham formed his views about race from the saddle, not the armchair. He had a strong interest in native peoples and was a gifted observer of customs, social structures, military matters, and a tribe's place within a larger landscape. But his perspective was often distorted because he viewed everything through the prisms of race and war.

Just as he never missed a chance to study native people, he never missed a chance to hunt big game. A family photo album from East Africa documents an array of trophies: hartebeest, warthog, sable antelope, giraffe, lion ("a ten footer"), black rhino ("almost a record horn"). Many of their heads ended up on the walls of Burnham's homes. A chapter in *Taking Chances* describes his pursuit of "Jungle Elephants," including what he calls the most dangerous animal in Africa, the "rogue" elephant. One of these creatures absorbed nine or ten high-grain bullets before it died. Its foot was sixty-one inches in circumference, and it was almost ten feet tall at the shoulder. From the tip of its trunk to its tail measured twenty-seven feet. Its tusks were six feet long and later decorated Burnham's home, one of several such pairs. He shot another elephant in the head but lost it in the bush; it survived long enough to ambush and kill a passing Maasai and shatter the arm of another.

Such tales about African big-game hunting, once popular, may now seem repellent. In his later years Burnham too had second thoughts. Like Theodore Roosevelt and other early conservationists, he grew alarmed at the destruction he had once relished. Africa's wildlife, he wrote, "is greater and more wonderful than that of all other continents combined," and it thrived "until the 'civilized' white man with his vaunted intelligence came with bullets and a hundred other means of destruction, including traps and poison. In one generation he turned almost half of Africa into a lonely sun-baked wilderness." He reviled hunters who went to East Africa to kill wild animals while also sidestepping danger, shooting high-powered rifles from vehicles and airplanes. "This mode of sport is, to my notion, about as thrilling as sitting on the pasture fence and slaying the pet cow."

Burnham embodied the paradox of certain groups—pioneers, prospectors, ranchers, commercial fishermen—who love wilderness and wildlife to death while extracting everything they can from them, and then are surprised when the game or the grass or the clean water or the fish begin to disappear.

—•—

In late summer of 1903, Blanche and Bruce left Naivasha for a six-day safari with Burnham. Blanche relished this return to a strenuous outdoor life, but admitted to her parents that each day left her exhausted. Perhaps, at age forty-one, she was losing her enthusiasm for the rigors of camping on the veldt.

After the quiet loveliness of Naivasha, she certainly had little enthusiasm for resuming colonial life in Nairobi. She began making plans to return to England with Bruce. She was delighted when Fred agreed to go with them in late October. Burnham seemed to sense that his time in Africa was ending. In a letter to his mother dated October 8, 1903, he wrote what sounds like a farewell, not only to Africa but to a way of life:

> It is with regret I leave this lovely camp with its lake and great mountains, its steaming old craters, solemn moss drooping forests. . . . I shall miss the roar of the leopards, the wail of the hyenas, and the soft calling notes of the bell bird. The nights are of such matchless splendor when the moon is full, and my wild naked Kikuyu sing a deep and lovely chant in keeping with the sounds that come from forest and plain. During the day the valley below is dotted with thousands of sheep and herds of cattle herded by [Maasai] who stand about in

little groups like ebony. A soft lowing as continuous as the sound of running water comes constantly and pleasantly over the boma walls—such a sound and scene as must have touched the shepherds of old. The wildest and sweetest land I have ever seen. It is I fear passing from me forever. Sometimes I wish I had never learned to read or form any conception of duty, civilization, religion, for I would have been and am at heart a splendid savage, nothing more, and now I am to return to London—to swallowtails, the club, soft carpets, soft food, soft life, soft men and women.

Burnham probably expected his hiatus from Africa to be brief. It was, after all, the place he often insisted would be his permanent home. But he wouldn't return for thirty years, and then as a tourist visiting old haunts. His African years had been filled with adventures, sorrows, violence, and triumphs, and had made him famous. "My boyhood dreams of Africa had all come true," he wrote years later. "I realized this with a sense of accomplishment and joy, although it had streaked the heads of both my wife and myself with gray."

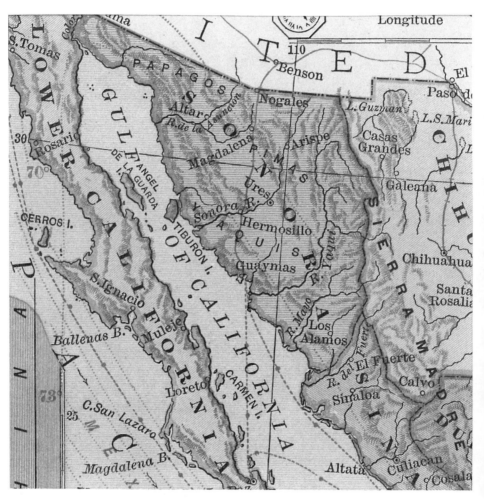

Sonora, Mexico. (From *Barnes's Complete Geography* by James Monteith, 1885.)

CHAPTER TWENTY-THREE

PROSPECTS AND LOSSES

IN MARCH 1904 Blanche elatedly wrote to her parents that she and her family were coming home to live for at least a year or two. The move made Rod "wild with joy," she wrote. They built a house in San Rafael Heights, an out-of-the-way neighborhood in what Burnham, in a letter to his mother, half-sardonically called "lovely, sleepy, sunny Pasadena, a safe *nook* of the world hid away on the *edge* of the world." In late March 1905, his mother, who five years earlier had remarried and found happy companionship, died of cancer. It shook Burnham.

As always, his need for action and money soon made him restless to escape this drowsy refuge. His financial interests in Rhodesia, Alaska, West Africa, and East Africa all were either dormant, kaput, or endlessly pending. So many prospects, so little cash flow. He needed money partly to fund his new plan for Rod: mining engineer. That meant college. The cost of four years at Stanford or Berkeley shocked him, but he told Blanche the sacrifice was necessary so that their son, unlike him, wouldn't suffer from lack of formal education. "In his blood and strength," he wrote to Blanche, "I see myself when I was a living volcano and men either loved or hated me, sometimes to their own undoing. Roderick *must* fit himself for the age of struggle in which we live."

Burnham was considering various money-making adventures when his friend, the romantic novelist Rider Haggard, delivered one to his doorstep. In April 1905 Haggard and his daughter visited the Burnhams in Pasadena. They arrived in California in the private rail car of Haggard's old friend, John Hays Hammond. In an era when mining was often in the headlines, Hammond was the most famous and wealthy mining engineer in the world.

As the private car clacked along the tracks toward California, Haggard had told Hammond the strange tale of Montezuma's "lost city." The novelist had heard it from a correspondent named J. G. H. Carmichael. Carmichael claimed to have discovered an old Aztec city hidden in the jungles of southwest Mexico, where Montezuma, frightened by the approaching conquistadores, had stored treasure worth £3 million. But after Carmichael stumbled upon it, the local Indians forced him to flee. He was determined to go back. He had learned the Indians' language, Quecchi, since that might help him retrieve the treasure, if he could find it again. He had sent his account to Haggard with an admiring note about the writer's novel *Montezuma's Daughter* (1893), and a request to fund his search for the lost city.

Haggard was a perfect audience for such a tale, which resembled one of his own. Some of Carmichael's statements checked out, so Haggard and a friend sent him a small sum. Carmichael plunged back into the jungle. When he came down with fever, his Indian carriers deserted him. He survived by catching catfish with a bent nail, but his health was broken and he died soon after returning to civilization.

That's the story Haggard told Hammond on the train. The jungle still protected Montezuma's lost treasure, he added, but if anyone could find it, it was the man he was going to visit in Pasadena. The tale fired Hammond's imagination. He agreed that Burnham, whom he knew from southern Africa, was the man to pursue it. After leaving Haggard and returning to New York, Hammond wired Burnham to come see him about the Mexican proposition. Burnham was there within a week.

The two men had many things in common. Both were Westerners. Hammond, six years older, was born and raised in San Francisco, where his parents had gone for the gold rush. He had degrees from Yale and Freiberg (a German mining university), while Burnham was self-educated, but both had the optimistic, adventurous temperament of prospectors, and both had come to manhood in roughneck mining camps and boomtowns all over the Southwest and Mexico. Both had left the United States in 1893 to seek their fortune in the new frontier of southern Africa, where they first met. Hammond started there with the Barnato brothers, who owned gold mines in the Transvaal. Cecil Rhodes quickly recognized his abilities and hired him away at a huge salary. Hammond more than earned it by convincing Rhodes to adopt the new technology of deep-level mining in his gold and diamond operations, which substantially multiplied Rhodes's wealth. It also made Hammond's reputation and his first fortune. Hammond admired Rhodes, but unlike Burnham stopped short of near-idolatry, partly because he was less prone to such ardors and partly because he had been drawn into Rhodes's disastrous plot to overthrow the Boer government of the Transvaal. When the Jameson Raid failed, Hammond was imprisoned in Pretoria as a conspirator and sentenced to death. He was released after Rhodes paid Kruger's extortionate fines.

By the time Hammond and Burnham met in New York, Hammond was the general manager and consulting engineer for the Guggenheim Exploration Company. His job was to find and evaluate mineral and oil prospects in North America, and he got a piece of any property the company bought on his recommendation. This deal, plus a magnificent salary, reportedly brought him a million dollars a year.

Guggenheim Exploration's masthead was crowded with five sons of Meyer Guggenheim, a tailor who had emigrated to the United States in 1847 and proceeded to amass one of the country's great fortunes, mostly through mining and smelting, before his death in 1905. His son Solomon (who later founded the Guggenheim Museum) was one of Guggenheim Exploration's managing directors. Another was Harry Payne Whitney, who had inherited $24 million from his father in 1904 and was married to the heiress Gertrude Vanderbilt, who later founded the Whitney Museum. For a prospector like Burnham who needed working capital, Guggenheim Exploration was a jackpot.

As an evaluator of mining prospects, Hammond had a reputation for thoroughness and honesty. Rhodes once asked him to assess the mineral wealth of the British South Africa Company's concession. Rhodes was hoping Hammond would report a second Rand, which would quiet skeptics and raise the company's stock price. Hammond bluntly noted that the deposits were scattered and unexceptional. Rhodes, to his credit, didn't attempt to influence the report and accepted it without complaint. When Hammond moved on to work as a consulting engineer in London and then New York, he hired experts to double-check his own appraisals, and often hired other experts to corroborate the experts. His judgments had made him trusted and wealthy. The Guggenheims and Whitney banked on his recommendations.

Hammond had worked in Mexico as a young engineer, and was intrigued by its unexplored possibilities. Carmichael's story rekindled his enthusiasm. In his youth Burnham too had wandered around Mexico, as a prospector and as a courier for the smuggler McLeod. He had also taken exploratory trips in the years since, and his attentive eye had noted many prospects. In New York he and Hammond no doubt stoked each other as they talked about Mexico.

By the end of April the Guggenheim Exploration Company had offered Burnham $500 a month plus expenses to take a prospecting trip to southwest Mexico. Or, if Burnham preferred a percentage, they would help him form a syndicate. Burnham, always anticipating a big strike, chose the latter option, and decided to offer the opportunity to some of his wealthy contacts in England. Exhilarated by his change in luck, he wrote to Blanche that after a few days in London he would swoop home to pick her up for Mexico, "and a whirl at fortune's wheel in which you will see me as of old, full of life and schemes and vim and worth your undivided love." He added that he weighed 138½ and felt healthy.

He and Hammond left for London. Burnham began studying Spanish four hours a day. By early May he had hooked a prominent financier named Arthur M. Grenfell on the Mexican prospects. Grenfell was the son-in-law of Burnham's friend and African business partner Earl Grey, who was also a director of the BSAC. The Mexican Southern Mining Syndicate was formed as a cooperative syndicate with Guggenheim Exploration.

But within a few days Burnham got tempted by a more exotic prospect dangled by another of his African contacts, Charles H. Villiers, who had ridden on the Jameson Raid and was also one of the directors of the East Africa Syndicate. On May 11, 1905, Burnham informed Blanche that once again there had been a sudden change of plans: they were going to remote China, far up the Yangtze River, almost to India. He would be working for a new gold mining syndicate formed by some of the investors from the East Africa Syndicate. He would get £150 per month plus 5 percent of sales and some deferred shares, and—perhaps most exciting—"it will all be new lands again." He would pick her up in California and they would keep going to the Far East. He sounded rejuvenated. "Just think how ancient I am—44. But I still am full of schemes and long to hold you in my arms as when I was only 22."

He was leaving the next day to meet Hammond in Germany to ask for a postponement of the Mexican venture, and to invite him into the China deal. (Hammond graciously agreed to the postponement and declined on China.) Blanche wrote that she was game for anything. "After this we are going to stay together even if we starve," she wrote. "We will go out into the wild and hunt and fish for a living."

Burnham assured her that China was certain. He also had been questioning Villiers about the delay in floating a new company for the soda lake, which Burnham expected to be a bonanza for him. The financier pledged it was in the works. "So once again things *look bright*," he wrote, "but bear in mind I have not as yet cashed a cent." They agreed that he needed to stay in London until the deals about China and soda were settled.

Both issues became more frustrating. Every few days Villiers swore that the soda lake syndicate would be floated in just a few more days. This loop played over and over throughout June. Likewise, Villiers and Edmund Davis, another principal in both the China syndicate and the East Africa Syndicate, constantly tantalized Burnham with the fragrance of China, but the blossom never produced fruit. In early July he wrote to Blanche that the financiers now expected to need two more weeks to collect the capital for China, and two more months to float the soda scheme. He was expecting to realize a small fortune—at least £10,000 from the soda company and between £10,000 and £40,000 from his shares in the East Africa Syndicate. "So you can see there is money in the air," he wrote, "but none in my pocket."

In fact, after paying expenses in New York and London for two and a half months, he was broke. He told Blanche to borrow $500 for him in Pasadena and wire it right away. "I can get it here but it would be fatal to let them know I was hard up." If things weren't settled soon, he wanted her to come to London with Bruce. "Life is too short to be apart so awful long," he wrote, ". . . we can't take our money into the grave and every week's loss of your love is lost forever." He signed it, "With unmeasured love, I am ever, your erratic lode star."

In September Blanche and Bruce joined Burnham in London. They had been separated for four months. They rented the same house at Bourne End where they had stayed after the Boer War, a comfortable place on the Thames. Bruce, now seven, still loved boats and was enthralled to be near water. He and his nurse often walked along the river.

Burnham and Blanche mulled over plans and possibilities. The soda lake loop kept repeating. The financing for the China syndicate never seemed to reach critical mass. Meanwhile, Burnham wasn't working and their expenses had increased with the obligations of London social life.

Sometime on October 1, Bruce went missing. Hours of frantic searching ended the next morning with a horrible discovery: Bruce's body floating in the Thames. He had slipped away to explore the riverside by himself. When Burnham saw his dead son, recounted Haggard, "he fell to the ground senseless as though he had been shot." Once again Burnham sent a terse cablegram to their family in California: "Bruce drowned. Coming soon."

The loss of another child plummeted Blanche into depression. Burnham dealt with his heartbreak characteristically, by forcing himself back into motion. He had responded similarly after his mother's death earlier that year. In a note of thanks to her doctor, he had written, "All my life I had so woven mother into my innermost thoughts that her loss seems at this writing beyond repair. This is of course contrary to nature and I shall plunge away into the wilds of Mexico very soon where nature and time will adjust all things anew." For Burnham, the antidote to defeat, sorrow, or despair was action.

Once again, the Burnhams had to adjust. Bruce was gone. The soda lake scheme kept receding into the future. China was a vanishing mirage. Blanche needed the comfort of her remaining child, and Burnham needed to lose himself in activity. The Mexican offer from Hammond and Grenfell remained on the table. Burnham grabbed it. He and Blanche reached Pasadena on November 20. He left almost immediately for the border.

Porfirio Díaz, president and virtual dictator of Mexico between 1876 and 1911, was determined to force his backward, impoverished country out of the eighteenth century and into the twentieth. To Díaz that meant modern industry and modern agriculture, which required huge infusions of capital. Like many poor countries, Mexico lacked money but was rich in resources. Díaz began taking his nation's assets from the poor and redistributing them to people who could exploit them. He awarded huge estates to cronies and threw open Mexico's doors to foreign investors. Torrents of money poured in, sweeping up minerals and land, depositing new towns and railroads, enriching a small group of Mexicans and Americans while pushing the great majority farther into poverty.

Díaz prepared the way for modernization and the flow of capital by removing possible impediments, such as indigenous people and the traditional rights of campesinos. For instance, in Sonora, Burnham's main area of activity for the next several years, Díaz's army cleared the fertile Yaqui Valley for development by decimating the Yaqui Indians who hunted and farmed there. Thousands were killed and thousands more were deported to work as slaves in the tropical Yucatán, where most of the desert Indians soon died.

By 1908, when Burnham's life and finances became entwined with the Yaqui Valley, the population of Yaqui Indians there had dropped from 20,000 to 3,000. That turned out to be more than enough to cause mayhem. Burnham would soon judge Yaquis the equals of Apaches as guerrilla fighters.

But that violence lay a few years ahead. In late 1905, as he entered Mexico for Guggenheim Exploration, the country's resources were ripe for picking. He met up with Blanche's brothers, John and Judd, and began prospecting. Testing ore with a horn spoon always made him buoyant. "Lovely weather, fine camp, good food, and I feel full of life and spirits again," he wrote to Blanche, adding, "I am hungry every day and hard as iron."

Blanche lacked his psychological resilience and his male avenues for recovery. In late December she told her sister Madge that she couldn't stop crying. "It seems as though two tragedies and three wars were enough for any poor woman to bear." Perhaps depression drained her energy; perhaps she found it impossible to reciprocate her husband's unsinkable optimism. At any rate she stopped answering his letters. On December 21 he mentioned that he hadn't gotten any replies. On December 22 he began, "Tomorrow will surely bring me a line." On December 23 he wrote, "Say, this is strange, not one whisper from you . . . What has happened. This is my fourth to you."

He kept writing, describing his prospects and the beautiful Sonoran landscape of oak, juniper, cactus, mountains, streams. As he sensed the reasons for her silence, his tone gentled. On December 28 he wrote that his Christmas had been lousy and he guessed hers was too. He added that he wouldn't expect many letters in Mexico, and that he was carrying her picture in his pocket. By January 4 he still hadn't heard from her, but furnished the excuse that the mails were irregular and she shouldn't worry about it. He signed off, "Lots and lots of love and several good hard hugs and pray we find our lost bonanza."

A week later everything looked brighter. "We are just sampling the biggest copper mine in the world we believe," he wrote. Equally wonderful, he had received her wire and they were linked again. "Take for yourself boundless love and continuous admiration," he wrote, "even after twenty two years of tempest and calm, obscurity and fame, poverty and plenty."

The copper mine was about ninety miles due south of Douglas, Arizona, and was called La Caridad (Charity). Over the next few days, the combination of his rich prospects and Blanche's letters swelled Burnham's exhilaration. He called the mine "the bonanza of the world" and wrote, "We are feeling pretty cock-a-whoop!" He had secured an option and Hammond was sending an engineer to examine it. It was the "biggest surface show of copper in Mexico," and Burnham was certain Hammond would want it. As a bonus, four letters had just arrived from Blanche and one from Rod. Top of the world.

The mining engineer visited and reported favorably. That convinced Hammond to form a new subsidiary of Guggenheim Exploration called the Western Mexico Syndicate, still in cooperation with Grenfell's Mexican Southern Mining Syndicate. Burnham went to New York in April 1906 to sign the contract. The initial funding was $25,000, with Guggenheim Exploration owning 51 percent and Hammond 49 percent. Other documents suggest that Hammond had a silent partner, the railroad baron Edward H. Harriman, president of the Union Pacific and Southern Pacific Railroads, among others. The contract gave Burnham $500 per month and his brother Howard $250 per month to scout mining properties for the syndicate in Mexico. If the syndicate took up any of the properties found by Burnham, he would get a 10 percent interest.

A few days later Hammond's hometown was shattered by one of the worst natural disasters in the country's history. The San Francisco earthquake destroyed most of the city and killed 3,000 people. Hammond immediately sent $10,000 to the relief fund and, according to Burnham, sent another $40,000 anonymously.

By late May Burnham was back in Sonora, scouting mines and waiting for a second expert sent by Hammond to evaluate La Caridad, where test shafts had been dug. "So very much is at stake in next 15 days," he wrote to Blanche, who was about to join him with Rod. If La Caridad was the bonanza he expected, his 10 percent would be worth a fortune.

The second engineer "very highly approved" of La Caridad, which stirred Hammond to send a third expert, a sign that he was getting serious about full-scale development. Word had gotten out about Sonora, and prospectors were swarming in. In Nacozari de García, the closest town to La Caridad, Burnham complained that he almost had to sleep on a cot in the hall at the Hotel de Nacozari, where the grub "ought to poison a sewer rat." But at least the floor wasn't encrusted with consumptive spittle as in his previous hotel there, and in the railroad's Pullman cars.

Meanwhile, *Real Soldiers of Fortune* (1906) had just been published, Richard Harding Davis's book of profiles about six modern adventurers, including Winston Churchill and William Walker. It opened with a frontispiece showing Burnham and Armstrong escaping after the Mlimo episode, and Davis gave the book's climactic chapter to Burnham.

In Mexico he was feeling more like a frustrated panhandler than a swashbuckler. La Caridad still wasn't settled. In December he went back to New York, hoping to raise another $250,000 to further explore his Sonoran prospects. Hammond had become his champion at Guggenheim Exploration and was going to recommend the purchase of La Caridad. "It will be success or failure in a few hours," he wrote to Blanche on December 7, "so just offer a short prayer to God for me, for you know I never pray to him except through your pure and dear heart. You are all that stands between me and perdition." Hammond also wanted him to meet with Harriman, the railroad magnate.

On December 11 the Guggenheims turned down all of his Sonoran prospects—La Caridad (copper), Lampazos (silver), and Mina de Mexico (silver). But the next day he wrote, "The wheel of fortune has turned again." Hammond—"his blood is up," wrote Burnham—intended to raise money for Mexico through other wealthy friends. Hammond was entertaining the idea of giving him $100,000 on his own. The day after that, the wheel took another sharp turn—Hammond now hoped to raise $250,000 right away for a million-dollar company.

Burnham tempered his excitement. "Am awfully afraid the boom is near its crest," he wrote to Blanche. A series of articles in *Ridgway's*, a muckraking weekly that was also serializing Joseph Conrad's new novel, *The Secret Agent*, warned against the wildcatters and speculators who were selling dud Western mines to gullible Easterners. The magazine described most buyers as suckers who were gambling, not investing. "I want to make good before crash," wrote Burnham, who had experienced several.

Further, Burnham and Hammond had a meeting with some brothers named Richardson, who owned nearly half a million acres in Sonora's Yaqui Valley. The Richardsons wanted investment partners for their huge agricultural development.

Money was hanging everywhere, just out of reach. "I do hope to God I get enough to last our tribe more than six months," wrote Burnham to Blanche, "but I don't suppose I will. Our wants expand so much faster than the power to get the money that it looks hopeless." All these pending deals meant that once again he wouldn't be home for Christmas.

Harry Payne Whitney joined the syndicate, as did the banker Darius Ogden Mills. Harriman seemed interested but was distracted by a new government investigation into charges that his Western railroad monopoly was restraining trade for smaller railroads, and further allegations that he was providing oil tanker space to John D. Rockefeller's Standard Oil and shutting out other oil companies. Henry Clay Frick also joined the syndicate. Frick, a partner of Andrew Carnegie in steel and coke, was notorious for hiring Pinkerton agents in 1892 to assault striking workers at the Homestead Works of the Carnegie Steel Company. Ten men were killed. The incident had helped sour Burnham on Gilded Age America before he left for Africa in 1893. But Frick had money, which Burnham needed to fund his own dreams of wealth.

The days ticked on. Nothing kept happening. Meetings, negotiations, requests for documents, cancelled meetings, conditional acceptances, withdrawals, requests for more documents followed by more delays—standard business practices, but they chafed Burnham's restless temperament as well as his latent class resentment. "It does make me hot," he wrote to Blanche, "to see all these swaggering rich around one who got nearly all by crooked work and they have everything on earth. . . . Probably tomorrow will upset every plan of today. Yet if I give up, everything in Mexico and everyone dependent on me go to hell at once. So I must hang on."

New York prices were staggering him. The maître d' at a first-class restaurant expected $10 to reserve a table. A fancy dinner might cost $50, and waiters now expected tips in dollar bills, not silver change. "This is the maddest ever," he wrote to Blanche. "Will it last is the question. $12,000 per front foot for vacant lots facing [Central] Park on 5th Ave and only 80 feet deep."

He noticed that constant proximity to wealth produced ugly yearnings. "It shakes one's resolution for integrity and accounts for a lot of this awful graft," he told Blanche. "'Tis so human to want to be as good as the next one in appearance." He was heartily sick of being separated, and felt adrift without her. "There are very many kisses long overdue," he wrote in early January, "and the worst of it is that I feel they cannot all be made up. It would wear you out. Though as you are going in for athletics with Isabel [Isabel Harrah, Rod's girlfriend and future wife], it might be done."

On January 9, 1907, the Western Mexican Syndicate finally closed, with initial capital of $250,000. Burnham left immediately for California, and from there for Mexico. He was elated. Maybe, finally, this would be his bonanza year.

—·—

During the next months he traveled all over Mexico. The members of his tribal payroll—brother Howard, brothers-in-law John and Judd Blick and Pearl Ingram—also were scouting with their horn spoons. Between them they found prospects in Jalisco, Guadalajara, and Baja as well as Sonora. Burnham wrote to Blanche that he was in the saddle nine hours per day, riding over steep mountains, feeling fine, happy to be in rough country again.

Hammond sent yet another engineer, the fourth, to evaluate La Caridad. This expert's report in September 1907 noted that so far the syndicate had spent $31,000 on the option and on test shafts, and that a final payment of $21,000 was due January 1 to buy the mine. The engineer was skeptical of its worth. He recommended cutting a few more test shafts before the deadline. His conclusion: if rich veins are found, make the final payment. "If not, abandon it."

Burnham strongly disagreed, but in November, Grenfell wrote to Burnham that he would not make his share of the final payment, and Hammond evidently agreed. The mine closed down. Decades later, others began collecting Burnham's bonanza: La Caridad became one of the world's largest copper mines and remains in operation.

—·—

Far from the wilds of Mexico, financial structures in the United States were wobbling. In 1906, in keeping with Roosevelt's promise to bust the monopolies, Congress passed the Hepburn Act, which gave the Interstate Commerce Commission power over railroad rates. This shook railroad stocks, which for years had been highly speculative and inflated, yet were used as collateral by banks and trusts. In March 1907, for instance, the price of Harriman's seemingly rock-solid Union Pacific dropped $50 per share.

Smaller railroads felt the shock. Then in August the government fined John D. Rockefeller's Standard Oil Company $29 million for antitrust violations. Trading on the New York Stock Exchange slipped by double digits. The financial system shuddered but didn't collapse.

That happened two months later. The cause was a scheme by F. Augustus Heinze. He had made his pile as owner of the United Copper Company in Butte, Montana, then bought his way into many local and national banks. Still avaricious, he, his brother Otto, and several bankers attempted to corner the copper market in October 1907. They failed, and the price of United Copper crashed. Heinze was ruined. That set off a run on banks affiliated with him, and several declared insolvency. The panic spread quickly. Millions were withdrawn from the Knickerbocker Trust Company in New York within a few hours, forcing it to close. That set off another cascade of bank runs. The Panic of 1907 (sometimes called the Knickerbocker Crisis) whirled across the country, causing mayhem at regional and local banks. A complete national collapse was averted at the end of the month when the financier J. P. Morgan propped up several banks with his own money and then shook cash from other financiers whom he forced to follow his lead. This crisis eventually led to the creation of the Federal Reserve System, to give the government more control over banks.

Copper's central role in the panic probably helped sour Burnham's syndicates on La Caridad. More broadly, the meltdown unnerved investors, who shied away from speculative ventures such as mining prospects in Mexico. The panic damaged the wealthy, but it crippled or wiped out smaller players such as Burnham. He called it "the financial tornado of 1907." Once again, just as he was about to grasp his bonanza, it had turned into smoke. An illustration: he owned 750 shares in Grenfell's Mexican syndicate. A few months after the panic, the handsome stock certificate was defaced by an inscription written in red ink: "First & Final Dividend of 0% per share paid June 15/08." Signed, "F. Roche, Liquidator." On the back, Burnham wryly scribbled, "First Class Wall Paper, Keep Carefully."

The news from Africa was also bad. He had expected to make a fortune from his interests in East Africa, especially the soda lake. A few years after he left, a railroad reached the lake. The company reorganized and became the African Lands and Development Company, Ltd. Burnham tried to collect his commission for a decade, but the new company always claimed there was no profit. Eventually he got a small settlement, made smaller when he kept his promise to share his portion with several men who had served under him in East Africa. Once again, his bonanza had turned into a pittance.

But there were always other prospects to explore.

CHAPTER TWENTY-FOUR

A PRESIDENT SAVED, ANOTHER FORTUNE POSTPONED

H IS MINING VENTURES were temporarily on hold, but Burnham wasn't idle. Eliot Lord, a go-getter and sometime literary agent in New York, had heard Burnham tell some of his African hunting stories, and convinced him to write down a couple of them. Eliot placed two of these with *Collier's*, a well-regarded magazine, and urged Burnham to compile his African hunting adventures into a book. Hammond was enthusiastic, promising to get Richard Harding Davis to edit it and Roosevelt to endorse it.

In small groups, Burnham was mesmerizing as a storyteller. Hammond once noted that Burnham had the rare ability to turn Theodore Roosevelt into a listener. Eliot Lord had noticed the same quality: "He has amazing power of visualization, of re-creating any scene in his life as he sits quietly in his chair," he wrote in a book proposal. "More than this, he has a vividness and felicity of description which make any paraphrase weak and insipid." Lord convinced Burnham to get "a talking machine" and narrate his adventures into it. He devoted several weeks to the project in the spring of 1908.

In August the railroad king Harriman invited him to Pelican Lodge, his camp on Oregon's Klamath Lake. This camp featured servants, a spacious lodge, and an ice plant. The guests' tents had wooden walls, velvet carpeting, electricity, bathrooms, and running hot and cold water. Hundreds of workers had spent the summer building a road between Pelican Bay and Crater Lake, thirty miles north, so Harriman and his guests could drive to the trout fishing there. Harriman had split the cost with the county.

Most of his fifty guests were millionaires and politicians such as Oregon's governor. Burnham's reputation preceded him, and a professional marksman challenged him to a match on the rifle range. Burnham was intrigued to hear that the man had hit forty-nine out of fifty targets, but then learned that he had done so at a distance of 100 yards instead of 200—"*quite* a difference," he wrote to Blanche. "I am going to make 100 straight this evening so it can't be beat." Harriman asked Burnham to take his fourteen-year-old son Roland on the boy's first bear hunt. A few days later a San Francisco paper ran a story headlined "Magnate Rejoices at Son's Prowess, Railroad Wizard's Younger Boy Proves Mighty Nimrod in Northern Woods."

Dictating African stories and supervising teenaged nimrods were tolerable diversions but didn't generate cash. As always, Burnham was chasing a potential bonanza: the Yaqui Valley.

———

He wasn't the first gringo to see dollars there. After President Díaz cleared out most of the Yaquis and expropriated the land, in 1890 he sold about half a million acres to a Mexican American ally, Carlos Conant, along with the right to irrigate this immense tract from the Yaqui River. With U.S. and Mexican investors, Conant formed the Sonora and Sinaloa Irrigation Company. When the mountain snows melted, the Yaqui River was a wide torrent, but in summer it dwindled to a trickle. Conant built a diversion dam to catch the spring melt. He also dug a wide canal and began dredging lateral canals. All of this enraged the remaining Yaquis, whose ancestors had been farming the valley since before the Spanish arrived. The Yaquis destroyed the canal dredge and frightened off prospective settlers. By the early 1900s Conant had sold less than 2,000 acres. The company went bankrupt.

While Conant was trying to farm the valley and tame the Yaquis, Davis Richardson came to Sonora to start over after his herd was wiped out by a terrible winter in the Black Hills (the same sort of disaster that ended Theodore Roosevelt's Dakota ranching days). Richardson found silver and grew wealthy. He brought his brothers south to help him expand into land development. When Conant went bankrupt, the Richardsons bought his concession and added to it. President Díaz gave them the rights to most of the Yaqui River's water, infuriating the valley's Yaquis and other small farmers. The Richardsons dug forty more miles of canals, attracted some settlers, and built a town, Esperanza (Hope), as the project's headquarters. But the enormous scale of the undertaking drained their finances. They estimated that completing the canal system would cost another $325,000.

They needed investors. Burnham heard about the Richardsons while crisscrossing Mexico. In November 1908 Burnham went to New York with Davis Richardson to sell the agricultural project to Hammond and his circle of investors. After two weeks of negotiations and delays, the deal closed. It was even better than Burnham had hoped. Harriman had declined to join, but Hammond and Harry Payne Whitney each put up $500,000. Hammond estimated that building a bigger storage dam and enough canals and laterals to irrigate the valley would cost about $12 million. Burnham would get a salary of $500 per month as managing director and vice president, plus about 100,000 shares that he expected to be worth a dollar each within three years. A bonanza. Potentially.

The new Yaqui Land and Water Company immediately began a marketing campaign in the United States to attract settlers. Posters, newspaper ads, and slick brochures touted the valley's deep rich soil, mild healthy climate, long growing season, and early harvests, four to six weeks ahead of California's Imperial Valley. The ads boasted that the company had miles of irrigation canals, with water rights guaranteed. Access to markets was easy. And Yaqui Valley land was cheap—only $16 an acre if you bought today, soon going to $25—at least ten times less expensive than comparable farmland in California. "Your investment will be absolutely safe," promised a sales brochure:

> More than $900,000,000 of United States capital is invested in Mexico, and the greater part of this immense sum has been invested in lands, by some of the most conservative bankers and financiers of this country. They see the opportunity and are taking advantage of it. Mr. E. H. Harriman is spending seventy-five million dollars to build the West Coast Line of the Southern Pacific Railroad through to the City of Mexico. None of these bankers and financiers would have invested his money in Mexico if it were not safe. Mr. Harriman KNOWS and the bankers and financiers KNOW it is safe. If it is safe for them it is safe for you.

So get in on this opportunity while it lasts, urged the ads, because the Yaqui land rush is on.

To Hammond and Whitney this wasn't mere hype. In addition to their heavy investment, they bought thousands of acres for their own pleasure and planned to start a winter colony of their friends. The hunting in the valley was superb, and so was the fishing in the nearby Gulf of California. Whitney, an avid horseman, intended to raise polo ponies and thoroughbred racehorses.

By the end of 1908 twenty-two new settlers had begun clearing and fencing land in the Yaqui Valley. They too sensed a bonanza. A year or so later more than fifty American families had bought land and started farming. In 1910 the new company had 700,000 acres. About half was reserved for agriculture, more than 200,000 acres for grazing, and 80,000 acres for timbering. The settlers were growing a wide array of crops: corn, hay, wheat, alfalfa, cotton, fruit (lemons, limes, melons, grapefruit, kumquats, tangerines). Some were raising cattle, sheep, pigs, and poultry.

Burnham's letters during these years are crowded with the tasks necessary to establish and run this grand scheme. The company published a crop calendar with recommendations for more than seventy crops. There was a thousand-acre experimental farm to test soils and crops, including half a dozen kinds of Burnham's old adversary, the orange. The company also had to arrange for goods and services necessary to attract and keep settlers: a general store, farm machinery, a sawmill and lumber yard, warehouses for grain, an ice plant so fruit could be preserved for shipping, an electric plant, a clinic with a doctor. The company brought in well-drillers and bricklayers, agronomists and pomologists. All this convinced many settlers to send for their wives and children. When he had time, Burnham also put in sessions with the dictating machine for Lord.

Sometime in 1908, while rambling through a forest of giant cactus in the Yaqui backcountry, he noticed a semicircular igneous rock, about eight feet wide, half-buried like a large tombstone. It was incised with strange swirls, scrolls, and circles, some with curving tails. Burnham suspected the forms were ancient Mayan hieroglyphics. He named the rock the Esperanza Stone. In 1909 he invited Charles Frederick Holder, a naturalist, sportsman, and author from Pasadena, to visit Yaqui for some fishing and incidentally to examine the stone. It excited Holder, who wrote a story about it for *Scientific American*. He wanted to donate it to Pasadena's Throop College of Technology (later renamed the California Institute of Technology), but the valley's people objected, and the Mexican government took possession of the stone.

———

In the autumn of 1909 Burnham took a break from his duties in the Yaqui Valley when Hammond asked him for a favor. Hammond was accompanying his friend, President William Howard Taft, on a railroad tour of the Midwest and Southwest. Taft had arranged a meeting on October 16 in El Paso/Juarez with Mexico's President Díaz, the first such meeting between presidents of the two countries. The leaders also would ride in a parade.

For El Paso and Juarez, the meeting was a great occasion, but for those in charge of presidential security, it was a nightmare. The border was volatile with malcontents and revolutionaries, and the security experts on both sides worried about assassins. By the day of the meeting, Mexico and the United States each had assigned about 2,000 men to guard the border and the parade route.

Nevertheless, Hammond was nervous. If either president was assassinated, it might spark a war. Hammond wanted to preserve his friends, Taft and Díaz, and perhaps also his Mexican investments. At his own expense, he asked Burnham to join the presidential train from California to Texas, and to assemble a special detail to bolster the presidents' protection in El Paso. "The President has had more kinds of guards on this journey than he ever saw in the same length of time before," wrote a reporter who was traveling with Taft for the *New York World*. He continued:

There have been Secret Service men, militia, regulars, cowboys, police, and rangers, and Chief Wilkie [head of the Secret Service] is to meet him at El Paso, but with Major Frederick Russell Burnham along, the necessity for Chief Wilkie's presence is not apparent. The Major is so well known along the border that it is said the fact that he is seen in the crowd will ensure the departure of all trouble makers. There is a superstition down here that he has eyes in the back of his head, and that he can produce a gun from the air, if necessary. . . . He is the most modest and the quietest blue eyed 5 foot 4 inch man yet encountered on the Presidential tour, though he has the record here and in South Africa of having killed at least twenty men, either in self-defense or in the line of duty as an officer.

Burnham gathered a band of scouts, cowboys, former sheriffs, and customs officers, who were sworn in as deputies. Small groups were assigned to each section of the parade route and instructed to watch the crowd, not the presidents. Any lone person who looked or acted peculiar would be approached by two deputies. According to Hammond, more than 100 weapons were temporarily confiscated in this way, though the owners were probably just Texans rather than assassins.

Burnham noticed a man loitering near the entrance of a hotel just as Taft and Díaz were arriving. The man appeared to be writing in a notebook but looked furtive. Burnham signaled a Texas Ranger named Charles Moore, and they closed on him. Moore hooked his arm through the man's as Burnham grabbed his wrist. Taft and Díaz were a few feet away. Concealed in the man's right hand they found a small "pencil gun," sometimes called a "palm pistol." Its stub barrel and cropped stock made it a perfect assassin's weapon. The man claimed to be a reporter, clearly the pretext of a scoundrel. He was jailed until Taft and Díaz left town.

Burnham touches on the incident in *Taking Chances*. With typical modesty he says, "I disclaim any important part" and gives credit to the sheriff of El Paso. He doesn't even mention his role in nabbing the man with the palm pistol, which may have foiled a presidential assassination.

—•—

In March he was back in New York hoping to convince the Yaqui investors to put in another million dollars. He got sucked into the required social whirl, calling on the Harrimans, Whitneys, and Vanderbilts. "I am trotting round in a plug hat too small for me and a tail coat whose sleeves hang over my knuckles, and the tail hits just back of my calves," he wrote to Blanche. He drew a cartoon of himself to illustrate.

Hammond raised another infusion of cash, including some of his own, to keep the project going. He was confident in it and in Burnham. Burnham shared his optimism. He traded about a third of his common shares in the company for 300 acres of the project's best land, figuring that in a few years it would be worth $100 an acre no matter what happened to the stock price. He got a financial boost when legal papers from London informed him that the Belingwe Development Syndicate, a small subsidiary from Rhodesian days owned by him, Pete Ingram, and John Blick, was being forced into liquidation. His 1,050 shares were worth a bit more than a pound each, a jackpot of about $6,000.

He kept shuttling between Mexico and California, sometimes with Blanche. In August they traveled to Cheyenne, South Dakota, to meet Roosevelt and see a "genuine wild west show"—one of the last, suspected Burnham, since "the race of the cowboy is fast passing away."

Throughout 1910 small brushfires of unrest had been flaring throughout Mexico. Burnham's letters began mentioning revolutionaries. In June President Díaz arrested Francisco Madero for daring to announce his candidacy for president. But events were moving beyond Díaz's control. As order broke down, belligerents and cutthroats took advantage. In July one of the Yaqui settlers came home to find his wife and two children murdered. In October, Madero escaped to Texas, and in November, he called for revolt. By the spring of 1911, revolution had spread across Mexico under Madero and others such as Pascual Orozco, Emiliano Zapata, and Francisco "Pancho" Villa. By the end of May Díaz had resigned and gone into exile, but Mexico remained turbulent.

The revolution spurred the Yaqui Indians to take back their ancestral lands. They rampaged through the valley, burning crops and running off livestock. Burnham directed defenses and tried to control the settlers' panic. On May 22, 1911, he sent a telegram to Hammond: "Things now much brighter. Found settlers very uneasy. They have heavy losses." At a meeting in mid-July the Yaqui settlers passed a resolution thanking him for his efforts to protect them "during the recent troubles." The troubles, however, were just beginning.

The revolution in Mexico loosed everything that had been repressed during the Díaz years, from reformers to brigands. Nasty political rivalries erupted between leaders of the landed gentry and the campesinos, and among factions within each group. President Madero couldn't control his own sometime allies such as Villa and Zapata, much less the countryside, which was claimed by rival bands of politicians, thieves, and Indians. The Mexican Revolution shattered into many revolutions, barely distinguishable from chaos. Madero was favorable toward the Yaqui project and similar developments, but American-owned enterprises were often targeted by angry Mexicans. In November a superintendent in the Yaqui Valley was murdered. Burnham tracked the criminals with a bloodhound, unsuccessfully.

By mid-December he was in New York. The project was nearly broke again, and this time Hammond didn't have the liquidity and influence to fix it. Mexico no longer looked like a secure investment. In anticipation of more trouble there, Burnham bought two more bloodhounds and a machine gun that shot 400 rounds per minute. He and Hammond had dinner with President Taft, but to Burnham's frustration didn't discuss Mexico. He wrote to Blanche that Taft was "blowing soap bubbles of peace and arbitration" while Americans and American property were under fire. In late December bandits murdered another settler in the Yaqui Valley. Northern Mexico seemed to be spinning out of control. Some American politicians and businessmen were pressuring Taft to send in troops to protect American interests, and incidentally to take control of the country.

On March 2, 1912, Taft responded to these pressures by issuing a proclamation that warned Americans to stay out of Mexico and advised those already there to leave. He declared the absolute neutrality of the United States and said he had no intention of intervening in Mexico's internal affairs, though he expected the Mexican government to protect U.S. citizens. Any U.S. citizens who did try to interfere in Mexican affairs would be prosecuted. Later that month he also forbade the sale or export of arms to Mexico.

Burnham was disgusted, not only with Taft but with a Yaqui Land and Water Company officer named H. A. Sibbet, the project's manager. Sibbet had told the settlers that the women and children should leave at the first hint of more danger, and that if the situation grew deadly, the men should abandon the project and save their lives. Burnham accused Sibbet of panicking. Better to fight, he wrote to Sibbet, like the settlers before the

First Matabele War; better to stick with it, like his ancestors in Minnesota and Kentucky. "Let us carry this thing through come what will," he wrote. "'Tis worth it and will outlast all of us." This was bedrock principle for him, he wrote. Nevertheless, he pledged to support Sibbet and work with him on the company's evacuation plan.

Burnham evidently also unloaded his bellicose views onto Hammond, because on March 21 Hammond sent a long stern reply. He said Taft's proclamation had stated the situation exactly. The only valid reason for the U.S. government to step in would be to save American lives, not American property. Intervening simply to decide matters for Mexico would be very bad policy for future relations between the countries. The same restraint was required by their company.

"I need hardly enjoin on you the necessity of our Company being absolutely neutral in Mexican political affairs," wrote Hammond, "and to commit no act which by any stretch of imagination could be regarded as aiding or abetting either the government in power or the revolutionists. What arms our settlers have must be used entirely for their own protection, and, of course, must not be sold or loaned to belligerents."

He agreed that the men probably could defend themselves and should take all measures to do so, but insisted that the decision to stay or go must be entirely theirs: "it would be almost criminal to give the settlers false hope as to their security in case trouble should arise. We on our part are in no position to guarantee them protection. . . . In any event, it is far more important to save their lives than to save their or our property. The charge of cowardice should not deter them from seeking safety when they have no occasion to fight for any principle and where there might be danger of assassination by bandits. . . . it would be selfish cowardice on my part," ended the letter, "to ask other people to defend property in which I am interested when I myself am at a safe distance."

The letter was politic, large-minded, and wise, with a perspective beyond the personal. It illustrated why Burnham placed Hammond just below his pantheon of Rhodes, Roosevelt, and Lord Roberts. But Burnham's character and values had been formed by fighting on frontiers, and he disagreed with most of Hammond's points. Pioneers must fight for their land, to the death if necessary, and anyone who fled was cowardly.

The two men did agree on one thing: the settlers needed protection, and they didn't have enough weapons. In mid-April Burnham went to Washington, D.C., to ask the Secretary of State to make an exception to Taft's recent policy about guns. He wanted permission to buy 100 rifles and 20,000 rounds of ammunition from the government, strictly for use by the 200 settlers still in the Yaqui Valley. Bandits and Indians were regularly attacking and killing people. Taft immediately granted the exception.

As Burnham was making this deal, Blanche wrote to him that things were worsening in Mexico and she hoped he wasn't going back. A week later he was in the Sonoran port of Guaymas, en route to the project. The railroad had been cut again. The company was set to evacuate the women and children, about fifty in total. The men were going to try to harvest the crops. In a feeble attempt to protect the settlers, the toothless Mexican government had sent 400 "convicts," in Burnham's description, to guard the valley. "The bandits and the savages are now running everything."

When he reached the project, he found chaos. Some women were resisting the imminent evacuation, but Sibbet was forcing them to go. A few men were leaving with their wives. "A clear case of too much skirts," wrote Burnham to John Hays Hammond's son Harris, calling one of the men "a good plucked one."

He found another problem: on April 22 a Los Angeles newspaper had claimed that he and 500 hardened fighters were camped on the Yaqui River and had smuggled an arsenal of weapons across the border, including several Gatling guns. Their purpose, said the story, was to guard the mining properties of the Guggenheims, Hammond, and J. P. Morgan.

The story was an ill-informed hash. The 400 "convicts" sent by the Mexican government had become 500 mercenaries hired by Burnham. The legitimate shipment of rifles en route from the U.S. government had turned into a smuggled arsenal including Gatling guns. Burnham had no association with Morgan, and the Guggenheims were not invested in the Yaqui project.

The story infuriated him but alarmed Sibbet and Richardson. They told him that his presence was endangering the project and insisted that he resign as director before the Mexican authorities invaded to capture him. They also informed him that he would be escorted to the border. Burnham signed the resignation, bitterly. But the settlers wanted him to stay, and he warned Sibbet ("that colossus") not to try to eject him.

The harvest proceeded. Burnham predicted it would be the colony's last until the chaos in Mexico ebbed. Abandoned farmhouses now dotted the valley. Two weeks later the bandits and Yaqui marauders had moved off, so he prepared to exit. At age fifty-one, it looked like ruin again.

"I wish I could get some of my salary—about $10,000 due me *now*, and nothing in sight but trouble," he wrote to Blanche the day before leaving for Pasadena. "Still we are not so bad off as some of our settlers and should be thankful that we have any cash at all. Love dear I will soon be holding you to my heart and all else is then forgotten and fades to mere nothingness."

—•—

The violence in Mexico continued throughout 1912. Properties owned by foreigners were often targeted. In the Yaqui Valley, crops and buildings were burned, cattle stolen. Most settlers didn't return. In January 1913 Hammond conceived an audacious plan and asked Burnham to join him as guide and interpreter. He wanted to get permission from Mexico's President Francisco Madero to ride into the Bacatete Mountains, stronghold of the rebel Yaquis, to negotiate directly with the warriors who were terrorizing the valley. He intended to give every family who left the mountains a free plot of land and the water to irrigate it.

Burnham immediately saw the similarity to Rhodes riding into the Matopos to meet the Ndebeles, an act Burnham considered one of the bravest in history. He agreed to go. Like Hammond, he admired the Yaquis in many ways, and understood their fury after decades of extermination and broken promises by the Mexican government. "I think it reflects wonderful forbearance, on the part of the Yaqui Tribe," he wrote to Hammond about the proposed journey, "that they have not fallen upon our settlement and destroyed it to a man."

President Madero seemed intrigued by Hammond's courageous offer, but the following month Madero was overthrown in a coup by Victoriano Huerta, who rejected the proposal.

In spring of 1914 the London bank owned by Arthur Grenfell, the British partner in the Yaqui project, collapsed due to Grenfell's reckless speculation in railroad stocks. His crash left the Yaqui project cash-poor and unable to pay salaries. Instead, Hammond gave Burnham another 500 acres in the valley and more shares. These could make them rich someday, Burnham wrote to Blanche from New York, "but will not help immediate cash a single dollar." But he told her not to worry, their bills weren't crushing, and he was working on new schemes, including buying another ranch, 500 acres on the San Joaquin River in Madera County, California. "I will pull it all out OK bye and bye," he wrote. The date was May 11, 1914. "Do you realize I am 180 years old today," he wrote. (He was fifty-three.) "But never mind, dear, I love you still with all the fire and passion of youth."

———

Not long after his election in 1912, President Woodrow Wilson made clear that he sympathized with the Mexicans fighting to overthrow their exploiters, including American companies with large Mexican concessions. If these companies suffered losses, said Wilson, so be it; he would not intervene. American citizens in Mexico should protect themselves by leaving the country.

He stuck to this policy for several years. Then in May and June of 1915, Yaqui Indians from the Bacatete Mountains raided the valley, burning and killing. The Mexican government couldn't control the Indians, and anyway was reluctant to risk Mexican lives to defend the remaining foreign settlers. Many Mexican soldiers resented the foreigners and pillaged them. The settlers appealed to the U.S. government for help. Wilson, fearing a massacre of American citizens, sent warships with Marines into the Gulf of California, and the U.S. Department of State informed the Mexican government that unless it protected U.S. citizens in the Yaqui Valley, the Marines would land and do so.

The countries seemed poised for war, a development urged by some U.S. businessmen and politicians who wanted to make Mexico a protectorate similar to Cuba after the Spanish–American War. The Mexican authorities insisted that the settlers leave the valley, for their own safety and to remove the goad to Yaqui violence. They warned U.S. officials that landing soldiers in Mexico would be considered an act of war. The remaining settlers had now been advised to leave by two governments. For Wilson, war was too steep a price to save a handful of stubborn colonists and the investment of some U.S. capitalists. He told the warships to stand down.

That averted the political crisis momentarily but infuriated the settlers and their supporters such as Burnham, who always took the martial view. Where Wilson saw obstinate squatters, Burnham saw stalwart pioneers. Where Wilson saw the need for political caution to preserve long-term relations with Mexico, Burnham saw the need for immediate action to uphold bedrock American principles. In letters he called the President "Woodenhead Wilson" or "that d–n capon Wilson."

In a rant to his old prospecting friend William Kettner, now a congressman from California, he complained bitterly about "the small band of yappers . . . blowing trumpets and waving paper doves" while Americans were being murdered in Mexico. Kettner, in his affectionate reply to "My dear old Scout," agreed with his friend, but added that people were frightened by the idea of war, perhaps because so many were then dying in Europe in the new World War. Among the thousands of letters sent to him about war with Mexico, he wrote, not a single one had supported the idea until Burnham's, and the majority must rule.

Burnham found that hard to accept. He saw American courage and readiness to act being eroded by fear and timidity, not just in Mexico but worldwide. He blamed "the wretched, piffling, cowardly Wilson and the little milksop, weak-kneed cabinet officers," and "the millions of mollycoddles" who supported them. He was ashamed that Wilson was preventing the country from joining Britain in the World War against the aggressions of Germany, especially after that country defied Wilson's warnings in May 1915, when a U-boat torpedoed the passenger ship RMS *Lusitania*, killing 1,198 civilians, including 108 Americans. While pacifists waved paper doves, the world was being hijacked by villains willing to die for their country and their beliefs. Burnham wrote to his brother Howard that he had been reading Nietzsche on the doom of democracies, which in his dark moments he feared might be true. "At times," he continued, "I feel that the political rock on which I was raised, of intense loyalty and patriotism, is crumbling under my feet."

———

Meanwhile, the Yaqui Valley project was essentially suspended. On March 7, 1916, Burnham wrote to ask William Richardson what was being done to protect the few settlers still there. "Bear in mind always," he said, "that I am ready to go any hour, anywhere." That same day, he wrote to Hammond that the pillagers in Sonora now included the government, which had just announced new strictures and heavy taxes on foreign landowners, with the obvious goal of repossession. Burnham wrote that he had been in contact with representatives from other American landowners in Sonora, who "are now lined up and ready to make any action possible to save this total confiscation and destruction of their properties in Mexico." He implied that a word from Hammond would light the fuse. It didn't come. Though Hammond stood to lose a fortune, he understood that sending a few armed men into Mexico to provoke an international incident was less a defense of noble values than a foolish suicide mission and a diplomatic disaster.

The provocation came from the Mexican side. On March 9 the rebel army of Pancho Villa, who was fighting against President Venustiano Carranza, raided Columbus, New Mexico. Four days later President Wilson ordered Major-General John J. Pershing and a force of 4,800 men, including some Apache scouts, into Mexico to capture Villa. They chased him for eleven months, with small success, before Wilson recalled them in the lead-up to the country's entry into World War I.

The Yaqui Valley project was again suspended by violence. So was Burnham's income. It looked like another fortune might get snatched away. In the meantime, he needed to scramble again.

CHAPTER TWENTY-FIVE

HIPPOS AND SPIES

D URING THESE YAQUI years Burnham found time and energy for another project that mixed the practical with the quixotic: the importation of African game animals into the United States. He began looking into the possibility in early 1905, corresponding with the world's foremost supplier of animals to zoos and circuses, a German named Carl Hagenbeck.

After Bruce drowned later that year and Burnham returned to the States, he took up the idea in earnest. His plan was to import animals such as the bushbuck, klipspringer, springbok, dik-dik, and duiker, then release them into the mountains, forests, and deserts that President Roosevelt had started claiming as federal lands. If some of these spaces were declared game preserves, U.S. sportsmen could experience the pleasures of hunting African animals.

Roosevelt liked the idea, and so did his chief of the Forest Service, Gifford Pinchot, who became one of Burnham's lifelong friends and correspondents. Burnham, Hammond, and a few others raised $50,000 to help fund the plan. In 1906 two California congressmen introduced bills to put it into action, but the idea was attacked as an attempt to use federal funds to set up a hunting reserve for Roosevelt's wealthy friends. The bills failed to reach the floor.

Burnham, of course, didn't give up. Around 1908 he and his brothers-in-law John and Judd Blick bought a 5,000-acre ranch near Three Rivers, California, on the edge of Sequoia National Park. He released some imported Mexican deer and javelina there as game animals. The experiment worked, confirming Burnham's interest in establishing non-native game in the U.S.

In February 1910 he published an essay in *The Independent* magazine entitled "Transplanting African Animals." His reasoning echoed the pragmatic conservation of Roosevelt and Pinchot: "Vast tracts of our lonely deserts could be teeming with life," he wrote, "interesting, beautiful, harmless, very useful for food and leather." He urged the importation of everything from oryxes ("Its meat is well-flavored and its hide is equal to the best calf") to Cape buffalo, ostriches, flamingoes, "and certainly the royal bustard." He envisioned warthogs snuffling in Southern swamps, giraffes browsing treetops on Texas scrubland, camels roaming the desert Southwest. And why not add some zebras "to dot our plains with color"?

Burnham presented the scheme as easy, practical, and profitable. The hard part would be stopping Americans from slaughtering the animals before they became established. "So intent are we on destruction," he wrote, "that we have become the wonder of the world. . . . Only a national law and a changed public opinion can make it possible to save what animal life we have or introduce new and valuable additions." But doing so would "add greatly to our national wealth, and furnish a reserve food supply."

This last point referred to the national worry about a shortage of meat. Supply wasn't keeping pace with demand as cities swelled with immigrants and rural refugees looking for factory work. The rangelands were showing the first signs of overgrazing, and the country was running out of new territory to exploit. During the heedless westward expansion of the nineteenth century, the supply of land, trees, grass, water, and wildlife seemed unlimited, but those days were gone—so alarmingly gone, in fact, that Roosevelt, Pinchot, John Muir, and others were insisting on conserving what remained. But the country's population continued to grow, and it was hungry. Burnham was not alone in seeing African wildlife as a sensible and renewable source of meat.

Among his fellow visionaries was Congressman Robert Broussard of Louisiana. The month after Burnham's essay appeared, Broussard sponsored a bill to investigate the feasibility of importing African animals into the United States. The timing seemed right. On March 24, 1910, at a hearing before the House Committee on Agriculture, he introduced three experts in support of the bill. A scientist named W. N. Irwin represented the Department of Agriculture. A second expert was Frederick "Fritz" Joubert Duquesne, a South African hunter whom Roosevelt had recently consulted before his celebrated hunting safari to East Africa. Broussard probably didn't know that Duquesne had emigrated to America in 1902 after escaping from a British prison camp in Bermuda. He had refashioned himself in the United States as a reporter, an occasional lecturer about Africa, and a handsome, charming hustler. But before all that he had been a Boer scout who had once vowed to kill Broussard's third expert: Burnham.

—·—

The relationship between Duquesne and Burnham makes this strange episode even stranger. Before the meat scheme, the two men knew each other as shadows. Burnham said that during the Boer War he feared only two men on the veldt: Daniel Theron, the Boers' best scout, and Duquesne, their second best. He considered Duquesne, nicknamed the Black Panther, far more personally dangerous because he was driven by hate.

It seems that during the war Duquesne had visited his family's homestead. At first he couldn't find it; nothing remained but charred rubble. A family servant still living nearby told him that the British had strung up his blind uncle and stabbed him to death with bayonets. They had repeatedly raped Duquesne's sister, then executed her, and then had raped his mother before dragging her away. Duquesne found his mother and her rape-baby in a nearby concentration camp. Both had syphilis and were near death from starvation. Duquesne blamed Lord Kitchener and vowed to kill him. He spent much of his life seeking vengeance on the British and their allies.

Because of his daughter Nada, Burnham understood Duquesne's bloodlust and how it could warp a man. Burnham knew he had escaped that fate through a lucky mixture of intrinsic optimism, devotion to an ancestral code, and the love of a supportive woman.

But in 1910 he and Duquesne found themselves allies in the unlikely scheme to bring African animals to the United States. Burnham testified before the Agriculture Committee that most of the meat eaten by Americans came from just a few domestic animals—pigs, chickens, cattle, sheep—none of them native to the continent. Surely Americans were adventurous enough to expand their palates, especially at a time of national need. Duquesne told the committee that many African animals were delicious sources of meat for European settlers there. He was especially rhapsodic about the taste of hippopotamus.

That last bit may have been aimed at the bill's sponsor, Representative Broussard, who had paid Duquesne to scout the bayous of Louisiana as a habitat for hippos. Among the possible imports, hippos were Broussard's focus. He envisioned them gorging on the Japanese water hyacinths that were choking his state's waterways. This invasive species, brought to New Orleans in 1884 as aquatic decoration, had proliferated so quickly and thickly that mats of it were smothering fishing areas and blocking navigation, important economic sectors in Louisiana. The plant had defeated every scheme to eradicate it. But Duquesne assured Broussard that hippos could munch the invader into submission and free the plugged, suffocating waters of Louisiana. And as a bonus, each of these rotund weed-whackers could be converted into a ton of tasty meat. The hippo solution was practical, ecologically pristine, and edible. Who could object?

Many newspapers enthusiastically agreed. "Denizens of Jungle to Come to Our Land," proclaimed one headline. "Toothsome Rhino, Succulent Koo-doo, Luscious Dik-dik and Tasty Trek-bok May Soon Supplant High Priced Beef on Bill of Fare." Broussard didn't get his bill onto that year's legislative agenda, but the idea had momentum. To keep it going, he, Burnham, and Duquesne formed an advocacy group, the New Food Supply Society. Eliot Lord, Burnham's sometime literary agent, jumped in and began soliciting money from wealthy supporters. That August, when Burnham met Roosevelt in Cheyenne at the Wild West Show and again in Denver, the former president said to quote him as a whole-hearted supporter.

Burnham did so in September, when he spoke in Pinchot's stead before the annual meeting of California's Humane Association. He urged them to seize the opportunity to do something original and significant by backing the importation bill. He asked them to support other innovations as well, such as the catalo—a cross between a cow and a buffalo (bison)—which he presented as a way to save the last specimens of a great Western symbol. "A splendid opportunity is before us," he said, "to do practical, lasting, sane work."

In the spring of 1911 Burnham met with Broussard and Duquesne in Washington to discuss introducing the bill that spring. Burnham also made plans to travel to South Africa to investigate animal importation, with help from his old Rhodesian friend Johan Colenbrander. But in the spring of 1911 Mexico combusted with revolution. Burnham had to cancel Africa and rush to Sonora.

President Taft wasn't as keen on the importation idea as Roosevelt, and Broussard postponed the bill again, perhaps until the fall. Fall became winter, and Broussard told Burnham perhaps in the spring. By then Burnham was busy helping beleaguered settlers in the Yaqui Valley. And so the dream of hippos in the bayous of Louisiana and giraffes on the plains of Texas passed peacefully away.

Years later Burnham came across his speech to the Humane Association. It was written on stationery from that other quixotic plan, the Yaqui Valley. After he reread his practical, optimistic vision of a more adventurous, more picturesque, better-fed America, he wrote on it, in the shaky handwriting of an eighty-three-year-old, "The facts are still unrefuted. F.R.B.—1944."

It's irresistible to add a postscript about Duquesne. After the New Food Supply Society faded away, he and Burnham lost touch. Burnham had hoped that the constructive dream of animal importation would untwist Duquesne, but the nature of the Black Panther was fixed. When World War I began in 1914, he became a German spy in the United States. Using multiple aliases and disguises, he loitered in dockside bars and bribed British sailors to smuggle out what they thought were rare orchid bulbs. Aboard ship, the bulbs exploded. Using this ruse and others, he sank twenty-two ships.

Or so he said. Like much else about him, this may be true, or partly true, or as fictitious as his many identities. His biggest claim has been disproven—that in 1916 he fulfilled his vow by directing a German U-boat to the HMS *Hampshire*, which went down with more than 600 on board, including Lord Kitchener. But later investigators did confirm the general accuracy of most of Duquesne's claims. He did sink ships, set fires, and kill Britons.

Consequently, the British authorities wanted him for murder, and the New York City bomb squad was investigating him for an arson in a Brooklyn warehouse. Clues and an informant led the bomb squad to a former British officer named Captain Claude Stoughton, who gave paid lectures about his dashing military career. In Stoughton's apartment they found photos of a handsome man in various uniforms, suspicious paperwork concerning insurance claims, and lots of newspaper clippings about unsolved explosions.

Stoughton was Duquesne. The New York police arrested him in December 1917. When the British heard about it, they wanted him for prosecution. Duquesne suddenly became deranged. His behavior was so alarming that he was sent to a mental hospital. Next came sudden paralysis below the waist. Skeptical doctors jabbed Duquesne's legs and toes with pins, but the crazy paraplegic didn't flinch. He ended up in the prison ward of New York's Bellevue Hospital, where he sat pitifully in his wheelchair, gazing through iron bars—that is, when he wasn't cutting through them with a smuggled hacksaw. One night, after seven months of paralysis, he miraculously recovered, jumped out the window, and disappeared.

In 1926 a certain Major Frank de Trafford Craven took a job in New York with a publisher of movie magazines. Four years later the city's police arrested Craven as the fugitive Duquesne. He denied his identity, futilely. But the British no longer wanted him and a judge threw out the charge of escape. He was free again.

For years, Burnham had covered the walls of his study with photos of people he admired. One of them showed Duquesne in his Boer uniform. Perhaps Burnham heard about his arrest in 1932 and wrote to his old foe, because in 1933 he received a note that he afterward kept at hand in his desk:

> To my friendly enemy, the greatest scout in the world, whose eyes were the vision of an empire. I craved the honour of killing him, but failing that I extend my heartiest admiration.
>
> Major Frederick Russell Burnham from Fritz Joubert Duquesne. 1933. One warrior to another.

In the mid-1930s, during Hitler's rise in Germany, Duquesne joined an American pro-Nazi group and resumed spying. He passed valuable information to the Reich about bombs, weaponry, gas masks, radio devices, ship movements, and other military secrets. A double agent betrayed him to the FBI. In June 1941 he and thirty-two others—known as the Duquesne Spy Ring—were arrested for espionage, still the biggest such bust in the country's history. Duquesne was sentenced to eighteen years in Leavenworth Federal Penitentiary.

"His doom fills me with sadness," wrote Burnham soon after, in a chapter about him in *Taking Chances*. Duquesne was "one of the most remarkable men I had ever met," he wrote, "regardless of the thousand rumors and irrefutable proofs of his black deeds—acts which could not be defended by any civilized code." Burnham hoped that someday a writer or historian "with an understanding heart, will show that this human epitome of sin and deception was but a product of the extreme hate to which we have all contributed, and for which we continue to pay the price." When *Taking Chances* was published in 1944, he pulled strings at the FBI to put a copy into Duquesne's hands. The spy's response, if any, is lost.

Three years into his sentence, Duquesne's failing mental and physical health, real this time, got him transferred to a prison medical center in Missouri. Worsening health led to his early release in 1954. Two years later, in City Hospital on New York's Welfare Island (now Roosevelt Island), the indigent seventy-eight-year-old Black Panther slipped away forever.

CHAPTER TWENTY-SIX

SCOUTING FOR MINES AND FOR ROOSEVELT

As THE YAQUI project was going dormant again, Burnham returned to his fallback pursuit: prospecting. In late 1915 he became a mining scout for A. Kingsley Macomber, a wealthy businessman. As a twenty-year-old, Macomber had pegged land for Burnham in Rhodesia, and had explored with him above the Zambezi River. Back in the United States, Macomber married an heiress connected to the Standard Oil fortune and augmented that with profitable investments in mines, banks, real estate, and thorough-bred horses. He had money and Burnham had a prospector's eye.

Hammond valued that eye as well. He once noted that only one in six mines paid off, so investors had to be prepared to absorb heavy losses. They might spend hundreds of thousands of dollars to sink shafts several thousand feet deep, as Rhodes did in the Rand, in hopes of finding a payable vein of gold. So investors prized scouts who had what Hammond called "a good nose" for a prospect. This required knowledge of geology and mineralogy, but also a more elusive quality: an instinct for ore.

Burnham had the nose. Unlike many scouts and mining engineers, he also had the integrity to report what he found. Cynicism about mining reports was universal and well-founded. "A collection of mining romances in the shape of reports on mines," noted one contemporary observer, "if published, would afford entertainment for readers of fiction unequaled by any modern publication." Burnham also had the prospector's inclination toward optimism—a necessary trait, but it could bend judgment.

In December 1915 he began looking into abandoned mining properties and was immediately excited by several, especially the old Black Bear mine in the Klamath Mountains of Northern California. After studying the mine's records, he knew that between 1862 and 1881 it had yielded more than $2 million in bullion. The mine's owner, John Daggett, was a man obsessed. He bought into the Black Bear in 1862, sold out in 1863, bought it back in 1866, sold out again in 1872. In 1884 its siren song lured him into buying it back. For the last thirty years he had been trying to interest investors, certain that another bonanza awaited just beyond the last shafts. Burnham wanted to believe. His letter to Blanche about Daggett and the Black Bear reads like a wistful parable of the mining life:

All day I have been mulling over flimsy copies of letters of men now gone, and other copies of letters of men who wrote and quarreled and swore and worked but are now tottering wrecks, gray, quiet, waiting calmly for the final act and *taps*. These letters are filed in big leather books like my father used to have. They tell of the struggles over the snows, the long pack trains, sick horses, broken wagons, holdups, rows over county seats, high taxes, $10,000 for freight for one little mill, etc., of a beautiful woman and her murder and his fate and hers, great finds of gold, over a million in two years from one shoot of ore in the Black Bear Mine. Then of its lost ore body and the long desperate struggle to regain it. Loss after loss, bankruptcy, and final crumbling decay like Kipling's jungle swallows it all, the creaking pumps can lift no longer, the timbers rot and crash. Finally the last engineer writes his farewell letter to the Co. Then silence save for the birds of the air or the sigh of wind in the gallows frame. One tottering man of

84 still dreams his dreams of another great bonanza, a little deeper. He has spent his all. . . . It lures one on yet I feel an icy chill at times when the thought comes of really asking friends to back my judgment. It may take *thousands* of feet to find it. Yet I, like the grand old man, believe it is still there.

By the next day, when he wrote his report to King Macomber, he was sober and pragmatic. The mine had once been a bonanza, he said, but as the years passed and the shafts went deeper, it had yielded less and less until mining stopped. Seams of gold might lie waiting somewhere below, but to reach them, if they existed, would take at least $50,000, maybe $75,000. When Macomber passed on it, Burnham was relieved.

He spent the next few years driving, riding, and hiking all over the West, checking out prospects. His letters came from up and down the Sierra Nevadas, from the Riverside Mountains and Death Valley in southeast California, from Skull Valley in Arizona. He found a strong prospect in Arkansas. Sometimes he camped, sometimes stayed in hotels. Blanche got letters on stationery from hotels in Globe, Phoenix, Bakersfield, and Blythe in the Chuckawalla Desert. He wrote while aboard the California Limited from "somewhere in New Mex."

He was chasing gold, silver, and copper, but also "war baby metals" now in demand to make the steel needed by the modern military: tungsten, manganese, vanadium, chrome, and molybdenum, "a coming metal." After a year of prospecting he had found enough paying mines that he could write to a friend, "Mexico very near put me on the bread-line, but I am now pulling out in pretty good shape, after all."

In September 1916, while prospecting in the high mountains, he was floored by excruciating pain in his abdomen. He suspected something fatal related to his old stomach wound in South Africa. On the eve of his surgery, he wrote jaunty farewell letters to his brother Howard and other friends. "I who have taken old death by the hand many times," he wrote to Harris Hammond, "may this time follow him over the border. But whether this be so or not matters little for I have led a concentrated tabloid life, of certainly twenty in one."

It was only appendicitis. It slowed him briefly, then he was back on the road, sniffing for prospects. In early February 1917 he boarded a train for New York, where he hoped to put together a syndicate for mining those "war baby metals."

––—––

As soon as the World War began in 1914, Burnham itched to go. Blanche must have been appalled. Nevertheless, he wrote to contacts in the British Army, asking them to help him get to the front. But he was fifty-three years old, and the skills of a frontier scout had limited appeal to generals waging a new sort of war with tanks, airplanes, poison gas, and trenches. He was politely ignored.

So he ranted about capons and mollycoddles, and mocked Wilson's slogans, "Peace with Honor" and "He Kept Us Out of War." Roosevelt, Burnham, and others saw democracy in urgent peril. The imagery in Burnham's letters was dire: swords hanging over heads, seeds of disaster ready for harvest. He joined the Preparedness Movement, begun by Roosevelt and others, including two former Secretaries of War, who were alarmed about the dreadful state of the country's military. Preparedness Day parades around the country drew thousands of supporters. Wilson, always wary of Roosevelt's presidential ambitions, worked to undermine the group.

Even after the sinking of the *Lusitania* in May 1915, President Wilson had resisted calls to embroil the United States in Europe's war. In September 1915, to keep the U.S. out of the conflict, Germany had pledged that its U-boats would stop torpedoing neutral ships. So on February 1, 1917, when the German government announced the resumption of submarine warfare against all vessels, Wilson's hand was forced. A few days later he broke off relations with Germany and began preparing the country for war.

Burnham, in New York, wrote to Blanche that the Germans' announcement had probably torpedoed his plans as well. He might be able to sell some manganese and tungsten, but all major financing was on hold. He also mentioned that Roosevelt was considering raising a division of fighters, and had contacted him. The old Rough Rider, now fifty-eight, had once said of Burnham, "He is a scout and a hunter of courage and ability, a man totally without fear, a sure shot, and a fighter. He is the ideal scout, and when enlisted in the military service of any country he is bound to be of the greatest benefit."

"If war comes," wrote Burnham to Blanche, "of course I am in it at once." But he thought President Wilson was all talk. That's why Roosevelt was exploring the possibility of a new, expanded version of the Rough Riders—for Burnham, an avenue toward combat. He must have known how Blanche would react to the prospect of losing him to another war. He expected to hear from Roosevelt the next day. Meanwhile, he wrote, he was going to watch *Madame Butterfly* from Mrs. Harry Payne Whitney's box at the opera.

The next day, February 9, he sent Blanche this run-on wire: "A great chance has come maybe I can serve my own country as effectively as I did England am offered Command under Roosevelt so am not too old . . . keep everything out of papers."

Blanche tore it into pieces. (Sometime later, probably for the sake of the family archive, she taped most of it back together.) On the same day, Burnham sent her a letter acknowledging that his decision might end their marriage:

My Love

Last night Geraldine Farrar sang at her best the sweet songs of the poor *Madam Butterfly*. Yet through all the soft cadences of the music ran the thought that on the morrow I must send a message almost as sad to my own sweet Madam Butterfly who for years and years had followed me from arctic snows to burning deserts, who had laid away her dear children, yet loved me as few men are loved by women. I have again like Captain Macklin kissed the sword. But this time in defense of my own land instead of that of strangers. I do not know how you are going to feel about this war . . . But I cannot live in peace with my own soul by any other course. Better death a thousand times. Yet I do not chide you in any way. Each must do according to the inner light.

So if this must change your feelings for me, it will not change mine for you. It is of you I think at the last moment of consciousness, and you I call for first on regaining it. It will be the same if I awoke in the Halls of Valhalla.

I love you above all women in the world.

. . . But no matter what your choice may be I give you as farewell the salutations of my inmost soul and beg of you think of me always at my best and of those countless hours of heaven and bliss in the days gone bye.

A new wine is in my blood. I am again the fighting Rhodesian that held and inspired men in those days. You could not help but admire me even if you turned me away from your heart. Yet mine is always yours if you want it.

My soul is my maker's and must be returned, my life is my country's, my heart I give to you.

Farewell dear,
F.

He wrote to her again the next day. "Everything seems to be crumbling to ashes in a way," he said, "—democracy, Christianity, the old family ties—all are breaking down. Why should I flatter myself I could retain the love of even *one* woman forever? Especially if I live as my soul dictates. So I am hardening it with fire day by day, making ready for the news that I have lost the woman as well."

On February 16 he got her reply by Western Union: "Two letters of 9th recd. I knew in my heart what you would do and love and honor you as always but it would have been easier for me if you had not wired."

He replied immediately, flooded with relief. Now he felt he could face whatever happened. "I am doubly armed you still love me." Roosevelt had chosen him as one of eighteen commanders for two divisions. For Burnham, it was a chance to salve his regret at being in the Klondike when Roosevelt had called him for his original Rough Riders. He had been meeting with Roosevelt and others about logistics and recruitment.

"Well it is all in keeping with my life," he wrote to Blanche, "from the desert to a palace, back to the clods, then sought by the mighty men of the world again. Why should all these strange things come to me again and again." He hadn't been able to shake any money loose for a syndicate. If nothing changed in two weeks, he planned to come home and go into the desert to look for prospects.

A few days later he got Blanche's follow-up letter to her wire. It is lost, but Burnham's fervent reply suggests its contents:

Sweetheart

Your beautiful letter now read and I feel at once that perfect understanding of each other, without which it is almost impossible for either of us to live. Full well I recall all your terrible losses—the death of Nada, your brothers in the firing line, your husband just escaping from a thousand dangers and now about to go on what seemed another desperate venture while dozens of unmarried men stayed safely in laager. I knew your despair. But I had promised; Col. Napier depended on me. I had saved his command once. If I yielded to my heart's love and her despairing cry the column might all perish and Bulawayo itself fall. It was a terrible hour for both of us, where *Great Love* and *High Duty* were at cross purposes. . . .

But now it is different loved one. I can proceed along lines of high endeavor and still have your love. It is not just what you would wish. Yet dear a month of life is more than years of just living, and you must know, ere this, to see me at *my* best there must always be *impending* danger and constant action. Even you then say I am worth loving.

Now we are old and grey. Only a few years can be left to us at most. Let us concentrate years into months and months into moments . . . Dream of my heart. Even *war* can never cloud it. You shall be with me forever.

F.

But Blanche didn't offer her support unconditionally. One of her next letters was scissored as if by a war censor. She had reconsidered some wounding words, she explained, and cut them out. Burnham replied that he knew she didn't like war, but time was running out, Wilson was a coward, and the Germans and Japanese were infiltrating Mexico with plans to attack the United States. This last anxiety stemmed from the Zimmerman telegram, made public at the end of February. The German government had sent a coded cable to the Mexican government asking it to become an ally if the U.S. entered the war. In return Germany promised to help Mexico regain territories lost to the United States. Mexico's President Carranza considered the offer but rejected it as too risky. To Burnham and others, it was another reason to occupy Mexico.

He left New York for the West. He had agreed to raise four companies for Roosevelt, about 22,000 men. He expected it to take three months of travel. But first he had to see King Macomber, to ask if working for Roosevelt would cost him his job as a mining scout. In any case, there was no pay in recruiting for Roosevelt, so he hoped to sell the Riverbend ranch on the San Joaquin River to ease their finances.

Blanche seemed ready to sell the La Cuesta ranch near Three Rivers too. "I have had to economize now for three years," she wrote, "and think it would be pretty fine to be able to buy pretty things as I used to do." As for Roosevelt and the war, she wrote, "We understand each other thoroughly now, and all is peace." But she would not write to him about these things anymore, she added, because they upset her too much.

The recruitment went splendidly. Burnham did newspaper interviews and wrote dozens of letters to friends asking them to join and to publicize the effort. Within a month hundreds of men applied, and a month after the United States declared war on Germany in early April 1917, he had 20,000 volunteers pledged to go. Roderick, now almost twenty-one, signed up and so did many of Burnham's friends.

The other recruiters had done just as well. In just over three months, many thousands of men had enlisted as volunteers and were waiting for the call. Congress authorized Roosevelt to take his divisions to fight in France. Burnham was sure he would soon be back at war, this time fighting for his own country. But on May 18 when Roosevelt asked Wilson for permission to activate his volunteers, the president said no. Roosevelt was expected to be the Republicans' presidential nominee in 1920, and Wilson, a Democrat, had no intention of giving the rival party's leading man a starring role in the war.

The next day Burnham wrote to Blanche, "I am too sad to write. The political crime overwhelms me." He saw only one bright spot—that she would be happy. He was going to Oyster Bay on Long Island the next day to commiserate with Roosevelt. "I wish I could take defeat as well as R. does," wrote Burnham. "I do fairly well and rebound in time, but it is harder as the years go by and one's star is sinking year by year to oblivion and great issues being decided with no chance to take a hand in the decision."

The second blow that month was the death of his only sibling, Howard, not quite forty-seven, on May 4 in Cannes, France. Burnham didn't hear about it immediately because of the war. The cause was Howard's old enemy, tuberculosis. While dying slowly in Cannes, not long after returning from Germany, where he had been spying for the Allies, he had tried to settle his affairs. He wrote long instructions about how his sons should be brought up and educated. He made his wife Constance swear to repay a $5,000 loan from his brother. It had been given without hesitation a few years earlier when, unknown to Howard, Burnham himself was scrambling for money.

There were some emotional debts as well. Howard thanked his older brother for indulging his youthful urges to roam deserts and take risks.

Unlike Fred, Howard was sometimes moody and snappish. In his gruff way, he thanked Burnham for watching over him and tolerating his prickles. "The one person," he wrote to Burnham, "who has never failed me, or others."

Burnham had borrowed $1,800 that year from Hammond because he "sorely needed it." But he wrote to Constance that he would never accept the loan repayment from her unless it didn't affect her finances or her boys' educations. Despite his own recent financial reverses, he told her, "so long as there is an acre of ground or a dollar left, we in California are always willing to share it with you and to help you and the children in any way." A tribe never abandons its members.

———

Like his father, Roderick Burnham was eager for battle. He enlisted in the U.S. Army and was ranked an officer because of his college degree (from the University of Arizona, where he was also captain of the football team). When he was assigned to train soldiers in the States and not fight in Europe, he vehemently protested. The army obliged by demoting him to private and shipping him to the western front.

It was a different war from those in his father's stories. Roderick was poisoned by chemical gas and lost all his teeth from trench mouth. But he fought and survived, and by the end of the war had made sergeant. The army wanted to send him to officer training school, but after experiencing the horrors of the front, he chose civilian life and became a successful mining scout and engineer.

One wonders how Roderick's father, always gung-ho about war, would have felt if he had gone into the fetid, muddy trenches with Roosevelt's division and seen the bodies piled high in no man's land, and the blistered, writhing victims of poison gas. Would the disillusioning nightmare later described by so many writers have diminished his enthusiasm for battle? It's doubtful. In the most famous poem to come out of the war, Wilfred Owen scorned Horace's celebrated lines, "dulce et decorum est pro patria mori" ("it is sweet and right to die for one's country") as "the old lie." But Burnham believed whole-heartedly in Horace's lines, without irony.

Burnham did find a way to fight Germany. To make steel for armaments, the U.S. military suddenly needed large quantities of little-known metals such as tungsten and manganese. But where to find these crucial war metals, formerly disregarded? Old geological surveys offered scattered clues, but Burnham had a better source: old prospectors. He knew many, and had renewed their acquaintance in the last two years while crisscrossing the West as a mining scout. These men had wandered over every inch of the desert searching for gold and silver, and Burnham thought they might remember patches of the strange black metals now in need. "I urged them to recall to memory some long-forgotten cañon with stained walls," he wrote in *Scouting on Two Continents*, "or some crags and peaks streaked brown and black, crumbling in the blaze of the desert sun."

One half-crippled prospector, seventy-four, remembered finding a vein of manganese thirty years earlier in the Chuckawalla Desert. He was sure, as prospectors always are, that he could find it again. For days Burnham followed him across sand dunes, through cactus, up steep mountains strewn with baking rocks. They wore damp handkerchiefs over their mouths and noses to protect their lungs from temperatures well above 100 degrees. The peaks in the distance quivered like candle flames, and the crystalline air trembled. "I could sit here and gaze on these mountains forever," said the prospector happily.

He and others like him led Burnham to neglected veins and forgotten mines near Tombstone, Mount Diablo, and other old camps. Loads of tungsten and manganese began rolling to eastern smelters to become steel, then weapons and munitions used against Germany. "It was certainly the desert people's best tribute to the nation," wrote Burnham. "It was the last fine rally of the long-beards."

CHAPTER TWENTY-SEVEN

CLOSING THE CIRCLE

Affter the last rally of the long-beards and the end of the war, Burnham fidgeted at La Cuesta, the family ranch on the western slope of the Sierras near Sequoia National Park. He was rattling around, with no focus for his still robust energies. Many men he admired had died during the war years: his brother Howard, Leander Starr Jameson, Lord Roberts. Frederick Selous had been killed by a sniper in German East Africa. Johan Colenbrander had drowned while trying to cross a flooded South African river for his role in a movie called *The Symbol of Sacrifice*. Roosevelt had died suddenly in January 1919.

He was fifty-eight. It was exasperating that some people saw him as a relic, too old to fight or compete, when he knew he could still easily outdo most men. His optimism about the future was undiminished. As always, he simply had to create it, and his drive to do so remained inexhaustible.

In early July 1919, on a business trip to New York to see John Hays Hammond, he pushed the investor to revive the Yaqui project. He needed action and was short of cash again, borrowing $500 from Hammond's son Harris. But he was sure that things would soon improve. Hammond had just helped him take advantage of a blip in the market to sell Howard Burnham's shares in International Petroleum, one of Hammond's companies, for $50,400. Howard had earned the shares by discovering lucrative oil fields for the company in eastern Mexico, but until recently the stock had been nearly worthless because of the ongoing Mexican Revolution. Now Standard Oil and another large company were sniffing around International Petroleum, so there were offers to buy I.P. shares. The money erased the financial worries of Howard's widow Constance, and also allowed her to comfortably repay the $5,000 loan, an unexpected windfall for Burnham.

He too owned I.P. shares, but despite his need for money he decided to hang on to them in hopes of a bigger payoff in the future. "So why worry?" he wrote to Blanche. "I have never let you go quite naked or starve to death." Meanwhile, he needed to stay in the East and tend to possibilities.

By mid-July he was at Lookout Hill, Hammond's coastal summer estate in Gloucester, Massachusetts. He spent nearly three weeks there discussing opportunities with Hammond on the golf course at the Myopia Hunt Club, or with Harry Payne Whitney on his yacht. Hammond was commuting to New York, working on an oil deal for International Petroleum. If it went through, Burnham could get $30,000 for his shares within a few months, or double that in a couple of years. For Hammond the deal would be worth $20 million.

These were giddy prospects, and they spilled glitter onto the Yaqui project. Hammond was optimistic about it again. He thought President Wilson would have to do something soon about Mexico, partly because of the continuing violence and partly because influential congressmen such as Henry Cabot Lodge were pressuring him to occupy the country. Hammond imagined Yaqui as his life's crowning work, and the oil deal could give him the capital to realize it, if the situation in Mexico permitted.

The possibility elated Burnham. Aside from his California ranches, his life savings had been wagered on the Yaqui Valley. If the project revived, so did his fortunes. "Gee I wish you were here," he wrote to Blanche on August 1. "I feel a little of my old joy and enthusiasm of things doing every day."

Burnham had always been a hard-rock prospector, but the recent months of excited talk had altered his focus. The twentieth century would require the new specialty metals, but the extractive industry of the future was oil. When Hammond offered to form a small oil syndicate with Burnham as a scout, he eagerly agreed. He would make only $100 a month at first, but also a percentage of any profits. They named the syndicate Burnham Exploration.

"I may make a splash yet," Burnham wrote to Blanche, "even if I am gray headed and *fat*." (He now weighed 148, ten pounds heavier than in his scouting days in Africa.) He told Blanche to start looking for a place to rent in Los Angeles, and joked that since they had lived at six different addresses in recent years, she might get arrested for vagrancy.

Hammond's oil deal went through in early September. Burnham could glimpse a payday just ahead. It felt like old times in southern Africa, with possibilities everywhere. Hammond was now turning his attention back to Yaqui, Burnham wrote to Blanche, "and I am in on Yaqui big in every way. So fix up your diet and health. There is lots to do and see and live for yet. I am going to hit the pace now for a while and you will need roller skates to keep up."

He hoped his energetic confidence would cheer her up. Her knees bothered her, probably arthritis, and she sometimes had to use a wheelchair to get around. She had bouts of neuritis. A dentist had recently yanked many of her teeth. These physical troubles were worsened by the gray loneliness that often draped her when Burnham was away for long stretches. He had been home for a couple of weeks after the formation of Burnham Exploration, but left again in mid-October.

A week later he sent a letter from New York assuring her that she was not "going on the rocks," and that "Nerves are very largely mental" and can be controlled. He asked her to cut back on social obligations, to think before answering the phone or promising to meet someone, to move slowly, take a sea bath, relax. And don't worry about finances, he instructed, because "it is all coming right." When he returned they would go soak on the beach at San Juan Capistrano and drive their new car to Agua Caliente and Lake Arrowhead, "and just trek when we want to and stop as long as we please, and I will love you just as ever and always, and you will get well."

In New York, the "little syndicate" that Hammond had started for Burnham was turning into something bigger. Burnham had recommended drilling on some patches of promising ground, and Hammond's expert had agreed. Drilling was expensive, so Hammond decided to raise $300,000 to capitalize Burnham Exploration. His longtime friends Harry Payne Whitney and Ogden Mills joined the syndicate as his partners. If just one drill struck oil, Burnham's shares would be worth a tidy fortune. Blanche got all this good news with the less welcome information that he had to go to Washington, D.C., then Texas and Louisiana, and didn't know when he would get home.

⸺

Shreveport, Louisiana, reminded him of Johannesburg in 1893—crowded, wide open, pulsing with energy and hustlers. "There are thousands of highbinders here from every oil field in the world." It was almost impossible to find a bed. He felt lucky to get a cot in a room with seven other men at the Hotel Youree, a mile outside town. He slept little because his roommates stayed up until the wee hours playing cards, smoking, spitting, and jabbering about oil and politics.

Gushers were being reported every week, and properties were trading hands quickly. To scout the oil patches, he rode local trains and then hired jitneys with chains on the tires to churn through the deep red mud. He bought one three-year lease on forty-five acres for $562 and a one-eighth share, "a good little bet." He had his eye on another $15,000 worth of leases, but he couldn't get the go-ahead from Hammond because wires weren't getting through to New York. Mail was almost impossible, too—heaps of it lay undelivered at the post office, and he wasn't getting letters from Blanche, a silence that always jarred him.

After a couple of weeks in Shreveport he was eager to exit and report to New York. "If I am long delayed in N.Y.," he wrote to Blanche on November 30, "it sure looks as if we ought to be divorced. I have not seen you for years and years and fear you must have changed a lot and maybe have forgotten me."

Blanche had recovered some of her health and good spirits by then. She had been writing to him, and felt bad that he hadn't heard from her; she knew how much he needed their connection. When he had left for New York in July, they never expected him to be away for so long, and now he had been gone for another seven weeks. But she also sounded her old notes of faith in him and the prospect of togetherness in the future. "I feel sure we are going to strike oil," she wrote, "and if we do I am going everywhere with you. We will not be separated for a *single* night."

By April 1920 Burnham Exploration had bet more than $80,000 on ten oil prospects. The investors were so pleased with their scout's work that they raised his salary to $400 per month. To finance more bets, and to avoid diluting the stock by adding investors, they needed at least one property to spurt oil. Burnham was sanguine, his confidence intact. The main thing was to have prospects in play. Just as important to him was Blanche's admiration of his enduring boldness. "I am still proving to you I am not a mollusk or a fixed star," he wrote to her. "I am a comet, maybe and liable to go up in smoke at any time."

———

The Yaqui project, however, remained on hold because of ongoing turmoil in Mexico. Between 1910 and 1920, the Mixed Claims Commission, formed by Mexico and the United States to consider claims against either government, took complaints from more than 3,200 American citizens and companies about losses due to violence. During the same period, more than 270 American miners had been killed. Yaqui Indians were still murdering people—poor publicity for land sales. Only about ten stubborn settlers remained.

President Wilson, in his final year of office, clearly intended to maintain his policy of nonintervention. Hammond and Burnham had a flicker of hope that things would somehow work out, but Harry Payne Whitney, who owned a third of the project, refused to sink another dollar into it. Whitney suspected that his $500,000 investment, like Hammond's, was as good as gone.

He was right. The new Mexican constitution essentially made it impossible for foreigners to own land. Hammond and the Richardsons sold their holdings to the government in 1926 for $6 million. In coming years the Yaqui Valley would become Mexico's agricultural heartland, just as Burnham had predicted. Another fortune lost.

———

In the old pueblo of Los Angeles everyone knew La Brea, named for the oily tar that seeped from the ground there. Burnham had discovered the pits one hot summer day while riding for Western Union, when his horse stepped into the goo and almost didn't get out. The tarred boy and his horse staggered to an adobe house on Rancho La Brea, where Greek George Caralambo helped them clean off. Soon after, the fugitive bandit Tiburcio Vásquez was captured in a shoot-out at Greek George's.

Now, fifty years later, oil derricks had sprouted all over La Brea and hundreds of other sites around Los Angeles. Oil had been discovered not far from the pits in 1890 by a gold prospector named Edward Doheny, who drilled and found fortune. His success drew other companies. Before the end of the century, more than 500 wells were pumping oil in the vicinity, and derricks were visible from any hill in Los Angeles.

By 1920 every parcel of promising ground near the city had been studied and probed by oil company geologists. So when Burnham told Hammond there was oil under Dominguez Hill, just twelve miles south of downtown Los Angeles, Hammond shook his head. The hill was named after the family who had owned a huge hacienda there since 1784, Rancho San Pedro. Several large companies, including Standard Oil, had drilled test wells to 3,650 feet at Dominguez as recently as 1916. All were abandoned as worthless.

Roderick had told his father that Dominguez deserved another look. Burnham knew every crease and slope in this landscape. As a boy, he had often ridden up Dominguez Hill. On the surface, Dominguez showed no seeps or other signs of oil, but Burnham's knowledge of the Los Angeles Basin, plus his prospector's instincts, told him that oil must be pooling beneath the old hacienda's vantage point. He also had faith in Roderick. Hammond scoffed. "That country had been gone over again and again by the biggest oil companies," he said later, "and it was impossible to believe they had missed something that was any good at all." Burnham insisted that Hammond come take a look with a geologist he trusted.

To Hammond's surprise, the geologist strongly recommended drilling. That would require another $300,000. Hammond's partners, Whitney and Mills, balked, reluctant to throw money at something already explored and scrapped by other companies. It was Hammond's turn to insist. He also supplied the first $100,000. The other two reluctantly ponied up. Burnham Exploration signed a lease on 902 acres in May 1922. A month later, to assure financing, the company sold a 50 percent interest to Union Oil. By fall they were spudding in the first well. In March 1923, they hit oil, and in September the first well went on-line, followed quickly by many more.

Dominguez turned out to be one of the most productive oil fields in California. By January 1925 forty-two wells were pumping 1,780,000 barrels a month from a formation estimated to contain many more millions. The three partners of Burnham Exploration had invested about a million dollars. Just fifteen months after the first well began producing, half of that was retired, followed three months later by the second half. The company expanded, drilling wells in Texas, Wyoming, and Canada.

The circle had closed. After seeking his fortune in rough spots all over the globe, Burnham had found his bonanza at age sixty-four in the golden place he had galloped over as a boy, dreaming of Africa and adventure.

CHAPTER TWENTY-EIGHT

AFTER THE BONANZA

SCOUTING ON TWO Continents was published in 1926 by Doubleday, Page and Company. It was "edited and arranged" by Mary Nixon Everett, an acquaintance of Burnham's who pushed him to put his life on paper, which he had previously attempted in fits and starts. Judging by Burnham's letters and essays, Everett contributed little to the book's agreeable writing and style, which are Burnham's. John Hays Hammond wrote the foreword. The book carried blurbs by Robert Baden-Powell and H. Rider Haggard, and was dedicated to Blanche, "My dear companion of many a mile."

It sold very well, and there were editions in Dutch, Danish, Swedish, and German. Reviewers all over the world were agog at Burnham's life, which spanned an era quickly fading into myth. The review in the *New York Times* was typical, beginning, "Here is a thrilling book," and adding that Rider Haggard's remark about Burnham being more interesting than any of his own romantic heroes "is the stark, simple truth." The *Saturday Review of Literature* called it "a series of adventures so varied and thrilling as to be almost incredible."

After the book appeared, writers sent Burnham screen treatments about his life, seeking his approval. Aside from gross biographical inaccuracies, they reeked with Western dialect and clichés about scouts that Burnham had always deplored. ("'Howdy pardner', drawled the stranger. 'Couldn't help but hear you're dickerin' with this hyar pirate. Y'ore plumb right—that there candidate for th' glue fact'ry never'd even get you off to a good start toward's [sic] Mashonaland.'") Burnham's usual comment on such stuff: "Godawful tripe." (Ernest Hemingway admired *Scouting on Two Continents* and bought the screen rights in 1958, intending to turn it into a television series for his friend Gary Cooper, but he didn't write a script before committing suicide in 1961.)

———

Burnham and Blanche savored their late-life wealth. They bought land atop one of the highest hills in Los Angeles, near the sign that spelled out the new development's name in huge white letters that would soon become an icon for the movie industry: Hollywoodland. The Burnhams bought two lots, one for themselves and one next door for Rod and his family. Burnham hired a well-known Los Angeles architect who was also a member of the tribe, Blanche's brother Joseph J. Blick.

While their new homes on Durand Drive were under construction, Burnham, Blanche, Roderick, and his wife Isabel took a memory tour around the world to the places that had shaped the family's lives: Britain, Rhodesia, South Africa, East Africa. They also visited China, Australia, and places in between.

Burnham and Blanche returned to a palatial home in the Spanish style, a lavish modern version of the casas where Burnham had delivered Western Union telegrams as a boy. Visitors came up the driveway to a parking area, then took an elevator to the main level. They stepped out onto a lawn with paths bordered by roses and other flowers, and on the way to the house passed a putting green. Palms and cypresses framed the sprawling house and its lovely geometry of rooflines and terracotta tiles. There were loggias with thin columns, stone staircases, and a round tower. The land fell away on both sides, affording spectacular views of places where Burnham had a long history: downtown Los Angeles, the San Fernando Valley, the Santa

Monica Mountains, the Pacific Ocean, Catalina Island (where the Burnhams had a cabin), and, far to the east, the snowcapped mountains where he had roamed and hunted as a boy.

Inside, in the trophy room, the mounted heads of big-game animals looked down on animal skins, elephant tusks, a rack of rifles, some spears, and a knobkerrie studded with brass, taken off an Ndebele chief killed by Burnham. In his study the walls disappeared behind rows of framed photographs, nearly 150 of them, many inscribed. He called the collection his Walls of Fame. There were family photos of himself, Blanche, Roderick, Howard, and assorted Blicks, but most of the space was devoted to people and scenes from his life. Buffalo Bill in his showman's fringed buckskin. Fort Victoria in 1893. Rhodes sitting with a pet dog. "Dr. Jim" Jameson and Allan Wilson. A group of scruffy scouts from the First Matabele War. A Gatling gun crew at the siege of Bulawayo. A Zulu medicine man. Klondike gold miners. Lord Roberts, Lord Kitchener, and Baden-Powell. The Britain-bound shipmates from the *Dunottar Castle*, including Churchill. Rider Haggard and Richard Harding Davis. Theodore Roosevelt as a Rough Rider. John Hays Hammond and E. H. Harriman. Fritz Joubert Duquesne. Such people. Such stories.

—————

As he aged, Burnham intensified his efforts for conservation. He lobbied for state parks and preserves in California. He became a vigorous member of the Save the Redwoods League and also worked on the issue as an appointed member of the California Park Commission. He felt a personal connection to these majestic trees since his beloved ranch, La Cuesta, abutted Sequoia National Forest. He also served for years on the executive committee and the board of trustees of the Southwest Museum of the American Indian in Los Angeles, now part of the Autry National Center.

In the 1930s his disgust at hunters who drove cars to desert waterholes to shoot bighorn sheep spurred him to take action. He convinced some prominent citizens of Arizona and the leaders of Arizona's Boy Scouts to help him lobby for protection of the desert bighorn, whose numbers had dwindled toward extinction. They began a "Save the Bighorn" campaign in schools and on radio. As a result, in 1939 Franklin Delano Roosevelt signed legislation creating the Cabeza Prieta National Wildlife Refuge and the Kofa Wildlife Refuge. These encompassed more than a million and a half acres, bigger than Delaware, in the rugged, mountainous deserts of southwest Arizona, where Burnham had once prospected and matched wits with Apaches. In March 1941 he gave the dedication speech that opened the refuges.

He also campaigned to stop fishermen from killing sea lions and to limit the purse seiners raking the seas to make fish fertilizer. In 1941 he wrote to FDR, asking him to stop the army from building a shooting range near Henry's Lake, just west of Yellowstone, because it was a resting place of trumpeter swans, the largest waterfowl in North America and highly endangered. "If I thought that the destruction of these birds would interfere by even one hour with our national defense," he added, "this letter would not be written."

Wildlife and wilderness were no longer resources to be exploited without limit, but treasured inheritances to be salvaged, preserved, and passed on.

These same progressive values about conservation shaped his conservative views about race and immigration, which narrowed and hardened as he aged. Neither he nor other progressives such as Roosevelt saw any contradiction in these perspectives. Rather, they seemed complementary attempts to halt decline and preserve American essences in danger of vanishing.

Burnham's friend and fellow member of the Boone and Crockett Club, Madison Grant, epitomized this conflation. His views about conservation and race dovetailed with Burnham's. Grant was one of the pioneering conservationists of the early twentieth century. He led campaigns to save California's redwoods and the American bison, and was instrumental in outlawing plume hunting, which had decimated many bird species. He helped start the Bronx Zoo. He fought for legislation to protect wildlife and to create many national parks and refuges, including Glacier and Denali.

Yet he also wrote *The Passing of the Great Race; or, The Racial Basis of European History* (1916), an influential justification of "scientific racism" and eugenics. The book put a scholarly halo around bigotry by presenting historical and scientific "proof" of the white race's superiority. Grant warned that "the Master Race" was being diluted and degraded by immigration and miscegenation. Contemporary reviewers, almost without exception, praised the book. Roosevelt admired it. So did Burnham.

Grant based his theories partly on the new science of wildlife management. To preserve valuable superior species, lesser species as well as the weak and diseased had to be sacrificed—culled, sequestered, castrated. Grant recommended similar policies to preserve "the great race." He wanted to exclude non-Nordic peoples from the United States, especially immigrants from Asia and southern or eastern Europe. He also advocated the sterilization of criminals, "imbeciles," the insane, and "worthless race types" such as blacks and Jews.

Grant's book helped to inspire the Immigration Act of 1924, which severely restricted the number of immigrants and banned any from Asia or India. The book also was used to justify state laws allowing "mental defectives" to be sterilized, laws upheld by the U.S. Supreme Court in 1927. Sterilization, wrote Justice Oliver Wendell Holmes, enabled society to "prevent those who are manifestly unfit from continuing their kind." Grant got a gushing letter about his book from a German admirer named Hitler. (During World War II Burnham would denounce the architects of the Third Reich and imperial Japan as "strange monsters of evil.")

In 1930 Grant coedited a book entitled *The Alien in Our Midst; or, "Selling Our Birthright for a Mess of Pottage"; the Written Views of a Number of Americans (Present and Former) on Immigration and Its Results*. Burnham contributed an essay, "The Howl for Cheap Mexican Labor," which called for an Exclusion Act against Mexicans similar to the one prohibiting immigration by Asians, in order to protect America's racial bloodlines. When Grant died in 1937, Burnham eulogized him in the Boone and Crockett Club's newsletter as a visionary conservationist and racial theorist.

In 1936 Burnham and Blanche visited Alaska. They marveled at the trains that had tamed fierce rivers and mountains. But memories couldn't stop the subtractions of old age, and the rest of that year was less happy. Burnham's great friend and supporter John Hays Hammond died in June. A few months later, as Burnham rounded a hairpin turn on one of Hollywood's narrow canyon roads, a speeding car in his lane forced him to swerve off and down the hillside. His car tumbled many times, pancaking the seventy-five-year-old Burnham inside. Once again he proved unkillable. Rescue workers pried him out. For several excruciating months he wore a steel-and-leather body harness.

On December 22, 1939, two months shy of her seventy-eighth birthday, Blanche died. Burnham, a prolific letter-writer, goes silent about this loss, which suggests how crushing it was. In the mid-1920s he had written to a friend,

> In boyhood it was my greatest good fortune to meet a girl who truly believed in me and that I would carry out the wild schemes and plans I confided to her. Fantastic as those dreams were, nearly every one has come true. The vision of all she would be called upon to endure amid appalling circumstances was mercifully hidden from her young eye, nor could she foresee how tragedy and sorrow would some day test her soul as by fire; yet, throughout all the hard experiences of our years together, no resentment of destiny ever showed in her manner or crossed her lips. A gentle heart, a pleasant voice, a loyal nature, with a wide understanding of life as it is—she has indeed met every situation with supreme courage and continues to be a clear fountain of inspiration to me and to all who know her.

In their last years, after so many separations, they had finally managed to spend almost every night together. Their love story spanned sixty years.

In May 1941, shortly after Burnham dedicated the Cabeza Prieta National Wildlife Refuge, the Boy Scouts held an eightieth birthday celebration for him in Carlsbad Caverns. More than 1,000 people came. (Burnham was a devoted supporter of the Boy Scout movement in America. Late in Robert Baden-Powell's life, Burnham arranged for a peak in California's San Gabriel Mountains to be named Mount Baden-Powell. After Burnham's death, the peak next to it was christened Mount Burnham.) In a photo taken at the birthday party, Burnham looks fit and dapper in a three-piece suit, high starched collar, and white fedora, surrounded by Boy Scouts and stalactites.

He began organizing materials and memories for another book. *Scouting on Two Continents* had been conceived as two volumes, but the publisher decided one was enough. That probably explains the miscellaneous nature of this second book, *Taking Chances*, which seems to consist mostly of leftovers from the earlier one. This suspicion is strengthened by letters indicating that Burnham and Mary Nixon Everett fell out over money when he decided to publish *Taking Chances* privately. The title page says Everett "elicited and arranged" it, but Burnham's main assistant on the book was his new secretary, Ilo Willits.

They sent the last pages to the publisher on October 25, 1943. "By that time I was hopelessly in love with him," wrote Ilo, "and he had found out he couldn't get along without me." He was eighty-two. She claimed to be forty-five but was probably forty-nine. He asked her to marry him. She agreed, but to forestall the suspicions of Roderick or anyone else that she was a gold-digger, she insisted on a prenuptial agreement that excluded her from Burnham's estate, most of which had already been given to Rod. Burnham agreed to this stipulation. Both he and Ilo would regret this, Burnham because he had failed to provide for her, and Ilo because of future financial struggles.

They were married on October 28. By that time Roderick was divorced from Isabel and had married his former secretary, Gayle Cranney, twenty-three years his junior. He seems to have looked askance at his father's new marriage, or at least that's what the overly protective Ilo thought, which caused some strain. She devoted her life to Burnham, answering letters, caring for him during his periods of illness, and sometimes insulating him even from family. She also started organizing his extensive papers.

Seven hundred copies of *Taking Chances* were privately published in early 1944 and distributed by Burnham to friends and acquaintances. "I only wish he were younger so that we might write a book from the mass of data which he has accumulated," wrote Ilo to a correspondent. "It would dim both his other books, I think. He hasn't told the half of it."

By then he had lived in the Hollywood Hills mansion for fourteen years, by far his longest steady residence, but now it was too large and also was haunted by memories of Blanche. He and Ilo moved to a smaller house not far from Griffith Park in Los Angeles. By early 1946 smog and crowds pushed them fifty miles northwest to Fillmore, in the Santa Clara Valley. Neither of them liked it, so they moved to a small house in Santa Barbara. Ilo was content, but Burnham, restless as ever at eighty-five, wanted to build another house on a bigger piece of land.

They found one on a hillcrest in Santa Barbara, with views of the Santa Ynez Mountains on one side and the Pacific Ocean on the other. Leveling and clearing the lot took weeks. Burnham insisted on building the garage first, so he and Ilo could move into it and enjoy their new panorama while the house went up. As soon as they did, he began a slow fade.

The house was still unfinished on September 1, 1947, when, after a lifetime of risk and adventure, he died at four o'clock in the morning in his sleep. He was eighty-six. His life had followed the sharp curve of history from scalps on the frontier to the atomic bomb. He was buried next to Blanche among their tribe of Burnhams and Blicks in the small cemetery at Three Rivers, near the La Cuesta ranch and the majestic sequoias he loved.

Burnham bristles with contradictions. Robber barons infuriated him, yet he worked for several. As a young man he advocated the socialist ideals of Edward Bellamy, but always acted like a capitalist entrepreneur. He left the United States in disgust, vowing never to return, but always did. Though irritated by meddlesome government, he became an eager tool of imperialism. He was happiest in wilderness and described himself as a savage at heart, yet mingled easily with high society in New York and London. He enjoyed his fame as "the American scout," but groaned when writers reduced him and his rigorous craft to melodramatic Western clichés. He proudly displayed the heads and skins of trophy animals, yet became an ardent conservationist. He was devoted to one woman for more than sixty years, but found normal domesticity almost unbearable.

War and its camaraderie excited him, yet his chosen means of waging it, as a scout, was done in solitude, preferably without firing a shot. He revered his ancestors for risking everything to seek freedom and opportunity in the New World, and he did the same thing by going to Africa, yet he opposed most immigration. His hot-blooded patriotism scorned less martial views, yet he called Rhodes's peace mission into the Matopos the finest moment in history. He detested unfairness and injustice, but helped take lands from their inhabitants. He studied native peoples closely on two continents and admired many of their traits, but couldn't escape the deforming racial attitudes of his era. Despite his insights into power and politics, he remained blind to some of their consequences, and with his amazing powers of observation he sometimes failed to notice what was right in front of him.

Burnham wouldn't see these as contradictions, since he contained them all. They fit together like shards of a mosaic that reflects its era and shadows ours. Burnham and many like him took the risks, endured the hardships, and spilled the blood that, for good and ill, formed our world. He noted that all decent people deplore war and violence, though usually after being cushioned by law and peace, and he remarked that those who followed the pioneers never complained about benefiting from their sacrifices and ferocities. Burnham surely identified with Roosevelt's well-known "man in the arena":

> The credit belongs to the man who is actually in the arena, whose face is marred by dust and sweat and blood; who strives valiantly; who errs, who comes short again and again, because there is no effort without error and shortcoming; but who does actually strive to do the deeds; who knows great enthusiasms, the great devotions; who spends himself in a worthy cause; who at the best knows in the end the triumph of high achievement, and who at the worst, if he fails, at least fails while daring greatly, so that his place shall never be with those cold and timid souls who neither know victory nor defeat.

Burnham's most fundamental trait was his optimism. Like him, it was nearly indestructible. Despite his many setbacks and sorrows, it always rekindled his energy for chasing dreams to the next place, the next possibility. Near the end of his life, as he witnessed another terrible war pitting democratic civilization against modern savagery, he wrote, "not even the world-wide harvest of death need dismay us." It was, after all, only "the dark dawn of a great New Era," "certain to be brighter than all the ages past. . . . Old fears are mostly groundless."

But he wasn't starry-eyed. He wouldn't have been surprised by all the subsequent wars, genocides, and fresh sources of barbarism, because he didn't expect evil to disappear, in himself or in others. But he rejected apathy and had little patience for self-pity or knee-jerk cynicism. He believed that every individual can help shape our shared history, and that if we can overcome our fears and stay alert and improvise intelligently, we will survive the territory ahead. He never lost confidence in that unknown frontier, the future, where a new present can be forged by bold action, and prospects abound.

APPENDIX
THE CONTROVERSIES

THE SHANGANI PATROL

In the 1960s and 1970s, Burnham's reputation got scorched in the firestorm of white Rhodesian nationalism and reactions to it. In those days of racial and political turmoil in Rhodesia, conservative whites sought inspiration from heroes with the right British bloodlines. On the other side, liberals sympathetic to black nationalism were hunting for imperialist villains. Burnham, as an outsider, was a convenient target for both. He was attacked mainly for his role in the assassination of a native priest several years after Shangani (see next section), but also for his part in the Shangani Patrol. Several white Rhodesian historians accused Burnham, Ingram, and Gooding of the most shameful military crime: desertion.

One of the first modern hints of this appeared in 1968 in a book by Oliver Ransford called *The Rulers of Rhodesia*. "There is a good deal to suggest in fact," wrote Ransford, "that Burnham was not ordered away from the patrol as he makes out, but deserted it with his brother-in-law Ingram when he saw the odds that Wilson's men would have to face." Ransford fails to offer a single shred from that "good deal" of evidence to support his vague slur.

In 1970, a Rhodesian writer named John O'Reilly came across a shred in the Rhodesian National Archives—in a letter written in 1935. It was from John Coghlan to John Carruthers, who had been a scout in the Matabele Wars. Coghlan wrote that "a very reliable man informed me that [Colonel Sir Aubrey] Woolls-Sampson told him" that Gooding had confessed on his deathbed to fleeing the patrol without permission. (Burnham and Woolls-Sampson knew each other from the Ndebele war and the Boer War.) O'Reilly exploited this brittle shred of second- and third-hand rumor and innuendo in his fictionalized account of the Shangani Patrol, *Pursuit of the King*, known to every Rhodesian. It depicts Burnham as a deserter, liar, and blowhard.

O'Reilly's evidence hardly bears scrutiny, but requires it. Gooding died in 1899. Thirty-six years later, in a letter, someone (Coghlan) mentions to someone else (Carruthers) that a third person ("a very reliable man") told him that a fourth person (Woolls-Sampson) told the unnamed reliable man at some unspecified date that Gooding had made a deathbed confession to which there were evidently no other witnesses. Perched on this slender reed, O'Reilly rhetorically asks why Wilson would send Gooding away with two expert scouts. Gooding provided the answer in his own contemporary account, which in all essentials matched Burnham's and Ingram's: Wilson asked Burnham to go, Captain Borrow told Gooding to accompany him, and Burnham asked if Ingram could join them. Captain Judd then said that Burnham should take two men to increase the chances that one could get through, and Wilson agreed. No innuendo or historical distortions necessary.

The next significant smear came in the foreword to a 1975 Rhodesian edition of *Scouting on Two Continents* by another Rhodesian writer, Peter Emmerson. He expanded O'Reilly's insinuations without the bother of proof. Emmerson postulated that Wilson, facing such long odds, wouldn't send three men back to Forbes, or at best that Wilson had given permission to escape to anyone who wanted to attempt it. So the trio either deserted and lied about it, or they ran away and lied about it. In any case, they were deceitful cowards.

Emmerson ignores the fact that on the previous evening Wilson had depleted his force by five men, sending back two before the gallop through the Ndebele encampment, and three after the encounter there. Wilson did this before Borrow's patrol arrived and added twenty-one men to the group.

More importantly, Wilson knew that the only way to avoid doom was to get word to Forbes about the patrol's hazardous situation, in hopes of quick relief with a Maxim. Wilson also knew that the best chance of getting this message through the Ndebele lines lay with his two American scouts. Wilson's logic, unlike O'Reilly's and Emmerson's, was based on tactical necessity rather than bias.

These attacks seem influenced by the popular Victorian notion that a soldier's greatest triumph was to die with insouciant bravery. This ideal was celebrated throughout British culture, in popular novels and dramas, and in omnipresent paintings such as Lady Butler's *Floreat Etona*, which portrays an officer, sword raised, riding gallantly toward certain death. It was epitomized by Tennyson's revered "The Charge of the Light Brigade":

> *Not tho' the soldier knew*
> *Someone had blunder'd:*
> *Theirs not to make reply,*
> *Theirs not to reason why,*
> *Theirs but to do and die:*
> *Into the Valley of Death*
> *Rode the six hundred.*

> *Boldly they rode and well,*
> *Into the jaws of Death,*
> *Into the mouth of Hell*
> *Rode the six hundred.*

> *When can their glory fade?*
> *O the wild charge they made!*
> *All the world wondered.*
> *Honor the charge they made,*
> *Honor the Light Brigade,*
> *Noble six hundred.*

The Wilson Patrol fit this image perfectly, turning military catastrophe into patriotic martyrdom, and the episode instantly hardened into myth. From the perspective of this ideal, it was almost unimaginable that Burnham would agree to leave his doomed comrades, and offensive that he didn't seize his opportunity for heroic death. But to others, such as the Apaches and the frontiersmen who learned from them—and also, as the British would soon learn, to the Boers—this ideal looked like military stupidity. It certainly got a lot of British soldiers killed unnecessarily.

In any case, the rumors, insinuations, and theories about Burnham's cowardice evaporate in the face of facts and evidence. None of the men who served with Burnham during that campaign and depended on him daily ever reported any doubts about his courage or his dedication to the mission. The Ndebeles called him "the white induna's eye" and gave him the admiring nickname He-Who-Sees-In-The-Dark. Contemporary journalists heard nothing but praise for Burnham from officers and troopers. Typical is the following passage from Charles L. Norris-Newman, who arrived in Matabeleland in 1894 and interviewed participants for his book about the war: "Too much praise cannot be given to Burnham, who led the night marches from this time [during the retreat of the Forbes column], and who seemed to possess a distinctive intuition of when difficulties arose and how they were to be avoided, and when it is remembered that the nights were dark, no stars being visible, chopping wind, and heavy showers, thick bush country, with no paths, and entirely strange to him, his wonderful powers of mind, heart, and body will better be estimated."

Even decades later his companions were clear about this. In 1944, in response to a story in the *Rhodesia Herald* about the Shangani Patrol and Forbes's column, a member of that column named M. E. Weale wrote, "I have always looked upon Burnham as the most efficient scout we ever had, and it was greatly due to his good scouting that we managed to get away on that memorable night when we left the tired horses and Maxim carriages behind and Commandant Raaf took over command. I have always felt that the honours were equally divided between these two men, to whom we owed our lives on that occasion."

THE MLIMO

The Mlimo episode is by far the most controversial incident in Burnham's life. Doubts about it festered for decades and eventually erupted among some Rhodesian historians, who alleged lies and cover-ups by Burnham and Armstrong. The first attack came in 1897, in a book called *With Plumer in Matabeleland: an Account of the Operations of the Matabeleland Relief Force During the Rebellion of 1896*, by Frank W. Sykes. He cited an anonymous source who claimed that Burnham and Armstrong had murdered a helpless old black man and then inflated themselves into heroes.

The next serious allegation was slipped into a book entitled *The Making of Rhodesia* (1926), by a Rhodesian civil servant named Hugh Marshall Hole, who had spent the war years as a BSAC clerk in Salisbury. In a footnote, without naming Burnham and Armstrong, Hole wrote of the Mlimo incident, "On their return they were greatly applauded for having achieved their dangerous errand, but some time later, when it was found that the Mlimo was still at work, an official inquiry was held, with the result that the whole affair was exposed as an elaborate hoax."

Hole offered no proof for this assertion. In private letters he claimed to have read Judge Watermeyer's report, and further claimed, uniquely, that it denounced Burnham and Armstrong. He added that the incident was clearly a hoax because the two men erroneously stated that the Mlimo's cave was "close to the Sashi River, and within about 30 miles of the Matopos Hills," which would put it fifty miles west of Mangwe, far from Njelele.

Such a claim did smell like a hoax, but neither Burnham nor Armstrong ever made it. In all of his reports and newspaper interviews, Burnham located the cave less than twenty miles *east* of Mangwe, near the Shashani River, not the Sashi. Hole's "proof" was a geographical error he copied from a report written in April 1899 by Armstrong's enemy, Chief

Native Commissioner H. J. Taylor, in response to a list of complaints by Armstrong that got the young man dismissed as a native commissioner. In the same report, Taylor also asserted that Jobani was not a priest of the Mlimo, despite all the local witnesses to the contrary.

Then in 1948 a man named Frederick Ramón de Bertodano (later the Marquis de Moral) donated a typed copy of his diary to Rhodesia's National Archives. He had written it, he said, while in Bulawayo for several months during the uprising. De Bertodano had been raised in Australia and had trained there as a solicitor. He arrived in laagered Bulawayo on May 19, 1896, aged twenty-five. He hoped to depart quickly after selling some mining interests for a British syndicate, but got delayed by the revolt. During his time there, he avoided military service and, based on his diary, spent most of his time drinking and gossiping in the Bulawayo Club. Later, in the Boer War, he served as a commandant and intelligence officer, but lost that appointment amid charges of fraud, corruption, and profiteering. In 1947, the year Burnham died, de Bertodano settled in Salisbury, Rhodesia, where he came across a copy of *Scouting on Two Continents*. In a note added to his diary in 1948, he wrote that Burnham's lies had inspired him to donate the diary to help set the record straight.

The diary was indeed damning. It chronicled contemporary talk that was sneering and disbelieving about Burnham, Armstrong, and the killing of the priest. De Bertodano and others described the two men as lying, boastful self-promoters. The entry for July 6, 1896, was typical: "Several of us talking at the club. Very strong opinion expressed of the shooting of the M'limo by Armstrong, Native Commissioner at Mangwe and Burnham the so-called 'Great American Scout.' Several men say that the whole thing is a farce . . ." In a note he added to the diary later, de Bertodano recalled that "Burnham in conversation could not get away from himself and young Armstrong was temperamental and conceited," though the diary was unclear about when or if de Bertodano ever met Burnham, seemingly an important event. In another entry de Bertodano described a stroll with Judge Watermeyer, during which Watermeyer told him, "The whole thing was a 'fake' and a lie of self-glorification of young Armstrong and Burnham. The 'M'limo' was an old native working in a kaffir garden."

Rhodesian researchers pounced on de Bertodano's diary. Terence Ranger's superb *Revolt in Southern Rhodesia, 1896–97* (1967) is the most influential book of history written about the uprising. For his account of the Mlimo episode, however, he relied heavily on de Bertodano's diary to conclude that Burnham and Armstrong killed a harmless old priest and then magnified the episode into a hoax.

Oliver Ransford, another Rhodesian historian, also trusted de Bertodano's diary as well as Hole's repetition of Taylor's erroneous report. Ransford adopted Hole's sneering tone and phrasing to make his case that Burnham and Armstrong were hoaxers: "After a cloak and dagger affair which was boisterously applauded at the time, Burnham claimed he had succeeded in shooting the oracle and was certain this would play a large part in ending the rebellion. . . . to make it now seem even more absurd the weight of evidence that has since come to light suggests that Burnham and his friend Armstrong 'faked' the whole affair for self-glorification and that the man they killed was an inoffensive peasant."

Historical assertions (and assumptions) build upon themselves. From seeds planted by Sykes, Taylor, Hole, and de Bertodano about Burnham sprang the judgments of Ranger and Ransford, which were accepted as accurate and have been repeated by other historians. But Sykes's and Hole's accusations were based on malicious gossip and errors, and de Bertodano's diary, which called Burnham and Armstrong liars, is rotten with fabrications. For instance, de Bertodano claimed to talk to Frederick Selous in Bulawayo on May 21, 25, and 29—but Selous was away (as was Burnham) from May 11 to May 31 with the patrol sent to meet the Salisbury column. In his entry for June 17, de Bertodano reported, "Long talk with P. D. Crewe, Selous (silent as ever!), Macfarlane & others." Perhaps Selous was silent because, as he wrote in *Sunshine and Storm in Rhodesia*, he was gone with Colonel J. A. Spreckley's column from June 7 to June 23.

De Bertodano's entries about Burnham and Armstrong are equally fraudulent. According to his diary, people at the Bulawayo Club knew on June 17 that Burnham and Armstrong had found the Mlimo's cave in the Matopos and were "trying to get him." This would have been news to Burnham, since on that date he hadn't yet heard about Armstrong's plan. The two men didn't leave until June 20, and it's doubtful that their secret mission had been broadcast in the Bulawayo Club. On June 21, de Bertodano again foresaw the future: "Widely reported that Armstrong and Burnham have shot the M'Limo in his cave or 'temple.' Several men don't believe it because they don't trust the yarns of either Armstrong or Burnham." The men's skepticism was understandable; the assassination wouldn't occur for two more days.

In the diary, de Bertodano ridiculed the two men for claiming to gallop away from the natives after the shooting, snorting that the rough terrain in the Matopos would not allow it. Putting aside that this was curious mockery from someone who evidently never left laagered Bulawayo to assist in its defense, anyone who has seen the landscape between Njelele and the Shashani River knows, as Burnham stated many times, that flat grassy areas are interspersed with kopjes, as opposed to the rugged landscape west of Mangwe, where Taylor and Hole incorrectly placed the cave. Inventive newspaper illustrators did sometimes portray Burnham and Armstrong escaping through rocky defiles where no horse could gallop, which may be the source of de Bertodano's secondhand misimpression.

Similarly, in his July 15 entry, de Bertodano scoffed at Burnham and Armstrong for telling people that after killing the Mlimo they had "A hard ride and running fight when they were nearly exhausted." In *Scouting on Two Continents*, written thirty years after the alleged diary, Burnham described "a long hard ride and a running fight over rough ground, until we were nearly exhausted." De Bertodano evidently plagiarized the sentence and inserted it into his "diary." And so on.

De Bertodano doubtless spent time in Bulawayo and kept a diary, but the document he submitted to the National Archives was so corrupted by fabrications that researchers should have dismissed it as historical fiction. It is valuable mostly as a manufactured specimen of bias against Burnham and Armstrong.

In a foreword to a Rhodesian reprint of *Scouting on Two Continents* (1975), the Rhodesian researcher Peter Emmerson did question the reliability of de Bertodano's diary, without explaining why, and also challenged Hole's assertion that Judge Watermeyer had censured Burnham and Armstrong. Further, he noted that the accusations against Armstrong by H. J. Taylor and others "may be of doubtful validity."

Nevertheless, he adopted de Bertodano's description of Burnham—"He was loud, brash, boastful and conceited"—despite scores of contemporary descriptions that remarked on Burnham's exceptional modesty, not to mention his own frequent admissions of failure in *Scouting on Two Continents*. To illustrate Burnham's self-aggrandizement, Emmerson evidently wrote on the flyleaf that Burnham, in *Scouting on Two Continents*, claimed he had "done Rhodesians a stupendous service by exploding the myth of the cave and destroying the M'Limo's power." But Burnham never made this claim about himself; the sentence Emmerson quotes was about Armstrong, whom Burnham always credited with breaking the Mlimo's power.

Like other Rhodesian writers, Emmerson also disregarded the friendship and accolades Burnham received from every leader who knew him in Africa—Rhodes, Jameson, Carrington, Baden-Powell, Selous, Earl Grey, Lord Roberts, and on and on. Some of these men made military decisions affecting hundreds of men based on their trust in Burnham's accuracy and truthfulness. Emmerson, like other Rhodesian writers, also disregarded Burnham's eager return to southern Africa to fight for the British in the Boer War, and his heroic service in that conflict. Perhaps all this is disregarded because it cannot be squared with a portrait of Burnham as a cowardly blowhard.

And so Emmerson, despite his doubts about the main accusations against the American, allowed himself to be persuaded anyway: "nevertheless the weight of evidence has become overwhelming that there was deception after the event, if not before." All doubts get swept aside in a wave of condemnatory rhetoric: "At best the incident would seem to have been a clumsy attempt at psychological warfare, which failed . . . At worst it was a cold blooded murder of an innocent noncombatant for personal gain." After writing such a sentence, Emmerson was forced to conclude that Burnham's book couldn't be believed: "Certainly this is so of the African chapters."

Yet the "weight of evidence" is hard to find in Emmerson's essay, where insinuations rather than proofs become overwhelming. Even Burnham's documented achievements are somehow discounted as fabrications and campfire tales. There is no hint that he could have been anything other than a boastful lying seeker of fame. Everything is twisted toward one end—diminishment of Burnham. There seems to be no room for the American scout in Rhodesian history, a peculiar snub of someone who loved the place and devoted so much sweat and blood to it. No similar bias against Burnham exists within South African history.

Still, parts of Burnham's account and subsequent claims about the Mlimo incident are troubling, starting with that two-hour chase. De Bertodano is wrong that the topography makes it impossible, but wouldn't two men on horseback in somewhat open terrain quickly outrun pursuers on foot? Did Burnham exaggerate the escape to make a better story?

On December 10, 1938, a man named E. C. Hartley wrote to the *Bulawayo Chronicle* about those long-gone days. Hartley had been the postmaster-telegraphist at Fort Mangwe in 1896 and claimed to be good friends with Armstrong (evidently one of a few, owing to Armstrong's spiky temperament). Hartley confirmed the basics of the episode as he had heard them from Armstrong: Armstrong learned the location of the priest's cave, he and Burnham volunteered for the mission of killing him, and Burnham did so. But then, according to Hartley, Armstrong's account diverged from Burnham's:

The return journey was accomplished without incident. A good deal of publicity was given this expedition which Bonar Armstrong very

strongly deprecated but owing to his official position could not pub-
lickly [sic] refute. . . . his version was that neither going nor returning
did they contact with any male natives and that the statements that
they were chased by natives etc. were absolutely untrue. This narrative which constitutes what actually transpired in connection with the
M'limo episode was frequently related to me by Bonar Armstrong
and which I had an opportunity of verifying from his official reports.
[These have disappeared.] It must however be conceded that the expedition was an extremely brave and dangerous undertaking.

Hartley went on to say that because of doubts about the episode, Armstrong insisted on an inquiry, and that Judge Watermeyer's "very exhaustive
investigation" confirmed that "the native killed was the Chief Priest of the
M'limo," though there may have been other important priests.

Hartley's version seems more plausible than Burnham's, with its dramatic two-hour chase, or the Rhodesian historians', with their reluctance to
acknowledge anything risky or courageous about the mission. If Hartley's
version is true, it certainly dents Burnham's credibility about the mission's
aftermath.

But Hartley may not be right either. A well-known correspondent
and illustrator named Charles Edwin Fripp happened to be at Mangwe
when Burnham and Armstrong returned from killing the priest. That
evening Fripp got the first version of the event from the two men, and
sent a story and sketch about it, datelined June 23, 1896, to the London
newspaper *The Graphic* (the story appeared on August 15). The basic elements
that appeared in subsequent stories and reports were all in Fripp's story.
The accompanying illustration, drawn by another artist from Fripp's sketch,
showed Burnham and Armstrong riding across a grassy, level landscape as
natives with spears pursued them. In the background, as Burnham often
described, the grass was on fire. "This sketch," noted the newspaper, "was
made from materials supplied to our correspondent by Mr. Armstrong." So

did Armstrong change his story for Hartley? Is Hartley misremembering or distorting what he heard? Did Burnham exaggerate? It seems impossible to know.

Burnham always claimed that the man in the cave was the chief priest of the Mlimo, and that killing him shortened the Ndebele uprising. In *Scouting on Two Continents* he wrote, "peace followed the downfall of the M'Limo." In 1896 and for years afterward, most people agreed with that assessment, as did official inquiries. In 1900, for instance, in *A History of Rhodesia, Compiled from Official Sources*, Howard Hensman wrote, "With the downfall of Wedza and the shooting of the M'Limo in a cave in the Matoppos by the American scout, Burnham, the Matabele rebellion may be said to have come to an end."

But both of Burnham's assumptions were incorrect. First, Jobani wasn't the only chief priest of the god. Even at the time, a few knowledgeable people suspected as much, and it soon became clear that priests in other parts of the country were urging on the rebels. This led to doubts that Burnham had killed the real oracle, doubts that festered into accusations of a hoax. Part of the problem was ignorance about the Ndebeles' religious organization. Njelele was just one of several major shrines to the Mlimo in Matabeleland, each of which had a chief priest.

That's partly why Burnham's second assumption was flawed. Killing the chief priest at Njelele didn't shorten the war; rather, it almost certainly worsened the situation south of Bulawayo. The settlers and their military men couldn't understand why the Ndebeles didn't close the vital road over Mangwe Pass, Bulawayo's lifeline for supplies. Nor could they understand why the natives in that region rarely attacked whites. Selous, Baden-Powell, Carrington, and Burnham, among others, all expressed puzzlement at these military conundrums. They assumed that the Ndebeles were leaving the road open either to encourage the settlers to give up and flee by that route, or to lure a large number of them into the pass for slaughter.

The truth was simpler but unknown at the time: the priest at Njelele had advised the people in his region to remain neutral in the uprising. The pass remained open and attacks were few because most of the area's natives weren't actively hostile. Ndebele impis did enter the region, and commanders did try to recruit the local people. Burnham and Baden-Powell, in their three-day scout into the Matopos just before the Mlimo mission, found signs of these impis and local cooperation with them. But scholars such as Ranger later showed that the priests most responsible for encouraging the uprising lived elsewhere in Matabeleland, and that the assassination at Njelele was a blunder that provoked the neutral population. It did more harm than good.

Later writers, especially Rhodesians, have attacked Burnham for not correcting his mistaken assumptions. "That he was aware of the doubts before he left is clear," wrote Emmerson, in a typical accusation, "as must have been the palpable falsehood that the killing ended the Rebellion. Even if he wasn't wholly aware of the situation at the time, he would certainly have been so by 1926, the year his autobiography was published."

Burnham surely did know about the doubts, yet never mentioned them, perhaps because he never saw things that way, or because the official inquiries supported him, or because he wanted to protect his reputation. But he couldn't have known about Hole's initial accusation of fraud when he wrote *Scouting on Two Continents*, because Hole's book appeared that same year, and Burnham apparently didn't read it until 1935. That year, Burnham's lawyer sent a letter to Hole asking for an explanation. Hole evidently answered, but nothing came of it. Burnham also must have known by 1926 that the priest he killed was not the sole oracle of the Mlimo—that became common knowledge after the assassination—but there's less reason to believe that he knew the priest was neutral or that the assassination didn't help end the war, since that information wasn't well-established by scholarship until the 1960s.

The Mlimo episode is fraught with ignorance, malice, inaccurate reports, conflicting stories, lost documents, fraudulent documents, antagonism between the people involved, and bias. Amid the murk, a few things seem clear, or at least less cloudy: the settlers and their military leaders believed that the priests of the Mlimo were guiding the uprising; Lord Grey and General Carrington thought it was militarily advisable to target the one priest whose whereabouts they knew, based on Native Commissioner Armstrong's information; Burnham shot the wrong priest, a blunder that may have worsened the situation. Finally, and most importantly, Burnham was following orders to assassinate someone he believed to be the prime mover of an uprising that had killed many of his friends as well as his infant daughter.

ACKNOWLEDGMENTS

In Zimbabwe, Rob Burrett was invaluable as a guide, historian, and sounding board, roles he continued to play long after I returned home. I'm grateful to David Scott-Donelan for connecting me to him. Johan Hattingh ably guided me for part of my travels in South Africa; my thanks to historian André Wessels for the recommendation.

The librarians at Yale and at Stanford's Hoover Institution, which hold the Burnham archives, made my lengthy visits pleasant as well as fruitful.

Fred Burnham, son of Roderick Burnham, welcomed my interest in his grandfather and invited me into his home in Tucson, where he shared family scrapbooks and other material. I'm especially indebted to Rod Atkinson, the nephew of Fred Burnham and great-grandson of Frederick Russell Burnham. Rod has spent many years researching his ancestor. He was always willing to share what he knew and to discuss any puzzling or thorny aspect of his great-grandfather's life. I'm also grateful that the Burnham family gave me unrestricted permission to use materials from the Yale archive.

My agent, Deborah Grosvenor, encouraged me to expand the frame when thinking about Burnham's life, which I hope led to a better book. My editor, Starling Lawrence, saw the prospects in Burnham's story and offered several essential pointers that helped to clarify my views. Ryan Harrington at Norton responded cheerfully to every question or concern, and smoothed the book's path toward publication. Copyeditor Allegra Huston sifted out a number of blunders and muddles.

As always, I was sustained by the heart and cheer of my wife Jude.

NOTES

Most of the book's quotations from Burnham come from several primary sources. He wrote two memoirs: *Scouting on Two Continents* (*S2C*) (Doubleday, Page and Company, 1926), and *Taking Chances* (*TC*) (Wolfe Publishing, 1994, reprint of 1944 edition by Haynes Corporation). The other primary sources are the extensive Burnham papers held by Yale University and by Stanford's Hoover Institution, which overlap but aren't identical. In the rare instances where the Burnhams misspell a word, I have usually corrected it to avoid distraction.

At several places in the text, the translations of historical dollar amounts into modern equivalents come from measuringworth.com.

PROLOGUE

1   The details about the flight of Burnham's mother from the Sioux war party are taken from *S2C* and various letters and newspaper reports in the Burnham archives.

Chapter 1: CHILD OF THE FRONTIER

5   The opening pages of *S2C* contain several errors. Burnham substitutes Red Cloud, the Oglala Sioux chief, for Little Crow, a Dakota Sioux, a mistake repeated countless times in newspapers and articles. He also says he was two when the war began; he was fifteen months old. He misdates the Sioux hangings—the year was 1862, not 1863. He identifies Minnesota's governor at the time as Sibley, but it was Ramsey. He also misspells Le Claire and Red Wing. These are understandable mistakes in a memoir written sixty years after the events, but they also suggest a degree of sloppiness by Burnham and Mary Nixon Everett, who "edited and arranged" the book. As far as I can tell, the rest of *S2C* contains relatively few factual errors, which will be noted as they come up.

7   Helpful on the Sioux War: Folwell, *A History of Minnesota*; Bishop, *Dakota War Whoop*; Wingerd, *North Country: The Making of Minnesota*.

10   "Pampered protégés" comes from *Dakota War Whoop*, p. 280. As of 2015, the Wikipedia page on Burnham erroneously said that he was born on a Sioux reservation.

15   Some of the material on books of Western adventure was taken from Billing-ton, *Land of Savagery, Land of Promise*, and from Smith, *Virgin Land*.

Chapter 2: A PUEBLO AND SOME PURITANS

19   The quotes from Burnham about the bounty of California and his sense of liberation after his father's death both can be found in the rough draft of *S2C* in the Yale archive.

20   The anecdote about the drayman Wood is from a speech Burnham made to the Sunsetter Club of Los Angeles, date unknown, in the Yale archive.

23   For background information about mining and freighting: Fisher and Holmes, *Gold Rushes and Mining Camps of the Early American West*; Nadeau, *City-Makers*; Rossiter, *Statistics of Mines and Mining in the States and Territories West of the Rocky Mountains, 32.*

26   Among the helpful sources on Tiburcio Vásquez: John W. Robinson, "Tibur-cio Vásquez in Southern California: the Bandit's Last Hurrah," *California Territorial Quarterly* 27 (Fall 1996); Will H. Thrall, "The Haunts and Hide-outs of Tiburcio Vásquez," *Historical Society of Southern California Quarterly* XXX, no. 2 (June 1948); and John Boessenecker, *Bandido: The Life and Times of Tiburcio Vasquez* (University of Oklahoma Press, 2010). Like other myths that turn Western thugs into heroes, the one about Vásquez as an idealistic revolutionary persists. The website of the Tiburcio Vásquez Health Centers in California, for example, explains that the founders "wanted to choose a name that evoked a sense of pride and fortitude in their community, and what bet-ter choice than the heroic character who—legend has it—defied authority in order to aid the downtrodden Californios?" Two California schools also are named after this criminal rogue.

29   The information about Clinton, Iowa, comes from *S2C* and *TC*, and from sec-tions deleted from these books, found in the archives at Yale and Stanford.

30   The description of the evangelical revivalist comes from her biography: John Onesimus Foster, *Life and Labors of Mrs. Maggie Newton Van Cott: The First Lady Licensed to Preach in the Methodist Episcopal Church in the United States* (Hitchcock and Walden, 1872).

Chapter 3: WANDERINGS AND APPRENTICESHIPS

33   For Prescott and life in early Arizona, see Corle, *The Gila*. Virgin Mary's menu appears on pp. 323–4.

34   Essential sources on the Apaches: Thrapp, *The Conquest of Apacheria*; and Haley, *Apaches*.

35   Several commentators have identified the old scout named Holmes who

taught Burnham as W. A. "Hunkydory" Holmes. This is incorrect. Burnham was eighteen when he met Holmes, which would be 1879. He describes the scout as "an old man then, and physically impaired," which makes sense for someone old enough to have served with Fremont and Kit Carson in the 1840s. Hunkydory Holmes, on the other hand, was born around 1839.

39   Burnham's peripheral vision: from *The Golden Penny*, a London illustrated weekly, undated clip in a Burnham family scrapbook in the Stanford archive.

40   Some of the characteristics of a good scout sound similar to those measured in the new field of "risk intelligence," defined as a cognitive skill allowing for good quick decisions on the basis of limited information in an atmosphere of uncertainty. See Alison George, "The Man Who Gave Us Risk Intelligence," *New Scientist*, May 21, 2012.

41   "the atmosphere of adventure with prospects everywhere": From Banning and Banning, *Six Horses*, 19 (foreword by Burnham).

Chapter 4: THE TONTO BASIN FEUD

43   Sources helpful for this chapter, in addition to those cited below: Barnes, *Arizona Place Names*; and Hodge, *Arizona As It Is; or, The Coming Country. Compiled From Notes of Travel During the Years 1874, 1875, and 1876.*

43   Angeline Mitchell Brown, from an excerpt of her "Diary of a School Teacher on the Arizona Frontier," in Moynihan, Armitage, and Dichamp, eds., *So Much To Be Done.*

44   Don Dedera's *A Little War of Our Own* is the most thorough and impartial treatment of the feud. Other sources consulted include Will C. Barnes, "The Pleasant Valley War of 1887," *Arizona Historical Review* 4 (October 1931 and January 1932); Forrest, *Arizona's Dark and Bloody Ground*; Herman, *Hell on the Range*; Pyle, *Pleasant Valley War*; and the chapters on the feud in Drago, *The Great Range Wars.*

47   The quote from P. P. Daggs comes from Dedera (*A Little War of Our Own*, 108), who found people in Pleasant Valley still reluctant to talk about those bloody events even a century later. Dedera correctly surmised that the family who befriended Burnham was the Gordons, who appear sporadically in contemporary newspapers such as the *Arizona Silver Belt*. Burnham's rough drafts in the Yale archives identify the family as the Gordons. Rod Atkinson, Burnham's great-grandson and a superb researcher, also dug up and shared useful information about the Gordons.

48   Some accounts of the feud mention Burnham, not always accurately. Forrest, in *Arizona's Dark and Bloody Ground*, refers to Burnham twice and makes two errors: he writes that Burnham didn't get sucked into the feud until 1887 and

that he was a "boy" at the time. Burnham likely got involved in the early 1880s while the feud was still brewing; by 1887 he was twenty-six, hardly a boy.

49   The description of Burnham's revolver comes from Jack Lott, "The Making of a Hero," who knew the weapon firsthand. A photo of it, perhaps taken by Lott, can be found on the Wikipedia page for the Pleasant Valley feud. Lott was a big-game hunter, an aficionado of firearms, and a knowledgeable writer about guns. He also wrote several articles about Burnham, whom he greatly admired, and he was a friend of Burnham's son Roderick, who died in 1976. Roderick evidently gave Lott his father's guns, including the Remington revolver and several weapons used in Africa. Lott committed suicide in 1993. Burnham's descendants have been unable to determine what happened to the guns.

49   The quotes about snap shooting with a revolver come from "The Revolver," an essay by Burnham, evidently never published, found in the Stanford archives.

50   Like every researcher so far, I was unable to find any contemporary mention of old Gordon's killing of the deputy and Burnham's association with it. Dedera, who has investigated the feud most deeply, categorizes this shooting as "among probable but thinly documented cases" (159).

51   Pleasant Valley, now called Young, remains lovely and isolated, with a population of about 650. Sections of the road to it are still unpaved. Among its few streets are Graham Road and Tewksbury Boulevard. Every July during Pleasant Valley Days, Young celebrates the feud that tore it apart, offering a parade, reenactments, and tours of sites where blood was spilled. Like so much violent Western history, the Pleasant Valley feud has become a money-making attraction.

53   The quotations about Burnham's eyes are from, respectively, the Introduction to *S2C* by Mary Nixon Everett, xix; and W. B. Courtney, "Great Scout," *Collier's*, October 19, 1935, 60.

54   "no moral anchors": Davis, *Real Soldiers of Fortune,* 199.

54   Peter van Wyk (the pen name of Peter Craigmoe) speculated that the young Kansan who turned to rustling was the outlaw Billy Claiborne. Van Wyk spent many years researching Burnham's life and wrote a fictionalized biography about him called *Burnham: King of Scouts.*

Chapter 5: TOMBSTONE

58   Helpful for this chapter, in addition to the sources cited below: Sonnichsen, *Billy King's Tombstone*; and Federal Writers' Project, *Arizona, the Grand Canyon State.*

58   James B. Hume is quoted in Philip L. Fradkin, *Stagecoach: Wells Fargo and the American West* (New York: Free Press, 2003), 104.

59   Lansing's description of Ed Schieffelin comes from an unidentified Arizona

newspaper quoted in Richard E. Moore, "The Silver King: Ed Schieffelin, Prospector," *Oregon Historical Quarterly* 87, no. 4 (Winter 1986): 367–8. I also drew on Moore's article for Schieffelin's whereabouts before Tombstone.

60 The anecdote about the Schieffelin brothers' survival plan if attacked by Apaches appears in Hammond, *Autobiography*, vol. 1, 78. Hammond, a mining engineer who later became good friends with Burnham, visited Tombstone and talked to the Schieffelins about a year after they opened their mines.

60 The names of mining claims come from Fisher and Holmes.

62 "Shooting from behind or shooting an unarmed man": Myers, *Tombstone's Early Years*, 94.

62 The anecdote about the death of John Heith (sometimes spelled Heath) from emphysema comes from Sonnichsen, ed., *Billy King's Tombstone*, 186–7.

62 "leading diseases": William H. Bishop, "Across Arizona," *Harper's*, March 1883.

62 On liquor in Western mining towns, Fisher and Holmes are informative and entertaining (183–93). Also Carmony, ed., *Whiskey, Six-Guns and Red-Light Ladies*.

63 Heidi Osselaer, an Arizona historian, has found more than 140 women who ran businesses in Tombstone during this era: "On the Wrong Side of Allen Street: Female Merchants in Tombstone, 1879–1884," unpublished paper delivered at the Western History Symposium, August 2012, in Prescott, AZ.

64 According to material exhibited at the Bird Cage (now a tourist attraction) and on many websites, the theater took its name from a popular song, "She's Only a Bird in a Gilded Cage." The story goes that the comedian Eddie Foy and a songwriter named Arthur J. Lamb were chatting in the theater one evening soon after the place opened under a different name. As they watched the beautiful women in feathers who flirted with customers before heading for the upstairs "cages," Lamb blurted the phrase that became the song's title. He sat at the saloon's piano and quickly composed a ballad. The famous singer Lillian Russell happened to be performing that night, the story continues, and she sang the brand-new song to many encores, whereupon the overwhelmed owner renamed the theater the Bird Cage.

A few of these details have some factual basis, but when mushed together they create an utter fabrication. Lamb did write the lyrics to the song, but he was born in Britain in 1870, so the story puts this lad on a barstool in a Tombstone brothel at age eleven. Eddie Foy and Lillian Russell did tour through Tombstone and may have entertained at the Bird Cage, but not with Lamb present. Nor was the Bird Cage's name changed because of the song—Lamb wrote it in 1900, eleven years after the place closed. Similarly, the Bird Cage features a large painting of a popular belly-dancer called Fatima, later known as Little Egypt. The theater museum claims that Fatima performed there in 1881 and sent the painting the following year. But the belly-dancer who performed as Fatima—Farida Mazar Spyropoulos—was born in Syria around 1871, which makes the bare-breasted curvaceous female in the painting ten years old. These are the kinds of widespread, self-perpetuating, and wonderfully seductive lies waiting to ensnare every researcher into the Old West, where random unrelated facts are woven together and embroidered into myths.

65   McLeod: Burnham identifies him only by his last name, but he is almost certainly Neil McLeod, well-known at the time in Tombstone and Globe. Rod Atkinson discovered some helpful news clippings about this man, including several reports that he was killed in August 1884 near Nacozari de García, a town near Fronteras, Mexico. This fits with information in *S2C*, where Burnham states that McLeod was "killed accidentally by his own men. This happened in a smugglers' camp near Fronterras." Also helpful was a story about McLeod by Roscoe G. Willson, who calls him "the all-time king of Arizona smugglers." ("Arizona Days," 9).

68   Coded messages: in addition to Burnham's comments in *S2C*, see *TC*, chapter 21, "The Grapevine," where he mentions several methods used by Indians, including messages sent via tiny woven baskets, scratched shells, logs in flooding rivers, and migratory birds trapped and stained in certain patterns, then released.

71   Apaches running hills with mouths full of water: Watt, *Apache Tactics*, 15. Apaches outrunning horses: Carr, *Old Mother Mexico*, 5–6. Carr, a popular editor and columnist for the *Los Angeles Times* who became Burnham's friend, wrote that Burnham told him an Apache could run next to a horse until the horse collapsed.

72   The footrace in Globe: John F. Coggswell, "World's Most Adventurous Man, Major Fred Burnham, D.S.O., Describes Greatest Peril He Ever Had to Face," *Atlanta Constitution,* November 1, 1931, SM10.

Chapter 6: THE TIGERS OF THE HUMAN SPECIES

73   In addition to Burnham, Haley, *Apaches*, and Thrapp, *The Conquest of Apacheria* and *Al Sieber*, the main sources for this chapter are the indispensable Cozzens, ed., *The Struggle for Apacheria*; Watt, *Apache Tactics*; Downey and Jacobsen, *The Red/Bluecoats*; Dunlay, *Wolves for Blue Soldiers*; Worcester, *The Apaches*; and Smith, *Captive Arizona*.

74   Sherman on Arizona: quoted in Thrapp, *The Conquest of Apacheria*, xii.

76   Bourke, "black night of despair": from his article "General Crook in the Indian Country," *The Century Magazine*, March 1891, 644–9.

79 "In [Apache] combats": from Crook's article, "The Apache Problem" (1886), found in Cozzens, *The Struggle for Apacheria*, 597–8.

81 Miles on Apache camouflage: from Miles, *Personal Recollections*, 525.

82 Crook, "so many birds": from "The Apache Problem," in Cozzens, *The Struggle for Apacheria*, 600.

83 "the torture of a journey": from Wesley Merritt, "Incidents of Indian Campaigning in Arizona" (1890), ibid., 155–6. Cavalry "as useless as gunboats": from Charles King (one of Crook's officers), "On Campaign in Arizona" (1880), ibid., 162. "Jagged, peaked, rocky": from Powhatan H. Clarke, "A Hot Trail" (1894), ibid., 635.

85 Burnham never mentions Clum but almost certainly knew him from Tombstone, where Clum founded the *Tombstone Epitaph* in May 1880. The paper supported the Earp faction. Burnham may have run into Clum (and Wyatt Earp) again in the Klondike during the gold rush of 1898.

Chapter 7: HUNTING TIGERS WITH TIGERS

87 Atrocities at a ranch near the Gila River: recounted in Thrapp, *The Conquest of Apacheria*, 237–8.

88 For the Globe Rangers, see Thrapp, *The Conquest of Apacheria*, 255, and *Al Sieber*, 247, as well as Will C. Barnes, "The Apaches' Last Stand in Arizona: the Battle of Big Dry Wash" (1931), in Cozzens, *The Struggle for Apacheria*, 277–8.

88 For the account of Burnham's scout for Burbridge, in addition to *S2C* and *TC*, I used Burnham's story "Half Jack-Rabbit, Half Wolf," published in *Boys' Life*, March 1928. This story, with minor changes, became a chapter in *TC*.

94 Two messengers, one mounted, one on foot: from Coggswell, "World's Most Adventurous Man."

94 Burnham's chapter in *S2C* on the Apache raids of 1882 contains several small inaccuracies. He identifies the chief of scouts at the San Carlos Apache reservation as Fred Sterling. He was Albert D. Sterling, known as Al, and his official title was chief of police, though his native police were essentially scouts. Burnham also says that Sterling and his successor, "Cibicue" Charley Colvig, were killed by Apache government scouts who turned on them. That view was common at the time but is incorrect. Both men were slain by renegade Apaches who came up from Mexico. Burnham also mentions being part of a rescue party that saved some settlers on Cherry Creek in the Tonto Basin, including "a small boy named Charley Meadows, famous for many years afterwards as Buffalo Bill's leading cowboy." Burnham's group undoubtedly saved a little boy, but not the famous Charlie Meadows, who was born in 1859 or 1860 and hence was slightly

older than Burnham. The Meadows family did have a ranch in Tonto Basin that was attacked by Apaches in July 1882, but it wasn't near Cherry Creek, and when the Apaches struck it, Meadows was serving as a scout under Al Sieber. Burnham also says that the grand jury report about corruption on San Carlos was written in 1883 rather than 1882.

Similarly, in "Half Rabbit, Half Wolf," his chapter in *TC* about his service during the Apache raids of 1882, Burnham says that when he returned to Globe from a scouting expedition after the Apaches raided McMillenville in July (he calls it McMillan), he expected to report to Sterling. This jumbles chronology, probably because of faulty memory. Sterling was murdered in April 1882, several months before the McMillenville raid. It's possible but unlikely that Burnham had been out of touch for months and hadn't heard about Sterling's death. In the same chapter, Burnham says he was scouting for signs of the band led by Chief Diablo, but this is mistaken. There were two important Diablos in Apache history, but both died before 1882. The renegade bands on the loose were led by Geronimo, Chatto, Juh, and Na-tio-tish.

Likewise, in both *S2C* and *TC*, he says that at the end of his scout around the Pinals for Burbridge, he met up with Scarface Charley, the famous Modoc chief. This is almost certainly a misidentification. The man may have been a Modoc and may have been called Scarface Charley—probably not an uncommon nickname in those days—but it's doubtful he was the Modoc chief who fought the whites in California in the 1870s and then led his people to a reservation in Oklahoma, where he died in 1896. I found no evidence that this well-known Indian worked in Arizona as a government scout in the early 1880s. Throughout his life, Burnham avidly read accounts of the West. If he had known an Indian of that name in Arizona, he may have assumed the two were the same man.

94   For the testimony of various Apache leaders given to Crook, and Crook's responses, see Cozzens, *The Struggle for Apacheria*, 295–313. For the grand jury's indictment, see ibid., pp. 318–20. For the *Silver Belt* and Tiffany, see Trapp, *The Conquest of Apacheria*, 258n.

95   Robert K. Evans: from his "The Indian Question in Arizona," *Atlantic Monthly*, August 1886, reprinted in Cozzens, *The Struggle for Apacheria*, 607.

96   The headline from the *Arizona Silver Belt*: April 7, 1883.

97   Bourke, "disgraceful page in history": from his *On the Border with Crook,* 485. Crook's defense of Apache scouts, from his "Resume of Operations Against Apache Indians, 1882 to 1886," collected in Cozzens, *The Struggle for Apacheria*, 587–8.

Chapter 8: A MINE, A WEDDING, A CHANGE OF PLANS

99   Burnham misspells the name of Buckey O'Neill as O'Neal, but the other details he mentions about the lawmen are correct. See Ball, *Desert Lawmen*. Other sources helpful on Arizona lawmen and Wells Fargo shotgun messengers: Charles Michelson, "Stage Robbers of the West" (1901), collected in Oliver G. Swan, ed., *Frontier Days* (Philadelphia: Macrae Smith, 1928), 405–13; Dale, *Frontier Ways*; and Virginia M. Hall, "Wells Fargo Treasure Boxes," *Calcoin News*, Winter 2002.

100   "kill or be killed": from Michelson, "Stage Robbers of the West."

102   Sources helpful on mining: Lewis, ed., *The Mining Frontier*; Paul, *Mining Frontiers of the Far West*; the invaluable Spence, *Mining Engineers and the American West*; William S. Greever, *The Bonanza West: The Story of the Western Mining Rushes, 1848–1900* (Norman: University of Oklahoma Press, 1963); Fisher and Holmes, *Gold Rushes and Mining Camps of the Early American West*; Dobie, *Apache Gold and Yaqui Silver*; Dobie, *Coronado's Children*.

103   For Cushman, see William Christen, *Pauline Cushman: Spy of the Cumberland* (Roseville, MN: Edinborough Press, 2006). In later years, her life worsened. After about ten years, she and Fryer separated. She moved between San Francisco, El Paso, and Arizona, sometimes working as a seamstress or charwoman. She began taking opiates for pain. In 1893, at age sixty, she overdosed and died in a San Francisco boarding house. In 1910, the army remembered her and reburied her remains with full military honors in Presidio National Cemetery. Her gravestone: "Pauline C. Fryer, Union Spy."

104   Dick Chilson's letter was published in Judge Hackney's newspaper, the *Arizona Silver Belt*, on January 5, 1884. The same page carried a story about the mine's sale for $90,000. Another account about the mine said the sales price was $60,000, but that was written nearly twenty-five years after the contemporary account in the *Silver Belt*: see *The Western Investors Review* 15 (October 1908): 10.

105   Shafts of sunshine on the Burnhams' wedding day: Family lore related to me by Burnham's grandson, Fred Burnham.

106   In *S2C* Burnham misspells Sirrine as Sirine.

107   Most of the information about Howard in this chapter comes from Burnham's chapter about him in *TC*.

110   Dobie, Corle, and Fisher and Holmes are entertaining on lost mines.

114   On the various corrupt "rings," see Lamar, *The Far Southwest*, 139ff.

Chapter 9: TO AFRICA

117   When the Burnhams decided to emigrate to southern Africa, they began saving letters, their own and those from relatives and friends. Consequently, the

primary sources about Burnham's life go from almost nothing to abundance. The letters quoted from this point on are in the Burnham archives held by Yale and Stanford. An excellent selection that covers the Burnhams' time in southern Africa is Bradford and Bradford, eds., *An American Family on the African Frontier.*

118	For background on the British South Africa Company, the best single source is Galbraith, *Crown and Charter.*

121	Background material about the Chicago World's Fair was drawn from Erik Larson, *The Devil in the White City* (New York: Vintage, 2003).

124	Churchill, "Aryan stock": quoted in Richard Toye, *Churchill's Empire* (New York: Henry Holt, 2010), 81. For Churchill's racial views, see also Lawrence James, *Churchill and Empire: A Portrait of an Imperialist* (London: Pegasus, 2014). In recent years, several books have addressed the thorny issue of Gandhi and race, most recently Ramachandra Guha, *Gandhi Before India* (New York: Knopf, 2014). The quotations here come from Joseph Lelyveld, *Great Soul: Mahatma Gandhi and His Struggle with India* (New York: Knopf, 2011), 54, 57, 58.

Chapter 10: TO THE FRONTIER

137	Description of the Burnhams' arrival in Fort Victoria: from Melina de Fonseca Rorke, *The Story of Melina Rorke, R.R.C.* (New York: Greystone Press, 1938), 123–4.

138	Not long after Burnham camped at Great Zimbabwe, a syndicate called the Ancient Ruins Mining Company began destructive operations there. When Rhodes found out, he stopped it and established laws against damaging ancient sites. But he was not absolutely opposed to pillaging such places, and he reserved interesting objects for himself. He later gave Burnham restricted rights to search for gold and artifacts at Dhlo-Dhlo, another of Zimbabwe's fantastic ancient sites, sixty miles east of Bulawayo. Burnham and his friend Pete Ingram took about 600 ounces of gold beads from there, and sold their interest to another syndicate for a few thousand pounds.

Chapter 11: WAR IN MATABELELAND

140	For background about the war of 1893 I consulted, among many others, Glass, *The Matabele War*; Blake, *A History of Rhodesia*; Keppel-Jones, *Rhodes and Rhodesia*; Wills and Collingridge, *The Downfall of Lobengula*; W. D. Gale, *Zambezi Sunrise: How Civilisation Came to Rhodesia and Nyasaland* (Cape Town: Timmins, 1958); and O. N. Ransford, "An Historical Sketch of Bulawayo," *Rhodesiana* 16 (July 1967): 56–65.

143 The original spelling of Lobengula's capital was Buluwayo, changed after the war to Bulawayo, which remains its name. For simplicity I use the modern spelling throughout.

146 In *S2C*, Burnham misspells the name of Robert Vavasseur, the scout who went with him to find Bulawayo, calling him Vaversol. Burnham also misspells the name of the man who entered burning Bulawayo with him, calling him Poselt instead of Posselt. He also misdates this excursion as November 2 instead of November 3.

148 Hilaire Belloc: from *The Modern Traveller*, 1898.

Chapter 12: THE KING'S SPOOR

151 Glass, *The Matabele War*, is especially helpful on the incident of Lobengula's stolen gold.

Chapter 13: THE SHANGANI PATROL

158 The literature about the Forbes column and the Shangani patrol is copious. In addition to the sources mentioned for the previous chapter, these contemporary sources were instructive for this chapter and the next: Burnham's account, with an interview, in two parts in the *Westminster Gazette* (January 8 and 9, 1895), some of which is repeated in Haggard, "Wilson's Last Fight"; Du Toit, *Rhodesia, Past and Present*, 135–50; "Diary" of William Napier, Historical Manuscripts Collection, MISC/NA4. National Archives of Zimbabwe, Harare; W. L. Gooding, "A Ride For Life," *Grey River Argus* (New Zealand newspaper), vol. XXXVI, issue 7986 (July 10, 1894).

158 Burnham's low opinion of Forbes is muted but clear in *S2C* and in his contemporary letters and interviews. For instance, Du Toit (cited above) includes this exchange between himself and Burnham:

> *"Do you think that Wilson's force could have kept their position or forced a retreat if Forbes had sent one Maxim with the reinforcements?"*
>
> *"I have not the least doubt, though this might have been less in accordance with military tactics."*
>
> *"What had Forbes to do, according to the general opinion of Wilson and his men?"*
>
> *"We were all of opinion that, if he did not wish to cross the river in the night with his whole force, he should have sent word to us to return at once."*

166 The guilty batmen: two years later, during the Second Matabele War, the verdict was nullified on grounds of insufficient evidence and lack of jurisdiction by the sentencing magistrate.

168 The fate of the Shangani Patrol was the emotional climax of a patriotic drama called *Cheer, Boys, Cheer* that ran in London for 177 performances in 1895. Another drama that opened in London in 1899, *Savage South Africa*, reenacted the incident, and was turned into a movie that same year called *Major Wilson's Last Stand*. Both starred Peter Lobengula, who claimed to be the son of King Lobengula. Peter led fifty warriors into battle against Wilson in two shows each day. The production was sensational in several ways. The theater featured a "native village" where the audience could mingle with the performers, most of whom were near-naked black men. This proved especially popular among female theatergoers, which led to censure in the papers. The role of Burnham was played by a Wild West performer with the stage name Texas Jack. A few years later, Texas Jack took a Wild West show to South Africa, where he hired a young American trick-roper called the Cherokee Kid, soon to be famous as Will Rogers—who, to complete the circle, became friends with Burnham in the 1930s in Los Angeles. I'm indebted to Rod Atkinson for much of this information.

Chapter 14: SPEARS INTO PEGS

171 Blanche's restful personality: letter from Arthur Bent to Burnham, April 10, 1907, in Yale archive.

175 "a ring of financing adventurers": *Truth*, December 14, 1893: 1273.

Chapter 15: CASHING IN

183 Haggard on Burnham: from his autobiography, *The Days of My Life*, vol. 2, 121. The section on Burnham covers pp. 121–30.

185 Burnham briefly tells the story about the copper bracelet in *S2C*. John Hays Hammond gives a longer version in *Autobiography*, vol. 1, 272–4.

189 Trek through thorn belt: in *S2C*, Burnham says he was looking for the Gwelo River, but this is a failure of memory. The group crossed the Zambezi at Victoria Falls, far to the west of the Gwelo. In a letter to his mother written just after the trek, he says he was trying for the Gwai River, which makes geographical sense.

190 Message carved on gunstock: Burnham mentions this in a letter to his mother and in *S2C*, but gives no details about the message itself. Burnham's son Roderick gave this gun to Jack Lott, who photographed it and wrote about it. See Lott, "Burnham, Chief of Scouts," 193–201, and "Do You Own a Piece of History?", 57–63, 80–1.

Chapter 16: WAR AGAIN

195   The literature about the Jameson Raid is extensive. Especially helpful for this chapter were Pakenham, *The Boer War*, and Wheatcroft, *The Randlords*.

       In addition to the sources already cited, these were helpful: Ranger, *Revolt in Southern Rhodesia*; Ranger, *Voices From the Rocks*; Oliver Ransford, "An Historical Sketch of Bulawayo," *Rhodesiana* 16 (July 1967): 56–65; O. N. Ransford, " 'White Man's Camp', Bulawayo," *Rhodesiana* 18 (July 1968): 13–21; Kennedy, *Islands of White*; Selous, *Sunshine and Storm in Rhodesia*; Baden-Powell, *The Matabele Campaign*; Clarke, *The Plumtree Papers*.

195   Churchill on the Jameson Raid: quoted in Wheatcroft, *The Randlords*, 10.

203   Bulawayo's "hanging tree" still grows alongside Main Street.

205   In *S2C*, Burnham states that Nada was "not yet three years old." In fact, she died twelve days before her second birthday.

205   White bloodlust: Selous, *Sunshine and Storm in Rhodesia*, 29–31. For his other remarks on the subject, see especially 34–7, 64–7, and 192–4. Among other examples of white vengeance aroused by native atrocities, he mentions the Sioux War in Minnesota (31)—an odd case for him to cite or know about; he probably heard of it from Burnham. Baden-Powell also was surprised by the settlers' strong desire for vengeance, until he heard the stories and saw the victims: see *The Matabele Campaign*, 29–31. In an account of the first war, C. H. W. Donovan described his change from rationality to vengeance: *With Wilson in Matabeleland*, 239–42.

Chapter 17: THE MOUTHPIECE OF GOD

209   Selous on Mlimo: *Sunshine and Storm in Rhodesia*, especially 15–17.

210   For Baden-Powell and the ideals of scouting, see MacDonald, *Sons of the Empire*.

210   Baden-Powell on Burnham: *The Matabele Campaign*, 70–1; on the importance of military scouting, 89–121. Throughout their long correspondence, Baden-Powell never stopped asking Burnham for more bits of woodcraft.

213   Various sources spell the name of the man Burnham shot in the cave as Jobani, Jobaani, Jobane, Tshobani, Dshobani, Dshobane, and Juane.

217   Stent's account was reprinted in his *A Personal Record of Some Incidents in the Life of Cecil Rhodes* (Cape Town: Maskew Miller, 1924). Stent's account and the Ndebele spokesman are quoted in Blake, *A History of Rhodesia*, 138. Rhodes's remark about "moments in life that make it worth living" is also quoted in Ranger, *Revolt in Southern Rhodesia*, 245.

219   Burnham's unpublished essay about Rhodes is in the Yale archive.

220   "Hasten forward quickly there": quoted in White, *The Eastern Establishment and the Western Experience*, 83.

Chapter 18: KLONDIKE

223   In his first paragraph about the Klondike in *S2C*, Burnham gets several things wrong: the strike occurred on August 16, 1896, not 1897, and the discoverer's name was Carmack, not Karmack. News of the strike didn't reach Seattle until July 1897. Later in the chapter, Burnham erroneously says that writer Joaquin Miller was among the flood of newcomers into Dawson in June 1898, but Miller had spent the previous winter there and nearly starved.

223   Books especially helpful for this chapter: Adney, *The Klondike Stampede*; Greever, *The Bonanza West*; Berton, *The Klondike Fever*; and Gray, *Gold Diggers*.

228   "reeking bog": Adney, *The Klondike Stampede*, 365.

231   "*swish, swish*": ibid., 412.

232   "still considerable": *Los Angeles Evening Express*, October 20, 1898.

234   Chopped bacon: Adney, *The Klondike Stampede*, 204.

236   Estimates vary about the worth of gold taken from the Klondike during the gold rush years. The figure of $29 million from 1897 to 1899 comes from *The Canadian Encyclopedia*'s article on the gold rush.

239   The cablegram from Lord Roberts: the Bradfords write that Burnham's son Roderick was waiting on the dock for the fresh newspapers that day, and that a purser gave him Roberts's cable, whereupon Roderick ran home with it (295–6). I found nothing in the letters or any other source to corroborate this pleasing story. Instead, I rely on the more likely version in Davis, *Real Soldiers of Fortune*, 217. Davis interviewed Burnham extensively at a time when Burnham's memory about the cable was still fresh.

Chapter 19: CHIEF OF SCOUTS

240   In addition to books previously mentioned, helpful books for this chapter and the next include Thomas Pakenham's matchless *The Boer War*; Belfield, *The Boer War*; Gooch, ed., *The Boer War*, especially Wessels, "Afrikaners at War," 73–106, and Glenn R. Wilkinson, " 'To the Front': British Newspaper Advertising and the Boer War," 203–12; Conan Doyle, *The Great Boer War*; Lowry, ed., *The South African War Reappraised*; Tuchman, *The Proud Tower*; Wisser, *The Second Boer War*; Wessels, *The Anglo-Boer War 1889–1902*; *A Handbook of the Boer War, With General Map of South Africa and 18 Sketch Maps and Plans* (London: Gale and Polden, 1910); Richard Danes, *Cassell's History of the Boer War, 1899–1901* (London: Cassell, 1901); and Reitz, *Boer Commando*.

The Boer War chapters in *S2C* occasionally jumble or condense events, as memories (and memoirs) are apt to do. For minor discrepancies, I have relied on contemporary letters and accounts rather than Burnham's later recollections.

242 "courage matched only by stupidity": Pakenham, *The Boer War*, 240.

242 Maoris and Canadian half-breeds: from an unidentified newspaper clip pasted into a scrapbook kept by the Burnhams, now in the Stanford archive.

243 Davis: "Major Burnham, Chief of Scouts," *Real Soldiers of Fortune*, 189–228. The book remains highly entertaining.

243 In *S2C*, Burnham gets two things wrong about "Long Cecil," an artillery gun built during the siege of Kimberley. The American engineer who designed it was George Labram, not Le Brun, and it fired a twenty-eight-pound shell, not a hundred-pound shell.

245 Conan Doyle, *The Great Boer War*, 257–8.

247 Letter from Burnham to Baden-Powell about importance of admitting failure: September 18, 1909, in the Yale archive.

249 The defaced illustration of Burnham: from the *Los Angeles Examiner*, March 10, 1907, pasted into a Burnham family scrapbook in the Stanford archive.

249 In a chapter of *S2C* entitled "The Pietersburg Failure," Burnham recounts his three futile attempts to scout the town of Pietersburg. He also says Pietersburg (now called Polokwane) is twenty-five miles from British headquarters south of Bloemfontein. But Polokwane and Bloemfontein are 400 miles apart. In letters written at the time, Burnham refers to scouting excursions towards Petrusburg, a hamlet on the road to Bloemfontein. Everett, the editor of *S2C*, evidently confused the better-known Pietersburg with Petrusburg, and Burnham didn't catch it.

Chapter 20: BEHIND ENEMY LINES

272 Lord Roberts's letter to Burnham is reprinted in *S2C*, 351. The letter awarding Burnham £2,000, sent on Roberts's behalf by C. V. Hume from Pretoria on July 31, 1900, is in the Yale archive.

Chapter 21: CELEBRITY AND HINTERLANDS

273 Burnham "as well as other celebrities" on the *Dunottar Castle*: in Major A. W. A. Pollock, *With Seven Generals in the Boer War: A Personal Narrative* (London: Skeffington, 1900), 283.

275 Burnham devotes a chapter of *TC* to Churchill, mostly about their time on the *Dunottar Castle*, the name of which he misspells.

276 *Mainly About People*: from a news clip of unknown date, sometime in the fall of 1900, pasted into a Burnham family scrapbook in the Stanford archive.

283   Burnham devotes a few pages to the War of the Golden Stool, with emphasis on the heroism of the British officers and native soldiers: *TC*, 46–8.

286   Burnham uses the older name for the Dagara (or Dagaaba) people, calling them the Dagarti.

287   The Burnham family scrapbook in the Stanford archive contains clips about Burnham's Gold Coast expedition from, among others, the *Daily Mail*, *African Review*, *Illustrated London News*, *West Africa*, *The Financier and Bullionist*, and *Gold Coast Globe and Ashanti Argus*. The quote "one of the very greatest gold-fields in the world" appeared in the last-named paper on July 9, 1901. The head-line from the *Daily Mail* appears on an undated article in the scrapbook, reprinted by the *New York Times* on August 12, 1901.

288   DSO ceremony and Burnham's worry about his sword: Family lore related to me by his grandson, Fred Burnham.

288   "uncivilized Afrikander savages": quoted in Pakenham, *The Boer War*, 530.

289   Burnham's devotion to Africa waned after Rhodes's death: from V. L. Ehren-clou, "Major Burnham—the Scout," *Union Oil Bulletin*, June 1925: 10.

Chapter 22: BRITISH EAST AFRICA

291   There is comparatively little written about the early days of the East Africa Protectorate. Helpful were Somerset Playne, ed., *East Africa (British): Its History, People, Commerce, Industries, and Resources* (London: Foreign and Colonial Compiling and Publishing Co., 1908–09); Lord Hindlip, *British East Africa, Past, Present, and Future* (London: T. Fisher Unwin, 1905); P. L. McDermott, *British East Africa; or, Ibea; a History of the Formation and Work of the Imperial British East Africa Company* (London: Chapman & Hall, 1893); and Kennedy, *Islands of White*.

291   In *TC*, Burnham writes that in 1902 "officers of the British East Africa Com-pany" engaged him to go to East Africa (75). That's misleading. Burnham was hired by a different entity, the East Africa Syndicate, a few of whose directors had previously been associated with the chartered company.

293   Dispute about the discovery of Lake Magadi: see M. F. Hill, *Magadi: The Story of the Magadi Soda Company* (Birmingham, U.K.: Kynoch Press for the Magadi Soda Co., 1964), 12–13. For another thorough history of the Magadi claim, which accepts Hill's version of its discovery, see Lotte Hughes, "Mining the Maasai Reserve: The Story of Magadi," *Journal of Eastern African Studies* 2, no. 1 (March 2008): 134–64. Lake Magadi contin-ues to be mined for soda.

301   Burnham's photo album of African trophy animals is in the Stanford archive.

Chapter 23: PROSPECTS AND LOSSES

306 Hammond's two-volume autobiography is an appealing neglected work. Burnham appears in it several times.

306 Haggard tells the story of Carmichael, Montezuma's treasure, Hammond, and Burnham in *The Days of My Life*, vol. 2, 128–30. Other information about the treasure appears in letters between Haggard and Burnham. As late as 1923, Haggard was still asking Burnham if his explorations in Mexico had ever turned up signs of Carmichael's lost city.

311 "as though he had been shot": *The Days of My Life*, vol. 2, 130. After the drowning, Bruce's nurse, Elizabeth Badrick, almost lost her mind. The Burnhams didn't hold her responsible and occasionally corresponded with her. She evidently fell on hard times. In 1926, Burnham sent a gentle letter with money to buy her a gravesite and a stone, with hopes that it would not be needed for many years. She died in 1931.

315 *Ridgway's*: William Justus Boies, "The Mining Flame and the Public Moth," November 24, 1906: 13–14, and Lindsay Denison, "The Gamble for Nevada Ores," December 15, 1906: 3–6.

Chapter 24: A PRESIDENT SAVED, ANOTHER FORTUNE POSTPONED

320 Burnham's story "Rogue Elephant" appeared in the October 1906 issue of *Collier's* magazine.

321 The details about Harriman's Pelican Lodge at Klamath Falls are taken from a contemporary account in the *Des Moines Daily News*, August 29, 1908: 2. The headline about the bear hunt appeared in *The Call* (San Francisco), August 19, 1908: 3.

321 On Mexico and the Yaqui Valley, the following were helpful: Sanderson, *Agrarian Populism and the Mexican State*; Dwyer, *The Agrarian Dispute*; Edwards, "The Protection of American Lives and Property"; Trow, "Woodrow Wilson and the Mexican Interventionist Movement of 1919"; Jeff Banister, "The Río Yaqui Delta: Early Twentieth-Century Photos from the Richardson Construction Company," *Journal of the Southwest* 40, no. 3 (Autumn 1998): 397–401; Hart, "Social Unrest, Nationalism, and American Capital in the Mexican Countryside"; Gonzalez, *The Mexican Revolution*; C. V. Whitney, *High Peaks* (Lexington: University Press of Kentucky, 1977); and Pamela A. Matson, ed., *Seeds of Sustainability: Lessons from the Birthplace of the Green Revolution* (Washington, D.C.: Island Press, 2012).

322 The sales brochure for the Yaqui Valley is in a Burnham family scrapbook in the Stanford archive.

324   Charles Frederick Holder, "The Esperanza Stone," *Scientific American*, September 1910: 196ff. I don't know the stone's fate and whereabouts. Holder later interested several publishers in a book about Burnham and wrote some chapters based on Burnham's dictation, but it was never published. The manuscript is in the Stanford archive.

324   Taft–Díaz meeting: in his autobiography, Hammond devotes two pages to Burnham's role in this, vol. 2, 565–6. In *The Secret War in El Paso: Mexican Revolutionary Intrigue, 1906–1920* (Albuquerque: University of New Mexico Press, 2009), Charles H. Harris III and Louis R. Sadler provide a thorough description of the Taft–Díaz meeting, including the security preparations, the seizure of the man with the gun (they identify Burnham's partner as Ranger Moore), and a photo of the type of "pencil pistol" confiscated: 1–16, 212–4. The news clip from the *New York World*, October 13, 1909, is in the Stanford archive. While writing his autobiography, Hammond asked Burnham for his recollections of the incident, which may explain why both men misdate the year as 1910 instead of 1909.

330   Smuggled arsenal: the story appeared in the *Los Angeles Evening (Herald) Express* on April 22, 1912. Other papers reprinted it the next day, including the *New York Times*.

Chapter 25: HIPPOS AND SPIES

336   In his chapter about Duquesne in *TC*, Burnham confuses congressional bills from 1906 and 1910, writing that the later bill was defeated because a congressman accused President Roosevelt of wanting to fund hunting safaris for wealthy friends. But the president in 1910 was Taft. In Burnham's address to California's Humane Association in 1910, when his memory was fresh, he gets it right, blaming the class-conscious congressman for the failure of the 1906 bill.

338   Most of the material about Duquesne and the importation of African animals was drawn from the archives at Yale and Stanford, and from Burnham's chapter on Duquesne in *TC*. An entertaining, exhaustive treatment of this episode is Jon Mooallem's "American Hippopotamus," *The Atavist* 32 (December 2013).

338   The biographical sources on Duquesne are as fantastic, and sometimes as credible, as their subject: see chapter 9 of Thomas Joseph Tunney and Paul Merrick Hollister, *Throttled!: The Detection of the German and Anarchist Bomb Plotters* (Boston: Small, Maynard and Co., 1919), which is available on Wikisource; Clement Wood, *The Man Who Killed Kitchener: The Life of Fritz Joubert Duquesne, 1879–* (New York: W. Faro, 1932); and, more reliably, Art Ronnie, *Counterfeit Hero: Fritz Duquesne, Adventurer and Spy* (Annapolis,

MD: Naval Institute Press, 1995). For the Nazi spy ring, see Peter Duffy, *Double Agent: The First Hero of World War II and How the FBI Outwitted and Destroyed a Nazi Spy Ring* (New York: Scribner, 2014).

339 "Denizens of Jungle": unidentified newspaper clipping about the Broussard hearing in March 1910, found in a Burnham family scrapbook in the Yale archive.

Chapter 26: SCOUTING FOR MINES AND FOR ROOSEVELT

344 Hammond's remarks about prospecting and prospectors come from a speech to the American Mining Congress in Chicago, October 27, 1911, in the Hammond archives at Yale.

345 Mining romances: quoted from *Mining and Scientific Press* (1893), in Spence, *Mining Engineers and the American West*, 100.

348 Roosevelt on Burnham, "He is a scout and a hunter": quoted in Davis, *Real Soldiers of Fortune*, 216.

353 The information about Roderick's service in the army comes from Rod Atkinson, Roderick's grandson.

353 Wilfred Owen, "Dulce et Decorum Est."

Chapter 27: CLOSING THE CIRCLE

359 Figures from the Mixed Claims Commission: Hart, "Social Unrest," 85n. Deaths of American miners: Spence, *Mining Engineers and the American West*, 294.

360 Whitney's shares in Yaqui: Whitney's son, Cornelius Vanderbilt Whitney, later claimed that he bought his father's certificates of ownership for $5,000 on the open market, without his father's knowledge, and immediately traveled to Mexico, where he sold them to General Álvaro Obregón, soon to become the country's president, for $500,000. According to C. V. Whitney, his father never knew about the episode, which provided the money C. V. used to help found Pan American Airways. See his autobiography, *High Peaks*, 17–24.

360 Helpful about Dominguez, in addition to the archives: Dodd, "Dominguez Oil Field"; and C. R. McCollom, "The Dominguez Field," *Union Oil Bulletin* (date uncertain), 11–13, in the Stanford archive. Today much of the old oil field is occupied by the Dominguez Hills campus of California State University, in Carson. Burnham's grandchildren still receive dividend checks from his oil stocks.

361 Hammond, "impossible to believe they had missed something" quoted in the *Boston Post*, September 1925, typescript of article found in the Burnham archive at Yale.

Chapter 28: AFTER THE BONANZA

363 "Howdy partner" screenplay: in the Yale archive.

364 After leaving his Hollywood Hills mansion, Burnham donated his animal trophies, along with the larger collection of King Macomber, to the Southwest Museum of the American Indian in Los Angeles, now part of the Autry National Center. Most of the trophies were ruined by years spent in a warehouse, but a few heads, including a massive Cape buffalo, are now on display at the International Wildlife Museum in Tucson.

365 On Madison Grant and the intersection of conservation with scientific racism, a helpful source is Jonathan Peter Spiro, *Defending the Master Race: Conservation, Eugenics, and the Legacy of Madison Grant* (Burlington: University of Vermont Press, 2008).

366 "strange monsters of evil": *TC*, ix.

367 Burnham's letter about Blanche was written to Everett and appears in *S2C*, xxii.

368 "hopelessly in love": letter from Ilo to Howell Wright in February 1949, in the Stanford archive. Wright accepted the Burnham papers for Yale.

368 Ilo's correct name and age are cloudy. Her maiden name was Willits, and she evidently was previously married to someone named Ferree or Ferre. I found documents that spelled her name Ilo Willits Ferre, Ilo Willits Ferree, Ilo Klore Willits, and Ilo Kay Willits. The universities to whom she donated Burnham's papers confuse things further. The Yale archive calls her Ilo K. Willetts; Stanford uses Ilo K. Willits [or Ferrce]. In several letters she claims to be thirty-seven years younger than Burnham, which would make her birth year 1898, but records list her birthdate as June 20, 1894; my thanks to Rod Atkinson for this nugget. After Burnham died she had to sell the hillcrest home in Santa Barbara. While organizing Burnham's papers she lived in small houses near Los Angeles, then in smaller apartments. Her letters refer to a book that she completed about Burnham in the mid-1950s, but the manuscript has disappeared. She died in Anaheim in 1982.

371 "The man in the arena" was part of a speech entitled "Citizenship in a Republic," delivered by Roosevelt at the Sorbonne in Paris, France, on April 23, 1910.

371 "world-wide harvest of death", etc.: from *TC*, viii–ix.

Appendix: THE CONTROVERSIES

THE SHANGANI PATROL

373 Ransford, *The Rulers of Rhodesia*, 331. Ransford's single sentence on Burnham and the Shangani Patrol manages to be factually sloppy as well as slanderous.

Ingram didn't become Burnham's brother-in-law for two more years. Perhaps Ransford used this premature tag to intensify the insinuation that the two men were spineless colluders.

373 O'Reilly, *Pursuit of the King.*

374 For Gooding, see earlier citation.

374 Peter Emmerson, foreword to *Scouting on Two Continents*, unpaginated.

374 For a thoughtful rebuttal of the desertion theorists, see Lott, "Major F. R. Burnham, D.S.O.: A Vindication."

375 For an interesting treatment of the Victorian ideal of a brave death, see MacDonald, *The Language of Empire.*

376 "The white induna's eye": *S2C*, 202.

376 Norris-Newman: *Matabeleland and How We Got it*, 128.

376 Weale, letter to the editor, *Rhodesia Herald*, December 22, 1944.

THE MLIMO

377 Sykes, *With Plumer in Matabeleland*, 259–61.

377 Hole and hoax: *The Making of Rhodesia*, 367n. For another critique of Hole's assertions, see Bradford and Bradford, *An American Family on the African Frontier*, xxii–xxiii.

378 Frederick de Bertodano's diary: Historical Manuscripts Collection, BE 3/2/1, National Archives of Zimbabwe. For comments about his service in the Boer War, see Craig Wilcox, *Australia's Boer War* (New York: Oxford University Press, 2002). My critique of de Bertodano's diary is deeply indebted to Peter van Wyk's dismantling of it in *Burnham: King of Scouts*, 565–8, and also in his papers in the Stanford archive.

381 Burnham's modesty: people who knew him always mentioned this, as did most newspaper stories. Many reporters noted that Burnham talked easily about anything except himself, and that his exploits had to be dragged out of him. A few examples will suffice: in a story written shortly after the Mlimo incident, a reporter for the London *Daily Telegraph* (August 23, 1896) noted that Burnham refused to elaborate on his report to Lord Grey with any dramatic details. The reporter called him "as quiet, unassuming a man as can be imagined.... His speech is soft and low, and he is as modest as a girl ..." In a 1901 profile of Burnham for *Pearson's Magazine*, the famous war correspondent Curtis Brown wrote, "Time and again attempts have been made to persuade Major Burnham to set down a record of these incidents in his own words and with the details that should clothe, as with flesh and blood, the bare skeletons of facts already known. But such efforts were unavailing despite all inducements. He would say 'that writing was not in his line,' or give some

other excuse. His thoughts never seemed to concern themselves in the least with spectacular effects or with popular applause. . . . The difficulty of getting from such a man, little by little, the details of some of the more exciting events in his career has been considerable, but the result has proved well worth the effort" ("Burnham the Scout," *Pearson's Magazine* 6, no. 5 [November 1901]: 507). A year earlier, in October 1900, after Burnham had been invalided home from the Boer War, Brown tried to get him to talk about the Shangani Patrol, the Mlimo, and his missions in the Boer War: "The Major refuses to talk of these things for newspaper publication—he says it wouldn't look right—but he had some shrewd and noteworthy observations to make concerning the warfare and the scouting of the future." Richard Harding Davis noted that, because of Burnham's modesty, it took five years to gather enough material to write the chapter about him in *Real Soldiers of Fortune* (1906). One of Burnham's Rhodesian critics, John O'Reilly, tries to reverse-spin all this, theorizing that Burnham's seeming modesty was a shield to fend off inquiries that could reveal his true base nature. No unbiased reader of *Scouting on Two Continents* can fail to notice Burnham's unpretentious voice and frequent acknowledgments of failure—odd traits for a lying braggart.

382   For Hartley, see Clarke, *The Plumtree Papers*, 43–5.

383   For the valuable observation that Fripp attributed the details in his drawing to Armstrong, I am indebted to Rod Atkinson.

384   Hensman, *A History of Rhodesia*, 232.

SELECTED BIBLIOGRAPHY

Adney, Tappan. *The Klondike Stampede*. New York: Harper and Brothers, 1900.

Baden-Powell, Robert S. S. *The Matabele Campaign, 1896: Being a Narrative of the Campaign in Suppressing the Native Rising in Matabeleland and Mashonaland*. London: Methuen, 1897.

Ball, Larry D. *Desert Lawmen: The High Sheriffs of New Mexico and Arizona, 1846–1912*. Albuquerque: University of New Mexico Press, 1992.

————. *The United States Marshals of New Mexico and Arizona Territories, 1846–1912*. Albuquerque: University of New Mexico Press, 1982.

Banning, William, and George Hugh Banning. *Six Horses*. New York: The Century Company, 1930.

Barnes, Will C. *Arizona Place Names*. Revised and enlarged by Byrd H. Granger. Tucson: University of Arizona Press, 1960.

Belfield, Eversley. *The Boer War*. London: Leo Cooper, 1975, reissued 1993.

Berton, Pierre. *The Klondike Fever*. New York: Carroll and Graff, 1958, reissued 1997.

Bigando, Robert. *Globe, Arizona: The Life and Times of a Western Mining Town*. Globe: Mountain Spirit Press, 1990.

Billington, Ray Allen. *Land of Savagery, Land of Promise: The European Image of the American Frontier in the Nineteenth Century*. New York: W. W. Norton, 1981.

Bishop, Harriet E. *Dakota War Whoop, or, Indian Massacres and War in Minnesota, of 1862–63*. St. Paul, MN: Wm. J. Moses' Press, 1864.

Blake, James Y. Fillmore. *A West Pointer With the Boers*. Boston: Angel Guardian Press, 1903.

Blake, Robert. *A History of Rhodesia*. New York: Alfred A. Knopf, 1978.

Bourke, John G. *On the Border with Crook*. New York: Charles Scribner and Sons, 1891.

Bradford, Mary, and Richard Bradford, eds. *An American Family on the African Frontier: The Burnham Family Letters, 1893–1896*. Niwot, CO: Roberts Rinehart, 1993.

Burnham, Frederick Russell. "Half Jack-Rabbit, Half Wolf." *Boys' Life*, March 1928, 9ff.

————. "The Howl for Cheap Mexican Labor." In Madison Grant and Charles Stewart Davison, eds., *The Alien in Our Midst: or "Selling Our Birthright for a Mess of Industrial Pottage,"* 44–8. New York: Galton, 1930.

————. "The Remarks of Major Frederick R. Burnham." *Historical Society of Southern California* 13, no. 4: 334–52.

————. *Scouting on Two Continents.* Garden City, NY: Doubleday, Page and Company, 1926.

————. *Taking Chances.* Prescott, AZ: Wolfe Publishing, 1994, reprint of 1944 edition by Haynes Corporation.

Carmony, Neil B., ed. *Whiskey, Six-Guns & Red-Light Ladies: George Hand's Saloon Diary, Tucson, 1875–1878.* Silver City, NM: High-Lonesome Books, 1994.

Carmony, Neil B., and David E. Brown, eds. *Tough Times in Rough Places.* Silver City, NM: High-Lonesome Books, 1992.

Carr, Harry. *Old Mother Mexico.* Boston: Houghton Mifflin, 1931.

Clarke, Mary. *The Plumtree Papers: A History of Bulalima–Mangwe and Life in Rhodesia up to 1922.* Bulawayo: Plumtree Foundation, 1983.

Collins, Charles. *An Apache Nightmare: The Battle at Cibecue Creek.* Norman: University of Oklahoma Press, 1999.

Conan Doyle, Arthur. *The Great Boer War.* 1900. New York: Cosimo, 2007.

Corle, Edwin. *The Gila: River of the Southwest.* New York: Rinehart, 1951.

Courtwright, David T. *Violent Land: Single Men and Social Disorder from the Frontier to the Inner City.* Cambridge, MA: Harvard University Press, 1996.

Cozzens, Peter, ed. *The Struggle for Apacheria: Eyewitnesses to the Indian Wars, 1865–1890.* Mechanicsburg, PA: Stackpole Books, 2001.

Cronon, William, George Miles, and Jay Gitlin, eds. *Under an Open Sky: Rethinking America's Western Past.* New York: W. W. Norton, 1992.

Cruse, Thomas. *Apache Days and After.* Lincoln: University of Nebraska Press, 1987.

Cunningham, Eugene. *Triggernometry: A Gallery of Gunfighters.* Caldwell, ID: Caxton Printers, 1962.

Dale, Edward Everett. *Frontier Ways: Sketches of Life in the Old West.* Austin: University of Texas Press, 1959.

Davis, Richard Harding. *Real Soldiers of Fortune.* New York: Charles Scribner's Sons, 1906.

Dedera, Don. *A Little War of Our Own: The Pleasant Valley Feud Revisited.* Flagstaff, AZ: Northland Press, 1988.

Dobie, J. Frank. *Apache Gold and Yaqui Silver.* Boston: Little, Brown, 1939.

————. *Coronado's Children: Tales of Lost Mines and Buried Treasures of the Southwest.* New York: Literary Guild of America, 1931.

Dodd, Harold V. "Dominguez Oil Field." *California Oil Fields* (California State Mining Bureau) 12, no. 4 (October 1926), 7–22.

Donovan, C. H. W. *With Wilson in Matabeleland, or, Sport and War in Zambesia.* 1896. Bulawayo: Books of Rhodesia, 1979.

Downey, Fairfax, and Jacques Noel Jacobsen, Jr. *The Red/Bluecoats: The Indian Scouts, U.S. Army.* Fort Collins, CO: Old Army Press, 1973.

Drago, Harry Sinclair. *The Great Range Wars: Violence on the Grasslands.* New York: Dodd, Mead, 1970.

Dunlay, Thomas W. *Wolves For Blue Soldiers: Indian Scouts and Auxiliaries with the United States Army, 1860–90.* Lincoln: University of Nebraska Press, 1982.

Du Toit, Stefanus Jacobus. *Rhodesia, Past and Present.* London: William Heinemann, 1897.

Dwyer, John J. *The Agrarian Dispute: The Expropriation of American-Owned Rural Land in Postrevolutionary Mexico.* Durham, NC: Duke University Press, 2008.

Edwards, Warrick Ridge. "The Protection of American Lives and Property: The Sonora Crisis of 1915." http://fch.fiu.edu/FCH-1993/Edwards.htm.

Emmerson, Peter. Foreword to reprint edition of Burnham, *Scouting on Two Continents.* Bulawayo: Books of Rhodesia, 1975.

Farish, Thomas Edwin. *History of Arizona.* San Francisco: Filmer Brothers Electrotype Company, 1918.

Federal Writers' Project, W.P.A. *Arizona, the Grand Canyon State: A State Guide.* U.S. History Publishers, 1940.

Fisher, Vardis, and Opal Laurel Holmes. *Gold Rushes and Mining Camps of the Early American West.* Caldwell, ID: Caxton Printers, 1970.

Folwell, William Watts. *A History of Minnesota*, vol. 2. 1924. St. Paul: Minnesota Historical Society, 1961.

Forrest, Earle R. *Arizona's Dark and Bloody Ground.* 1936. Tucson: University of Arizona Press, 1979.

Galbraith, John S. *Crown and Charter: The Early Years of the British South Africa Company.* Los Angeles: University of California Press, 1974.

Gard, Wayne. *Frontier Justice.* Norman: University of Oklahoma Press, 1949.

Glass, Stafford. *The Matabele War.* London: Longmans, 1968.

Gonzalez, Michael J. *The Mexican Revolution, 1910–1940.* Albuquerque: University of New Mexico Press, 2002.

Gooch, John, ed. *The Boer War: Direction, Experience and Image.* London: Frank Cass, 2000.

Goodwin, Grenville. *Western Apache Raiding and Warfare.* Edited by Keith H. Basso. Tucson: University of Arizona Press, 1971.

Grant, Madison. *The Passing of the Great Race, or, The Racial Basis of European History*. New York: Charles Scribner's Sons, 1916.

Gray, Charlotte. *Gold Diggers: Striking It Rich in the Klondike*. Berkeley, CA: Counterpoint, 2010.

Greever, William S. *The Bonanza West: The Story of the Western Mining Rushes, 1848–1900*. Norman: University of Oklahoma Press, 1963.

Grey, Zane. *Tonto Basin*. Waterville, ME: Thorndike Press, 2004. Reprint of *To the Last Man*, 1922.

Haggard, H. Rider. *The Days of My Life*. Vol. 2. London: Longmans, Green and Co., 1926.

———. "Wilson's Last Fight." In *The Red True Story Book*, edited by Andrew Lang. London: Longmans, Green, and Co., 1895.

Haley, James L. *Apaches: A History And Culture Portrait*. Norman: University of Oklahoma Press, 1981, reissued 1997.

Hammond, John Hays. *The Autobiography of John Hays Hammond*. Two volumes. New York: Farrar and Rinehart, 1935.

Hanchett, Leland J., Jr. *Arizona's Graham–Tewksbury Feud*. Phoenix: Pine Rim Publishing, 1994.

Hart, John Mason. "Social Unrest, Nationalism, and American Capital in the Mexican Countryside, 1876–1920." In Daniel Nugent, ed., *Rural Revolt in Mexico: U.S. Intervention and the Domain of Subaltern Politics*, 72–88. Durham, NC: Duke University Press, 1988.

Heard, Isaac V. D. *History of the Sioux War and the Massacres of 1862 and 1863*. New York: Harper and Brothers, 1864. Reprinted Millwood, NY: Kraus Reprint Co., 1975.

Hensman, Howard. *A History of Rhodesia, Compiled from Official Sources*. London: W. Blackwood and Sons, 1900.

Herman, Daniel Justin. *Hell on the Range: A Story of Honor, Conscience, and the American West*. New Haven: Yale University Press, 2010.

Hiley, Alan R. I., and John A. Hassell. *The Mobile Boer: Being the Record of the Observations of Two Burgher Officers*. New York: Grafton Press, 1902.

Hodge, Hiram C. *Arizona As It Is; or The Coming Country. Compiled From Notes of Travel During the Years 1874, 1875, and 1876*. New York: Hurd and Houghton, 1877.

Hole, Hugh Marshall. *The Making of Rhodesia*. 1926. London: Frank Cass, 1967.

Kaplan, Amy, and Donald E. Pease, eds. *Cultures of United States Imperialism*. Durham, NC: Duke University Press, 1993.

Kennedy, Dane. *Islands of White: Settler Society and Culture in Kenya and Southern Rhodesia, 1890–1939*. Durham, NC: Duke University Press, 1987.

Keppel-Jones, Arthur. *Rhodes and Rhodesia: The White Conquest of Zimbabwe 1884–1902*. Kingston, Ontario: McGill-Queen's Press, 1983.

Lamar, Howard Roberts. *The Far Southwest 1846–1912: A Territorial History*. New York: W. W. Norton, 1970.

Lamar, Howard Roberts, and Leonard Thompson, eds. *The Frontier in History: North America and Southern Africa Compared*. New Haven: Yale University Press, 1981.

Lewis, Marvin, ed. *The Mining Frontier: Contemporary Accounts From the American West in the Nineteenth Century*. Norman: University of Oklahoma Press, 1967.

Limerick, Patricia Nelson. *The Legacy of Conquest: The Unbroken Past of the American West*. New York: W. W. Norton, 1987.

Lockwood, Frank C. *Arizona Characters*. Los Angeles: Times-Mirror Press, 1928.

Lott, Jack. "Burnham, Chief of Scouts." *Guns and Ammo Annual*, 1973, 193–201.

———. "Do You Own a Piece of History?" *Guns and Ammo*, January 1979, 57–63, 80–1.

———. "The Making of a Hero: Burnham in the Tonto Basin." In Craig Boddington, ed., *America, The Men and Their Guns That Made Her Great*, 77–91. Los Angeles: Petersen, 1981.

Lott, J. P. "Major F. R. Burnham, D.S.O.: A Vindication." *Rhodesiana* (Salisbury: The Rhodesiana Society) 35 (September 1976): 43–7.

Lowry, Donal, ed. *The South African War Reappraised*. Manchester: Manchester University Press, 2000.

Lutrell, Estelle. *Newspapers And Periodicals Of Arizona 1859–1911*. Tucson: University of Arizona Bulletin, July 1949.

Lyon, William H. *Those Old Yellow Dog Days: Frontier Journalism in Arizona 1859–1912*. Tucson: Arizona Historical Society, 1994.

MacDonald, Robert H. *The Language of Empire: Myths and Metaphors of Popular Imperialism, 1880–1918*. Manchester: Manchester University Press, 1994.

———. *Sons of the Empire: The Frontier and the Boy Scout Movement, 1890–1918*. Toronto: University of Toronto Press, 1993.

Miles, Nelson Appleton. *Personal Recollections and Observations of General Nelson A. Miles*. Chicago: Werner, 1896.

Moynihan, Ruth B., Susan Armitage, and Christiane Fischer Dichamp, eds. *So Much To Be Done: Women Settlers on the Mining and Ranching Frontier*. Lincoln: University of Nebraska Press, 1990.

Myers, John Myers. *Tombstone's Early Years*. Lincoln: University of Nebraska Press, 1995.

Nadeau, Remi. *City Makers: The Story of Southern California's First Boom, 1868–76*. Los Angeles: Trans-Anglo Books, 1965.

Neill, Rev. Edward Duffield, and Charles S. Bryant. *History of the Minnesota Valley:*

Including the Explorers and Pioneers of Minnesota and History of the Sioux Massacre. Minneapolis: North Star Publishing, 1882.

Norris-Newman, Charles. *Matabeleland and How We Got it: With Notes on the Occupation of Mashunaland*. London: T. Fisher Unwin, 1895.

O'Reilly, John. *Pursuit of the King: An Evaluation of the Shangani Patrol in the Light of Sources Read by the Author*. Bulawayo: Books of Rhodesia, 1970.

Pakenham, Thomas. *The Boer War*. New York: Random House, 1979.

Paul, Rodman Wilson. *Mining Frontiers of the Far West*. New York: Holt, Rinehart and Winston, 1963.

Pearce, Roy Harvey. *Savagism and Civilization: A Study of the Indian and the American Mind*. Berkeley: University of California Press, 1988.

Pyle, Jinx. *Pleasant Valley War*. Payson, AZ: Git a Rope! Publishing, 2009.

Ranger, Terence. *Revolt in Southern Rhodesia, 1896–97: A Study in African Resistance*. Evanston, IL: Northwestern University Press, 1967.

———. *Voices From the Rocks: Nature, Culture, and History in the Matopos Hills of Zimbabwe*. Bloomington: University of Indiana Press, 1999.

Ransford, Oliver. *The Rulers of Rhodesia*. London: John Murray, 1968.

Reitz, Deneys. *Boer Commando: An Afrikaner Journal of the Boer War*. 1929. New York: Sarpedon, 1993.

Rickey, Don, Jr. *Forty Miles a Day on Beans and Hay: The Enlisted Soldier Fighting the Indian Wars*. Norman: University of Oklahoma Press, 1963.

Rossiter, W. Raymond. *Statistics of Mines and Mining In the States and Territories West of the Rocky Mountains*. Washington, D.C.: Government Printing Office, 1875.

Sanderson, Steven E. *Agrarian Populism and the Mexican State: The Struggle for Land in Sonora*. Berkeley: University of California Press, 1981.

Scott-Donelan, David. *Tactical Tracking Operations: The Essential Guide For Military and Police Trackers*. Boulder, CO: Paladin Press, 1998.

Selous, Frederick Courteney. *Sunshine and Storm in Rhodesia*. London: Rowland Ward and Co., 1896.

Sheridan, Thomas E. *Arizona: A History*. Tucson: University of Arizona Press, 1995.

Siringo, Charles A. *Riata and Spurs: The Story of a Lifetime Spent in the Saddle as Cowboy and Detective*. Boston: Houghton Mifflin, 1927.

Smith, Henry Nash. *Virgin Land: The American West as Symbol and Myth*. Cambridge, MA: Harvard University Press, 1950.

Smith, Victoria. *Captive Arizona, 1851–1900*. Lincoln: University of Nebraska Press, 2009.

Sonnichsen, Charles L. *Billy King's Tombstone: The Private Life of an Arizona Boom Town*. Caldwell, ID: Caxton Printers, 1942.

Spence, Clark C. *Mining Engineers and the American West: The Lace-Boot Brigade, 1849–1933*. New Haven: Yale University Press, 1970.

Sykes, Frank W. *With Plumer in Matabeleland: An Account of the Operations of the Matabeleland Relief Force During the Rebellion of 1896.* London: Archibald Constable and Co., 1897.

Thrapp, Dan L. *Al Sieber, Chief of Scouts.* Norman: University of Oklahoma Press, 1964.

———. *The Conquest of Apacheria.* Norman: University of Oklahoma Press, 1967.

———. *Victorio and the Mimbres Apaches.* Norman: University of Oklahoma Press, 1974.

Trow, Clifford S. "Woodrow Wilson and the Mexican Interventionist Movement of 1919." *Journal of American History* 58, no. 1 (June 1971): 46–72.

Tuchman, Barbara W. *The Proud Tower: A Portrait of the World Before the War, 1890–1914.* New York: Macmillan, 1966.

Utley, Robert M., ed. *The Story of the West: A History of the American West and its People.* Washington, D.C.: Smithsonian Institution, 2003.

van Wyk, Peter. *Burnham: King of Scouts.* Victoria, BC: Trafford Publishing, 2003.

Watt, Robert N. *Apache Tactics 1830–86.* London: Osprey Publishing, 2012.

Wessels, André. "Afrikaners At War." In John Gooch, ed., *The Boer War: Direction, Experience and Image,* 73–106.

———. *The Anglo-Boer War 1889–1902: White Man's War, Black Man's War, Traumatic War.* Bloemfontein: Sun Press, 2011.

West, James E., and Peter O. Lamb. *He-Who-Sees-in-the-Dark: The Boy's Story of Frederick Burnham, the American Scout.* New York: Brewer, Warren and Putnam, 1932.

Wheatcroft, Geoffrey. *The Randlords: The Exploits and Exploitations of South Africa's Mining Magnates.* New York: Atheneum, 1986.

White, G. Edward. *The Eastern Establishment and the Western Experience: The West of Frederic Remington, Theodore Roosevelt, and Owen Wister.* New Haven: Yale University Press, 1968.

Wills, W. A., and L. T. Collingridge, eds. *The Downfall of Lobengula: The Cause, History, and Effect of the Matabeli War.* London: *The African Review* Offices, 1894.

Willson, Roscoe G. "Arizona Days." *Arizona Days and Ways,* March 28, 1954, 9.

Wingerd, Mary Lethert. *North Country: The Making of Minnesota.* Minneapolis: University of Minnesota Press, 2010.

Wisser, John Philip. *The Second Boer War, 1899–1900.* Kansas City, MO: Hudson-Kimberly, 1901.

Woody, Clara T., and Milton L. Schwartz. *Globe, Arizona.* Tucson: Arizona Historical Society, 1977.

Worcester, Thomas Emmett. *The Apaches: Eagles of the Southwest.* Norman: University of Oklahoma Press, 1992.

INDEX

Page numbers 389–409 refer to endnotes; page numbers in *italics* refer to illustrations.